Adrift In
Aesthetic Latitudes

For Those at
Sea about Art

by

BIRNEY QUICK

VOYAGEUR PRESS — 1980

DEDICATION

I wish to dedicate this book

TO MARION

my staunchest supporter,
my most honest critic,
my wife.

ACKNOWLEDGMENT

Special gratitude is due to Walter MacDonough,
Professor Emeritus of Literature at the Minneapolis College of Art and Design, for his fre-
quent encouragement and careful perusal of
these essays.

Editor: Raymond Bechtle

Copyright © 1980 by Birney Quick

All rights reserved

First published in 1980 by Voyageur Press,
    9337 Nesbitt Road, Bloomington, MN. 55437

Library of Congress catalog card number: 80-50930

ISBN: Regular Edition 0-89658-019-9
ISBN: Limited Edition 0-89658-020-2

Printed by North Central Publishing Company,
    St. Paul, Mn.

CONTENTS

Introduction   Quik 79

INTRODUCTION

When I was seven, my father introduced me to the art of trout fishing. He did not take me to a major trout river but rather took me to a little stream that meandered through a nearby farmer's pasture. I did not catch anything, but I got my feet wet and I got bitten at an early age by the trout-fishing bug. Since that introduction I have fished all the major rivers of this state and some in Canada.

This book is much like that stream in the pasture: a place where people can get their feet wet without foundering in the turbulent and shifting mainstream of art. My hope is that my book will give those who read it a feeling of confidence and will then tease them into eventually trying the mainstream.

I OF SUBJECTS AND OBJECTS

"The only criterion for inclusion in these essays is simply that each represents personal experiences or opinions."

making an
artist

Quick 77

MAKING AN ARTIST

I decided it might be a good thing if I were to write something about myself in order that the reader may browse in the growing part of my life.

When I meet people for the first time, they often ask what I do for a living. My answer is that I am a painter — knowing full well I will have to explain further that I paint pictures, not houses. Then, they say, "Oh, you're an artist," instantly putting me into a higher cultural but lower financial slot.

I feel obliged to explain still further that the label "Artist" can't be bestowed on a person simply because he or she paints pictures. First, the title is earned through the approval of his work by his peers, and by society, after they have scrutinized that work for many years.

Often questions continue about techniques and the value of art. Even though I have been asked these questions a great many times, I always go slowly when answering them. The historic answers are more or less set, but the proliferation and variety at the growing edge are very involved and are constantly changing. For the mainstream of Art is much like the Mississippi: long, slow, and meandering all over the landscape, finally depositing all the material it has carried on a broad delta at its mouth.

I have been a part of this stream for over fifty years, sometimes at its center, and at others in little tributaries that dry up. My contributions to the delta are in drawing, painting, printmaking, and education, with an occasional foray into the area of writing articles about art.

The metaphor concerning the Mississippi and art is an apt one for me because I was born in 1912, quite near the river's source in the northern Minnesota town of Proctor. I was the third of four children born to a father who was a poet at heart but a railroad conductor by necessity, and to a mighty mite of a mother, a true human dynamo. Neither was ever daunted by the hardships they saw coming when they headed their children into life as painters, musicians, and educators.

Proctor was, and still is, a tough little town clustered around the railroad yards and repair shops. It could never be called a cultural center. Its activities rotated around the iron made from the ore of the Mesabi Iron Range. Fast freight engines would pull the trains to Proctor and there switch them to "mallies" for the steep dangerous run to the docks in Duluth. I think some of this iron got into the souls of those who grew up there, and helped them fight for recognition in the larger world.

Often, little things influence destinies and give direction to the growth of little boys. My grade school teacher sent a drawing of a robin, one of my first works, to the State Fair; and it came back with a blue ribbon pinned to it. My proud mother started to think of her son as an artist and at this early moment began guiding him toward a career in art.

Two steel engravings hanging on the walls of the school library gave me my first impression about art: one was a portrait of Lincoln and the other was a copy of *Washington Crossing the Delaware*. In 1918, the small-town schools of America were not filled with art as they are now. The walls were covered with propaganda for the First World War to end wars, and art was at the bottom of the list of important things to think about. So my mother's hopes for me were not the usual kinds of hopes that a mother would have had at that time and place.

Our family eventually left the little brown house on Second Street in Proctor to move five miles down the hill into an antique mid-Victorian mansion in the port city of Duluth. This fanciful new home was a great place for kids to grow up with its backyard, the carriage house, and a tremendous sweeping view of the river, harbor, and lake. Environment has a profound effect in shaping all of us. Another influence was the brightly colored reproductions of Vincent Van Gogh hanging on the walls of my new school. At the same time in art history classes I first heard the tales of his tortured life.

The next big step in my life occurred in 1930. In that year I went to Andover, Massachusetts, a small town which was the opposite of Proctor. I was sent there to the home of an aristocratic, autocratic aunt who was to watch over me for the next three years while I studied art in Boston, a commuter's trip away.

My parents had to stretch every dollar in order to cover the essentials for living and at the same time provide for their children's education. How they did it during the years of the Great Depression still mystifies me. They set goals for all their children; and when their children achieved any one of those, that made them feel rich because of the achievement rather than poor because of their sacrifice.

At this time my father's connections with the railroad were economically very useful because of the free transportation they provided. Later, you will see how these benefits seemed to work against me.

It was a thrilling experience to board a Pullman of the Northwestern Railroad for the overnight trip from Duluth to Chicago; then, next morning to make the transfer by taxi to the New York Central's crack train for a day-and-a-half trip to Boston, with the Pullman being switched while you slept to the Boston and Albany Line. I feel sorry for the air passengers of today who have never experienced the feeling of luxury that was part of rail travel of the Thirties. To be called for breakfast by a four-toned chime struck by the dining car steward is a thrill I will never outgrow. In those days any of the meals served in the dining cars were gourmet experiences that had all the style of a three-star restaurant while you were swaying along, and America was speeding by outside the window.

There was romance for me in the appearance of all my fellow passengers. I thought they must be on journeys every bit as exciting as my own. The incipient artist in me was already reading the stories in the faces of the people I met or saw. I remember talking to a man with a handlebar mustache who told me he was on his way to Germany via rail and ship for the sole purpose of purchasing a gun to take on a safari in Africa. That wouldn't be too impressive today because it would only mean two days by air. By the fastest way in those days, however, the trip would take at least three weeks, but you really would have known you had been someplace!

The trips East in the fall and the vacation trips home at Christmas tied in with the work of getting an education in the competitive world of art, and made this period of my life extremely stimulating and, I think, in addition gave me a sense of urgency to achieve some recognition as soon as possible in order to be able to continue to enjoy these sorts of experiences.

My aunt's home was a historic one on High Street built just a few years after the colonies were founded at Plymouth. It was filled with rare antiques collected by her and her husband on their trips across the Atlantic and to other points in the world.

She was able to open doors and introduce me to the many cultural possibilities in the town of Andover.

Within a short time after my arrival I had a studio home located between the two preparatory schools in town. In my first studio I began my career as a painter. The whole environment indeed was very helpful.

I heard Sergei Rachmaninoff play and Lotte Lehmann sing on the stage of the Phillips Andover Auditorium. I had my first one-man show in the Addison Gallery of American Art, and became friends with many of the professors at the school. All this was taking place while I was a student at the Vesper George School of Art in Boston, where I studied for three years.

The shaping of many, but not all artists has to do with both environment and education, and those were the forces that influenced me. The Depression was all around us in the Thirties; consequently, I found myself being taught by the top professionals of the time in every field. Their loss was my gain, for they came to teaching after the work in their own profession had completely dried up.

In my education I moved from commercial art to illustration to fine art. While looking over the shoulders of my fellow students involved in these different areas, I came to the conclusion that although it was a risky life, the place where the artist came closest to being his own man was in the field of painting. I have never been sorry about the decision.

During this process I made the first change in my inner being and my outward appearance. I dropped the uniform and attitudes of the advertising man, put on the clothes of the rebel Bohemian, and left both Boston and Andover for the rural summer art colony atmosphere of the Woodstock Art Colony in New York State.

There I met many New York artists who lived in Woodstock during the summer season in order to escape the heat and doldrums of New York City. It was my first taste of real professional attitudes toward art. I was 24 years old at the time.

From this group I heard of grants to be had and fellowships to be won. While living in a leaky-roofed studio that once had been the stable of a horse called Ronny, I tried for a Tiffany Fellowship and, amazingly, won it. This moved me from a stable in rural New York to the five hundred and eighty acre Tiffany Estate at Cold Spring Harbor, Long Island.

If there ever was a story of fromrags to riches, this certainly was it. I got off the train in Oyster Bay, Long Island, a day before the date I was actually to arrive at the Tiffany Foundation.

From the decorative iron gate at the entrance to the grounds, it was exactly one mile through gardens and arches covered with laurel to the front door of Laurelton Hall, the Long Island residence of the late Louis Comfort Tiffany. A little fearfully I knocked on the door, hoping that I would meet the man whose letter had told me that I had won one of the fellowships. The door opened, and there stood a very large, elegantly dressed person. I said, "Mr. Nichols?" And he said, "No sir, I am Edward, the butler." Art has a way of opening doors at all levels, from high to low.

Mr. Hobart Nichols, a little man dressed in a rumpled suit, smoking a hand-rolled cigarette, then popped out from behind the imposing Edward.

From this moment on I lived an idyllic life for quite a while in the company of seven other young artists, from different parts of the world: Holland, France, Cuba, Poland, Finland, and the United States.

Along with many other beautiful features the estate had an eight-sided art gallery. I don't know if this was the reason that eight fellowships were given each year, but each fellow was allotted a wall on which to hang his works as he completed them. The competition for the attention of famous art visitors who came from New York almost weekly was very keen. Their opinions and criticism, complimentary or not, were very important to all of us.

One of these visitors was Albert Sterner, a prominent painter of the time. Like Edward, he was a very impressive person, having the girth, rosy complexion, long white hair and beard of Santa Claus. Wearing a finely tailored suit, carrying a cane, exuding the sophistication, polish, and knowledge of a Lord Duveen, the eminent art dealer — such was the presence of Albert Sterner.

One afternoon he came to the gallery at the request of Mr. Nichols to give all of us the benefit of his experience, and also an assessment of the quality of our work. He proceeded to move around the room in a very precise pleasant way, saying something complimentary about everyone's work until he came to mine. There he stopped and spent one whole hour tearing it apart, because of both content and technique. When he finished, I had not a shred of courage or self respect left. I sneaked out of the gallery to sit on a bench and look at the sea through very misty eyes. I don't know how long I sat there before Hobart came out and put his arm over my shoulder and said, "Albert says he thinks you have a lot of promise, and he wants you to try for the Chaloner Award. He is one of the judges."

Thus, Albert Sterner taught me one of the lessons of good teaching in art. That is, save your toughest criticism for the students that you think might make it in the profession. The others will gain what they need to use in art in other related ways.

I did try the very next year for the Chaloner Award which consisted of an all-expense-paid year in Paris complete with studio and transportation. I almost won this award; in fact, I did win second prize which was a consolation award of five hundred dollars, but I learned a valuable lesson. I learned what not to do if you are trying for a prize of this kind.

I received a letter from the judges of the Chaloner saying they wanted me to come to New York to be considered for the award and that they would send me money to cover the expense of the trip. Through my railroad father I was qualified for free tickets on the train so I made my very first mistake. I sent word to the jury that I would immediately come to New York but that I could take care of the travel expense.

The second mistake was that, having recently sold a painting to my old high school for three hundred dollars, I immediately went out and bought a very handsome tweed suit to travel in. I really presented quite a grand picture when I was all decked out in it. Then, the third mistake took place when I arrived in New York. I was met at the railroad station by my old friend Hobart Nichols. He asked where I was going to stay while I was there. I said, "I don't know." He said, "Why not stay at my club? I will put you up as my guest while you're here." His club was one of the most posh in New York City. Needless to say, it didn't take the jury long to decide who needed the prize and who didn't. So with all things equal I might have done better, but pride got in the way.

With the European experience postponed I returned to my home state and to the country and people I knew best.

The suit I bought for the trip to the big city became very frayed at the cuffs, elbows, and seat. The polished shoes gave way to boots, the bon vivant was fast becoming a romantic rebel artist. The happy paintings devoted to the good life disappeared; paintings of protest started to appear, for the struggle of being an artist during the Depression years was upon me.

My studio over a frame shop in Duluth had once been used as a storage room for the art store that ran the frame shop. The proprietor of the art store had hopes that I might turn into something of an artist so he risked renting this space to me. A couple of small openings were cut in the floor, and grates were put into them so some heat could escape from the frame shop below, ostensibly to keep me warm in the winter. This system was far from adequate in Duluth's forty-below-zero weather; and so, many a time I painted in an overcoat with a scarf around my neck and overshoes on my feet while even the oil paints would become stiff.

During these years I struggled with a few private students and a once-a-week class at a private girl's school. One day, finally, with things at their very lowest, I had to do something. I remember I was freezing and broke. I left the studio and started to walk up and down the streets of Duluth. After several hours I happened to look up and saw a sign advertising a painting contractor; it must have been my guardian angel who guided me to his office. I walked in and saw a fat man with his feet perched on a desk while he fiddled with the pencil in his hands. I told him my situation. He listened to the whole story because I guess he had nothing really to do at the time. It turned out he was the contractor. I feel this was a major changing point in my career. He said that just by chance he was bidding on a contract to paint a large public school on the Iron Range; and if I would help him make some color swatches to show at the bidding, he would see if he could get me the job to paint two murals at a price of one thousand dollars.

I had been desperate, and now in a short while I had a thousand dollars. Not only that, I got another mural commission for a medical building in Duluth. With all this prosperity around I figured it was time to pursue a certain girl seriously and get married, and that is exactly what happened. Now three children and two grandchildren later I am still happily married to my staunchest supporter and most honest critic.

In 1942 when the second war to end all wars was in full swing, I was in it as an Air Corps artist. At that time it was legitimate to be an Air Corps artist; but as time passed, someone in Washington decided that the war could do without our artistic efforts. So we went underground at the request of and connivance with our commanding officer; perhaps his portrait hadn't been finished. It was a simple thing to do. Over the door of our studio barracks we erected a sign which said in large letters CIVILIAN TELEPHONE EXCHANGE to deceive any inspector general coming to the base. Civilian departments were out of their scope.

This is similar to another case in our oufit. We had a great pastry chef. Every time it was rumored that there was to be an inspection, this cook was given a three-day pass and told to get lost. The commanding officer also loved his apple pie. Inspecting generals were not above doing a little proselytizing.

On Saint Valentine's Day in 1946, I was given my honorable walking papers with a Good Conduct Medal thrown in for good measure. I once again had to face an uncertain future in art, but along came my guardian angel and took me by the hand and led me to the doors of the Minneapolis School of Art (now the Minneapolis College of Art and Design). Still dressed in my Class A uniform, I went to see the registrar of the school. She looked up from her desk and said, "Sorry, soldier, we don't have any more room for students." I said, "I've had some teaching experience." The words were hardly out of my mouth before I was ushered into the director's office, and I had a job as a teacher of painting, and drawing. It was much easier to get in as a teacher than as a student. Actually these two roles are so interchangeable it is amazing to me that so much importance is given to the differences — a point to be pondered later.

I spent thirty happy years teaching and learning what I could at the college. During this time there were many ups and downs — commissions of all kinds, portraits, murals, even a one-year stint as director of the college's Junior Year Abroad in Holland and England. Now I am Professor Emeritus of the college.

Quick "79"
The Proper
Pot.

THE PROPER POT

Art students come from every walk of life, from every geographical location. I have had Indians from India, Indians from America, students from South Africa to Alaska, from city and country; and each one arrives, usually in his teens, already shaped in character by family and roots. To make for these roots a proper pot of the right dimension, filled with the proper soil for growth, is the task of the art teacher.

I think most art teachers agree that you cannot teach anyone to be an artist; however, I believe you can provide an environment that will assure the student of an opportunity to grow.

What should be the mixture in that pot which will make the roots develop? I would like to suggest traditional materials because, historically, they have proven themselves by producing the great flowering of art we are heir to.

What are the traditional materials? One is the teaching of art history. It is like digging into a compost heap where everything pertaining to art, both good and bad, has been piled down through the ages. The material is often left to ripen and blend for centuries only to be dug up again and again to be worked into the earth surrounding the roots. When this soil is warmed in the light of new ideas, chances are that there will spring up a garden of infinite variety which can be traced to the variety of roots that have been planted.

There will be hybrids, mutations, and, yes, even throwbacks — all so beautiful that each should be worthy of our attention. In my town, for example, there are great quantities of old-fashioned rugosa roses. I don't think we should ignore them because some new hybrid is growing nearby. But to ignore traditional painting by considering it out-of-date is an attitude that seems to persist among many young artists and makes their shoots grow off at odd angles. I believe this happens because their art teachers have failed to enrich the soil by adding an appreciation of art history. To paraphrase Pablo Picasso, "There is no such thing as new art or old art, there is just good art or bad art." In the nature of growth the new feeds upon the old. I suppose this could be considered a law of nature, so it follows that it also could be a law of art because art and nature are closely linked.

Another additive that should be worked into the soil around the roots for their protection and growth is a mulch made up of information discovered during the act of drawing. The pencil, pen, brush dig into nature, uncovering hidden truths which will give the support and protection, that knowledge gives to the emerging artist. We are seldom hurt by what we know, but often we are hurt because of what we don't know.

There is a rather recent phenomenon in the technique of producing crops in which the weeds are killed off and the roots grow and flourish with spectacular results. But then we find those apparently healthy plants have been poisoned by indiscriminate use of harmful herbicides. I wonder if the same danger is not present in producing an artist: possibly by killing off all other growth around him, he will grow tall but lack that strength and sweetness which comes from combating the weeds of natural existence. (It always comes home to us, when we eat wild strawberries or huckleberries which have ripened among brambles, that these wild fruits have the sweetest flavor.)

The teacher should tread lightly around the growing plants and not overprune their tendency to wildness. When the shoots start to show, the pot should be placed where it catches all the light possible. Young plants always turn to grow toward the light. It is well to keep turning them so all sides are exposed to the light; then they fill out in all directions.

The light for the growing artist is the light of new ideas. Without this light the young artist will be overshadowed by the figures of the past and not really develop his roots to their full potential. This light can be an exposure to new materials, new elements of design, and new ideas in environments and conception.

Finally, the earth should be watered. One of the loveliest passages of Shakespeare comes in *The Merchant of Venice*, "The quality of mercy is not strain'd; It droppeth as the gentle rain from heaven Upon the place beneath." It is well for the teacher to have this kind of gentleness and, at the appropriate time, use it to refresh the student when his ideas have dried up and he needs encouragement and understanding.

I believe if we want to have a world filled with a great variety of beauty, all we have to do is nourish the artists' roots.

On Drawing   Quick 79

ON DRAWING

Drawing is commonly the first discipline learned and the last love forgotten by artists. It delineates the underlying structure of painting, sculpture, and architecture. It is woven into every process by which a work moves from nothing to completion. The first stroke is drawing, the last mark is drawing.

The dictionary devotes several paragraphs to the word "drawing," but, strangely enough, only a line or two about putting marks on paper. What does the dictionary say then? It says the carpenter draws nails, the farmer draws water from the well, a scientist draws conclusions. In other words, drawing is getting something out of something else.

The artist looks at the subject; he draws a conclusion; he makes a mark, then another, and another in sequence. Perhaps at the same time he is drawing from the object or subject, he is also drawing from his mind related material which can be used to enrich the final result.

He is also drawing from the drawing itself. As the line emerges from the point and gradually starts to take the form of an image on the paper, a tentative searching process begins. The inscribing point keeps turning over the ideas, hoping to find answers which will add to the quality of the final work. Sometimes the probing results in accidental discoveries that eventually may also become a part of the artist's technique.

But that describes drawing as if it were only a process, a verb, but it also is a noun, an object. Most artists make drawings as preliminary studies for larger works where matters such as anatomy, action, and composition are resolved; but, of course, drawings are also made as the finished work.

Drawings have their own special qualities that set them apart from other art forms. Their charm often lies in the directness with which they are done, in the relationship of the image to the otherwise unworked surface, and in the quality of the lines, as in Japanese brush drawings where the brush is handled skillfully — moving from dark to light, thick to thin, indicating great detail with the simplest and most direct means.

Drawing can be compared to a single line of music played on a violin where both the line and the sound take on weight when the performer bears down on the pen or the bow. There is a flowing melodic line in the drawings of Matisse, for instance.

The action of a point on paper or an etching plate is like an incision that goes deeper than the surface, into it like intaglio. This in all likelihood is the basic thing that makes the viewer come in close for a more intimate study of the work.

Painting, on the other hand, lies on the surface, covering it and creating a new surface which often takes on the quality of a cameo due to the thick impasto and, because of the rough surface, drives the viewer back to view the work from a distance. This is the reverse of the way people look at drawings.

Drawing moves easily into the areas of etching, engraving, lithography (really just a natural extension of drawing techniques), and then has the added virtue of availability to many instead of one while still retaining the hand mark of the artist.

The study of drawings and prints by both the artist and the connoisseur can be very engrossing because often there are so many subtle messages; the way to see them is to hold the work in hand and with bowed head examine it under a glass. Then you can move along through the rest of an exhibit with head thrown back, eyes in neutral, and look at the works of the outer world done by the painter and sculptor and expect them to come to you rather than your having to go to them.

Print Making   Quick '80

PRINTMAKING

The coppery glow of the etching plate, the polished surface of the freshly ground litho stone, and the warm tantalizing surface of the wood block — all cause the artist's fingers to itch with anticipation at working with these beautiful materials.

Sculptors, so I hear, can see within the stone a form to be released. So also engravers and woodcut artists find in the wood grain messages to be brought forth in the finished print.

In this book I am only writing about those aspects of art with which I have had some personal experience. So I have left out important techniques such as aquatint and intaglio. I have also left out the silk-screen process because I feel it is more closely related to painting than printing.

I used many burnished copper plates when I was a young man struggling with the chancy etching process. My courage has waned since those days, for I can no longer bring myself to deface the lovely glowing surface with the etching needle. The wounds to the plate are permanent. I think I have heard plates scream, "Don't touch me!" as they have seen a fumbling draftsman coming into view. It's too bad there aren't more Rembrandts. The carefully numbered prints from his hand are treasured the world over. In his case I believe the scars in the copper are justified.

The cutting of the plate is not done in just one operation. There may be many trial proofs; and, after each, more cutting and digging may be necessary in order to achieve a desired velvety dark or a stronger statement of line. In addition to the cutting there also are immersions in acid baths. This process will eventually destroy that beautiful surface and, therefore, is only for the strong of heart. I wish etchers well, but this risk is no longer for me.

On the other hand, the lithograph stone beckons. Here instead of cutting the surface, I pamper it by using a grease crayon as the drawing tool. Then in the printing process there follow alternating layers of ink, water, and grease — each of which is kind to the surface. The crushing weight of the presses is present in all the printing processes, but again the litho stone is treated well as it is eased

23

through the press, sliding under a greased surface as the printmaker pulls the print.

Finally, there is the woodcut or wood engraving in which all the unwanted surface is carved away, leaving a void that remains a void, or, "as the artist likes to say," becomes a negative space in the finished print. Only by creating these negative spaces can the artist produce the positive statement of line, plane, and — yes — color.

The earliest and purest prints of the woodcut artists were all done in black and white, an extension of the drawing technique of the artist, but now he has at his disposal the method of reaching a larger patronage through duplication.

Color is possible in both lithography and woodcuts but only with the use of additional stones or blocks, one for each color.

Japanese woodcuts in color made their appearance in Western Europe as wrappers around other oriental products. It took a Whistler and a Van Gogh to discover the charm of these prints and bring them to the attention of the art world. The same intensity of color appeared in the work of Van Gogh and in the delicate qualities of the prints in the paintings of Whistler and Cassatt.

Prints and printing have developed far beyond their early beginnings. The process still best serves the artist with a bent towards draftsmanship by allowing him to express his message in line and tone for many viewers. This is important to both the artist and the viewer as it provides a means for the artist to reach a larger market and the opportunity for the art lover with limited funds to own original works. This, of course, is the beauty of and the prime reason for all printmaking processes.

Quick 79'

On Painting

ON PAINTING

North light falls on a battlefield whose measurements are forty-two inches by forty-two inches. It is a most lonely war where one combatant struggles with himself trying to tear or wrest an elusive thought and spirit out of his very being. The weapons for the action are paint and brush, and the struggle is with the white surface that resists all change from its two-dimensional integrity to an illusionary feeling of depth.

Forever, it seems, this conflict has been going on. In an instance or two in the long history of art the victory has gone to the canvas. The painter has grown tired of the struggle and has said, "Let the surface be. Let it keep its integrity." Thus paintings became just that; the artist concluded that paintings were just color on a flat surface. Some will say this is great simplicity; others will call it a retreat and defeat. I do not want to take sides in this issue. I don't work that way. I only want to record my personal experiences in the field of painting, to speak from my own particular struggles with paint and brush.

If the painter has in front of him a square flat surface of canvas with nothing on it, he has something that is absolutely devoid of life and movement except perhaps for the light reflected off the canvas. But if he changes the square shape into a rectangle, it starts to have movement, either vertical or horizontal.

One of my first concerns, then, is to give a sense of movement or to quicken the surface. This movement is not real, of course; it is illusionary. That is the clue to all art, for it is not reality. At times, however, art even borders on trickery or magic such as *trompe l'oeil*, or "deceive the eye" painting. Art can lead the viewer into believing and feeling many things. It can bring elation, smiles, or tears.

Locked away in a closet art is nothing; hanging on the wall it is a message in tone, line, and color. The message needs an interpreter, and so the eternal round of painter, paintings, viewers is set in motion. The viewer begins to understand the message, and a flow of understanding is established between him and the painter with the painting itself in between. If the painting does what it should, then the sensations once felt by the painter should be experienced anew by the veiwer. To produce these moods, the painter may use many media such as tempera, encaustic, gouache, fresco, casein, acrylic, oil, and watercolor.

I have devoted a lifetime to working in oil and watercolor; therefore, I shall speak only about them. The properties of each are quite different and demand a different attitude and mood when you approach them. Watercolor demands much skill, for the painter has to be right the first time. I think his best chance for success in the watercolor technique lies in putting on the mantle or hat of the devil-may-care swashbuckler; in oil, where the surface can be developed slowly, the painter can adopt the role of the thoughtful philosopher.

The medium of watercolor is transparent, elusive, fugitive; it is rapidly absorbed into the paper (sometimes, indeed, as the painter is looking at it), and can never be taken out again. The color is put on the surface as pigment mixed with water, and is drawn down and down into the paper with the color settling at different levels, depending on how much or how little water is used. The painter thereby creates a sensation of space as he repeats the process. If very little water is used, the color becomes opaque with hard edges that lie on the surface of the paper and create a great sensation of space when contrasted with those vague transparent colors with the blurred edges lost deep within the paper.

In both oil and watercolor, to make color recede or come forward is a device many painters use not only to fool the eye but also to lead the viewer into the depths of a landscape or the dark corners of an interior or the background of a still life. The painting surface gives one the horizontal and vertical dimension, but the painter controls and makes the space he needs beyond that surface.

Some artists like Paul Cezanne spent a lifetime working within a carefully controlled depth. Cezanne occasionally painted watercolors, and he would worry about his predecessors' losing the viewer in the misty distances of a romantic landscape. Therefore, he stopped the viewer by constructing paintings that only allowed the eyes to go so far, and then they had to go across the space or return to the surface. On the other hand, the great English artist, Joseph Mallord William Turner, whose major effort was in watercolor, would not care whether he lost the viewer in the sky or behind a distant mountain.

What the viewer chooses will depend on himself. One will choose the security of a Cezanne while another will prefer the adventure of a Turner. As for me, I prefer to work, sometimes limiting my space to the surface of the painting, at other times deepening my space back into the painting; for I like the variety of space that is suggested by the subject — be it mouse or elephant.

To move from the matter of technique to that of theory, I believe painters start to lose the meaning of art when they say there is a theory that can be followed. Somehow, watercolor has become the medium that attracts the largest number of show-offs in art. These painters, after becoming very skillful in technique, turn out one book after another of the how-to-do-it variety and lead many young painters into the shallowness of mere rendering. Great watercolors deny analysis and resist a display of clever technique.

Shortly after my tour of four years in the army I fell into the trap myself. After getting the job as a watercolor teacher at the college, I thought I should brush up on my skills in order to have something to pass on to the students. Setting up one still life after another, I slavishly copied them and soon was able to show the fuzz on peaches without any trouble. At that time there was only one pro-fessional gallery in town. The dealer's name was Harriet Hanley, and her gallery was the Hanley Gallery. Mrs. Hanley was an angel to many young artists and helped them get atarted by showing their works. To make me, a newcomer, known in Minneapolis, she gave me a one-man show of these watercolor still lifes. My first exhibit in Minneapolis!

People came and were polite and told me I was very clever with watercolor, but no one found the paintings so interesting that they wanted to own one. The exhibit came down and was tucked away and forgotten in the gallery's storage room.

Several years later I was helping Mrs. Hanley clean up the storage room, and we came upon the watercolors. What a shock it was for me! I said, "Harriet, I want to burn these." She said, "Good, I will help you." She continued, "They never did say anything to me. They were only clever renderings." And so I learned another lesson the hard way.

Excessively finished art is similar, in a way, to spoon-feeding. The viewer, much like an infant, is fed by the mother (the painter) who makes sure that nothing escapes being consumed or assimilated. Being spoon-fed eliminates the possibility of making choices. It even eliminates the excitement of occasionally making a mistake. An artist friend once told me that he never finished a painting; he always stopped while it was still becoming something. Usually, he said, the viewer will finish those parts not completely resolved, to his own liking, and therefore he himself becomes part of the creative process.

The Japanese watercolor, with its hard edges sharply delineated and its soft edges blending into the paper, leaves much to the imagination of the viewer. Thus it is not strange to find that Japan is a leader in the art of watercolor painting. To discover that America is equally as important in this tradition is quite unexpected.

To watch a Japanese artist at work soon explains his affinity for watercolor. The painter, kneeling on the floor with the paper laid out flat before him, is in the perfect position to control the liquid flow of the medium because water seeking its own level is very hard to control on an inclined surface. As the artist works in this kneeling position, he takes on the rapt expression of a supplicant pleading for the vision to appear. He is truly in touch with his inner self because, flowing from the end of the brush simultaneously, a painting and a poem written in caligraphic brush strokes appear on the paper. To arrest the fleeting image of a bird on the wing, fluttering from one branch to another, in both a haiku and the medium of watercolor, is a *tour de force* that appeals to the Japanese mind.

I think the American artist chooses the medium of watercolor for other reasons. As I review the names of American watercolorists, I find them to be a restless lot, moving about all over the world, often at the seaside, crossing the prairies of the West, or deep in a forest. I am thinking of James John Audubon, Winslow Homer, John Singer Sargent, Charles Russell, Frederic Remington, and John Marin. These great watercolorists were among the first American artists to make an impact on the international art scene. Their restlessness was a trait common to most Americans at the time. Restlessness, and the necessity for quick results, led to the invention of a kind of painting shorthand. In that day men didn't travel in vans large enough to be studios; they traveled in canoes or boats, on a mule or on horseback. Their kits were packsacks filled with sketch books, brushes, and colors. In that day watercolor was often a method of notetaking to be enlarged into oil paintings later when the artist got back to his studio.

Homer, Sargent, Marin regarded watercolor as a true art form in itself; and much of their creative work, particularly in later life, was done in watercolor. It is said that Sargent called portrait painting a pimp's profession, and he gave it up entirely to do watercolors.

As for myself and my preference, I have often been asked — which is more important in my mind, watercolor or oil painting? It would seem that because I do both, I don't have any real preference. This is true and not true at the same time. As I said at the beginning of this discussion of painting, each medium is approached with a different attitude, both by the artist and the viewer. (This is probably true of all the media in painting.)

Watercolor certainly lends itself to the light touch and the catching of a fleeting moment. Therefore, when the artist feels the pressure of limited time or within himself the urgency to make a statement in a hurry, he turns to watercolor. This, however, doesn't mean he has a preference for watercolor. At other times when he knows he has in his mind only the germ of an idea that is going to have to ripen and grow over a long period of time, he probably will turn to oil. Since all pigments are basically the same "powdered color," it is the medium that the artist responds to. The sheer transparent effect of watercolor is answered by the lush fullness of oil. Watercolor reveals the painting surface beneath while oil covers the surface with one newly created by the artist. There have been many instances where the oil surfaces built up by certain old masters have outlived the canvas beneath, and restorers have been able to remove and transfer them to a new surface.

Some of the most meaningful moments are slow to materialize, and the endless plastic qualities of oil give the creator the time to realize his vision. They say it took seven years for Da Vinci to complete the *Mona Lisa*. It is a pleasure to hear interior house painters talk about the properties and possibilities of oil paints. They use such terms as lean and fat, brushing and covering qualities, slow and fast drying, glossy and flat, undercoat and finish coat. Basically, the house painter and artist use the same terms and experience the same pleasure when manipulating their exciting materials.

The child when given finger paints exhibits joy both in the feel of the material and admiration for the colors that appear. So does the painter but to a much higher degree. He discovers, as he becomes more proficient, the unlimited possibilities for nuances of expression far beyond his initial understanding. These possibilities are the crux to me of a dilemma and a joy always present in each painting. There is *always* the question of the balance, of how a thing is said in relation to what is being said. There is *always* the question of restraint and freedom.

I believe the center of our emotions lies in the subconscious. The viscera becomes inflamed and builds up great power which surges through the whole body and finally finds release at the end of the brush as it touches the canvas. To keep from exploding some artists have had to pour, throw, or even shoot (with bullets filled with paint) their message onto the surface in order to gain this release. Examples of such artists are Jackson Pollock and Salvador Dali. (One wonders if examples could not be found of individuals whose inability to release this power resulted in madness and death.)

To be aware of this great power is absolutely necessary to all creative persons. I am sure mothers at birth experience feelings very much akin to those of the artist when he has completed a painting which has been a long time on the easel. To express this power, there is no question in my mind that the balancing of the message and technique is more sure with oil than with watercolor. With this knowledge in mind the painter in oil is likely to attack larger and more involved subject matter. At least, I find this true of myself.

The opportunity to explore a subject and figure out the answers and brush them onto the surface at a pace that fits the mood of the painter is perhaps the single most important feature of the technique of oil painting. The artist can walk to the back of his studio, sit down in his favorite chair, and mull over what he has done while he was standing at the easel — out of touch with the outside world but in touch with those inner forces boiling up from the subconscious about the concepts he is trying to guide and convert into meaningful marks upon his canvas. It's dangerous, but in my case I often work most of the day without taking the trip to that comfortable chair. Then late in the afternoon I will go there, maybe pour a glass of sherry, and sit and sit and stare and stare at the canvas with the distance giving my eyes the opportunity to see the whole work rather than just that part which is at the end of the brush. Often after this period of relaxed reverie, I am able to write myself a note which I affix to the canvas. This will help me to get back to the place and mood of the subconscious mind that I had when I left off painting for the day. In addition, I carry with me a consciously thought-out plan of action for the future.

About the subconscious mind, I tell my students that calling upon it is like putting a car into neutral, going to sleep, and rolling down a mountain road at breakneck speed. It is absolutely necessary that the subconscious mind immediately recognize a slip of the brush or an error in judgment which will jar the artist awake so he can apply the brakes and once again put the mind in gear in order to avoid wrecking the work in progress. When the student reaches this point of automatic reaction, he is well on the way to being a totally free creative artist.

In the subconscious effort I find my brush being directed to pat, stroke, scrub, smear, and caress the surface — each action being a response to the messages I am receiving from the subject being painted. While these strokes are happening, the brush is being dipped into colors of different hue, value, and consistency — following the messages received from the subject but also responding to my personal sense of beauty in color relationships.

This beauty may be apprehended on the surface of the painting. Here the viewer may see the love the oil painter has for the surface. The kind of love the artist has for the surface can be traced from passionate to gentle with all the nuances in between. This can be done simply by letting the eye or hand travel over the surface. I suspect certain scholars of art could even pick out some artists' names by touching the surface. (They say the great Polish pianist Paderewski could glance at the massed notes on a score that was across the room and tell the name of the composer.)

Some examples of how this love is expressed might be seen by, say, the three R's in art. Rembrandt's surface and the way it is built up reveals an honest earthy love. The Flemish artist Rubens expresses a sumptuous elegant love. And Renoir, the French painter, displays an unembarrassed sensual love. Renoir once said he knew when the painting was finished because he came to a point where he felt more like touching than painting.

But, there is also the virtue of restraint. I always like to feel that the orchestra could reach a louder crescendo, the operatic tenor could go a note higher, the sculptor could achieve a brighter polich on the marble, and the poet could reduce the line to two words and still make the same good sense. What is important, however, is for me to accept these without the necessity of proof. For even though the exotic dancer removes only one piece of clothing at a time, revealing more and more information about anatomy, the viewer is finally completely informed and completely disillusioned. Oh, to have some of the mystery still hidden behind a veil.

I still have many things I could say about painting, but I want to stop to let the reader ponder the idea that mystery in painting is one of its choicest attributes.

Quirk 79.
Pose Please.

POSE, PLEASE

The model stand is a whole way of life, a microcosmic reflection of the world. Sadness, joy, laughter, pain — all have occupied the platform in turn. The model is a device for projecting ideas. The model is a symbol that reveals the elements of story and design. A single gesture can provide the definition of the limits of a life or of a whole system of balances and parts.

The stories told of and by the models cover the gamut of human experience:

Laura was a bony little creature, all eyes, frightened at the prospect of posing in the nude for the first time. The art teacher, old in the profession and aware of Laura's emotional state, was very kind. He turned to the class and said, "Please note the beauty of her bone structure." Then, he urged them to make use of the special opportunity to study this aspect of anatomy. Laura grew to love the school and its students — maybe too well, for she became pregnant and left to have a baby.

Something must have gone wrong because a month or two later a box arrived at the school. In it was Laura's skeleton, bequeathed to the school. Now her beautiful bones are studied every year by the students, and she is still a part of the school.

Lilian, alias Dirty Gerty, occupied the stand over several years. She looked like a Michelangelo sculpture except for a cat tattooed on her thigh. Her villain's role in the local wrestling ring gave her the name of Dirty Gerty. She often arrived to pose covered with assorted bruises and with black eyes, always claiming her opponents looked even worse. In addition, Lilian had other jobs such as swallowing swords, jumping out of airplanes and out of cakes at men's smokers.

All this she did to raise a daughter kept hidden away far from her mother's world in a girls' school where the priority was to train young ladies in the social graces. Lilian worked hard so her daughter could step into another kind of world.

The fruit in the still life shrivels and rots, the flowers fade and are discarded. But models say, "We're not objects, we're personages and deserve better treatment." They come and go like migrant workers, many never quite seeming to be there at all. Perhaps more of them should be like Renoir's Gabriel. After her flesh lost its glow, she became his cook. From then on she lived in his paintings, an eternal glorious tribute to her beauty.

Models like Gabriel have become famous and immortal in marble, bronze, and paint. Their likenesses have been fought over, stolen, purchased at fabulous prices, and auctioned again and again at ever higher prices. The model stand in these cases becomes an expanding space that is larger than life. This prospect must be what has led many to answer the call, "Take the pose, please."

Paintings of the undraped charms of Gabriel, Mademoiselle O'Murphy, Dianne de Poitiers, the Duchess of Alba, along with legions of others must have stirred the libidos of those early connoisseurs of the female form. Today the models have much competition from the theater, rap houses, and bars, but the back-bar nude still stands a better chance of survival than those who dance upon the bar among the glasses.

Nudity versus the draped figure became the basis for an interesting model strike that took place at my college. For years, the idea held that disrobing to display one's body should be better paid to compensate for the possible loss of modesty. However, as nudity became more common, the validity of this claim seemed to disappear so the models became worried. The strike was based on this new thought, that it was just as difficult to put clothes on as it was to take them off. Because special costumes were necessary, there was more preparation necessary before the models could take the stand. Needless to say, they won the strike, and now clothed models are paid the same fee as nude ones.

Models have been an aspect of art since the earliest times. One of the Venus figures discovered by archeologists had twelve breasts. She, of course, was a goddess, symbolic of fertility. Gods and goddesses have figured prominently in the development of the models' world.

Vanity, vanity, thy name is not necessarily woman. It is also the male that struts onto the stage and preens himself. Forget Venus; think Apollo, Hercules, and Atlas. These are the types that the modern body-building muscle man patterns himself after.

Alvin Narcissus had a 60 inch chest, 18 inch biceps, 20 inch waist, and every one of his muscles rippled and twisted like the convolutions of a boa constrictor. He stood in front of a mirror day after day pumping himself up in either the discus-throwing or the Atlas pose.

This limited repertoire soon lost its attraction, like the stilted poses taken by fashion models.

Another model was a prize fighter who shadowboxed an electric light cord for half an hour before class, giving off a sweaty sort of realism quite unlike the perfumed, painted exhibitionist who reeked of Passion Flower.

Not all the male models fitted these odd patterns. There were red caps, vaudeville dancers, symphony cellists, actors, and many others whose paycheck left them a little short. Often, it was augmented by selling blood or posing.

There was one male model, like Laura all skin and bones. His skin was dark mahogany; his ancestors came from Bombay, so he said, and were practitioners of yoga. One day to prove his case he took a pose standing on one foot with the other foot on his knee, balancing with a staff. He did not blink nor show any other sign of life for three hours. The bell rang for the class to be finished, but still he stood for another five minutes. Then snapping his fingers, he relaxed the pose, which had been an exercise in self control.

As Shakespeare said, the world is a stage; certainly, the world of the model stand is. The best models are intelligent people with a feeling for the stage and for acting. This is the land of the mime and of the painter.

The Studio   Qualk 79

THE STUDIO

If a play were ever written about a visit to an artist's studio, the opening speech, as the actor makes his entrance, would have to be, "I love the smell of turpentine and paint." No other line would be authentic. If you entered Grandma's kitchen on baking day, you would have to say, "I love the smell of fresh-baked bread." Or in the barn, "I love the smell of new-mown hay."

The studio experience starts with the nose, but then impressions flow in through other senses. Most studios never start out to be a studio but end up being one, after having been used for other purposes for years. Quite often, these buildings are one step away from the wrecker. This fact may have some relationship to the public's view that the artist is a very romantic fellow, living always on the perilous edge of life. He has settled in such rundown places as the Left Bank, Paris; Greenwich Village, New York; and the French Quarter, New Orleans.

The artist's studio should be a place where he can study alone, but he also wants to have quick access to friends and fellow artists in neighborhood gathering places such as cafes and bars. In addition to the danger of being destroyed by a wrecker's ball, an even greater danger for the artist's studio is that people of affluence gradually find the areas quaint and start to move in and renovate the studio buildings, raising the rent to a point where the artists have to move out and start all over again in some other lean corner.

But in the meantime the artist has given the cities areas with special character that have made these cities famous and loved. Again, think of Paris, Rome, Florence, Amsterdam, New York, New Orleans, and San Francisco. All these cities should say thanks to the artists who were poor in pocket but rich in ideas.

But now to return to the studio itself, because that is where the work takes place and, consequently, where the interest lies. To look behind the scene is the way to become an aficionado in any field. Take knothole gangs at the baseball parks, sidewalk superintendents of excavations, peekers under tents at the circus, or peerers over the artist's shoulder in his studio — they all belong to the same inquiring group hoping to find out what goes on. The artist has no reason to be upset by this interest because this is what he himself does all the time as he observes the world and the actions of the people in it.

I have been in many different studios in my life and can give a composite description of what you might find in them. The arts very often overlap, so you might be greeted along with the smell of paint by the sound of music. It might even be that the type of music you hear will give you a clue to what kind of art you will see. I understand that in the studio of Stuart Davis you would hear the most advanced jazz of his day. They say El Greco always had a string quartet play for him as he worked, or at least when he dined. In my own studio I generally try to have Dixieland jazz, traditional jazz, or classical symphonies. Sometimes I am very lucky; the sound completely fills out the mood I am in, and the painting just seems to flow to the rhythm of the music. But those moments seem to pass quickly.

In most studios the artist himself is the housekeeper; contrary to what people might think, the artist is a capable housekeeper. The place may look quite cluttered and dusty on first impression; but the paints, brushes, and palette probably will be in shape for immediate use.

The job of making a painting generally means bringing order to many various ideas and putting them down in a planned organization on the canvas. Therefore, it is relaxing to have a jumble of odd shapes, textures, and colors for the eye to rest upon. Not only that, but the artist is often stimulated by the shape, color, or type of object that stands, sits, or lies around.

The clutter of objects generally reflects the geographical location of the studio. For instance, in Holland, where many artists had a great interest in the art of still-life painting, if you saw books scattered around, you probably would be in either the university town of Leyden or at Den Hague, the seat of government. If you saw blue pottery and glass, you would be in Vermeer's hometown of Delft. And if you were at the seaside towns, either in Holland or America, there would be fishing gear, and fish would pass through the studio — to be painted on their way to the frying pan.

All this has to do with the still-life painters, and there have been great ones, both in the past and the present. Some copied the objects so carefully that they seemed to step from the still-life table to the canvas on the easel. Other more modern studios may have canvases hanging on the wall with the subjects dismembered through cubism, but still holding to the basic qualities of the subject matter.

In the studio of the landscape artist the outside will have been moved inside; and on a winter visit to the studio, as on a winter visit to a conservatory, you will find summertime all around you. The lure of travel to far-off romantic places has often appealed to the artistic temperament, especially to a landscape painter. To see the oceans, mountains, and rivers of the world is always a stimulant to creativity, and so there also may be many landscapes of foreign places among the works within the studio. A winter visit may satisfy the visitor's hunger both for summer and far-off places at the same time.

Generally, the studios of portrait painters are more elegant than those of other artists, simply because they feel that with the proper bric-a-brac they will instill confidence about their own good taste in the mind of the sitter. This would not be the case in the average artist's studio. It frequently is as cluttered as the city dump.

Most artists have several works in progress at once, so you most likely will find many partially finished works leaning against the walls. At least, this is the situation in my studio. Bonnard's studio always had many works in progress, but instead of being on stretched canvases the paintings were tacked to the wall all around the room. He would walk into the middle of his studio each day, and with a fresh eye he would see what was to be done and would move from one painting to another, working on them as the spirit moved him. This must have been a very colorful studio to visit.

Often the artist not only paints but sculpts or makes prints. The variety of tools and equipment increases with each additional activity, and so the clutter becomes even more interesting. Just imagine, for example, a visit to Michelangelo's studio. There you could have found plans for the Vatican, half-revealed saints on stone, sketches for the Sistine ceiling, scraps of paper with original poems scribbled on them, and — not least — in the corner the lute which Michelangelo could play superbly. We are not all Renaissance men, but often artists have a number of interests that you will find reflected in the atmosphere of the studio.

If you are lucky, not only will you smell paint and see paintings and drawings, and hear music, but also you may begin a friendship because most artists view an interest in their studio as an interest in them personally, and a new friendship might become the most valuable reward of a visit to the artist's studio.

The Fallow time   Quick 79.

THE FALLOW TIME

The time that falls between the artist's schooling and the first step across the threshold of professionalism is the fallow time. The soil has been plowed over and over again at the college of art, and now the student faces the harrowing torment of finding his own level or place in art. This is the period that will try his soul and affect the rest of his life to a greater degree than any other that has gone before. How it is faced can make or break a career.

I have watched hundreds of students and felt for them as they have faced this time; therefore, I would like to draw a variety of truthful and sympathetic portraits of a few of them. I think, in fact, I will do two portraits: one drawing as they were during this period and a second one showing what they became several years later. The names are fictitious, but perhaps some students will think they are the subjects. However, there are so many common problems and answers that could apply to any number of students. Before these portraits are revealed, I would like to state that the life of an artist is so insecure that almost anything that he might do to get through this period should be acceptable.

The first subject that comes to my mind is Pat, an extremely talented boy from a mining community. He had the aesthetic look of a hungry poet. All eyes and with expressive hands appended to a gangling bent frame which looked much older than it was. He did not last out the four years of art school because he was too anxious to get on with the task of becoming an artist. He stepped into the period of growing up much faster than most, and his struggles resemble several counterparts in the world of art. Most people would say he was too immature to do what he did, but it happened anyway.

The studio at this juncture is often a lonesome place, and so one answer is to share it with someone else. Pat had his own personal dreams to follow which he did not wish to share with another artist, so rather than sharing his loft over a barn with an artist, he took a wife instead. Pat's mother had great faith in him and was able to understand her son's loneliness to a point that she was willing to help support him and his wife — and soon a child.

49

At first, this seems to be a portrait of a weak character. However, the later portrait shows that Pat accepted the poverty and the problems that went with it, stayed true to his concept that the artist should never do anything to compromise his art, yet would accept any help and would be ready to turn his hand to anything to support his life as an artist. Pat went from restoring paintings to frame-making to being a museum guard.

Meanwhile, by staying at his creative work, he was building up a following of patrons who came to treasure his paintings, drawings, and etchings — including the very loving paintings done of his wife and daughter as well as many still lifes and romantic cityscapes. The art world is certainly richer because of him, and any early debts incurred by him to anyone have been repaid a hundred times over through his commitment to art.

How is success counted? Was Van Gogh a success, or Gauguin? Tom O. came to the art school from the army and from behind the counter of a small family grocery store; six feet, four inches tall, with the muscle of a young Hercules, completely at odds with the popular image of the emaciated artist. Inside that big frame was a heart equally large which, unexpectedly, cried out with a longing for beauty. In school his fumbling hands only formed one or two oil paintings, a few drawings and watercolors. Each was a struggle towards perfection not in terms of realism but in terms of harmony of color, form, texture, and mood.

Tom never left any place — he just extended himself to include a new place while always leaving a generous part of himself behind for his friends to live with. With his minimal production in art you could almost say his entire life was a fallow time, but his life as an artist was a success because it produced what he wanted. His struggles with the tools of the artist gave him an appreciation of the worth of a completed work, and so he came to understand artists better than if he had remained outside their circle and only observed. He did not produce art *per se*, but he produced an artistic life that, viewed by others, made them aware of the sweetness or sensitivity that can be built into a life by living and moving in a circle of art.

He died at the age of fifty-two, alone in New York City, a failure in most peoples' eyes but a success in mine. He had made a conceptual piece of art of an entire lifetime. This same story can be told about legions of students who have attended art schools. They are not now, and never have been, practicing professional artists, but to call their lives in art failures would be a mistake because they have become a part of the milieu of artistic life, and for this reason will enhance any part of life which they touch. In the ongoing process of creativity they cannot be called anything but successful.

In doing some portraits you may find yourself working in the poor light of a back parlor or from a fragment of a faded photograph. This is the way I feel about drawing Carla, but the very vagueness of the subject makes her interesting. Carla was one of a number of women who came to the college with a wedding band on her finger and with a feeling that she had a male anchor locked to her leg. The scenario that follows has been repeated over and over again to my knowledge; however, in Carla's case it had little bearing on the major outline of her portrait. The coloring and dynamics have more to do with her id and the timing of her entrance onto the stage of art.

Though small of stature and timid almost to the point of not speaking, she had the brilliance of a diamond. The marriage soon failed, and the anchor was struck away to give Carla the freedom she felt she needed to create her art. Huge canvases started to appear, and — long before their general acceptance — they had all the abstract qualities of an orgiastic experience. These paintings created a sensation around the college. I always felt they were a fantasizing on the love she failed to receive from her erstwhile husband.

This may appear to have little to do with the fallow time that followed when Carla, the fine artist, sank from sight into the anonymity of the sea of graphic design. The survival period was upon her, and she did not shrink from the dangers of taking the lure of steady well-paying creative work in the neighboring waters of commercial trade. To tear yourself free from such a tender trap takes courage that only the true artist has. The time was upon her to bring forth those works in fine art of which she felt herself capable.

I know Shakespeare's Caesar was speaking to his legions when he said, "There is a tide in the affairs of men which when taken at the flood, leads on to fortune." Possibly a captain of a legion of Valkyries or Amazons said the same to women such as Carla; at least, she was picked up in the flood of the women's liberation movement, and she now is riding on its crest and wisely is taking a part in guiding the wave against a formidable barrier reef erected by the male chauvinists in art — of which there were and are many.

Her portrait shows a transformation through her art from a fearful girl child to a leader of women. Her career certainly will set a pattern that many graduating students could follow with clear conscience; therefore, I consider her life in art a real success.

I expect that if this were to be written in the next decade, the ratio of one woman to four men would be inaccurate, but at the present time I believe it is a fair proportion in relation to those achieving recognition in the world of art, so let's turn to Dick and Harry.

Happily, during my tenure at the college of art, there was a very broad curriculum, and so everyone who attended had a chance to fit into a program that suited his personality. In the case of Dick, it was a program that suited his very high I.Q. To him the studio meant what it is supposed to mean: a place to study, and study he did. The art history class was not a frill on studio work; to him it was a catalog of information. The lessons in color were not merely to find those which looked good together but rather to learn all the theory in order to know what additional uses color could be put to. The figure on the model stand was to him not just a beautiful girl but also a human machine that worked, driven by chemical and electrical impulses that give power to the muscles which in turn control the structural frame of bones through a series of pulleys and levers. This machine can lift weights and be moved by its own power from one place to another to carry on the work of the world.

Dick, in the study of anatomy, found the vehicle through which he would express his artistic message for several years. But we are getting ahead of ourselves and skipping his story in the fallow time.

Dick had a pragmatical view of life, a facet of character seldom found among artists. He set his goal to be a success in art through education and plotted his course accordingly. Fifteen or twenty years ago, without question, the broad highway to security for the artist was to take employment in a college as a teacher of art. To be honest, this was and is the sinecure of jobs because while providing a living wage, these jobs also leave the artist free time to do his own creative work. That's why they were pursued so avidly by the artist. Now so many have followed Dick's path that all teaching openings have hundreds of applicants. What was once a broad highway has turned into a narrow trail leading into a desert.

Dick eventually found one of these jobs, but first he, like Carla, put in quite a stint as a graphic artist at a rather ordinary advertising firm. Though the advertising world did not appeal to Dick, he realized that the same principles of design, color, and form applied to the field of graphics as to the fine arts, and that he had the opportunity to practice them until the time came when he would be able to apply them to his own fine-art ventures.

All of Dick's study and talent found their outlet in the academic world. Out of the free time came hundreds of dramatic oil paintings and prints based on that early study of the muscles and bones found in the human form. His name is no longer needed in the lower corner of the work to proclaim it as his from across the room. This is the real stamp of success, and we must remember that Dick has achieved this while risking his identity by satisfying the demands of clients in advertising.

It is important to realize that both Carla and Dick have proved this, and it should help to put to rest the quarrels that continually flare between the two disciplines.

A final example of the fallow time is found in the artistic career of Harry, who came to the college from the wide-open spaces of the West. He was a handsome athletic type with a slight bow to his legs, as many of his growing years were spent in a saddle while working on his family's ranch. Fortunately, he was a strong-willed person, as many of our students are because they have to fight for what they believe, often against the awesome power of a professor with a grade book in hand. I'm sure Harry had done his share of breaking horses to a saddle and knew all their bucking tricks to avoid being ridden. At least, he was able to escape that experience himself and came into the school with an idea of what direction he wanted his art to take. Four years later he left with his dream still intact and polished up to a point where it was starting to shine in a limited way on a small coterie of art buyers.

His dream was to do paintings of horses and riders, in the style of his heroes, Charles Russell and Frederic Remington, the popular painters of the romantic Old West. A student comes to the college seeking a way to reach his goal or dream and is not sure how to go about it; he will find that trial and error play as large a part as guidance does in reaching the goal.

This was true of Harry who came to paint and ended up in sculpture. His attempts at color proved him color blind; after several failures in painting, he turned from it, first to drawing, and finally to sculpture. This proved to be his forte. He did not carve but modeled in clay and cast the final product in bronze. I vaguely recall he worked as an apprentice for a number of prominent sculptors, doing castings and finishing, the manual labor of the athletic and aesthetic profession of sculpture. The next I heard he had left America and gone to the country of his ancestors, the Netherlands.

Years later I was made the director of studies abroad and took up a residence in the Netherlands to supervise the education of thirty

American art students. There I became reacquainted with Harry, who is now one of the country's leading sculptors and doing many important commissions for the government.

The cowboy from Montana, a member of the oldest art club of Amsterdam which was started with such members as Vincent Van Gogh, Anton Mauve and others of this rank, is still true to his first love, animals, and has now raised his interpretations of them to a very high level of sophistication. The last work which I saw in progress in his studio was a life-size modern version of Pegasus springing skyward from the body of Medusa — a far cry from the cowboy on a bucking bronco.

All these students I have written about have completed this fallow time, and it has proven to be very important. The fledgling artists have now become professional artists; but their struggles, in aiming for success, seem to have given them a touch of humility.

Quick 79
Getting in the
Mood

GETTING IN THE MOOD

Do not speak to an artist of nuts and bolts and then expect him to create. This is like dropping anchor and then shouting, "Set sail!" The artist has to prepare himself in spirit before the flow of creativity can take place.

There are many exotic examples of this preparation in the annals of art.

One ancient story is told by a servant of the Emperor of China who wished to have the walls of the palace decorated. Word was sent out to all corners of the realm for the artists to assemble at the palace and present themselves with their credentials to the Emperor so he could make his selection. When the artists were all assembled, many spread out examples for him to see, others spoke of great things they had done, others prepared their brushes and pigments. One, however, only bowed to the Emperor and left.

The Emperor called to a servant and said, "Follow that man and see what he does." The servant came back, and the Emperor asked what the man did. The servant said it was very strange. He followed the artist as he returned to his home and here he took off all his clothes and sat down naked and spraddle-legged in the middle of his room.

The Emperor said, "Dismiss all the others and hire that man, because he has prepared himself perfectly by ridding himself of all pretentions so he could serve both art and his Emperor."

Another story concerns the practice of the Oriental artist who contemplates the subject for weeks and weeks until he feels he is the subject. Then and then only, he returns to his studio and re-creates the scene from memory. He hopes, by this process, to eliminate detail and to catch the essence.

It is said that Giotto and Fra Angelico never picked up a brush without first praying, that Da Vinci painted the Mona Lisa in a black-walled room to the accompaniment of music by a string quartet.

Some artists prepare themselves by assuming a role. This may mean putting on a suitable costume. A very successful member of

57

the "action painting" school said that the canvas was a battlefield; therefore, he did not paint without first donning a military uniform.

For many years almost the whole body of artists wore distinctive clothing: berets, smocks, or, for the more elegant, Windsor ties and velvet jackets. By assuming this Bohemian attire artists were able to divorce themselves from the humdrum aspects of society and prepare themselves *in toto* for the free spirit they felt necessary in order to create.

The artist is not just a hand and an eye but is a laughing, suffering human who has to prepare himself as everyone else must. This does include, of course, getting involved with nuts and bolts; but there is a time when they have to be put aside so that, with an unencumbered mind, he can approach his art.

Quick 79.   There's Something Wrong With the Nose

THERE'S SOMETHING WRONG
WITH THE NOSE

John Singer Sargent, the famous American portrait painter, once was asked what a portrait was. He replied, "It is a painting of someone's face with something wrong with the eyes, nose or mouth." Artists can paint poor landscapes, still lifes, and even poor abstract studies, and escape the criticism of the public, but once they do a portrait, even if it is a masterpiece, they become fair game because everyone is certain Grandma's nose is not like that.

The great *Night Watch*, a large group portrait by Rembrandt which hangs enshrined as a national treasure in the Rijksmuseum in Amsterdam, was so severely criticized by his public that it brought Rembrandt to bankruptcy. Fortunately, the criticism acted in the opposite way on him aesthetically. (Often, unfair comments have positive effects.) From that moment on he worried less about catching the exact likeness of the sitters and more about the psychological impact of the painting. After that he did his greatest works.

A friend of Picasso found him sitting very dejectedly in front of a canvas in his studio. The friend said, "What's wrong, Pablo?" He said, "There's something wrong with the nose." "Well," the caller said, "why don't you fix it?" Picasso said, "I can't find it."

Henry VIII, like many other monarchs, before the invention of the camera, had portraits done of foreign princesses so he could have a preview before he added them to his long list of wives. It certainly must have given the artist Holbein pause. He had to please a princess and fool a king.

With the entrance of the camera following shortly on the heels of French painter Ingres, the problem for kings was solved, but the portrait painter found himself in straitened financial circumstances. As much as most of the painters disliked painting portraits, the money they made in the field paid for their more interesting adventures in other areas of art.

Gainsborough said his wife kept him in the harness as a portrait painter while he would much rather have ridden in the wagon, playing his viola da gamba, or painting landscapes.

In the early days of American art, portrait painters, loaded with rolls of canvases all with prepainted costumes and backgrounds, traveled the back roads. If you were a prosperous farmer, you could have your wife's face and head added to the most elegant gown already posed in front of a many-columned country home. All this could be done in the front parlor.

From the bust of King Tutankhamen to the most recent likeness of a president, portraits trace the history of nations while noting the life style, clothing, housing, and grooming of the times. Obviously, a portrait has value far beyond that of mere likeness. Thus, in the history of art, it makes little difference if there is something wrong with the nose.

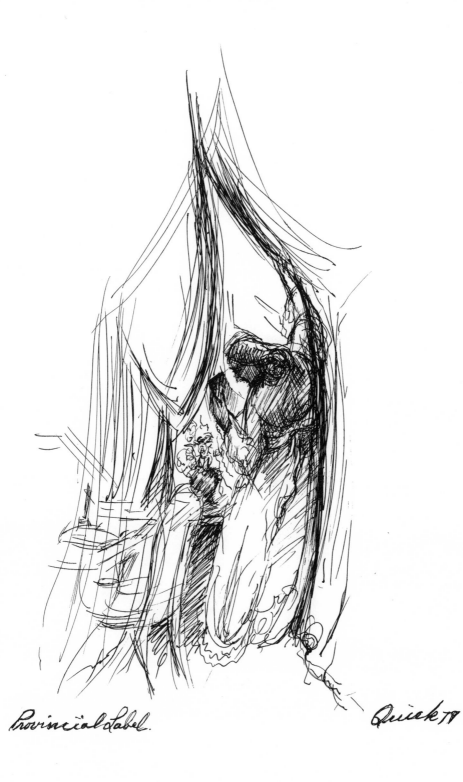

Provincial Label.   Quick 79

THE PROVINCIAL LABEL

"A prophet is not without honor save in his own country . . ."
Matthew 13:57

Going to the other side of the earth to find a sculptor, painter, or architect may at times show extra perception on the part of a patron, but at others it shows fear — the fear of being branded with the label of provincialism.

This fear, as the leading quotation from the Scripture seems to suggest, has been with us for a long time. These words of Christ also suggest that the fear is unwarranted.

People of stature and taste do not suffer from this fear; rather they seek diamonds in their own backyards and revel in the experience when they occasionally discover one. It is almost always the mature and experienced who enjoy this simple pleasure.

In the introduction I spoke of how my father initiated me to the art of trout fishing by taking me to a small stream in a nearby farmer's pasture and how I did not catch anything. Since then I have fished far and wide, but I have returned to this first fishing hole in the farmer's pasture. Now there is a difference. I catch trout there and hear the nearby village church bells chiming at the same time.

Provincialism has most always been associated with isolation, but is this true? A number of our first great artists in America who helped destroy the tag of provincialism, a label left behind from our colonial days, were such people as painter Albert Ryder, poet Emily Dickinson, and philosopher/writer Henry David Thoreau. These three became almost hermits as they retreated to their studio, rooms, and cabin, seldom leaving them and never moving from their native states.

Thoreau once remarked, "I have traveled much in Concord." Ryder in only one instance was lured away from home territory by a friend's bait of a free boat ticket to England. After boarding the ship in New York, Ryder left his cabin only at night to stare at the moon on the sea. On arriving in England, he did not even disembark but stayed aboard ship until it returned to New York. He went back to his studio to paint still another moonlit version of the sea. In this

65

retirement these artists studied the nature of man, animals, plants, sky, sea, and earth — curriculum for unlettered country peasants. However, from this vantage their unique contributions flowed back into the mainstream of art with an originality and a purity quite impossible to achieve while bumping against all the other artists spinning about in the whirlpool of art activity in the marketplace. This bumping and spinning has the time-effect of grinding the individuals into sizes and shapes that are as much alike as pebbles on a beach. This is contrary to the spirit of art which cries out for originality. Therefore, we should not use the word "provincial" to disparage but rather elevate and celebrate it as it relates to the places individuals go to find inner direction undisturbed by the clamor of the marketplace.

Looking back through history, we see mountains, rivers, oceans as barriers, barriers which controlled to a large degree the movement of people. Thus, the thoughts and products of these confined people had to grow to great heights before the results could be seen from afar. The obvious difference today is that the ideas and products are hardly launched before they become the common property of the world; they are flung back and forth from one corner of the earth to the other by planes, ships, radio, and television.

I suspect there is something positive and negative to be said for both situations, but it appears to me that the lot of the individual tends to become more difficult as these barriers disappear. Unless the provincial scene can be preserved, the individual may well become an endangered species.

Quick 79.
The artist in the market place.

THE EXHIBIT
OR
THE ARTIST IN THE MARKETPLACE

An exhibit is something that most artists, especially the mature ones, enter into with mixed emotions. Hope and fear are both present, and this never changes. To exhibit is a bit like a father introducing his children to the world, wanting them in a general way to look like other human beings but also to be different — and, specifically, to be like the father himself. I tell students to be careful in the selection of things they are going to exhibit because what they are really doing is hanging up a bit of themselves to be studied by the world.

I find it very strange indeed to see an artist work, perhaps for years, on his creations which are often born in as much pain as that present in childbirth, and then casually turn these children over to a stranger — for instance, the art dealer — to do with what he wishes. I have seen this happen often. Then the artist becomes upset if he sees his offspring mishandled.

The motivation of the art dealer is not always in harmony with the aspirations of the artist. Therefore, they both should be present at the installation of the exhibit to assure a blend of both the aesthetic and monetary concerns. This collaboration of dealer and artist is very important since one owns the gallery and the other owns the paintings. They both have an important investment in the gamble. For gamble it is; the only one more chancy is the publishing of a book of verse.

The exhibit of a body of work is like putting a number of paintings in a single frame or environment. This frame should be as flattering as it can be. The artist should never feel his work is complete until it is framed within the time and space of a gallery. (With regard to the very frame itself, they say Renoir would sell his work for somewhat less if the purchaser promised to put a handsome frame on it.)

It perhaps seems strange to mention the timing, but the artist who hopes to have a successful exhibit wants it to take place when there are people around to see it. As a young artist just starting out, you

69

might get an exhibit at a good gallery, but at a very bad time like the middle of July. That means you will have to work your way up through August and September to get into the prime time for the exhibiting of art. This may take a long while because most galleries operate on a yearly schedule, which means a year's wait. In the interim you may learn to starve.

In an exhibit much goes on behind the scene that is nothing like the exciting work of painting pictures. For example, you must determine the cash value of each individual work to be shown. A technique I have used to lighten this distasteful task is to ask a couple of friends, people familiar with the art world, to spend a day with me in my studio. There I place each work on the easel, and these friends write down privately the figure they think each work is worth. I do the same. At the end we take the average of the three figures, and that will be the one that goes on the gallery's price list. This is not a perfect answer, but it is better than a single opinion.

Edvard Munch considered his works his children, and he never sold any. But most artists are not born rich so they have to live by their work; hence, one reason for an exhibit is money to live on. Of course, there are other reasons. There is no question but that the ego has to be fed as well as the stomach. The artist's lifework has to go on — with wire, screw eyes, glass, mats, frames, invitations, wine, art dealers, and critics.

Most of the exhibits I have been involved in have taken place in the northern part of the United States. Like a farmer, the artist has to be fortunate in regard to the weather at the time of harvest or exhibit. I'm afraid I have had several openings of exhibits with howling snow- or sleet-storms outside. Much as the gallery-goer wants to be part of the gala opening of a show, he may not be able to make it. Premiere performances of plays, musicals, and exhibits have a way of setting the tenor of the whole run. Often one of the main reasons the gallery-goer goes to an opening is to see or to be seen by other goers. It is a social event for many; the more serious art lovers, however, will go back a second time to see the work.

A large crowd milling around, saying nice things about what they see while drinking wine and peering over shoulders, has a stimulating effect on the group and quite often encourages collectors to make investments in the work, or at least the artist hopes so. Some might say this is a crass attitude; but if there are sales, this pays for studios, time, material, and, yes, even pork chops — all very necessary so the artist can carry on his work.

The artist's life is like a round robin: a period of creative work, an exhibit, a sale, and back to work in the studio. In some cases I suspect this circle is almost like a necklace. In Paris in 1967, at the Orangerie, I saw an exhibit of the work of the Dutch painter Jan Vermeer, where one painting after another was hung along the gallery wall. I couldn't help but think that they came from the hands of an artistic alchemist. The color from the tubes had been changed to gold and jewels on the canvas; and the spaces in between, looking back to time spent in that quiet Dutch studio, had to have been golden to have produced such precious works.

Directly across the street at the Grand Palais, on the same day, I say the exhibit honoring Picasso on the occasion of his 82nd birthday. All of Paris seemed to have turned out to honor this man and his work. Again we looked at jewels, but this time they were of a much more exotic kind. They might have come from Africa or from the treasure chest of an Aztec chief. Jewels they were, and I'm sure the connecting links of creation were periods molded of fire and fury. With each artist the scale and value of the works may change, but each artist follows the same general rhythm of joyous work and display.

In the midst of all these exhibits are the dealers. Art dealers are a breed unto themselves, for the risk is so great in running a gallery that it only attracts men and women entrepreneurs of courage with a bit of larceny in their souls.

An example of a dealer who epitomized this type was Lord Duveen who may have been the greatest art dealer who ever lived. One trait that makes a dealer successful is that he believes that the results justify the means. Duveen once loaned a Washington apartment, rent free and decorated with fabulous bric-a-brac and old masters from the Duveen galleries in New York, to Andrew Mellon. Mellon became so attached to all the masterpieces that he had to own them, and later they became the premiere part of the National Gallery. The results certainly justified Duveen's ploy.

I think there are more art lovers among private art dealers than among museum directors because the personal risks are much higher in the private sector than in the public one. The rewards can be as long in coming to art dealers as they are to artists.

The best dealers love to build private collections that reflect their own tastes, and they are not above playing one collector off against another while still building up the value of the art in the process. The collector is fortunate to have a dealer who has what is called a good eye. This means that even when he looks at new art, he can see the quality in it and is willing to take risks with it. A good dealer has seen enough art in his time to enable him to ignore the name in the lower corner when making his judgment.

The dealer likes to build a "stable" of artists who will make it easy for him to supply collectors of differing tastes with work of equal quality but of different points of view. This may keep the artist poor but can make the dealer rich. In the past, dealers used to promote the artists shown in their galleries by trying to place their works in national and international group exhibits. One after another of these exhibits has been discontinued so this role of the art dealer — at one time very important — has declined, and the artist has less reason for being involved with the dealer.

Nowadays the artist gets a body of work together and arranges to show it at an individual exhibit. Some artists have large audiences that in general appreciate some of their work. Other artists have small audiences that become fanatic lovers of all their art. All these attitudes have a healthy effect on art and keep it from becoming set in its ways.

The exhibit is a marketplace that brings the artist in contact with buyers. All marketplaces down through history have produced some of the most interesting bits of daily experience. This is as true of art as it is of the farmers' market day.

Summer and Nature   Quick 79

SUMMER AND NATURE

The circling seasons lead us in and out through the year, imperceptibly weaving us into a pattern ordained by nature. Like the springs of summer, we are alternately filled and emptied in a rhythm set by the sun.

In spring as artists emerge from the studio into the sunlight, they are empty because they have used up their supply of nature's bounty during the winter's hibernation. It becomes necessary for them once again to complete the circle and fill their eyes, ears, and noses with the sights, sounds, and scents of nature.

Art teaches us to see, and nature fills our eyes. Like the squirrel in summer, we store up our collected impressions to be drawn upon during the long winter months. When winter draws to an end, the artist finds himself starved and drained and drawing upon his primary supply of colors — red, blue, and yellow. Where are the pinks, oranges, and purples of flowers? The green foliage that shades to blues at the horizon — all lost in a fading memory. Not only are the colors gone but also the shapes and forms. We are reduced to making unadorned ones that only depend on each other for their validity. We need a spring tonic, such as viewing the thrust of rocks and the crash of waves, or seeing a web of budding branches against the sky. Simply, artists need to return to nature to refill the wellsprings of their creativity once again.

This renewal has become increasingly important since the Impressionists moved the artist outdoors into the sunlight. I don't think the landscape painter will ever return to simplified statements of local color but will depend on the magic of sunlight to quicken his work.

The studio environment is so controlled: the weather is always the same — 65 degrees and sunny. It makes little difference whether the light is from a modern daylight fluorescent tube or from a north-light cut into the roof. Obviously, this sort of situation is comfortable to work in, but it brings with it the evils of the protected life. The main evil is that the artist loses contact with the real world of nature where there are other weather reports besides "sunny" and "holding."

Think of the painted storms of Winslow Homer with their Atlantic waves crashing on the shores of Maine and Florida, or the turbulent rain clouds of John Constable sweeping over the meadows of England, or, at the other end of the spectrum, the warm sun-drenched landscapes of the Hudson River Valley painted by George Inness. In other words, landscape artists paint weather reports as well as terrain. The paintings have more validity if painted in the presence of nature where changes in the weather work on and through the more constant elements of the land.

I find that certain names of places trigger my mind into thinking about the debts artists owe to nature. Tuscany, Provincetown, Barbizon, Arles, Grand Marais. (Notice the French derivations even on United States soil.)

Barbizon painters hadn't made the scientific discoveries in color of the Impressionists, but they were well aware of the resources for artists to be found in the study of nature.

Shortly before the Barbizon painters, Gustav Courbet was making a break with the Romantic painters' subject matter of the past and stating his manifesto of a new realism; this act was to create a bridge to nature which the Barbizon painters timidly crossed, carrying with them the asphaltum-made gloom of the studio to overlay their genre studies in nature of the French countryside. (Asphaltum is a glazing mixture used to give an artificial aging to a painting.) It was left for the Impressionists to make the complete break with both the subject matter and color of the studio and to create a new world of art where we can all revel in the sunshine by painting directly from nature.

For thirty years I have returned every summer to a small city called Grand Marais. (Roughly translated from the French, it means "large swamp.") This community is located in Minnesota twenty-five miles below the Canadian border on U.S. Highway 61. It is squeezed in between the largest freshwater lake in the world, Lake Superior, and a vast wilderness called the Superior National Forest. I go there with about a hundred and fifty other artists and art students to refill the wellsprings of creativity.

Why is a place like this chosen to be the site of an art colony? The answer is simple; here you are able to see the fundamental forces and character of nature that are not yet harnessed or altered by man.

If the artist-student sees a rock cast up on the shore or rolled down from a cliff, or a wind- or lightning-felled tree damming up a river, which in turn creates a black deep pool — a home for trout, he is seeing the forces of nature at work creating natural relationships in which all things come together in harmony. Winslow Homer saw such a setting in Maine; and since he was in harmony with nature, he realized he had to make the trout leap from the depths in front of a fallen tree in order to complete the scene and, incidentally, be the inspiration for a watercolor called the "Leaping Trout."

Along the rugged coast of Lake Superior the winter forces have been at work with the melting/freezing process, chipping away at the cliff's face; and at the cliff's base lie the huge angular shard pried loose by the freezing wedges of water. Already the waves of the lake have started to reshape them to conform to the other rounded forms molded over the centuries. The angular giants dropped beyond the reach of the waves have other elements at work on them. The lichen spreads its lace patterns over their surfaces while minerals bleed through to color their planes with spots of brilliant orange, red, and violet; all of these impressions flow in to expand one's imagination.

In addition to these created memories of color, shape, and form, there should always be memories of the changes wrought by the dynamic overriding factors of time and weather. Think of Monet with a half-dozen canvases, painting the same haystack at regular intervals during a single day and producing six different color schemes as the earth turned. Time and weather have to do with color and mood, and nature is constantly proving it — by itself or through the works of artists.

Quick "79"
Two weeks in Europe.

TWO WEEKS IN EUROPE

I have been asked a number of times where I would go in Europe if I only had a short time for such travel. Here is my answer.

The traveler likes to dine and stay at the best places while looking at the greatest art and most dramatic views of nature. If I wanted to live on such a rich diet for two weeks, I would ask to be dropped into the city of Salzburg, Austria.

People will say, "What about Paris, London, Madrid, Rome, Amsterdam, Athens, and others?" These all are great art centers; but remember this is only for a two-week stay, and you will find that each one of these cities only partially fills the list of initial requirements. After almost two years and twenty thousand miles of travel in western Europe, I chose Salzburg because within an arm's length, not vulgarly extended to a boarding-house reach, is almost everything a traveler with an epicurean appetite will be able to digest in this short time. He will be able to taste the cuisine, art, music, and landscape of Germany, Austria, Italy, Switzerland, and France.

Just think of it! Austrian pastry, Italian pasta, Swiss chocolate, German wurst and sauerkraut, and French wine and quiche. Visits to the houses of Mozart, Schubert, and Johann Strauss, Jr. Italian museums filled with the works of the Renaissance giants. The mountaintop school of vision of Oskar Kokoschka, the modern galleries of Basel, Zurich, and the ancient Pinakothek Museum of Munich — all located in the beautiful settings of the Swiss, Austrian, French, and Bavarian Alps along with the Italian Dolomites. In Salzburg, one can find the best of many cultures.

Some of the greatest aesthetic experiences arise out of moments of leisure when the mind is rested and receptive to seeing new places. I travel with my eyes wide open and with brush and sketch book in hand just as my fellow traveler does who gathers memories through his camera's eye.

In a brief flight I have left far behind a modern American city and a familiar studio, and exchanged them for an ancient city where all the sharp contours have been eroded by time and thus are restful and interesting to a jaded eye used to seeing only contemporary architecture in carefully planned relationships. To achieve this sort

of rest and new stimulation is the reason for travel; familiar surroundings seem to put our powers of observation to sleep, and
travel in unfamiliar places awakens them again.

A broad look at the cities of this particular region points up a star-
tling difference between the old and new worlds. The difference in
appearance, I'm sure, can be traced to the common human feelings
of fear and self-preservation, the results being the dramatic perspectives of cities built on mountaintops. Since oceans separated us from
invaders, we in America were free to build our cities on the most
convenient level land. These very virtues make for mundane sites.
This flatness means most of our American cities are more interesting
when approached from the air, as the two-dimensional man-made
design is apparent from there. On the other hand Salzburg and
other cities in those snowy Alps, from a height of twenty thousand
feet, look like unfathomable Rorschach blots. The design of those
cities depended on how the buildings could be fastened to the jag-
ged contours of the mountains. Such cities are most striking when
seen from below while traveling on foot.

When one travels to Europe, it is generally a trip back in time, not
only to old cities but to antique sculpture and old master paintings.
People will say we have imported much of this art to America. That
is true, but in Europe we find the art on the buildings for which it
was designed. In Florida, for instance, there is a very faithful copy of
Michelangelo's David set in a lovely sunny garden, but the sculpture
lacks the impact of another copy of the youthful David standing on
the original site against the stark rugged stonework of the Medici
Palace in Florence. (The original is in a nearby museum, placed there
to protect it from the weather.)

It is fortunate that this particular sculpture could be moved, but
unfortunately much painting and sculpture could not be because
they were built into the buildings or painted directly on the walls.
So we have to go where they are in order to see them. In addition
to those works of art permanently fixed in place, the new laws of these
countries of western Europe have declared that the works of the old
masters are national treasures and will not be allowed to leave their
countries.

That is why I suggest, for the short but broad cultural experience,
that it would be difficult to find a more centrally located place as a
base for travel, and for the enjoyment of music, art, cooking, and
looking, than Salzburg. This is especially true during the time of the
Mozart Festival when world-famous artists and musicians gather
there to stage and perform the music and operas of the composer in
his beautiful native city.

II OF THEMES AND CONVERSATION

"My life has been spent trying to help people enjoy life more."

Quick 79

How it all began.

HOW IT ALL BEGAN

Huddled figures crouched close to a fire, a gift stolen from the gods, so we are told. Why not believe it? As you will see, what transpires later is even more fantastic. From the grunting gesturing pack a lumbering creature emerges carrying a blackened brand. His eyes gleam either from the reflection of the fire or from an inner creative spark.

To the cave's wall he goes, and there makes a mark, then another, and another: a hairy bison, a small deer, several hunters with weapons appear. With each stroke, as recognition of familiar shapes reaches primitive minds, his watchers stand amazed.

Was what they saw art? No, of course not, even though some historians and critics have called it that. What was appearing was the first alphabet. Art was not intended, but communication was.

If the critics have called it art, can't we then say that art is communication imaginatively done? The alphabet becomes more colorful, more polished, in the hands of the Egyptians at 3000 or 4000 B.C. The letters become words and sentences. The polishing and shaping make use of exotic materials where the symbols of animals and man become almost illuminated manuscripts in the use of gold, silver, and engraved granite. All these embellishments have the earmarks of art.

Mystical, royal Byzantium took the language away from the people for the first time and converted it strictly to the use of the intellectual aristocracy by the simple device of converting the natural forms into abstract ones. However, in Greece the natural forms were retained, and after much sublimation of detail a refined classical style emerged which was to become the basis of visual communication in western art. Letters became words; words, sentences; and sentences took on poetic nuances as they communicated in visual terms something important about the daily affairs of men.

Somehow, from that beginning in caves when man was only interested in what was being expressed, his skill developed until he now finds joy in how it is said. And this combination of *what* and *how* can be called art.

Quick 79
It's a matter of
Seeing –

IT'S A MATTER OF SEEING

"Behold," "sense," "detect," "visualize," "contemplate," "deduct" — these are all manners of ways of seeing.

The child's inquisitiveness sharpens his eye to find detail. The old man's eye shuts out the detail so he can see the larger meaning. The child's eye looks through a microscope to see the minutiae of the world. The older eye develops a telescopic lens so it can see distant relationships. The child looks at the world with wonder. The old man wonders as he looks at the world.

I have beheld very few works of art, but I have looked at thousands. A shock seems to have to come first before we can behold anything. The eye becomes lazy and automatic in the presence of familiar things. The viewer relaxes and lets all the senses lead him through an ordinary day.

Suddenly it's different! In the Church of the Santa Croce in Florence, Italy, I came upon the fresco by Masaccio of Adam and Eve being driven from the Garden of Eden. My hands flew up beside my head, my palms turned to the work, and I stepped back in wonder as I beheld its symbolic magnificence. I experienced a similar feeling upon the sudden appearance of a humpback whale, and on seeing the glaciers of Alaska. I have experienced this sensation only a few times in my life as I have looked at man-made things.

The word "behold" has a Biblical ring to it that engenders thoughts of revelation and worship. There are a number of works of art that have become idolized or venerated to the point of being worshiped by both the knowing and the unknowing. They are often the works that were created at the zenith of the artist's power of perception, insight, and technique. To name a few which might stand along with Masaccio's *Expulsion of Adam and Eve*, are Da Vinci's *Last Supper*, Michelangelo's *Last Judgment*, and Rembrandt's *Night Watch*.

"Deduction" is also an inward act of seeing. It is a strange word that somehow means opposite things. It means both to add and subtract. In this final act of inward deduction we discover by adding all the traits of our personality, ourselves, and we discover our places by subtracting when we look out to the stars.

Fooling with mother nature.

Quick 79

FOOLING WITH MOTHER NATURE

Verisimilitude caught in the lens of the eye and then transferred slavishly to paper or canvas seems to be what much of the public thinks is the highest form of art.

Often when artists are outdoors painting from nature, someone will come up and look over their shoulders. The observer's opening words are often about an aunt they have who can paint every leaf and brick.

This is a sort of reverse criticism of the artist's work because obviously he is not painting every leaf and brick. Yet, with all his training and experience, he is not quite so good as that amateur artist aunt who never took a lesson in her life.

Artists generally have quite a different view of what's important, as do many collectors, connoisseurs, and ordinary viewers.

There are degrees of realism and non-realism which are accepted and appreciated by large audiences. Let us say you were to come upon a quiet pool of water in a forest. Reflected in the water is a perfect image of the landscape.

This would please the largest number of viewers. They would react and exclaim about its perfection; but then what if some water birds were to fly in and settle on the water, disturbing the surface and distorting the image slightly but at the same time adding the suggestion of motion? The slight ripple would not drive away all the people who enjoyed the perfect image, but many would find it less worthy of their attention. Finally a boy comes upon the scene; seeing the birds, he throws a rock at them. The water erupts with a splash. The ducks fly away and disappear. So does the image, but what is left is color, design, movement, and sunlight — still beautiful but not holding a mirror up to nature, as Shakespeare suggested we should do in order to hold a dwindling audience.

Perhaps what Shakespeare should have said was that artists should approach nature as students — to learn and to be transformed by it.

If, as students of nature, you look at the Great Masters, you will find the way to unlimited appreciation within a timeless structure of

97

art. How relaxed that makes our approach to seeing and understanding the world and works of the artist.

In the limitations and freedoms taken from and with nature by
artists, you can trace the history of art.

I think all artists, even the most avant-garde, will admit that they
have their roots in nature. The viewer can start at this point as well.

Detours from Reality

Quick 79.

DETOURS FROM REALISM

In order to look back down a road, you have to travel it first. In art, if you were to look back down the road, you would see a place called REALISM. However, you would have a great many detours to take in order to return to it.

You see, many artists grow tired of following the same old route and decide to break new trails, to move through new territory. The problem is that many of these pathfinders have spent too little time on the main road, and the trails they break peter out in swamps of confusion or in deserts barren of ideas.

The art world is full of examples of artists claiming they have found a new reality which all society should accept as the straight way to the ultimate destination of art. However, the paths they recommend are often as disorientated as the wanderings of a Don Quixote. The disaster is that the remains of their eager followers can be found scattered all across the landscape of art.

In defense of these pioneers in particular, and all pioneers in general, the bones of great numbers dot the prairies of the West, but in spite of that it would be a fool's statement to say their struggles were for naught.

For me some of the choicest lines of the late Robert Frost are found in his poem, "The Road Not Taken." "Two roads diverged in a wood, and I — I took the one less traveled by, and that has made all the difference." *And that makes all the difference.* I believe what I have been trying to say is that always, always the search for new paths should go on, but realism, based on the study of nature, should constantly be present, like the North Star, in order that we have a fixed point from which we can strike out — and to which we can return.

It is regrettable that so many students, artists, critics, and, yes — even viewers, ignore, reject, or forget this fixed point and become disorientated and disappointed with the world of Art. They give up when perhaps all that is needed is to find solid ground on which to stand while they get their bearings for a new direction.

Quirk 79.
Tell me and Artist born or made.

TELL ME — ARE ARTISTS BORN OR MADE?

Loren Eisley, in his book *The Immense Journey*, says we go back past fur, fin, and grunt to find our beginnings in the gaseous mass burning before the sun.

The genes start to fall into place away back in the great unconscious memory of tribes lost in the depths of time.

This gene seeks one pattern, that one starts another — one goes down the path toward science, another toward business, and still others toward art, music, dance, and literature.

Yes, artists are born, but then they must be shaped and polished; so we must say that they are also made. It seems there have to be both the carborundum of suffering and the oil of love to do this.

The time, the place, and the family are the main ingredients in the shaping and the education of the artist.

For example — the time, the Renaissance; the place, Italy. The family was made up of people who believed that man was the measure of all things. The products of this arrogant assumption: Michelangelo, Leonardo, Raphael, Donatello, Cellini, on and on and on and on — *ad infinitum*.

The leading question   Quirk 79."

THE LEADING QUESTION

The trap is ready to snap as you take the bait. What do you think of Norman Rockwell? Is he an artist? What do you think of Picasso, or those conceptual cats, this exhibit, or students today?

The questions are loaded, and the "quizzee" or "quizzor" is going to be hard to answer because, very often, his mind is made up. The best thing to do is to parry these questions by asking him what he thinks.

If you get an answer, you will probably at the same time get a clue to the direction the conversation will take; perhaps you can guide it into productive channels. You will talk about art but seldom come to specific conclusions about it because the appreciation of art is based on many personal experiences. Since these experiences are always being added to, they should encourage a person to develop a completely open mind on the subject of art.

Take the question, *What do you think about Norman Rockwell?* What the questioner is really asking, often with a chip on his shoulder, is do you think illustration is fine art? This is a question that has been a contended bone in the art world for generations. In many ways fine art and illustration speak the same language and seek answers to the same questions, but the emphases fall on different phases of creativity and speak to audiences that are seeking different answers. So it is much like asking the artist to compare apples and oranges, or even to choose between them.

The art world is full of places where the distinction between illustrator and artist is slight, for they are both interested in communicating to an audience, but the illustrator will be more inclined to emphasize the message while the artist will put the emphasis on how the message is said.

Most great works of art either tell or illustrate stories dealing with mythology, religion, and history, or they depict morality, love, hate, *ad infinitum*, about the human condition. Now the simple treatment of these subjects does not make a work of art, no matter how clearly the story is told. But the mere fact that a work is illustrative does not make it "non-art" either, because if it did, we would have to throw out the majority of the world's art.

Fine art and illustration can walk hand in hand down the same path, but they can and will find diverging paths and end up following them to different goals. Norman Rockwell is one who chose to follow the path of the illustrator. He had achieved great popularity in this field and certainly should be called a superb illustrator, but not a fine artist. Now, consider Picasso, Daumier, Goya, Lautrec, Homer, Hogarth, Blake, and Rembrandt — all have artistically illustrated stories, from the daily paper to the Bible, and have not lost face in the eyes of their peers or their public.

Another loaded question is — *What artist's work do you like best?* If you are not careful in this dialogue, you can end up either in the camp of the rear guard or of the avant-garde when you aren't in either one. I long ago switched from liking artists to liking specific works by a great number of different artists from different periods, countries, and media. It is much more accurate and exciting to pick from a larger field. The collection I have in my mind would include works from the cave man to works in neon and electrical sparks, with a garden or two as well. This may not satisfy the curiosity of the person who would like to catalog you, but it should open up another line of more profitable questions or topics for discussion.

Is there anything to the conceptual art movement? This is an easy one to answer as the questioner is as vague as the questioned on the subject. Of course, there is something to the movement because at least it drew the query in the first place, and two minds have started to defend or deny the thought that there is such a thing as conceptual art. Perhaps a Japanese garden is a distant relation to conceptual art, or the opera where the visual presentation is described and supported by words. As I understand it, the conceptual artist is asking the viewer to become an actual part of the work and to participate in the production from the inside on two levels, the cerebral and the emotional. I suspect he is asking an awful lot.

At times going to openings of exhibits can be very trying especially if there is some question in your mind as to whether you like it or not. There may be many people there, and you can sink into the anonymity of the crowd, but if you are an artist, you cannot escape without being asked to give your opinion of the exhibit. To be cast in the role of critic has never appealed to me, but this is what the questioner is doing. A student once asked me to pick a favorite quotation so she could embroider it on the back of a shirt for me. The one I chose was, "Live and Let Live."

With the ongoing action of art an exhibit is often just a visual hesitation in the process of development and certainly can be treated as such in any evaluation. Remember that fortunes fluctuate; Rembrandt and many other great artists have gone from rags to riches and back to rags again. There are many stock phrases that always will be acceptable to both the questioner and artist; they seem to say a lot but really say nothing at all.

An artist friend and I were once discussing the problem of facing a mother who is proudly showing off her new baby. All of us are very aware that babies can be ugly with purple faces, flopping ears, and pointed heads. We decided this was the best thing to say, "Now that is what I call a baby." It pleased the mother very much, and it let us off with a feeling that we had been perfectly honest. I think you might get off with the same statement to the artist or gallery-goer, "Now that is what I call an exhibit."

There are also a number of single words I have used to parry the question. Some of them are "interesting," "colorful," "current," "unique," but the best answer is not just one word but to say, "I haven't made up my mind, and I want more time to study the exhibit so I'm coming back later." The most flattering expression, of course, is to buy something.

For thirty years I have been a part of the life of a college of art, and year after year I have attended the spring exhibit of the students' work. Proud mothers, fathers, friends, and relations all come to see and comment on this final display.

It is my observation that the spread of quality is very much the same from year to year. So the question, *"What do you think about the students?"* always raises the hair on the back of my neck, especially at the time of this final exhibit. After all, these students have just completed a four-year course through a curriculum with a faculty guiding them. If a finger is to be pointed, perhaps it should be in a different direction.

Fortunately six or seven hundred students are a power that can exert extreme pressure and so affect the quality and direction of their education, whether it means a return to a traditional curriculum or striking out in revolutionary new directions. I believe it will be the students' wishes which ultimately will decide the matter. What do I think of the student? I think he is youthful and will outlast all of us. He will have the final word.

Quick 79

I don't know anything about
art but I know what I like

I DON'T KNOW ANYTHING ABOUT ART, BUT I KNOW WHAT I LIKE

There was an old man with keen piercing eyes who had been look-ing and looking for years and years. Those eyes had seen almost everything between birth and death, and he knew nothing about art. All the while he was looking at the very subject matter of art. Even this old man told me he knew nothing about art, but he knew what he liked.

The eyes educate the brain; however, the route is a two-way street and so the brain should be able to educate the eyes to see beauty when they are looking at newly created things called art.

A lady on a beach asked me, "How can people say they like that stuff they hang on walls when nobody knows what it is?" As she spoke, she kept admiring and turning over in her hands brightly colored and oddly shaped pebbles she had gathered along the beach — abstract art made by nature.

Quick "79"

The artistic
Lunch.

THE ARTISTIC LUNCH

On the boulevards the indoor and outdoor tables are crowded. A buzz is heard, like that of bees in a flowering garden sucking the choicest sweetness out of life. While the wine flows, so do the ideas back and forth among the diners, each pollinating the thoughts of the others.

The tablecloths become canvases; the napkins turn into sketch paper; and, under the influence of the festive occasion, creative people find the courage to express that budding idea or potential manifesto often difficult to articulate at other times.

This vignette of Parisian cafes is repeated again and again wherever artists gather in any numbers to eat. Knowing how to dine is understanding a creative process.

The chef knows he is an artist; the maitre d'hotel and waiters create the ambiance like a frame in which to display the art produced in the kitchen.

Frank Lloyd Wright said that to set a table is an opportunity to create a work of art. I wonder why some conceptual artist doesn't take it as a theme?

It doesn't have to be only painters, sculptors, or architects who are caught up in the expansive moment produced by good food and wine. That is the beauty of it. The table becomes a crossroad where everyone can meet — the butcher, the baker, the candlestick maker, the surgeon, banker, prize fighter, bartender, salesman, and artist — all these can add their special flavors to the conversation, which should complement the food and the wine.

Artists are students of life to a higher degree than most people. The sidewalk cafe becomes a classroom, laboratory, lecture hall, and sometimes a debater's podium.

There never was a formal school of Paris; but Paris and its environment, especially the cafes, provided an informal academy that students flocked to from all over the world.

The graduates are legion — Monet, Manet, Matisse, Cezanne, Lautrec, Hemingway, Fitzgerald, Picasso, Stein, Camus, the Kohn sisters, Braque. The list of alumni goes on forever, it seems.

The ideas found on tablecloths and napkins could have been impressionism, cubism, abstract expressionism, existentialism, non-objective art, surrealism, stream of consciousness. However, the separation of the parts is not important; the material chewed over and over and digested at these tables is, and always will be, important. The world is better off because of these lunches. Art can grow and flourish out of such moments of leisure.

In Defence of the
Ivory Tower.

Quirk 80

IN DEFENSE OF AN IVORY TOWER

Come, all you dreamers. It is time once again to defend the ivory tower. Give purpose and meaning to your life by fighting for your sanctuary. The tower is besieged on all sides — and front and rear — by pragmatical busybodies, critics, crusaders each armed to the teeth with weapons peculiar to their kind.

Remember how your ancestors were forced time after time to retreat into the sanctuaries available to them in order to attain the quiet necessary for the contemplation of the larger visions of life? One early visionary retired for forty days to the wilderness. Another climbed Mount Sinai. After these experiences they returned to change the laws of Israel and the philosophy of all Christendom.

In the Dark Ages bridges lifted over moats, great gates clanged shut, doors of cells closed, and monks disappeared to cut themselves off from all contact with the outside world. "Dreadful," said the inhabitants outside the walls, as they fell sick and died in ignorance. In this earth-dark fallow time seeds of dreaming produced a rich harvest of manuscripts illuminating and detailing the ideas of mankind. When the doors and gates finally opened and the bridges fell once again into place, out flowed a great flood of riches to fill the minds and hearts of men.

On top of man's shoulders at the tip of the first cervical vertebra sits the skull. Inside the dome-shaped space are the many chambers of the mind, all protected from the outside world by this ivory-hard helmet. One of these chambers must be set aside for dreaming because it is here the artist enters most often. It is a private and delightful space where dreams coalesce and take on substance.

Invaders can enter by the eye or the ear, and it becomes necessary on occasion to flee to a mountaintop or a tower in order to protect such a delicate thing as a forming dream. It takes very little to upset such a birth. Critics, crusaders, and busybodies, often with the best intentions, seem to have to intrude with their ill-considered simplistic views which can destroy a dream at its very conception.

The flow of creativity from dream to song, painting, or sculpture depends upon many things, but perhaps the most important is that the artist is lord of his own private ivory tower.

Soliloquy. Quick 79

SOLILOQUY

The insolence of office, and the spurns
That patient merit of the unworthy takes.
                    Shakespeare, *Hamlet*

The artist who talks to himself is driven to it by outside forces over which he has little control. Some of these forces are so powerful and so uncontrolled that fear of destruction is always present in the artist's mind when his work is exhibited. Mad men do roam the galleries. *The Night Watch* of Rembrandt slashed, the *Pieta* of Michelangelo smashed, the works of Turner and Schubert burned, paintings of the Impressionists spat upon. These are extreme examples of criticism, but one wonders whether some ill-considered words by critics may not cut as deep and do damage equal to the madman's knife. What kind of situation is responsible for these ill-considered words? "That," as Shakespeare would say, "is the question."

Is the college music major or art history student turned free-lance critic really qualified to write on the merits of a professional painter for publication on the arts pages of a newspaper? There is a question in my mind about newspaper ethics — whether any newspaper should publish this material in any place but the "Letters to the Editor" section which is open to the amateur to enable him to state his views on all sorts of subjects.

I have heard frightening tales of reporters wandering through the publishing world, and of neophyte artists ambling through the art world, only to find themselves lacking in the ability to do creative work; after this discovery they accept jobs as critics. Here certainly the question of ethics still lingers. And we may have to deal with not only an unqualified person but a bitter one.

In *Hamlet* we read of poison being administered through the ear. This also can be done through the eye. This poison can be in the form of words, words that corrode and take away the power of the mind and hand to work, often for long periods of time.

The ego often spawns badly chosen words, and they can be

127

either excessively laudatory or uncomplimentary; they can lead both the artist and the viewer into reaching faulty conclusions. Humans frequently are plagued with a belief that they can see what others can't see and hear what others can't hear. This tends to give them a sense of superiority. We allow ourselves to be misled through flattery into a situation such as is told in the tale, "The Emperor's New Clothes." Often, the critic is guilty of this fault to an excessive degree.

Fortunately, Shakespeare in *Hamlet* shows us through example the great opportunity to be a teacher as well as a critic in Hamlet's advice to the Players: "Whose end, both at the first and now, was and is, to hold, as 'twere, the mirror up to nature; to show virtue her own feature, scorn her own image, and the very age and body of the time his form and pressure." The play within the play is built on this speech. Hamlet, as the director, tries to steer the players away from pitfalls. The critic can and should do the same.

There are and have been great critics who, through positive and courageous criticism, have helped artists to realize their potential. Not always with a pat on the back but always with the thought that the faults are transitory and that they can be considered and corrected without loss of face or of confidence by the artist. After all, it is important to the critic that the artist keep producing; otherwise, the material to criticize will disappear. The critic as teacher gets paid for finding fault, and it is not a pleasant task; but if the criticism is combined with suggestions of ways to correct those faults, the artist as student becomes grateful.

Oskar Kokoschka, the great Austrian painter and teacher, told me this once about his teaching technique. He said he liked large classes and would pick out the most talented student to compliment or, as he said, "Feed sugar-coated bonbons." The other students couldn't help seeing this special treatment for this favorite. They would look over his shoulder and copy his way of working, each one improving in the process; and the level of the whole class became higher. Then, as Oskar had planned, he would reverse the treatment of this special student, partly because his head had started to swell and partly because Kokoschka wanted to use this student as a pawn to teach the rest of the class and influence their growth.

In front of the whole class Kokoschka would give him a severe criticism making sure it didn't end until the student was in tears. The student would leave swearing never to return, but he always did. Oskar would start the bonbon treatment all over again. In the meantime the rest of the class would have reflected that the favorite wasn't so great after all; now, instead of copying him, they would do their own thinking, even though influenced by his example. What they learned would become part of their technique.

This is a rough old-world way of teaching, but it is still effective. Within the studio classroom this is a continuing process, not a one-time event, that becomes a positive and creative strategy.

The time element makes this technique impossible to use in news media reviews. There is a long period of time between reviews, and the artist has no way of protecting his work or himself. His very life may depend greatly on the quality of the review, whether it damns or praises his work.

And so it is important that a newspaper not hire a critic willy-nilly, or let an unqualified person wield such power over the creations of the artist who is stretching every fibre to add something to the world of art. The critic is a bystander, an observer who has it in his power to make either creative or destructive observations about artistic efforts. By so doing he may have a beneficial or adverse effect; this can indeed be a great filip to the critic's ego, but the hand-maiden of power is responsibility.

Hamlet is a drama of revenge. I expect my tying the critic in with the tragedy is an effort on my part to avenge some of the outrageous slings and arrows loosed by those occasional unworthy critics who have caused pain to the patient artist trying to bring something new and beautiful into men's lives.

Quirk 79

The Bittersweet Aspects of Art.

THE BITTERSWEET SIDE OF ART

I like to think that great art serves a very basic human need, that it will touch everyone and anyone without their knowing how or why.

In art, as in jazz when the blues are played, a bittersweet mood comes on, making us feel and know that life is made up of both joy and sorrow. The knowledge that somehow there is somewhat of a balance between the two is an important and accepted point of view.

People have come to my studio when they were very sad and depressed, and have said, "I want to buy a painting." They have taken it away with them, clutching it as if it were their last straw.

It is said that if a suicide-bound woman were to buy a new hat, the crisis would be passed. Being touched by something beautiful will lift one up with the buoyancy of a life preserver.

These bits of beauty are not always from the hand of a painter; they can come from a poet, composer, architect, sculptor. They are not always portrayals of the joyful and beautiful side of life; often, they depict the sordid, sorrowful, lost, painful, and despairing aspects.

When the artist successfully depicts the tragic theme, he may do two things; he may bring us to the edge of tears, but then through his knowledge of and sensitivity to the human condition he may lift us up to a new plateau of courage and understanding. We are filled with bitterness and sadness at the sight of the dead Christ stretched across Mary's lap in Michelangelo's *Pieta*, but then we find the balancing emotion when we become aware of the deep compassion shown in every gesture and expression of the sorrowing mother.

The martyrdom of the saints by many anonymous artists, Hieronymus Bosch's views of hell, *The Disasters of War* by Goya, *Guernica* by Picasso, the bread lines of the thirties by the Soyer brothers, and even the old, decaying, red barns of the amateurs — all these portray the bitter side of life. Why do these works occupy such an important place in art? The answer is quite simple: We identify with them. We cast ourselves in the role of the subjects. We echo the sad-faced clowns of Marsden Hartley. We die with Desdemona and Pagliacci. We no longer are just the viewer or audience; we are on the stage, we are within the frame. The minor notes of the symphony are within us; they entered through the ear. The crucifixion is in us; it entered through the eye.

We are inextricably woven into a pattern started by the artist. The sunny skies of the Impressionists are balanced by the darkened clouds of Goya.

Let us simply accept the idea that there are both bitter and sweet aspects of art that can be reconciled in the hands of a master.

Lost at Sea in
Aesthetic Latitudes

Quick 79
79

LOST AT SEA
IN THE AESTHETIC LATITUDES

Almost all artists set forth in boats that reflect the fragility of their calling. Their destinations are generally vague, and years away. In spite of these dangers they push off with stars in their eyes, reflecting those in the heavens that they expect to be guided by. In the North is Rembrandt; in the South, Da Vinci; in the East, Hokusai; and in the West, Ryder. If not these stars, then they choose others of equal brilliance in other systems.

Joseph Conrad in his book, *The Nigger of the Narcissus*, says, "To be born is to be thrown into the sea." When a person makes up his mind to follow art as a career, he has to be born again to the life of an artist. There is no other way he can make it, or even survive. To be thrown into the sea means you become a piece of flotsam subject to all of the sea's various moods and forces — the currents, tides, rocks, shoals, storms, calms, fog. You have to learn how to survive.

Libraries hold hundreds and thousands of books devoted to art. These are published in every country of the world; their contents go back to the beginning of history. The world asks the artist to be original in the face of all this; strangely enough, it is possible.

The artist at his center should have a gyroscope of convictions so that he is able to steer through all the various forces he is bound to encounter. These encounters are necessary to enrich him, but they should not put him off course.

In a fog laid down in the eighteen hundreds by the critics in Paris, little craft set forth that eventually made landfalls in all the art centers of the world. Then, the critics and fog faded away as the Impressionists, true to their gyroscopes, brought the world of art into the sunlight.

The art dealers cause the tides to rise and fall. Their silver dollars, shining like a million moons, draw the artist to a high tide of momentary financial success — such as the "pop artist," for instance — and then leave him stranded on the beach while the tide returns once again to the depths to find another movement to be brought to flood, only to be left high and dry once again.

This ebb and flow continues on and on through the history of art.

The academy says, "Don't rock the boat, boys; stay calm, and perhaps that conceptual electrical storm will pass, just stirring the canvas enough to get us out of the doldrums."

Finally, with a safe harbor in sight, the most subtle danger of all comes to entice and lure the artist into the soft languorous arms of the temptress of mere rendition. The shoals are dotted from one end to the other with newly liberated sirens singing their songs of love and flesh. Until these artists learn a new song, this danger of subject matter overshadowing creativity will be present.

Whether you are a practicing artist or connoisseur, the attraction of debating and evaluating the aesthetic creative process always ends up with the inner gyroscope of conviction deciding the final direction. That is the way it should be, as art is a personal thing.

Quick 79.
In appreciation

ON APPRECIATION

On a shelf sit a skull and a shell, both former homes of long-dead creatures. In one, caged for a long time, lived an animal called man. In the other lived a mollusk which was able to come out and go into its home at will, tethered to it by a single muscle. One has beauty of form, color, and surface. The other's beauty is found only in its relationship to function, but the Great Source of life more than strikes a balance by giving only one the ability to appreciate the beauty of the other. This ability is often taken lightly, is seldom used; without use it dies.

That is why appreciation of beauty should be taught. With the lessons learned, the learner becomes more beautiful within that helmet called a skull. The inner being will grow and transcend the limited space of the skull as Oliver Wendell Holmes envisioned when he wrote "The Chambered Nautilus." The shell, a spiraling marvel of nature, starting with a domed cell no larger than the head of a pin, grows until it is approximately ten inches in diameter, adding a slightly larger domed space each year into which the little builder moves, sealing the old behind it.

It seems as if this tiny architect is seeking always to enlarge and beautify its environment; but then, uncaring, rejecting what it has made, it sloughs off last year's shelter and looks forward only to that new living space. By this action it produces beauty but fails to appreciate it, unlike the two-legged creature who finds the pearly shell on the beach and appreciates both the creative process and the result.

Quick "79"
Connoisseurs
and
Collectors.

MY FRIENDS, THE COLLECTORS
AND CONNOISSEURS

It is wise to criticize your enemies with great care as they will be quick to take offense and strike back. Friends behave differently, for they recognize the source and accept the ribbing, innuendos, and criticism as coming from a friend. They take it all in their stride, and little damage can be done. Perhaps much good can come from it. Therefore, when I speak of my patrons, the collectors, I am not afraid to speak about some of the unusual quirks that develop as they become addicted to collecting art and later to becoming connoisseurs.

They say magpies have strange collections in their nests. Among human magpies are tin-foil and string savers, sea shell collectors, and Johnny-down-the-street who, by virtue of a strong hand and keen eye, has managed to accumulate the largest and most varied collection of marbles in town.

You probably have heard of the Elgin Marbles. These are not the same as Johnny's, though they also were collected by a person with a keen eye and a strong hand, at least strong enough to wrest the pieces from their places on the Parthenon in 1802 after they had been loosened by an explosion of Turkish gunpowder stored within the temple. Subsequently Lord Elgin himself suffered a blast from the pen of poet Lord Byron who was furious over what he thought was a desecration of the Greek Temple of Athena. I'm sure Lord Elgin must have defended himself by saying that the works would suffer less from vandals and the weather when they were safely installed in the British Museum than when they were neglected by both the Greeks and Turks on the original site.

Often collections have been started in just this way. People with an expert's eye have found beauty in the shards of others, the cast-offs of past civilizations. Very often after the collection has been assembled and put on view, others have seen the beauty and intrinsic value. But the original finder may unjustly earn the name of robber.

Collectors will go to almost any lengths to enlarge their collections. I have seen elderly women wading up to their knees in icy Lake Superior, risking pneumonia to try to reach, with hands already covered with several diamonds, a highly colored agate a few inches beyond their outstretched fingers; their consuming objective is to add to their collection of other rocks in a bucket on the beach.

It is just a short step from that lad returning from summer camp with a collection of moths and butterflies to the man collecting Japanese prints a few years later. After all, butterflies and prints have the same fragile qualities of brilliant coloring and veined black lines emphasizing their design. The driftwood collector from the same boys' camp may eventually collect sculpture because of this early interest in form. Collectors, like artists, are born; and environment shapes them and gives them direction.

The concept that beauty is in the eye of the beholder is perhaps the single most important characteristic in developing the catholic taste of the collector. If this trait did not exist, originality would disappear from art, and vision would become narrower to the point of disappearance.

I have heard that male bowerbirds decorate the areas around their nests with pretty string, flower petals, pebbles, etc. as enticements to the female. This is not unlike a gentleman asking a lady over to view his etchings. For there are many reasons for collecting, and mating could be one. Or a person may collect because he is thus able to create an image; by exhibiting what he collects, he shows what he likes which in turn shows what kind of person he is.

Most collectors I have known are lovable gregarious types who have a zest for life and knowledge. They can drink the wine of the region and enjoy it fully as much as the rare imported vintage. They know the grass is as green in their own front yard as across the fence.

But then often the collector undergoes a metamorphosis and becomes a connoisseur. Often, the chrysalis of the connoisseur has been nourished by all the blooms in the garden of art, but he may emerge with a specialized appreciation of a single strain. This seeking for singular perfection is a very commendable attitude, but in art as in highly restricted diets, there can be serious side effects and, possibly, trouble, especially if the connoisseur happens to be a museum director.

In addition to these official connoisseurs in museums, there are private ones. It is not quite so serious a matter when the connoisseur is building his own private collection, but even here the specialized preference can be felt by the practicing artist if the names of the connoisseurs have such stature as Berenson, Kress, Mellon, Kohn, and Barnes.

The power of collectors and connoisseurs will be felt in the marketplace. As they help to set standards and scope, they should be not only interested in gratifying their own tastes but also aware of the effects of their specialization on emerging art forms. Like the critic who fancies himself a connoisseur, they should realize that the handmaid of power is responsibility.

As I stated at the beginning, my patrons — be they collectors or connoisseurs — are my friends; and thus, it is safe to carry on explosive discussions with them. The connoisseur justly deserves sincere thanks for giving us deeper insights. The collector deserves gratitude for his broad view of art and for keeping the field open to the young artist.

On Top of Mount Everest.   Quick 79.

ON TOP OF MT. EVEREST

In the rarefied atmosphere of a mountain peak one stands alone. I sat alone in a small cafe, waiting for my lunch to be served; a few ice cubes were all that was left in my glass, the remains of a perfect Manhattan. The night before I had watched a television documentary on an ascent of Mt. Everest. Now all around me were the clatter of dishes and the clamour of voices. The lonesome mountaintop and the crowded cafe were about as far apart as situations could get. But this thought crept into my mind: what happens to the psyche of the mountain climber can also happen to the psyche of an artist. It depends on whether the artist pushes his commitment to his life's work as does that climber.

I thought of how parallel the struggles and testing of the courage of a mountain climber and an artist are and how similar the rewards seem to be, at least in two respects. They are private and lonely, and they can only be understood by those who have committed themselves to an extended struggle and survived the ordeal. The mountain climber says that if one hasn't been to the top of the mountain, one won't be able to understand how it feels. So also says the artist at the ultimate peak of his career; if one hasn't experienced it, one won't understand the joys.

Mountain climbers climb in teams and share the struggle, but each climber finds his own satisfaction. The artist travels alone.

For the mountain climber and the visual artist, the joy comes from seeing things from unusual private perspectives, things that few will ever see. The artist is anxious to reveal as many of his insights as possible, but in some cases he reaches an impasse because of the limits of material, hand, or mind. Often the brightest visions are the most elusive and thus have to remain pent-up within him, all the while providing a joy that cannot be shared with anyone else. These glowing images produce the light that leads the artist on until the moment arrives when he will be able to reveal these secret joys to others through his work.

Some might say it's the Manhattan talking through the man. Not so, say I; all it did was to give him enough Dutch courage to expose a vagrant thought.

Of Mausoleums,
Banks & Museums.

Quirk 80'

OF MAUSOLEUMS, BANKS, AND MUSEUMS

Is art living or dead? It all depends on how you look at it. Is it a part of the past or something yet to be discovered? Most places that exhibit art seem to take one extreme view or the other. Seldom do you find one that is near the center. One claims to be showing modern art; the other, the old masters. They both neglect to make the point that art is timeless. If art is timeless, the age of a work of art is pointless. Seldom do you find a museum with a director who has the desire to strike a balance.

The museum *per se* only became a fact in the eighteen hundreds. Compared to the six-thousand-year history of art, it is a very recent phenomenon. Originally the director and staffs were charged with the task of displaying and keeping the art works safe from the effects of time and the elements. These housekeeping duties seemed too demeaning for men of taste and knowledge, and directors soon started to assume the role of arbitrators of what people should see.

Before the advent of the museum the artist had always dealt directly with his patrons and the public. These individual contacts afforded a great variety of views that had their effect on a healthy and expanding image of art. It seems strange that either the artist or patron was willing to relinquish to an art dictator the right to this free exchange, but alas it is true now to a large degree. The world of art, which was in the hands of many, is now in the hands of a few.

I would be very happy if I thought these few were all directors because they loved art, but in my fifty years of being an artist I have met only three who in my mind qualified as true lovers of art. The rest loved the art scene with all the glamorous ambiance that surrounds the acquisition and display of great, expensive works of art.

Often the museum director thinks like a banker in terms of blue chip investments to add to the treasure in the vaults. At times, looking at the market, he is willing to trade this work for that work in order to develop a portfolio of special works in different directions and at the same time to increase their value. All this has little to do with art and often gives a false value to it, and it may keep some artists from showing their work while it may corrupt others who get involved in the process.

155

I have heard both banks and museums referred to as mausoleums. The likeness does go deeper than their frightening and imposing facades that intimidate visitors to such a degree that they talk in whispers as they wander either in the lobby or through the galleries. In the presence of the dead you always whisper; but if for you art lives, there is no need for whispers. The funereal atmosphere of a mausoleum should be dispelled from a museum by the staff. But it is not dispelled. Rather the mood is heightened by the solemn curators, watchful guards, and careful guides who want you to be completely impressed with a sense of the value of the things you are seeing.

The final thought I have about the museum's relationship to a mausoleum or a bank is that they all have vaults. In the museum vault those treasures that are not viable or current in the minds of the curators may be buried until they are resurrected because of some art upheaval that recalls them to light.

The most complimentary comparison seems to be to liken a museum to a bank. They both house treasures which are guarded carefully from thieves and the elements. They also both keep records of their assets and from time to time publish a list of these holdings. This is the way it should be as their assets are held in public trust. But here a misunderstanding about a museum can occur. The museum catalog lists a work of a certain size, medium, period, etc., as belonging to the museum. The truth of the matter is that art be-longs to all those who see and understand it.

All artists want to think of their works as being alive in the memories and lives of others — like melodies or songs that keep running through the mind, not as frozen images in vaults or on walls or pedestals within a mausoleum, bank, or museum.

Art and Religion.   Quick 79.

ART AND RELIGION

The two words "art" and "religion" often are spoken in the same breath, along with words like "spiritual," "sublime," and "elevating." Why is this so? The answers to the *what* and *why* of the relationship are much less obvious and much more interesting to think about.

In order to handle the two subjects simultaneously, I find it necessary to behave like a juggler, first touching on *what* lightly and then turning to *why*, back and forth, hoping to catch both at the end in one hand.

Four times I have marched down an aisle behind a singing choir, side by side with a minister or priest, to take his place in the pulpit to talk on this subject. The congregation is waiting not to hear that there is a relationship between the two; history has demonstrated that with thousands of examples in paint and stone.

As we walked down the aisle, I was aware of the minister at my side dressed in his robes and carrying the attributes of his office. With the putting on of his robes he stepped out of the secular world and into the spiritual world of his creed. I was not dressed in an artist's smock; but when I go to my studio and change to a smock, I am aware of the symbolic as well as the practical meaning of the gesture. My mind turns to the process of translating the images that come to me into a message of line and color for an audience. In a small way the putting on of robes is one expression of the *what* relationships between art and religion.

To bring the first *why* relationship into play I would like to repeat a very old and familiar Bible story. God created a garden which was a perfect work of art, a heaven on earth. As the story unfolds, it tells how, due to human frailties, the two first people were driven out of that garden in disgrace, and the garden was destroyed behind them. *Why* is this story related to art? We know its relationship to religion, but why to art? The two driven out were lost physically and broken spiritually. They probably stopped outside the gate and looked back at the garden and guiltily realized that, because of them, the garden was destroyed. Their next thought had to be, "What can we do to redeem ourselves?" The only possible answer was to try to put the

159

pieces back together again. Man, since that day, has been charged with the task of once again trying to create a heaven on earth.

Now think! In the perfect world of the garden there was no need for a priest or an artist or workers of any kind, but in the imperfect world following the destruction of the garden there has been a need for every kind of worker. So at this earlies moment we find an answer to *why* art and religion are necessary and related. Their combined efforts are aimed at the goal of uplifting mankind. The artist and priest have donned their robes together to accomplish this task.

In *what* ways do we find parallels in attempts to reach that goal? The Gothic architect said, "Let me build towers so high they will reach the heavens."

The painter said, "Let me paint the domed ceiling of the cathedral the deep blue of the firmament and fill it with the heavenly host." *Why*? The painter answers that that way the people will know there is a heaven, and he wishes to paint it for them to see.

The preacher, on the other hand, points with pride to his *why* answer: This is the "Word" that stirred the populace into seeking salvation by supporting the efforts of the artisans to build such monuments to an idea.

These answers are both ancient and current. In 2000 B.C., the call went out to the woodcutters of Lebanon to cut cedars to rebuild the temple. The workers in the mines of King Solomon were driven to supply the copper and gold for the service of the altar. Today, rightly or wrongly, an all-glass church has been built to the glory of the Word.

The *why* frightens me at times, and I question the validity of the sumptuous decorations of the church. Are they made to please the ego of man or to please God? My thoughts turn back to a picture of the Word being preached to the people on a hillside under an open sky. Of course, this was by the Master Teacher who did not need the teaching aids of a Sistine ceiling or a visually documented *Last Supper*. But the *why* becomes apparent once again as we become aware that the sum total of all our creative efforts falls far short of those of that Supreme Creator who made the garden.

In a traditional church such as the Sistine Chapel, there rises behind the high altar the *Last Judgment* of Michelangelo. I wonder how often the same sermon about this judgment has been preached in front of it by the Popes of Rome. The *what* relationship lies in the content, quality, and style of the message — in words or paint.

We do not need to stay in the sanctuary to find these *what* answers to the question of the relationship of art and religion. They occur in every phase of our daily lives. Often the secular works painted by artists create a more religious mood than those specifically painted to decorate a church. A good example might be the paintings, *The Gleaners* and *The Angelus*, by the French painter Jean Francois Millet. Under his hand, workers in the field became human symbols imbued with a religious spirit.

There are thousands of genre art works that moralize every bit as much as a minister in the pulpit. The English painter, William Hogarth, created a whole series of paintings devoted to making object lessons of the seamy side of the London of his day. Across the channel the French painter, Honoré Daumier, did the same in Paris. Many other artists have done works with social commentary as a theme.

This brings us once again to *what* will be my final *why*. I know there is a force inside both the artist and pastor which rises up like a daemon awakening and driving them to reveal their thoughts about the unrevealed mysteries of life with words, gestures, and paint. These pour forth in a creative flood and by example are meant to fill the minds of men. Yes, there are relationships between art and religion that go beyond mere illustration, at the very heart of these two worlds they live in.

IN ANCIENT EGYPT THE ONION WAS ACCORDED DIVINE HONOR

The Onion '79

IN A FIELD OF CONVERSATION GREW AN ONION

Many years ago I attended a play by Anton Chekhov entitled *The Cherry Orchard*, a play dealing with conversation, a long conversation, and little else. It made a great impression on me. All these years, one line in particular has stayed in my memory, a line spoken at a party in the first act, at a party much like the one taking place in my living-room right now where the ideas for this essay are just forming. The theme of that *Cherry Orchard* party we hear echoed at my party, a theme that will recur at parties, *ad infinitum*, still to come. Chekhov's important line is "Let's philosophize."

These two words express with great poignancy the human longing for conversational companionship, companionship that for me and others of like interests, is not only one of life's most important preoccupations but a necessity as it is the fuel that feeds the fires of creativity.

Join the party at my house and see what is garnered from the field of conversation. Would you believe a harvest of ideas concerning a comparison of the art world to the many-layered onion?

The rhythmical beat and harmonious sound of a piano float in the air of the dimly lit and crowded room. Each vibration from the struck strings sends titillating waves up the spines of the listeners, and the mood created by the pianist becomes a part of each of them; they respond with foot-tapping, handclapping, eventually answering the musical invitation to dance — thus demonstrating the power one art form has over another. The Pied Piper's magic is eternal. Like the onion when one layer is peeled away, music reveals another underneath waiting to add its aura, color, aroma, and flavor to the whole sphere, whether it be like that of the lowly onion or of the elevated world of art. Most artists are aware of this layered effect and will claim that their particular art form is the premiere one and should be at the center of the onion.

This evening while I sat beside the pianist and talked with him, as I had many times before, there seemed to be some question in both our minds as to whether being at the center is better, or whether being on the outer skin is best.

At the risk of alienating some of the artists at the party who believed the center was best — and that is where their art form should be, I introduced into the conversation some of my own personal thoughts about the structure of the world of art. At the same time I tried to express that I believed love and fellowship exist among all the arts, no matter where they fall within the sphere.

It is all very well to argue and discuss, to have strong opinions within a family, but I don't know that it is wise to shout them to the world because the public will be quick to decide that there is more trouble than harmony within the group. I believe, however, that disparate views can be safely expressed in the written word because here the statements can be referred to and checked for the true spirit of the discussion. To me, it also seems right to discuss these views while sitting near a piano, for the sound of the music mutes the loudly voiced opinions and keeps the conversation from interrupting equally engrossing discussions going on in other parts of the room.

So here I began to state my views at some length to the group that had started to gather around the piano, my first words having to do with the initial meeting of man with his brother. For me this raised questions — "How did he behave?" "What was his first reaction?" I think he must have stared in disbelief at seeing another so much like himself. This could have caused him to panic because in the beginning he had been the only one to own the world, and now he had to share it. I would guess that he became the first mime actor the world ever knew; as such, he either tried to frighten this new creature away with wild actions and expressions or to act out the fact that they were much alike — indeed, imitations of each other in many ways. Then they came to feel they should join together.

Probably, in the beginning, at the center of the onion, the first artist was an actor who stepped wordlessly onto the stage of civilization and communicated silently through signs and gestures. These in turn have been reproduced on walls, canvas, and paper, down through history to convey an artistic message to the viewer. We owe a debt to this earliest art form. How can our appreciation be expressed?

First, through understanding and then by accepting mime as the nucleus for all future art forms to grow around. I see the dance, with some sort of beaten rhythm, falling into place behind mime; next, I see the grunting gesturing actor, not yet blessed with speech. We should understand our body language and the way it speaks through movement as it responds to rhythm or to that inner force — intuition.

I know homage has not always been paid to the art of the dance. In many periods of history the natural movement of dance forms was suppressed. Even today in some places music and the dance are called expressions of the devil; to practice them is to risk censure, or worse. But we recall that camaraderie, *espirit de corps*, and love often come from shared misfortunes. Other arts have suffered from restraints. There have been the destruction of religious sculpture by the iconoclasts, the whitewashing of religious murals by certain religious sects as they purified church interiors, the burning of books and their authors, and the banning of movies, operas, and plays. These abuses have helped draw artists closer, compressing them to form a protective sphere which I find much akin to the onion. At this point I stopped to breathe.

My piano-playing friend reminded me that I had been carried away and had wandered off the original theme of the conversation about structure, mutual aid, and appreciation. I wondered why he worried about it, for he himself often goes so far astray and extends his musical improvisations to such lengths that it is difficult to remember the original tune.

In deference to this comment and to that of another friend, my mentor in the field of architecture, who had taken a seat at the other end of the piano bench, I said, "Let's get back to structure and appreciation."

I knew these subjects appealed to the architect, and it didn't take any prodding to get him to enlarge on these topics. The word "structure" especially caught his fancy; he maintained that you first have to have structure, and that everything that comes later is merely embellishment within or upon the basic form. In a practical sense I agree he is right; after all, like the onion, the globe earth is a structure, and man and the architect's buildings are embellishments upon it. But, really, in creation what comes first, which is the most important? Is it the forces which come first to construct, or the finished object, the completed structure? Again, it appears we have lost our way and have ended up with something similar to the old riddle of the chicken and the egg; a discussion like that can lead us farther astray than ever. So we had better return to the original theme and pick up the trail — that path which, at least, should lead us to discover where and when the various art forms appeared. Perhaps we can even establish which art form is at the core and which is on the skin of the onion.

The architect stated that, without question, the visual artists appeared on the scene before the architect, but at a very early date man felt the need for permanent shelters. So, in a primitive way, the profession of architecture was born shortly after the visual artist became aware of the need to put down in more permanent form the fleeting messages from the gestures of the mime actors, dancers, and narrating hunters. Messages when told in the interpretive arts disappeared as soon as they had appeared and only survived in the memories of the viewers.

Referring to the idea of appreciation, the architect said he would like to defend the apparent change of patronage of other art forms by most of the architects in his profession. He started by saying that he had noticed that if there is the slightest bruise on any layer of an onion and any pressure is applied to that surface, it will slip off easily and leave the rest as clean and beautiful as ever, minus one protective layer. He went on to say, "I believe the layer of architecture suffered a bruise when it underwent a change of patronage itself from having to answer only to the single strong voice of a king, pope, pharoah, or emperor to the present where we now have to respond to a buzz of many voices quibbling over expense, direction, size, and concept." "The Committee," like sandblasters, wears away with its bombardment of conflicting opinions most attempts at enrichment of surface or form. The end result is that there are only a few architects who still work side by side with all the other artists, such as stonecutters, sculptors, muralists, stained glass and mosaic workers, all trying to create from the foundation up an organic structure that satisfies the complete spectrum of man's tastes.

The architect went on to point out that today he has to treat the other arts as applied ones, using them in and on the building after the original construction has been completed. This has some advantages; but it puts an architect in the role of patron rather than co-worker, and he feels estranged from the family of art.

The pianist said, "It does appear that your status has changed, but perhaps you have just moved a few layers away from the center and are now nearer the skin, and that might be better because you encompass more layers within."

At this point the local poet left another conversational group, where she had been paying only half-attention, to join ours. She leaned over the piano player's shoulder and whispered a request for him to sing the lyrics to the Gershwin tune he was playing. Without a break in the rhythm, the words of The Man I Love started filling the room, and we all joined in — the haunting blue mood of the music touching us. The poet then remarked that Ira's words always seemed to fill out and complement the beautiful music that his brother George composed. In reflecting on the harmonious combination of words and music, I remembered how it is always an added pleasure to have someone with unusual gifts and insights join a conversation and add a special flavor to it. She told of the operas and musicals she had seen and heard, from Wagner to Scott Joplin, where the contributions of sights and sounds by the playwright, choreographer, designer, composer, actor, singer, and even the audience, overwhelmed one with the many overlapping layers of art.

I was reminded that years ago another author said something to me which I had never forgotten. Talking about a similar party where people conversed like these gathered around the piano, he said he could live on conversations of this kind for weeks. Frederick Manfred's words have stayed in my memory as long as the "Let's philosophize." of Chekhov.

Words spoken by poets, sung by minstrels, written by historians, or discussed by this group gathered around the piano, bind all the arts together.

So the evening filled with music and talk passed but only after leading us, almost aimlessly, through the world of art. The conversation left me feeling richer and more convinced than ever that art is an exalted sphere which has much in common with the lowly onion. Moreover, this sphere has an inner core where man first communicated at the most primitive level of sign language; he has since climbed out of this ignorance by way of a series of layers of art (not the least of which is conversation, in my view), to find the highly sophisticated art of literature and language inscribed on the golden, final, outer skin.

The Final Word: Quick '80

A FINAL WORD

Though I have tried my best to express in words the depths of feelings I have had concerning my chosen life's work, I realize now, as I finish this book, I have not been so successful in this effort as I wished to be.

The contents are a mere fragment of the real thing; however, if you pursue art, perhaps you will find that which will be as singularly sublime for you as what I have found for me.

J. R. R. Tolkien, the great English scholar and storyteller, in his last book called *The Silmarillion*, describes the beginning of his perfect world as starting with harmonious sound. Beethoven summed up his world with the *Ninth Symphony*, as did Bach with his *B Minor Mass*, and Handel and Haydn in their great oratorios. The idea that abstract music may be the best vehicle for describing heaven appeals to me, but it puts the burden on you to accept on faith, as in the Scriptures, that man can achieve a heaven on earth

through his work.

FINDING
ST. PAUL
IN FILM

FINDING ST. PAUL IN FILM

Richard Walsh

t&t clark

NEW YORK • LONDON

T & T Clark International
Madison Square Park, 15 East 26th Street, New York, NY 10010

T & T Clark International
The Tower Building, 11 York Road, London SE1 7NX

T & T Clark International is a Continuum imprint.

Cover art by Brueghel, Pieter the Elder (c. 1525–1569). *Conversion of Saint Paul*. Oil on oakwood (1567). Credit: Erich Lessing/Art Resource, NY.
Caravaggio (Michelangelo Merisi da) (1573–1610). *The Conversion of Saint Paul*. Courtesy of Scala/Art Resource, NY.
Caravaggio (Michelangelo Merisi da) (1573–1610). *The Conversion of Saint Paul*. Courtesy of Scala/Art Resource, NY.
A scene from *Harvey*, A Universal-International Picture. Copyright © 1950 Universal Pictures Company, Inc. Courtesy of Photofest.
Harry Dean Stanton as Saul/Paul in *The Last Temptation of Christ*, A Universal Release. Copyright © 1988 Universal City Studios, Inc. All rights reserved. Courtesy of Photofest.
Gregory Peck as Elmer Gantry in *Elmer Gantry*, A Universal Release. Copyright © 1960, Universal Pictures Company, Inc. Courtesy of Photofest.
Jake Gyllenhaal and Jena Malone in *Donnie Darko*. Copyright © 2001 by Twentieth Century Fox Home Video. Courtesy of Photofest.
Robert Duvall in The Apostle. Copyright © 1998 by Universal Studios Home Video. Courtesy of Photofest.

Design by Wesley Hoke

Library of Congress Cataloging-in-Publication Data

Walsh, Richard.
    Finding St. Paul in film / Richard Walsh.
        p.   cm.
    Includes bibliographical references and index.
    ISBN 0-567-02850-X (pbk.)
        1. Motion pictures—Religious aspects.   2. Paul, the Apostle, Saint.   I. Title:
Finding Saint Paul in film.   II. Title.
PN1995.5.W29   2005
791.43'651—dc22
                                                                                                2005012987

Printed in the United States of America

01 02 03 04 05 06 07 08 09 10   10 9 8 7 6 5 4 3 2 1

Contents

Watching Paul:
Icon and Villain

For though I am free with respect to all, I have made myself a slave to all, so that I might win more of them. To the Jews I became as a Jew, in order to win Jews. To those under the law I became as one under the law (though I myself am not under the law) so that I might win those under the law. To those outside the law I became as one outside the law (though I am not free from God's law but am under Christ's law) so that I might win those outside the law. To the weak I became weak, so that I might win the weak. I have become all things to all people, that I might by all means save some. (1 Cor 9:19–22)[1]

Paul's Limited Film Exposure

Jesus is a film celebrity. He has appeared frequently in Hollywood, independent, and foreign films. He has appeared as himself and in various disguised roles.[2] In striking contrast, Paul, often considered the cofounder of Christianity, has languished in relative obscurity. In fact, my search of "Saint Paul" at the Internet Movie Database (imdb.com) found only two movies. Of these, only one is actually about the apostle Paul, *San Paolo*, directed by Roger Young for Italian TV in 2000 (and released later in English).

Young's effort deserves some mention because of his importance as a director of "biblical" films. Most famously, he directed *Jesus* for CBS TV in 1999, a family-TV version of the Jesus story. Young offers Jesus by turns as the divine Christ of tradition and as the generic everyman. The latter allows Young to imagine Jesus as a modern, subjective individual struggling to understand God—a characterization the gospels and the epic Jesus films do not provide.[3] Young places this struggle within a standard family drama. Jesus, that is, finds himself and his mission vis-à-vis his father (Joseph), mother (Mary), and friends (Lazarus, Martha, and Mary):

> This story is a standard hero tale. The hero separates himself from his youthful embeddedness, undergoes various trials and temptations, and finally takes on his heroic (kingly) career. Following contemporary trends, Young has

modernized this tale into a Freudian family drama. Thus, Jesus becomes messiah only when he "gets over" his father Joseph. . . . Mary's continuing importance suggests, however, that Young is not completely satisfied with the
Freudian drama, and that emphasis, along with Jesus' departure for the
"spirit world," may indicate a Jungian conclusion. . . . Jesus, then, fulfills both
halves of the contemporary, psychological hero story by divorcing himself
from his earthly father and by reuniting thereafter with his mother (a symbol
of the unconscious for Jung) and with his heavenly father.[4]

In short, Young's Jesus is a successful modern hero. In particular, he epitomizes free
choice and makes the same available for everyone else.[5] Despite his divine trappings,
then, Jesus' story is everyone's story, if they achieve psychological maturity.

Young's treatment of Saint Paul is similar.[6] Once again, Young combines a nostalgic treatment of the canonical record with an understandably modern family
drama. Thus, Young follows the story of Acts fairly closely, although he does
emphasize the role of Paul. Young's Paul, for example, is far more outspoken in
Jerusalem about the need to include the Gentiles and ultimately campaigns that the
apostles themselves give up much of their distinctive Jewish traditions. Young, that
is, reads Acts through the lens of Galatians or, more likely, later emphases in
Western gentile Christianity.

Young transforms Paul into a modern figure by providing him with a psychological dilemma. Young's Paul must choose between two different types of Judaism,
each represented by an elder figure whom he respects. Young situates Paul between
Gamaliel's tolerant Pharisaism and Reuben's ethnocentrism.[7] The resulting portrayal
resembles Nicholas Ray's portrayal of Judas in *King of Kings*. In that film, Judas is
caught between a messiah of war and a messiah of peace and ultimately chooses
wrongly. Young's Paul, of course, chooses rightly. Like Young's Jesus, Paul matures
when he chooses a "spiritual" path, a liberal message of love and tolerance, of freedom of choice, rather than the violent attempt to maintain ethic distinctiveness.
The choice between the pathway of two rival elders, Gamaliel and Reuben, makes
Paul's choice and move toward maturity resemble that of Young's Jesus, but the
dynamics of this movie work differently. The movie lingers on the intimate relationship between Reuben and Paul so that the drama becomes a sibling rivalry. As
is so often the case in such stories and films, the dynamics also focus on the different "fates" of these two "brothers."

Reuben, Young's imaginative addition to the narrative of Acts, opposes
Christianity as heresy and apostolic "dirty tricks." Narrow-minded Reuben even
opposes Gamaliel's Pharisaism because its acceptance of the resurrection sounds
too much like Christianity. Not surprisingly, Reuben is the violent persecutor of
early Christianity. He enlists Paul in this service, pressing a stone into Paul's hand
at the stoning of Stephen, but Young's Paul is too kindhearted for killing. He sim-

ply stands and watches. Finally, however, Reuben convinces Paul that Jerusalem's fragile peace with Rome depends on the annihilation of Christianity.[8]

The Damascus road conversion sets Paul at odds with Reuben. Reuben tries to kill Paul, but Barnabas, Ananias, and Dinah[9] help Paul escape. Thereafter, Reuben becomes the pawn of various powers (Herod and a Roman administrator named Gaius) who bribe and threaten Reuben into further murderous plots against Paul. After the fashion of the numerous near escapes in Acts, Paul escapes Reuben's traps again and again. Reuben's final plot against Paul during his Jerusalem imprisonment fails when Dinah exposes the plot. Finally, Gaius kills Reuben and then sends Paul to Rome. After the miraculous escape from the shipwreck, Paul arrives at Rome in chains. Despite the chains, the movie clearly depicts two different fates for Reuben and Paul. Reuben's violence is the road to destruction. Paul's message of love and tolerance is the liberal future.

Pier Paolo Pasolini's *San Paolo* differs dramatically from Young's liberal, family-values Paul. Pasolini's Paul is far more apocalyptic, but in a distinctively Marxist form. Although he never filmed the movie, Pasolini left a full script.[10] That script follows the story of Acts closely but sets the story in modern America and Europe.

> Rome is New York, capital of American imperialism. Jerusalem, cultural seat occupied by the Romans, seat also of intellectual conformity, is Paris under the German heel. The small, nascent Christian community is represented by the Resistance, while the Pharisees are the Pétainists.
>
> Paul is French, from a comfortable bourgeois background, a collaborator, hunting members of the Resistance.
>
> Damascus is the Barcelona of Franco's Spain. The fascist Paul goes on a mission to see supporters of Franco. On the road to Barcelona, traveling through southwestern France, he has an illumination. He joins the camp of the antifascist Resistance.
>
> We, then, follow him as he travels around preaching resistance, in Italy, in Spain, in Germany. Athens, the Athens of the sophists who refused to listen to Paul, is represented by contemporary Rome, by those petty Italian intellectuals and critics whom Paul detested. Finally, Paul goes to New York, where he is betrayed, arrested, and executed in sordid circumstances.[11]

The transubstantiation of the story from antiquity to something like the recent past makes Pasolini's message quite unmistakable. It is the same message that animates his *Il Vangelo secondo Matteo* (*The Gospel according to Saint Matthew*); poets—like Jesus, Paul, and Pasolini—can combine Marxism and (Catholic) Christianity in such a way as to lead the people to liberation.[12] For Pasolini, both Jesus and Paul are revolutionaries acting on behalf of the lower classes. Their poetry—and this is part of the reason that Pasolini repeats Jesus and Paul so literally—is important.

By literally following Matthew's "stylistic accelerations"—the barbaric-practical workings of his narration, the abolition of chronological time, the elliptical jumps within the story which inscribe the "disproportions" of the didactic, static moments such as the stupendous, interminable, discourse on the mountain—the figure of Christ should finally assume the violence inhering in any rebellion which radically contradicts the appearance and shape that life assumes for modern man: a gray orgy of cynicism, irony, brutality, compromise and conformism.[13]

Like Antonio Gramsci, Pasolini sees artists and intellectuals in the forefront of the revolution.[14] Poetry—Jesus', Paul's, and Pasolini's—is important. Unfortunately, the poet is quickly swallowed up by the powers that be. In fact, *San Paolo* ends much less optimistically than *Il Vangelo*. The church and the priest have swallowed Paul. Luke, the author of the Acts that Pasolini modernizes, is the main culprit. Pasolini is, of course, also commenting on the unhappy institutionalization of Marxism.[15]

Scorsese gave Saint Paul a different exposure in a supporting role in *The Last Temptation of Christ*. Saul is a member of the Zealot band that sends Judas to kill Jesus. Jesus makes crosses for the Romans and helps them crucify messianic claimants. The Zealot group has little sympathy for this collaborator. Jesus, however, suborns Judas to his own cause (although Judas threatens to kill Jesus if he strays from the plan). When Jesus brings his traveling show to Jerusalem, Saul corners Judas:

> Judas, what are you doing with this magician? You had orders to kill him and you haven't done it. Now, he acts like a prophet and you follow him. . . . We took an oath against Rome . . . I don't see anything against Rome around here. All I see are Jews against Jews.[16]

Immediately thereafter, Saul and other Zealots visit Lazarus, and Saul stabs Lazarus to remove the proof of Jesus' miracles. Saul, that is, chooses zealotry over Jesus.

Saul, now Paul, appears again in Jesus' fantastic last temptation on the cross. In the visionary sequence, Jesus enjoys the benefits of choosing physical pleasures rather than the tortured spiritual quest the movie has shown up to this point. Late in the vision, an aging Jesus meets the converted Paul preaching to a small group. Paul lists his sins, embroidering the list after the fashion of a revival preacher, mentions his persecution of those who broke the law, and builds to his conversion on the road to Damascus. Struck blind by a white light, he heard the voice of Jesus who made him Paul. He now offers a gospel about Jesus, the Son of God and of the Virgin Mary, who was punished for our sins and resurrected to heaven. Paul's Jesus conquered death, forgave our sins, and opened the world of God to everybody. Jesus is understandably perplexed:

Jesus: Did you ever see this Jesus of Nazareth after he came back from the dead? I mean with your own eyes?

Saul: No, but I saw a light that blinded me. And I heard his voice.

Jesus: You're a liar.

Saul: The disciples saw him. They were hiding in an attic with the doors locked and he appeared to them.

Jesus: Liar. He's a liar. . . . I was never crucified. I never came back from the dead. I'm a man like everybody else. Why are you telling these lies? I'm the son of Mary and Joseph. . . . Who are you talking about? . . . So don't go around telling lies about me or I'll tell everybody the truth.

Saul: Just a minute. What's the matter with you? Look around you. Look at all these people. Look at their faces. Do you see how unhappy they are? Do you see how much they're suffering? Their only hope is the resurrected Jesus. I don't care whether you're Jesus or not. The resurrected Jesus will save the world and that's what matters. . . . I created the truth out of what people needed and what they believed. If I have to crucify you to save the world, then I'll crucify you. And if I have to resurrect you, then I'll do that too whether you like it or not. . . . You started all this; now you can't stop it. All those people who believe me will grab you and kill you. . . . You see, you don't know how much people need God. You don't know how happy he can make them. He can make them happy to do anything. He can make them happy to die. And they'll die. All for the sake of Christ. Jesus Christ. Jesus of Nazareth. The Son of God. The Messiah. Not you, not for your sake. You know, I'm glad I met you because now I can forget all about you. My Jesus is much more important and much more powerful. Thank you. It's a good thing I met you.

While Scorsese does not show the miracle, the reason for Saul's conversion from murder to Paul's evangelism is the Damascus road conversion (Acts 9); nevertheless, Paul has apparently changed very little. As in the scene with Judas and Lazarus in the passion, Paul once again chooses something else—now his Christ—over Jesus. He is still quite willing to kill Jesus, at least rhetorically, if that is necessary for his gospel. He is certainly willing to walk away from Jesus in favor of his message about his saving Christ. Paul's Christ, not Jesus, is the figure who will "save the world."

This ethically questionable Paul is hardly Saint Paul. On the best possible interpretation, he sounds like Leclerc, the priest in *Jesus of Montreal* who tells Daniel that the truth is not important. Instead, what is important is what people need to hear. On this reading, Scorsese's Saul passes out pleasing illusions. On a less charitable reading, Scorsese's Saul is a charlatan, like Elmer Gantry or Jonas Nightengale, who peddles what people will pay to receive. Actually, he is worse. He is not only willing to suppress the truth; he is also willing to kill (Jesus and Lazarus) or to let people die (those who accept his message) to realize his goals.[17] In that regard, Scorsese's Paul is far more like the evil cardinal in *Stigmata*, who covers up the words of Jesus, which threaten the opulent church, with whatever means necessary. Like Pasolini's script, Scorsese's *Last Temptation of Christ* imagines the church as a question-able institution, but Scorsese's Paul is more clearly complicit in this nefariousness.

A Christian Proteus

Despite Paul's limited exposure in film, he has had three delightfully different roles: icon of psychological maturity, Marxist revolutionary, and murderous charlatan. Young and Pasolini follow Acts closely, but both modernize the story. Young mod-ernizes characters, while Pasolini modernizes setting and cultural background. Despite his faithfulness to Acts and Paul's words, Pasolini dramatically challenges Acts, while Young treats Acts far more nostalgically. Scorsese's Saul is a far more limited character. He is simply not the protagonist of *The Last Temptation of Christ*. As a result, he floats in and out of the story. Probably the message of this Paul is clos-est to that of the Pauline letters. More importantly, Scorsese offers by far the most negative portrayal of Paul. The Pauls of Young and Pasolini are iconic. Scorsese's Paul is reprehensible.

These dichotomous differences are hardly surprising. After all, Paul, in the words of Wayne Meeks, has always been a "Christian Proteus."[18] Read in one way, Paul's own words in I Cor 9:19–22, the epigraph to this introduction, sound like an authoritative mandate for this chameleon nature. Meeks's description of Paul as Proteus ends the Norton volume entitled *The Writings of St. Paul* that Meeks edited. After an annotated text of the Pauline epistles, Meeks includes selections culled from the history of Pauline interpretation. In the ancient church alone, Weeks dis-cerns four very different "Pauls."

The first of these Pauls is the Paul of Acts and the post-Pauline letters. In Maurice Wiles's pithy phrase, this Paul is the "domesticated apostle." This Paul ulti-mately became the canonical Paul or the Saint Paul of Christian tradition, the author of thirteen books of the New Testament, and the "real person" described by the author of Acts. This Paul incarnates the move of Christianity to the Gentiles. He is also, along with the gospels and Peter, the apostolic basis of imperial, *una sancta apos-tolica* Christianity.

Seen in retrospect—that is, after the establishment of "Saint Paul"—Meeks's three other ancient Pauls are the products of various heretics: of second- and third-century Jewish Christians who saw Paul as the apostle of Satan, of Marcionites who saw Paul as the only apostle who understood Jesus' new, strange God, and of ascetics who saw Paul as the model for their radical lifestyle. To these Pauls we should, of course, add the equally ancient Gnostic Paul, the spiritual Paul of heav-enly insights and mystic visions.[19]

In short, in the beginning of the formation of Christian discourse, "Paul" is a debated, constructed term. Paul is Pauls.[20] Saint Paul, however, eventually became the dominant construct. It had imperial (both political and religious) support.

Critical, academic discourse on Paul is parasitic on this tradition, but academics situate themselves vis-à-vis the powers by penetrating the canonical Paul to discover the real, actual, or historical Paul. Their results profane Saint Paul. Their work rejects the myth of *una sancta apostolica* harmony for glimpses of the historical Paul's competition with other apostles, of his ongoing problems with his churches, and of his struggles to legitimize his gentile churches vis-à-vis Jewish followers of Jesus. Further, instead of the thirteen canonical letters, scholars typically reduce their historical Pauls to the seven undisputed letters (Romans, 1 and 2 Corinthians, Galatians, Philippians, 1 Thessalonians, and Philemon) and sometimes to the four *Hauptbriefe* (Romans, 1 and 2 Corinthians, and Galatians). Scholars also see these letters as occasional, situational responses to particular situations, not as canonical pronouncements. These occasional letters do not dictate. They seek to persuade followers and to manage a mission field. They are not so much systematic statements of theology, then, as they are corrections of specific misinterpretations of Paul's desired myth and ethos.

While reducing the canonical data, scholars have once again increased the number of Pauls available, and they have, at least, indirectly called attention to the constructed nature of Paul. They have also publicly reopened (or continued) the polarities of antiquity.

> The history of Paulinism, as we have noted earlier, contains a peculiar ambivalence. The "most holy apostle" of the sacred traditions is at the same time, again and again, "the apostle of the heretics." There is singular irony in the fact that the great system builders of Christian doctrine quarried their choicest propositions from Paul's letters, only to have later generations discover that they had thus built time-bombs into the structure that would, in a moment of crisis, bring the whole tower of syllogisms crashing down. Paul has become the foe of all authoritative systems, although he himself—and that is the strange part—was not a revolutionary in any sense of the word. "Paulinism has proved to be a ferment in the history of dogma, a basis it has never been."[21]

This political debate continues unabated in the recent academy.

We might reduce the dominant academic image of Paul from Augustine to Rudolf Bultmann to the slogan of "justification by faith alone." Once loved, this construct is now abhorred. It has been challenged and replaced to a great extent by the so-called "new perspective" on Paul. That Paul is far more politically correct (that is, less anti-Semitic and less patriarchal). Not surprisingly, other academics have challenged this "new perspective" as a surreptitious attempt to legitimate political correctness. These recent scholars call attention, then, to the politics involved in (the historical) Paul and in his interpretation.[22] Even philosophers have recently turned to Paul in the quest for an engaged political ethics.[23] Despite the diversity, Paul remains just as highly value laden as he was in antiquity. He is something to hate or to love, to resist or to extol. He represents either everything that has gone wrong with the church or culture (as with the ancient Jewish Christians) or the sacred truth beyond human corruption (as with the ancient Marcionites). He is villain (Scorsese) or icon (Young, Pasolini).

Pauls—the canonical, the heretical, the academic, the "new" Paul, and the political Paul—are cultural and ideological constructs devised in polemical contexts and used to gain political advantage. In no case do we arrive at the "real" Paul. We are always dealing with constructs, with signs, with interpretations, and with politics. Here, I see no need to privilege one of these Pauls or to claim that I have found yet another "really real" Paul. In what follows, I will attend to canon and to critics (in roughly reverse order). When I speak of Paul in the following chapters, then, I will have in mind the figures and constructs of Christian discourse briefly summarized here. My Paul is a construct of that discourse, but my Paul has multivalent possibilities. My Paul is Pauls.

Hard to find in Brueghel's painting (he lies on the ground, near the painting's center, between the evergreen trees and the horseman facing away from the viewer), Paul is even harder to find in film.

I start in chapter 1 with the new, politically correct Paul of historical-critical scholars. That Paul comfortably belongs among us; however, the very pleasantness of this construct troubles me. That discomfort leads me in chapters 1 and 2 to a less familiar Paul, to a Paul who is a troublesome apocalyptic visionary and the psychotic precursor of Christianity. This fractured Paul, the apostle of cruciform Western Christianity, and his troublesome gospel of death take center stage in chapter 3. Chapter 4 leaves the Christian Paul behind for a Paul, like that of many post-Holocaust scholars, who is quite Jewish. Chapter 5 returns to where we began, Saint Paul. That chapter and the epilogue reduce Saint Paul, as do ancient Christian debate and present scholarship, to a highly questionable authority.

Throughout, then, I highlight the constructed nature of all our Pauls and seek to pit Pauls against one another. Critical debate has revealed serious cracks in the facade of Saint Paul. Moreover, without some myth-ritual support or outside some imperial hegemony—like that of the canon—none of our Pauls brings all the data into a harmonious, impervious whole. Today, "Paul," devoid of his sainthood, is condemned to meaning. The ideology that construes "Paul" provides his meaning. We tend, quite humanly, to take our ideology/myth for the truth, whether we consider our ideology/myth divinely granted, scientifically discovered, or simply the "natural" way of things; therefore, we need constant lessons in politics and in the cracks in our ideology.[24]

"Outing Paul" at the Movies

Such anomalies and inconsistencies become noticeable in stress or in dialogue with others. My method is dialogue or the attempt to bring various Pauls into conversation with each other and with contemporary movies. As the movies belong more completely to our culture than does Paul, they nicely expose Paul's strangeness. Reading Paul with the movies does not "save" Paul so much as construct him as an alien interlocutor. That may help to prevent his co-option by our ideologies.

In the enterprise of discovering Paul at the movies, I consciously follow the lead of several energetic, enterprising scholars. With respect to the specific topic of Paul and the movies, I am most conscious of my debt to Robert Jewett, Larry Kreitzer, Roland Boer, and Adele Reinhartz.[25] While I differ from their interpretations at points in the chapters that follow, I appreciate their work. Like them, I have chosen films that have only metaphorical connections with the Pauls of Christian and academic discourse. After all, Paul does not often "star" in film. The films discussed below, then, relate to Paul only as my interpretations of the films and of Paul render a Paul as the films' precursor.

Five major topics structure the following conversations with particular Pauls: (1) grace, (2) apocalypse, (3) death-obsession, (4) ethics, and (5) Paul's "canonical" status. Chapter 1 pits the notion of grace as individual transformation against the notion of grace as an apocalyptic upheaval of the "world." Chapter 2 pits the apocalyptic apostle against apocalyptic nuts, questions the apocalyptic Paul's sanity, and challenges his benefits as precursor to our society. On behalf of a responsible humanism, chapter 3 questions the obsession with death in Paul's gospel and its corresponding debasement of humans, theology, and ethic. Chapter 4 juxtaposes ethics and grace by exploring the ethical problems poised by grace and Paul's own abandonment of grace for social norms. Chapter 5 raises questions about the appropriateness of the politics and ethics implicit in the very notion of "Saint Paul" in a multicultural world. In each chapter, then, I try to exploit tensions in Pauls. I try, that is, to be true to the discussion about and construction of Paul from antiquity to the present.

By pursuing the issue of multiple Pauls in Christian discourse and at the movies, I wish to make it difficult to render Paul our ideological ally. Put simply, Paul scares me too much for that process to stand unchallenged. Paul needs to be watched most closely when he belongs too securely to us. If we do not see our Paul as a construct, no gap at all really exists between us and him. If our construct is "Saint Paul," we arrogate divine authority to ourselves and to our plans. When I speak of watching Paul, then, I am really talking about watching those of us who construct Paul for our own agendas. Accordingly, as I bring various Pauls and movies into conversation, I try to push the issues toward humility, humor, and responsibility. At the end, I allow myself a fantasy of a repentant, smiling Paul, one, I think, who differs noticeably and importantly from the Pauls I have known.

Notes

1. Unless otherwise noted, the Scripture quotations contained herein are from the New Revised Standard Version Bible, copyright © 1989 by the Division of Christian Education of the National Council of Churches of Christ in the U.S.A. Used by permission. All rights reserved.

2. By "himself," I mean films in which Jesus—either a historical, confessional, or misplaced Jesus—is the protagonist. By "disguised roles," I refer to films that may be described as Christ-figure films, that is, films in which the protagonist resembles Jesus. These are not hard and fast distinctions. They easily bleed back and forth. See Richard Walsh, *Reading the Gospels in the Dark: Portrayals of Jesus in Film* (Harrisburg, Pa.: Trinity Press International, 2003), 29–33.

3. See Walsh, *Reading the Gospels in the Dark*, 25–29, 33.

4. Ibid., 29. The upbeat tone of the struggle and its successful conclusion make the subjectivity of Young's Jesus quite different from that of Scorsese's equally subjective but haunted Jesus in *The Last Temptation of Christ*.

5. The villains in Young's *Jesus*, notably Satan and Judas, try to deny freedom of choice to others. The Gethsemane scene is particularly important in the twin characterization of these villains.

6. For a helpful plot summary of *San Paolo* by an anonymous reviewer, see http://www.imdb.com/title/tt0270621/plotsummary (accessed August 7, 2004).

7. Following Acts, Young's Paul is, at first, Saul. As Young's Paul is always Saint Paul—that is, as Young offers a nostalgic picture of Christian traditions—I have not tried to reproduce the name shift in this synopsis.

8. Interestingly, Young's Paul resembles recent scholarly views on Paul at some points. For example, some of the scholars who represent the "new perspective" on Paul (see below) argue that Paul's quarrel with Judaism and his "Christianity" was a choice for universalism over ethnicity. Despite Gamaliel, Young sees this as a conflict between Christianity and Judaism. The "new perspective" on Paul typically sees the conflict as intra-Jewish. Young's notion that Paul persecuted Christians because he felt they threatened the Jews' precarious détente with Rome is also an idea sometimes advanced in recent Pauline studies.

9. Dinah, another Young creation, is the obligatory romantic interest. Caught between Reuben and Paul, she marries Reuben, but she remains attracted to Christianity and Paul. Dinah repeatedly comes to Paul's assistance vis-à-vis Reuben. At one point, Jesus' mother, Mary, even assists Dinah in leaving Reuben!

10. A synopsis of the script is available in Alain Badiou, *Saint Paul: The Foundation of Universalism*, trans. Ray Brassier (Stanford: Stanford University Press, 2003), 36–39.

11. Ibid., 37–38.

12. See Walsh, *Reading the Gospels in the Dark*, 95–120.

13. Pasolini, cited in Naomi Greene, *Pier Paolo Pasolini: Cinema as Heresy* (Princeton: Princeton University Press, 1990), 27; however, Pasolini also claims that he offered Matthew by analogy, not exactly. See Oswald Stack, *Pasolini on Pasolini: Interviews with Oswald Stack* (Bloomington: Indiana University Press, 1969), 82.

14. On Gramsci's influence on Pasolini, see Greene, *Pier Paolo Pasolini*, 27–35, 54–60. Her entire book is an illuminating discussion of Pasolini's films and writings in light of his tumultuous relationship with Marxism.

15. See Badiou, *Saint Paul*, 38–39. The negative attitude to "priests" sounds like Nietzsche's negative analysis of Christianity in *The Antichrist*, in *The Portable Nietzsche*, ed. and trans. Walter A. Kaufmann (New York: Viking, 1954), 23–27, 42–43. Of course, for Nietzsche, Paul, not Luke, is *the* Christian priest. Pasolini also observes "priestly" elements in Paul (Badiou, *Saint Paul*, 39). Protestant interpretations of Paul have, of course, been as anti-priest as they have been anti-Semitic. The Catholic Pasolini's animus may come either from his aestheticism or his Marxism.

16. Unless otherwise noted, quotations from films are my own transcriptions.

17. To my knowledge, no other film incarnation of Paul is so unequivocally focused on death, but see chapter 3.

18. Wayne A. Meeks, ed., *The Writings of St. Paul* (New York: W. W. Norton & Co., 1972), 435–44.

19. See ibid., 149–213. David L. Barr, *New Testament Story: An Introduction*, 3rd ed. (Belmont, Calif.: Wadsworth, 2002), 176–207, has a similar treatment of ancient Pauls, as well as a helpful bibliography for these different constructs. For more detail on the interpretation of Paul in antiquity, see William S. Babcock, ed., *Paul and the Legacies of Paul* (Dallas: Southern Methodist University Press, 1990). James D. G. Dunn, "Introduction," in *The Cambridge Companion to St. Paul* (Cambridge: Cambridge University Press, 2003), 1–15, provides a helpful commentary on Meeks's selections. The classic treatment of the Gnostic Paul is Elaine H. Pagels, *The Gnostic Paul: Gnostic Exegesis of the Pauline Letters* (Philadelphia: Fortress Press, 1975).

20. The essays in Babcock, *Paul and the Legacies of Paul*, frequently call attention to the plural and constructed nature of Paul in antiquity. Calvin Roetzel ends his popular book *Paul: The Man and the Myth* (Minneapolis: Fortress, 1999), 176, with similar reflections about the interpretation of Paul in general.

21. Meeks, *The Writings of St. Paul*, 435–36. The last sentence quotes Adolf von Harnack's famous aphorism about Paul from his *History of Dogma*, trans. Neil Buchanan (London: Williams & Norgate, 1894), 1:136.

22. Many of these scholars have been associated with the SBL Paul and Politics Group. See Richard A. Horsley, ed., *Paul and Politics: Ekklesia, Israel, Imperium, Interpretation: Essays in Honor of Krister Stendahl* (Harrisburg, Pa.: Trinity Press International, 2000).

23. Roland Boer introduced me to the Paul of the philosophers in private correspondence. He also offered a public lecture on the topic in October 2004 at Duke University. He kindly provided me a copy of this lecture, which divides the "Pauline" philosophers into two diverse, unengaged groups operating with mirrorlike Pauls. Even here, then, Paul remains a debated construct, tending in conversation toward polar positions. Boer tries to bring those groups into conversation. On that agenda and the Paul of the philosophers, see also his editorial introduction to the new electronic journal, Roland Boer, "Editorial," *The Bible and Critical Theory* 1, November 2004, http://publications.epress.monash.edu/doi/full/10.2104/bc040001 (accessed January 18, 2005).

24. Roland Barthes, *Mythologies*, trans. Annette Lavers (New York: Hill and Wang, 1972), 109–59, has an excellent discussion of myth as a mechanism of the "natural" or "the cultural dominant." He opposes myth with politics.

25. See Robert Jewett, *Saint Paul at the Movies: The Apostle's Dialogue with American Culture* (Louisville: Westminster John Knox, 1993); idem., *Paul the Apostle to America: Cultural Trends and Pauline Scholarship* (Louisville: Westminster John Knox, 1994); idem., *Saint Paul Returns to the Movies: Triumph over Shame* (Grand Rapids: William B. Eerdmans, 1999); Larry Kreitzer, *Pauline Images in Fiction and Film: On Reversing the Hermeneutical Flow* (Sheffield: Sheffield Academic, 1999); Roland Boer, "Non-Sense: *Total Recall*, Paul, and the Possibility of Psychosis," in George Aichele and Richard Walsh, eds., *Screening Scripture: Intertextual Connections between Scripture and Film* (Harrisburg, Pa.: Trinity Press International, 2002), 120–54; and Adele Reinhartz, *Scripture on the Silver Screen* (Louisville: Westminster John Knox, 2003), 114–43.

Chapter 1

Saving Paul:
Modern Liberals and
Apocalyptic Criminals

[The Jews shouted,] "These people who have been turning the world upside down have come here also, and Jason has entertained them as guests. They are all acting contrary to the decrees of the emperor, saying that there is another king named Jesus." (Acts 17:6–7)

There is no longer Jew or Greek, there is no longer slave or free, there is no longer male and female; for all of you are one in Christ Jesus. (Gal 3:28)

Tender Mercies: Acceptance as Transcendence

Modernity has left transcendence in short supply, metaphysically and socially.[1] The notion of a world above has vanished. Social commitments have diminished. The modern individual stands alone. Movies often fantasize the end of this alienation with stories about romantic love in which a botched, limited hero or heroine comes into his or her own by finding that special human other. The pattern is so common that examples are superfluous. In short, the movies offer romantic love as the acceptable version of transcendence for the modern, expressive individual.[2]

Bruce Beresford's 1983 film *Tender Mercies* is a strikingly unsentimental version of this modern gospel. A washed-out drunk, Mac Sledge, has lost his country western music career and his family by incarnating his "whiskey-drinkin', hard-lovin'" lyrics all too literally. As the movie's opening credits roll, Mac passes out in a drunken stupor in a cheap Texas motel. The appropriate background music is "It Hurts to Face Reality." The next day, he asks the motel owner, Rosa Lee, for a job because he cannot pay for his room. Rosa Lee gives him work and breakfast. Thereafter, with little fanfare, Mac remains at Rosa Lee's roadside motel and rights himself through the new opportunity that Rosa Lee and her son, Sonny, provide him.

Mac's transformation, replete with temptations, detours, and setbacks, is quite realistic. An early scene at the local Baptist church is typical of Beresford's understated style. After the pastor talks to Sonny and his mom about Sonny's upcoming

13

baptism, he asks Mac about his religious history. When Mac admits that he has never been baptized, the minister coyly says, "We'll have to work on you." Ultimately, of course, the love and acceptance of Rosa Lee and Sonny socialize Mac. Fittingly, the music that punctuates this part of the movie is "Learning to Love Again." After two months of sobriety, Mac proposes haltingly to Rosa Lee as they work in her garden, "Will you think about marrying me?" She replies cryptically, "I will." Beresford never shows us Rosa Lee's acceptance or a marriage ceremony, but the next scene, which shows Sonny at school, presumes the marriage.

Buoyed by his new family, Mac returns to songwriting and to the temptations associated with that career. Early on, Mac sings "I've Decided to Leave Here" as he teaches Sonny to play the guitar in the family's kitchen. Playfully, Mac adds sotto voce to Rosa Lee, "Not really," but subsequent trials do cause Mac to consider his options. He goes to Austin alone to watch Dixie, his former wife and partner, sing and to offer one of his new songs to her manager, Harry. Later, Harry visits the motel and crushes Mac's dreams, rejecting the song as "no good." Rosa Lee comforts Mac by telling him that she thanks God every night for God's tender mercies, notably Mac and Sonny. When Mac tries to sing his new song, "If You'll Hold the Ladder (I'll Climb to the Top)," for her, his voice falters. Crestfallen, he leaves home for a bar and a bottle while "It Hurts to Face Reality" plays in the background again. Rosa Lee waits faithfully, if impatiently, at home. As Rosa prays for God to teach her "her path," Mac returns proudly because he is not drunk and because he has not been able "to leave here," an allusion of course to his playful song. Fittingly, the Madonna-like Rosa Lee rises from bed to provide a late supper. She surprises Mac by telling him that she gave his new song to a group of young musicians. As the reunion scene ends, they hug and sing part of "If You'll Hold the Ladder."

When the youthful musicians record his song, Mac's glory days return. He also begins to accept his own past. Thus, as he walks down a street one day, a woman asks him, "Were you really Mac Sledge?" Amused, Mac replies, "Yes, ma'am, I guess I was." Mac is still, however, only partly transformed. Thus, when his long-lost daughter, Sue Ann, visits, he refuses to endorse her childhood memory of him singing "(On the) Wings of a Dove" to her. As she leaves and he stands alone in an empty room, however, we hear him singing the song. Although baptized with Sonny in the Baptist church, their conversation on the way home also underscores the uncertainty of Mac's new life. Sonny declares, "I don't feel that different. I'm not a changed person. Are you?" Fittingly, Mac answers, "Not yet." Nonetheless, another scene demonstrates his ongoing progress. In a bar, the family listens to the band that recorded Mac's song. Then, onstage, Mac sings "If You'll Hold the Ladder" completely for the first time to an adoring, supportive Rosa Lee:

You're the only dream I've ever had that's come true. . . .
And if you just hold the ladder, baby, I'll climb to the top.
If you'll just stand beside me all the way,

I'll do all the things that didn't matter yesterday.
And I'll be everything this man can be before I stop.
If you'll just hold the ladder . . .

The joy is short-lived, however. When the band brings the record of Mac's new song to the motel, Mac and Rosa Lee lock up the motel in order to go to a band member's house to hear the song. As they are leaving, the phone rings, and Mac returns to answer it. Meanwhile, Rosa Lee dials in Mac's new song on the radio. Mac comes to the truck, turns off the radio, and returns to the porch. As Rosa Lee approaches, he tells her that Sue Ann was killed in a car accident. Thereafter, the background music is, once again, "It Hurts to Face Reality." Strikingly, no character ever makes sense of this tragedy. In fact, near the end of the movie, as he hoes the garden again, Mac says angrily to Rosa Lee,

I was almost killed once in a car accident. I was drunk and I ran off the side of the road and turned over four times. And they took me out of that car for dead, but I lived. And I prayed last night to know why I lived and she died. But I got no answer to my prayers. I still don't know why she died and I lived. I don't know the answer to nothing, not a blessed thing. I don't know why I wandered out to this part of Texas drunk and you took me in and pitied me and helped me to straighten out. Married me. Why, why did that happen? Is there a reason that happened? And Sonny's Daddy died in the war. My daughter killed in an automobile accident. Why? You see, I don't trust happiness. I never did. I never will.

Like the rest of us, Rosa Lee has no answer.

In the denouement, however, Sonny comes home from school to find a gift, a new football, from Mac. He goes outside to thank Mac, who is singing "Wings of a Dove." As they play catch, a smiling Rosa Lee watches from the porch while background music plays:

Tenderly, you gathered up the pieces of my life.
Lying in your loving arms never felt so right.
The hard luck road behind me is reflected in your eyes.
And the glory of the bright lights can't compare to this feeling when you smile.
You're the good things I threw away
Coming back to me every day.
You're the best it could ever be.
You are what love means to me.

In short, Mac has no answers, but he does have a new life, however fragile.

Realistic Romance—and Religion?

Literally and metaphorically, *Tender Mercies* brings country western music to the screen. An old joke avers that if you play a country western record backward, your sobriety, dog, truck, and girl return. The joke, of course, plays on the fact that many country western songs are whiny, crying-in-your-beer music. Of course, any long-time listener knows that country western music, like all popular music, comes in two forms: laments (about lost trucks, dogs, and girls) and thanksgivings (for good things found or returned).

These two forms reflect the two emotions of pain and pleasure. Religious language reflects the same two emotions when worshipers petition or praise God. Both forms of prayer appear in *Tender Mercies*. Rosa Lee thanks God for her "tender mercies" and petitions God to show her "the path." These two religious forms establish a connection between *Tender Mercies* and Psalms. In fact, the phrase "tender mercies," which appears as the movie's title and in Rosa Lee's description of her nightly prayers, appears throughout the King James Version of the Psalms (see Pss 25:6; 40:11; 51:1; 69:16; 77:9; 79:8; 103:4; 119:77, 156; 145:9).

Mirroring the human experiences of pain and pleasure, the Psalms appear in two general types: laments and hymns. The former reflects a situation of loss and petitions God for redress (see Pss 6; 13; 22; 44; 79). The hymn—sometimes subdivided into the hymn and the thanksgiving—praises God either for his creation of the gracious world in which the worshiper lives (the hymn, see Pss 78; 100; 105; 106) or for some recent, specific deliverance (the thanksgiving, see Pss 32; 34; 92; 138). While the lament petitions God's action, the thanksgiving provides the decorous response to God's deliverance. In fact, the lament itself typically moves from complaint and petition (see Pss 13:1–4; 22:1–21) to praise (see Pss 13:5; 22:22–31). The divine action—if there is any—that sparks the move from complaint to praise is off the page altogether.[3] In the Psalms, human speech dominates the present.[4] Instead of divine drama and miracle, then, the Psalms offer human religious experience lived within the disparate conditions and emotions of life.

Both lament and thanksgiving appear in *Tender Mercies*, but in the form of country western music. The lament-like "It Hurts to Face Reality" begins the film and reoccurs during Mac's subsequent temptations and trials. In short, although we never hear Mac pray, the movie reflects an "out of the depths"[5] understanding of the human condition and of Mac's specific life. Further, like the laments, *Tender Mercies* offers a nonmiraculous resolution of Mac's difficulties.[6] The drama—Mac's glittering career, boozy downfall, and conversion (if there is any such dramatic moment)—is all offscreen. Onscreen, Mac struggles to find life and sobriety at a dilapidated roadside motel. Similarly, Mac and Rosa Lee's marriage is offscreen, but their attempt to forge a life together in the midst of past and ongoing disappointments is onscreen. Sue Ann's fiery death is offscreen, but Mac, with all his questions unresolved, goes on with life onscreen. Both psalm and film, then, leave drama aside for the business of daily living, of going on—after, and with, suffering and joy.[7]

Like the Psalms, *Tender Mercies* eschews the intellectual struggle of theodicy. *Tender Mercies'* response to the evils of life, to reality, is "If You'll Hold the Ladder," Mac's paean to Rosa Lee's loving acceptance, and "Wings of a Dove."[8] They are the hymns that answer the lament "It Hurts to Face Reality." For *Tender Mercies*, one must be buoyed up to face reality. In contrast to the Psalms' ritual resolution of the lament, however, *Tender Mercies* offers a more modern solution: Mac's acceptance by his new loving family. *Tender Mercies*, then, is a *secular* psalm. Despite biblical allusions (and country western music), God is further offstage than in the Psalms. Mac's new family, not God, restores Mac. Accordingly, Mac, through country western music, gives thanks to Rosa Lee. Only Rosa Lee gives thanks to God, and we hear only her report of that prayer, not the prayer itself.

Of course, this attenuated transcendence contributes to *Tender Mercies'* modern realism, for, as we have seen, transcendence is in short supply in modernity. If God intervened more directly in this movie, we would be in the arena of fantasy, of weird, unexplained phenomena (although some character would proffer a scientific explanation), science fiction, religious horror, or some misplaced biblical epic. For moderns, Beresford rightly understates, and *Tender Mercies* rightly marginalizes God.

Modernizing Paul

Robert Jewett interprets the divine absence in *Tender Mercies* as a "mystery" and compares that mystery to the invisible, unexpected workings of Paul's God.

> But what is of particular interest is that such tender mercies are largely invisible. Both for Paul and for Foote's story [the author of the play upon which the movie is based], faith is required because the mercies of God are elusive, intangible, and off camera. In a mysterious way, the God of Abraham "gives life to the dead and calls that which does not exist into being," to use the language of Romans 4.[9]

Like Paul's grace, Mac's "tender mercies" are undeserved and unexpected. Love and salvation come to Mac "for no apparent reason, as though salvation were his destiny."[10] Like grace, then, "tender mercies" come seemingly ex nihilo and create a new life/situation (see Rom 4:16–17). The "tender mercies" resurrect Mac. Metaphorically dead at the beginning of the film, Mac moves from solitary drunkenness to a new family life. Fortuitously, for Jewett's reading, Mac is even baptized, raised to walk in newness of life.

For Jewett, Mac's story reveals the hidden plot of every life, a plot that only faith deciphers.

But unlike the usual miracles of film and television fantasy, this one occurs mysteriously, off camera. That's what dazes us. It is a matter of faith, elusive and intangible. All we can witness is that a person who was once almost nothing becomes something at the end of the story, singing his own new songs and tossing a football to his newfound son.[11]

Faith sees the ordinary as divine destiny or as God's tender mercies. Such sight— or, at least, Jewett's interpretation of the film—drags mercy, if not God, into the limelight. Jewett ends his analysis with his pastoral goal: "So the final question is this: can Americans, who prefer pragmatic evidence, learn to gaze beneath the surface of their lives to discern the hidden plot of tender mercies?"[12]

Jewett's intriguing reading modernizes Paul in at least two distinct ways. First, Jewett reads Mac's resurrection, symbolized by his baptism, modernly. For Paul, baptism demarcates a worshiper's new life in Christ.

Do you not know that all of us who have been baptized into Christ Jesus were baptized into his death? Therefore we have been buried with him by baptism into death, so that, just as Christ was raised from the dead by the glory of the Father, so we too might walk in newness of life.

For if we have been united with him in a death like his, we will certainly be united with him in a resurrection like his. (Rom 6:3–5)

Paul's followers die to sin, death, and old authorities when they are baptized into Christ's death. Thereafter, they live with and "in Christ" and in the spirit, foretastes of the resurrection, the upcoming apocalyptic finale (Rom 8:18–39). Pauline baptism, then, admits worshipers to the apocalyptic event of Jesus Christ's death and resurrection.[13] Admittedly, Paul elongates this apocalyptic moment. The new life is "already, but not yet." Paul's followers have only entered the antechamber of the new age through baptism. Accordingly, Paul's letters spell out what Christian (ethical) life should be like "in Christ," a peculiar interim between death and life (see Rom 6:12–19). Nonetheless, the apocalypse still impends, and Paul's baptized followers die and live in the shadow of that grand finale (Rom 6:5–11; 8:18–39).

Later churches made baptism an entry rite for an ongoing institution (see Col 3:1–4:1). This sacramental use of baptism liberates it from apocalyptic scenarios. Baptism—and the death-resurrection it symbolizes—becomes a ritual introducing one into institutional life, into a new status in this world, not into the apocalypse. Jewett reads *Tender Mercies* similarly. Death/life and baptism become metaphors for new possibilities in this life, for a second chance at family. In *Tender Mercies*, no grand apocalyptic finale awaits. All that matters are transformational possibilities within secular modernity.

Second, Jewett's reading modernizes Paul's notion of faith. Jewett's reading of the "hidden"—or is it absent?—God of *Tender Mercies* is a very pragmatic, pastoral response to modernity.[14] After all, mystery makes far more religious sense in modernity than miracle does. God—or his modern spokesman—cannot really afford miraculous signs. He needs to appear incognito to be taken seriously. Accordingly, movies like *Grand Canyon*, *Powder*, and *The Green Mile* have replaced biblical epics in recent cinema.[15]

Jewett's reading of the hidden God in *Tender Mercies* resembles the phenomenology of Mircea Eliade, for whom religion originates in a hierophany, a manifestation of the sacred in some profane object or event, which paradoxically retains its profane identity while simultaneously suggesting Rudolf Otto's "wholly other."[16] Of course, the nonbeliever can simply fasten upon the material reality.[17] God's modern elusiveness, then, is a double-edged sword. On one hand, unlike apocalyptic scenarios, this elusiveness protects religious interpretations of life from falsification. Who can say that God's mercies are not part of the *hidden* plot of every life? On the other hand, who is to say that they are? What if there is nothing behind or beneath the curtain?[18]

John Wisdom's famous parable of the gardener nicely encapsulates this debate. Two men carry on a running discussion about a long-neglected garden. One finds a design that suggests an unseen, mysterious gardener. The other finds too many weeds and too little evidence for the gardener hypothesis. Despite additional experience and ongoing debate, they reach no consensus. While neither expects anything different from the garden, they "feel" differently toward it.[19]

Appropriately, then, Mac is quite taciturn. He never speaks of God's tender mercies. His only speech about God, which he delivers as he hoes Rosa Lee's garden near the end of the film, reports his unanswered prayers despairingly. Mac concludes, "I don't trust happiness. Never did. Never will." Given the expressive individualism in modern America, "happiness" is not far from "God." Even without that translation, Mac's speech sounds more like an unanswered lament, and a lament that does not make the psalm's ritualistic transition from complaint to praise, than it does Paul's dramatic, apocalyptic gospel. In the movie, only Rosa Lee speaks positively about and to God. If we focus on Mac as the movie does, then we are left with a story that we may read religiously or not. Why should we look "beneath" the story of Mac's redemption by Rosa Lee's maternal love? From this perspective, the final background music is wonderfully vague.

Tenderly, you gathered up the pieces of my life.
Lying in your loving arms never felt so right.
The hard luck road behind me is reflected in your eyes.
And the glory of the bright lights can't compare to this feeling when you smile.
You're the good things I threw away
Coming back to me every day.

Why should we see those arms as divine? The movie's "message," if it is appropriate to speak so of a movie, is quite vague. It offers an overarching sense—despite the death of Mac's daughter in a drunken car wreck—that life is ultimately good, perhaps even better than it should be. Specifically, Mac does not deserve the love and acceptance of Rosa Lee and Sonny. Broadly, that message does resemble some of Jesus' parables and Paul's notion of grace, but it is a very profane version. It hardly seems a hierophany. It is far more similar to the children's story *Where the Wild Things Are*, in which Max misbehaves, is sent to bed, fantasizes adventures to far-off lands, and returns home to find his dinner still hot. In *Tender Mercies*, too, the graciousness of life is most materially obvious in the mother's meals.[20]

Jewett finds an elusive God behind all this. The merit of this interpretation for the propagation of the Christian faith—and the merit of Eliade's notion of religion as hierophany—is that it modernizes Paul's "faith."[21] While Jewett's emphasis on seeing the hidden God resembles the miracles of spiritual sight in, and advocated by, Mark and John, it turns "faith" into a debatable perspective or an interpretation. Admittedly, this interpretation fits the wholly privatized religion and limited transcendence of modernity quite well. Certainly, it belongs to the world of Wisdom's parable and of *Tender Mercies*. As a translation of Paul's "faith" and "grace," however, it also lacks something.

Generally, scholars explain Paul's "faith" as "faithfulness," "trust," or "commitment." The Jewish background is the henotheistic demand to "have no other gods before me" (Exod 20:3).[22] For Paul, "faith" is to be "in [Paul's] Christ" so fully and completely that if Paul's gospel is wrong, he and his followers "are of all people most to be pitied" (I Cor 15:19). Faith, then, is life in Christ. This life or "faith" means a certain ethical lifestyle and, often, public acts of devotion (like contributions to Paul's collection for the saints).[23] Mac's faith is rather different. He lives in his new family and in his recovered music. Other than that, Mac is not publicly committed to anything, certainly not to anything overtly religious.

What Mac finds in *Tender Mercies* is acceptance by Rosa Lee and Sonny. This acceptance socializes Mac into a new life. We might, if we wish, explain the conversion of Gentiles to Christ by Jewish missionaries like Paul in a similar way.[24] If so, Paul's "grace" equals the acceptance of the Gentiles by Jewish missionaries like Paul. Since the work of Krister Stendahl, scholars have increasingly read Romans in such a "social" fashion. If grace equals acceptance of the unlovely, the religious Rosa Lee's acceptance of the reprobate but gradually repentant Mac is an intriguing analogue of Paul's grace.

The socialization of the Gentiles in early Christianities, however, differs from that transpiring with Mac in *Tender Mercies*. What happens in this film is far more like the reading of Paul by older Protestant scholarship from Martin Luther to Rudolf Bultmann. Those scholars—and evangelical Protestantism like that expressed in Billy Graham revivals and in tracts like "The Four Spiritual Laws"—see Romans, for example, as the story of an introspectively troubled, guilty individual's recognition of his sin and, therefore, of his need for grace.[25] Romans, then, is the story of the individual's conversion to Pauline Christianity. Stendahl's more social reading of Romans challenges this older Protestant reading of Paul by pointing out that it anachronistically assumes the perspective of a modern, subjective individuality.[26] That older understanding also universalizes that modern individual. By contrast, Stendahl and many scholars since him read Romans as the story of God's salvation of the world, Jew and Gentile. This focus shifts the center of gravity from Rom 1–4 to Rom 9–11. So read, Romans justifies the inclusion of the Gentiles, not an individual sinner, in God's ongoing history with Israel. Romans becomes a theodicy for grace, the Jewish acceptance of the Gentiles, not a Pauline gospel pitting grace against law in the battleground of the individual conscience. "Grace" equals the inclusion of the Gentiles. Some late biblical prophets' idea that God would include the Gentiles in the eschatological kingdom becomes a reality. Paul becomes the key player in this eschatological mission to the nations. The completion of the people of God (all Israel) and the onset of the apocalypse lurk on the horizon.

On this post-Stendahl reading of Romans, Paul and *Tender Mercies* are worlds apart. First, Paul's grace is far broader than the "family values" socialization transpiring in this film. Paul's notion embraces his entire world, Jews and Gentiles, that is, Jews and everybody else. Second, this "new," social reading of Romans actually alienates Paul from us. The Protestant trend from Luther to Bultmann, by contrast, saves Paul for modernity, modernizing Romans as the story of *individual* salvation. Individuals are at home in modernity. The notion of the Jewish incorporation of Gentiles into the Israel of God is not. Not surprisingly, then, Jewett's reading of *Tender Mercies* highlights Mac's very individual salvation. Third, unlike the understated *Tender Mercies*, the "new" reading of Paul makes him incredibly dramatic. Paul and his mission are the harbingers of the apocalyptic end.

This Pauline tendency toward drama is the chief contrast between Paul and *Tender Mercies*. Even if Paul's "grace" equals—or justifies—his social/religious acceptance of the Gentiles,[27] he does not describe "grace" so profanely. Paul describes grace as an apocalypse, a miraculous revelation of God's plan for him and the world.

> For I want you to know, brothers and sisters, that the gospel that was proclaimed by me is not of human origin; for I did not receive it from a human source, nor was I taught it, but I received it through a revelation [*apokalupseōs*] of Jesus Christ. (Gal 1:11–12)

For Paul, that hierophany is neither private nor subjective. It apocalyptically interrupts and transforms the ordinary fabric of Paul's life. The persecutor becomes the apostle, the one sent, to the Gentiles (Gal 1:13–17). Notably, no psychological preparation or guilty introspection precedes this miraculous transfiguration (compare Phil 3:4–11). No wonder, then, that many recent scholars (since Stendahl) prefer to speak of Paul's "call" rather than his "conversion."

Thereafter, Paul incarnates this divine interruption. He is an ongoing apocalypse, for he declares that God "was pleased to reveal [*apokalupsai*] his Son in [that is, by means of] me, so that I might proclaim him among the Gentiles" (Gal 1:15–16).[28] Paul's own hierophany becomes a cosmic event transfiguring the whole world. Appropriately, then, the words translated "revelation" in Gal 1:12 and "to reveal" in Gal 1:16 are both forms of the Greek *apokalupsis*, "apocalypse."[29] That word suggests, largely in light of the New Testament and its interpretation, not merely a revelation, but the apocalyptic interruption of this age by the arrival of the new age of God's kingdom or, at least, the vision that such is about to occur.

For Paul, as we have already seen, the apocalypse begins with the death and resurrection of Jesus Christ *and with his own hierophanic call*. Once again, those are cosmic, not individual, matters potentially transforming the status of the world—Jew and Gentile—before and in God/Christ (Rom 3:21–26). Thereafter, even if haltingly, the world slouches toward Paul's new age. As Jewett points out, Paul's God "gives life to the dead and calls into existence the things that do not exist" (Rom 4:17).

This ex nihilo imagination simply does not match Beresford's eschewal of drama. Paul's God is not elusive at all. Divine transcendence impends everywhere. Accordingly, Paul's message is not about going on with ordinary life beyond suffering (the cross) and joy (resurrection). Instead, Paul uses his death-resurrection gospel to dramatize life. Accordingly, entry into "in Christ," a sectarian community within the Roman Empire, becomes an apocalyptic event comparable only to a dying cultic hero's resurrection.[30] The ordinary people entering "in Christ" become the chosen of God, living martyrs (Rom 12:1–2), heroes, or incomprehensible knights of faith (Rom 4).[31] While Mac struggles to live within the larger, mysterious forces that constrain his life, Paul engages in something altogether more outlandish and more religious. He creates a new world.

> It can thus be said that religion has played a strategic part in the human enterprise of world-building. Religion implies the farthest reach of man's self-externalization, of his infusion of reality with his own meanings. Religion implies that human order is projected into the totality of being. Put differently, religion is the audacious attempt to conceive of the entire universe as being humanly significant.[32]

Audaciously, Paul writes himself, and his dying-rising Christ, onto the world. This (Pauline) world thereafter revolves around Paul and his followers.[33]

No wonder, then, that the book of Acts tells the story of the beginnings of gentile Christianity even more dramatically than Paul does. In Acts, Paul's "conversion" is the result of a show-stopping heavenly light that literally floors Paul. Blinded by the light, yet another miracle allows Paul to see anew, that is, to see in terms of the story of divine providence unfolding in Acts (Acts 9:1–22). Combining Paul's story with that of Peter's equally miraculous acquiescence to gentile evangelism (Acts 10), Acts provides a mythic foundation for gentile Christianity.[34] This twin hierophany is so important in the economy of Acts that it repeats each story, Paul's twice (Acts 22:3–21; 26:2–23) and Peter's once (Acts 11:1–18). After an administrative approval (Acts 15:1–35), the gentile mission proceeds as providentially (under the leadership of the Spirit) as it began. While this myth is historically suspicious, its onstage presentation of providence is quite consistent with Paul's dramatic imagination.

Domesticating Paul

Acts and the post-Paulines transform Paul's dangerous apocalyptic claims into an institution's founding myth. The resulting domesticated Paul "founds" the world of the institution that exists rather than raising apocalyptic signposts about the imminent end of the present world with all its institutions. The resulting Paul is a traditional hero.

By contrast, for modern historical critics, Paul is a revolutionary hero at odds with the larger world, but oddly (or not) at home in modernity. Put succinctly, like the post-Paulines, modern historians domesticate Paul in order to save him for their respective times. After all, the revolutionary hero is the modern hero, and this hero/heroine and his/her construction is deeply embedded in and reflective of the modern myth.[35] Such figures appear in countless novels and movies. Like those heroes, the historical Paul is an alienated individual negotiating his difference from his cultural surroundings.[36] This very modern hero serves to justify the modern individual, the individual who knows himself/herself as distinct and different from his/her cultural surroundings. The villain in this story is any group, institution, or tradition that would inhibit or prohibit the hero's self-expression. For the Protestant patriarchs who first created this historical Paul, the villain was, of course, the early catholicism of the post-Paulines and other "late" New Testament documents. That is, the villain was a sacramental institution at home in the world. By contrast, of course, Paul was a free man (*liber*), the mythic icon of modern liberals.

Since Luther, scholars have re-signified the liberal—that is, the modern—Paul repeatedly. Instead of arraying a Protestant Paul versus early catholicism, for example, more recent scholars tell stories about a feminist Paul and a later patriarchal church and stories about a Jewish Paul and a later anti-Semitic church. In each case, Paul becomes a revolutionary figure within his culture and modernity's ideological ally. Stephen Moore nicely describes the historical Jesus as the beautifying "makeover" of an ugly original.[37] The historical Paul salvaged from the ruins of tradition by many recent scholars is a similar figure. Instead of a troubling pre-modern, Paul becomes a politically correct figure. This construct gives no offense. Redeemed, Paul speaks for us and as we should on all crucial issues. He is thoroughly egalitarian. As we cannot publicly advocate aristocracy, anti-Semitism, patriarchy, or racism, neither can he. Otherwise, he would cease to authorize our politically correct ideologies and programs.

Despite the historical Paul's revolutionary aura, the historical project domesticates Paul for modernity as much as the post-Paulines did for antiquity. The genuine, historical Paul renders Paul a modern liberal. That persona, hero, and story are too common in modernity, and in film, to be revolutionary. They are, instead, quite mythic. They constitute modernity; they do not challenge it. As a famous line chanted by the crowd in *Monty Python's Life of Brian* puts it, "We're all individuals." When the laughter subsides, we may notice that it is our unthinking, mythic devotion to individualism that renders us modern and, accordingly, indistinguishable from all other moderns.

Robert Jewett's *Paul the Apostle to America*, the companion volume to *Saint Paul at the Movies*, domesticates Paul quite openly. Jewett believes that only "contextual interpretation" renders the gospel effective, so he reads Paul as the apostle to America. Vilifying the Protestant European interpretation of Paul as an authoritarian chauvinist, Jewett resurrects Paul as the apostle of freedom, equality, and cultural pluralism. Jewett recovers this Paul by eliminating the parts of the New Testament picture unacceptable to this social project (the post-Paulines), by rejecting previous aristocratic (European) interpretations of Paul (as too patriarchal, anti-Semitic, or pro-slavery), and by practicing historical criticism on the genuine letters (to find egalitarian communities beneath the canon).[38] The result renders Paul our ally in the quest for a democratic, tolerant society within the context of pluralism.

This salvage operation continues a project that Jewett began in the 1970s with *The Captain America Complex*. There, he saved Jesus from apocalyptic, zealous nationalism. While he does the same for Paul here,[39] he also adds another salvage operation, saving Paul from dogmatism and aristocracy as well. In *The American Monomyth*, he and John Lawrence also save Jesus from popular culture. *Saint Paul at the Movies* obviously works differently. For Jewett, while popular culture has misappropriated Jesus, it has largely ignored Paul. Ostensibly, then, Jewett recovers a Paul that is more American than his 1970s Jesus was. Actually, however, Jewett critiques the "popular" in both cases. Where he rejected the popular view that "Jesus is us" in the 1970s, he rejected the popular view that Paul had nothing to say to us in the 1990s. Thus, he remains as critical of popular culture in the 1990s as he was in the 1970s. Hence, in the second half of *Paul the Apostle to America*, Jewett uses Paul to reject our cultural preoccupation with economic self-sufficiency, our servitude to consumption and culture, and the zealous nationalism that views violence as redemptive.[40] Jewett, then, reads Paul (and Jesus) on behalf of the politically engaged Christian liberal, whose loyalty to community defines himself/herself.

I frequently find Jewett's readings of Paul intriguing and convincing. I suspect, however, that the basis of my agreement with Jewett is the modern ideological commitments that I share with him rather than an objective appraisal of Paul. Both Jewett's Paul and mine are modern (or postmodern?) constructs. As a result, the conclusion that Maurice Wiles reached after studying the early Christian domestication of Paul is worth repeating.

> We have come to the end of our study and the question that immediately arises in our minds is the question "How far then did the early commentators give a true interpretation of Paul's meaning?" Yet the very form in which the question arises is not without danger. It implies the assumption that we have a true interpretation of Paul's meaning—or at least a truer one than that of those whom we have studied—in the light of which theirs may be tested and judged. It may be so; but we as much as they are children of our own times and there may well be aspects of Pauline thought to which we are blinded by the particular presuppositions and patterns of theological thinking in our own day. If therefore we seek to pass judgement on other interpreters it can only be in the recognition that we also stand in need of judgement, even and perhaps especially when we are least conscious of that need.[41]

Given Wiles's salutary warning, three things trouble me about Jewett's Paul. First, he is able to claim Paul as the apostle to America only by reducing Paul to the genuine letters.[42] As a result, an invented historical figure replaces the, admittedly, equally invented canonical Paul. Second, Jewett explains the remaining texts with an exacting, detailed historical exegesis. From this explanation, an arcane, academic Paul replaces both the popular Paul and the historical Paul created by mistaken scholars. What we may not notice, of course, is that the historical critic is indispensable to this reading. The historical critic replaces the Pauline text with an allegorical truth, whose source is the scholar's knowledge of antiquity. Only the initiate—and Jewett is an expert—in the historical mysteries can practice this allegorical exercise. Third, the reading invests the critic and the method with an impressive authority. Throughout, Jewett's invention of the American apostle plays a difficult, if not impossible, game. He strives to keep Paul's canonical authority while saving Paul from the canon. The canon simply does not, as it stands, authorize Jewett's modern religious and political program. Jewett needs a new Paul, one liberated from past cultural captivity, to speak to the present.

In fact, this risky, prophetic mode is Jewett's métier. Thus, in *Saint Paul Returns to the Movies*, Jewett embraces the rejection of the modern, Protestant Paul more fully.

In particular, he tries to use contemporary movies to move beyond the preoccupation with individual sin, guilt, and forgiveness in the Protestant, academic tradition and in Western Christianity generally. He does so by espousing ancient constructs of persons, focusing on the group and dyadic personality as opposed to modern individuality, and by concentrating on the very public issue of shame rather than guilt. For Jewett, Paul's shameful message of Christ crucified calls us to forgo self-destructive lies with which we try to hide our shame and to cease the proud contests for honor in which we routinely engage. Paul's crucified Christ makes possible the unconditional acceptance (grace) of all, even the most shameful, and founds communities of love, not honor. In essence, Paul rejects the honor-shame culture that was the moral basis of Greco-Roman society for radically egalitarian communities.[43]

Here, Jewett has significantly raised the stakes. He has dared to undercut, to an impressive degree, the modern myth-making enterprise installing the expressive individual as the sacred center of culture. This prophetic mode leads him, not surprisingly, then, to be quite critical of film, one of the major vehicles of this myth. Jewett's Paul, however, is still us. While this Paul is not quite as at home in modernity as earlier historical Pauls, Jewett decisively connects us with Paul's message. This Paul still justifies historical criticism and erudite academics like Jewett. It does not justify the typical modern audience of the movies, however. Now, this Paul justifies a sectarian Christian community, prophetically rejecting what Jewett sees as destructive tendencies in American culture.[44] To his credit, Jewett is quite honest about his commitments here. Nonetheless, he does elide differences between the past and his present with his construct of the historical Paul.

As Wiles reminds us, we all do something similar as we interpret. We efface a text or the past with our present ideological concerns. Or, as Kermode puts it, we replace interpretation with our truth.[45] For me, Jewett is particularly dangerous because I agree so wholeheartedly with his liberal politics and his critique of jingoism and economic individualism. In fact, I would say of Jewett's Paul what Alan Segal has said about the religiously tolerant Pauls of Stendahl, Gaston, and Gager: his Paul makes better sense for our pluralist world than any previous Paul does.[46] Of course he does, for this Paul is a modern construct at home in certain parts of the academy and Western Christianity. Therein is its peril. The construct is too easy for us to identify with and gain divine or apostolic authority thereby. Such identification transubstantiates politics and rhetoric into Barthes's myth,[47] or our ideology into the true or historical Paul. To recognize our interpretative work and to avoid the peril of having Paul speak simply our truth, we need to embrace "Pauls," not Paul. Pauls call attention to our constructs, which consist of fact and fiction and which participate in some ideological grab for power. Pauls, of course, alienate rather than domesticate Paul. As a result, Pauls are less authoritative than the post-Pauline Paul(s), the canonical Paul(s), and the historical Paul(s).

Disruptive Grace: Turning the World Upside Down

While he now disassociates himself from such individualistic readings,[48] Jewett's reading of Paul with *Tender Mercies* facilitates an interaction between Paul and modern religious notions of conversion. Paul's apocalyptic death-resurrection gospel becomes a story of individual rebirth. Troublesome, dramatic miracle vanishes in favor of the secular, materialist "grace" of the family. The family, the quintessential small community, saves the erring individual by incorporating him into its loving embrace.[49] Despite the persistence of pain and suffering, this gracious re-creation reveals the world to be a fundamentally good—in fact, a sacred—place. This translation is better—that is, more at home—in modernity than Paul's frequently nasty texts are. *Tender Mercies* and the politically correct Paul offend none of the powers that be. As we have seen, they avoid offense by carefully reducing Paul. They remember well Paul's gracious acceptance of the Gentiles, but they efface Paul's ex nihilo (or deus ex machina) understanding of grace. As we have seen, Paul traces grace to a divine interruption. Where modernity and *Tender Mercies* are short on metaphysical and social transcendence, Paul is not. For Paul, grace is a disruptive miracle. Such miracles do not merely transform chaos into order. First, they transform someone else's world into chaos.

Villains in the book of Acts remember this quite nicely, for they warn that Paul is one of those "turning the world upside down" (Acts 17:6). They are villains, of course, because Acts envisions Paul and others as the founding hierophany of gentile Christianity. As that Christianity exists within and at the sufferance of the Roman Empire, Acts cannot afford to be too clear about Paul's anarchy. In fact, Acts tendentiously demonstrates the innocence of Paul and others before various Roman authorities (for example, Acts 25:8). These protestations ring hollow, however, alongside Acts' gospel of the resurrection, for the resurrection message apocalyptically undoes the world. Acts, however, renders the resurrection a myth. It is part of the foundation of gentile Christianity, not the apocalyptic end of the "world." Nonetheless, even in the mythic work of Acts, the resurrection's apocalyptic pedigree remains dimly visible as Paul causes trouble for Greco-Roman administrators (Acts 17:6).[50]

Paul's own language is more obviously scandalous, and the world stumbles upon his gospel (I Cor 1:22–23). Paul's offensive gospel, a gospel meeting no "worldly" expectations, grounds his argument against the Corinthians' pride, their attempt to locate themselves in positions of worldly power through connections with impressive patrons (I Cor 1–4) or through glamorous spiritual gifts (I Cor 12–14). Versus their pride, Paul sets his lowly status—even though he is their founding apostle (I Cor 2:1–5; 4:8–13)—and his ironic gospel (1:18–2:5).[51] For Paul, this seemingly foolish, weak gospel is actually divine wisdom. In brief, it is the sacred source of a new world of meaning and life. Others—even the Corinthian follow-ers of Paul—stumble upon this hierophany because they act as if the world of the Jews and Gentiles—the ordinary world—is still in place.[52] Paul's ironic gospel, by contrast, reads that world as already past its expiration date. Detached from and discontent with the larger cultural world,[53] Paul's gospel consigns that world to apocalyptic chaos as it strives to found a new world miraculously (see 1 Cor 7; 15).

Reading Paul with *Tender Mercies* simply does not reveal the anarchic disruptive-ness inherent in Paul's miraculous grace. *Star Trek II: The Wrath of Khan* is more enlight-ening here. As the film opens, Lieutenant Saavik, in charge of the *Enterprise*, enters Klingon space to respond to a distress signal from a troubled ship. The Klingons attack and destroy the *Enterprise*, killing Spock and others. Then, miraculously, Admiral Kirk strides onto the bridge to stop what we just now realize to be a sim-ulation called the Kobayashi Maru Test. When Saavik complains to him that the test is insoluble, Kirk replies that it tests character, because how we deal with death is as important as how we deal with life.

As every Trekkie knows, the movie faces (the) death (of Spock). Three related circumstances set the stage: (1) the Genesis Project; (2) the return of Khan; and (3) Kirk's jaunt on a cadet training cruise on the *Enterprise*. The *Reliant* cruises space look-ing for a barren planet to test the Genesis Project, cutting-edge science designed to bring life from lifelessness by reorganizing molecular structure at a subatomic level. A barren planet is necessary because the Genesis Project will reorganize any existing "life" out of existence. During its search, the *Reliant* inadvertently encounters the superhuman Khan who commandeers the *Reliant* in order to wreak his revenge upon Kirk. The wrathful Khan, of course, returns from an episode in the first year of the *Star Trek* TV series. In that episode, the *Enterprise* came upon Khan and his crew in suspended animation. Awakened, Khan tried to wrest control of the *Enterprise* from Kirk, but Kirk defeated him and marooned him on an isolated planet. That world later became a barren waste because of an interplanetary mishap, and Khan, a char-acter reminiscent of *Moby Dick*'s Ahab, now lives only for vengeance.

Khan, in command of the *Reliant*, attacks the unsuspecting *Enterprise* when it responds to a scrambled message about the Genesis Project. Under attack, Kirk beams a squad, including himself, to the science station to look for the Genesis Project. Finding the station destroyed, they rescue two members of the *Reliant* left behind by Khan and follow clues about the Genesis Project into the heart of a nearby planetoid. There, the two rescued members betray the squad, enabling Khan to acquire the Genesis Project and leaving Kirk and his squad marooned. Of course, Kirk is still in touch with Spock, and the *Enterprise* beams them back aboard.

Khan attacks again, and Kirk takes the crippled *Enterprise* into a nebulae to even the odds. There, he defeats Khan, but the dying Khan initiates the Genesis Project. Spock sacrifices himself, fixing the engines in a radiation-saturated environment, to save the crippled *Enterprise*. Dying, Spock jests with Kirk about Spock's solution of the Kobayashi Maru Test. After a funeral, replete with a bagpipe rendition of "Amazing Grace," the *Enterprise* ejects Spock's casket into space. The film ends with Spock's casket resting on the Edenic surface of the new planet and Spock's voice intoning the mission statement of the *Enterprise*.

The Genesis Project is the intriguing element in the film. After watching a video about the project's creative potentials, Spock remarks that it "literally is Genesis." Less sanguinely, Bones observes an important difference: "Myth said it was done in six days; now we can do it in six minutes." Bones's concern is remarkably akin to the anxieties of Gen 3, for he doubts that humans are capable of handling such a device and worries that they may set loose a universal Armageddon. Genesis 3 and Gen 11:1–9 also worry that arrogant human knowledge will disrupt fragile, traditional orders. Modern film, as *The Wrath of Khan* indicates, is as conservative here as ancient mythology.

Against this backdrop, Paul's lack of concern about the dangers inherent in his apocalyptic knowledge and in his anarchic, ex nihilo grace is striking.[54] More specifically, reading Paul with *The Wrath of Khan* highlights the destructive features of Paul's gospel. His grace simply does not bring something out of nothing (contrary to Rom 4:17). Instead, Paul's apocalyptic grace destroys existing life in order to bring a new life into being. Like the Genesis Project, Paul's grace starts with existing material. An old joke expresses the point well. In the joke, scientists challenge God's creative uniqueness, claiming that they, too, can bring forth life. God invites them to try, and they create life from "dirt" like the God of Gen 2. God then wittily rejoins, "Get your own dirt." They have not operated ex nihilo. Neither does the Genesis Project nor Paul.

While the Genesis Project reorders at the subatomic level, Paul's grace reorders at the social and interpretative levels. Paul's grace "counts" a previous order as chaos and a previous life as death in order to reorder anew.

> Yet whatever gains I had, these I have come to regard as loss because of Christ. More than that, I regard everything as loss because of the surpassing value of knowing Christ Jesus my Lord. For his sake I have suffered the loss of all things, and I regard them as rubbish, in order that I may gain Christ. (Phil 3:7–8)

Paul's grace, then, is an interpretative miracle that engenders new social arrangements. We should briefly concentrate, however, on the interpretative quality of Paul's grace. After all, the apocalyptic death-resurrection has occurred only for Paul's Christ. Baptism and Paul's "in Christ" communities simulate it for or apply it to Paul's followers. Similarly, in *The Wrath of Khan*, only Spock undergoes an apocalyptic death (-resurrection). Everyone else lives because of his sacrificial act. They face death only in the Kobayashi Maru simulation. The dogfight scenes are the typical "near escapes" demanded by the action genre and, accordingly, do not constitute "facing death." Kirk's final speech even admits that he has "cheated." By rewriting the Kobayashi Maru Test, he has never really faced death.[55] Reading Paul alongside *The Wrath of Khan*, we may also wonder whether Paul's simulations face death any more squarely or whether they simply rewrite previous life and social orders as "death."

Only those not living well in present orders interpret existing orders as chaos and death rather than life. In other words, grace makes sense only to the socially dislocated and to those marginalized by present orders, to those "in the depths," to the botched and bungled, to Nietzsche's "resentful," to sectarians and criminals. To those ensconced in present orders, grace is anarchy. Grace simply does not make sense within an existing world. Within a world, justice is the desideratum. Thus, the story of the Exodus makes sense only to Hebrew slaves, not to Pharaoh and his army, and certainly not to the horse and rider cast into the sea. Equal pay for unequal work makes sense to those who have worked an hour, not to those who have borne the heat of the day. Slaying the elder brother's fatted calf to celebrate the prodigal's return makes sense to the prodigal, but not to the elder brother outside his own party. Paul's miraculous grace is similarly anarchic and unjust to those outside its benefits. Now, however, Paul's grace, understood sacramentally or as the conversion of introspective individuals, has become part of the institutional powers that be. This complex needs deconstructing if we are to see grace as anarchy.

To this end, it is worth observing that Khan, the dying super-criminal, initiates the Genesis Project and threatens all life in the vicinity. By contrast, the movie's heroes are defenders of existing order and life, of truth, justice, and the American way. Hollywood movies seldom offer anything other than slightly idealized forms of the cultural present. They may challenge corruption, but from Capra to the present, they awaken the audience to the value of the present world. Thus, while *End of Days*, for example, flirts with apocalyptic imagery and mythology, it does not truly imagine the coming of a new world. Instead, its hero defends the world that is. As a result, grace plays less of a role than justice or melodrama at the movies. Generally, the movies distribute goods to heroes and punishment to villains. What else but defense of American truth and justice—and Toby Keith songs to that effect—would we expect from products of the American Empire? At the movies, "[American] justice is the one thing you should always find."

From this perspective, Paul's miraculous grace, unless we domesticate it as the story of the conversion of an introspective individual like Mac, is anarchy, and Paul himself is as criminal as Khan is. From this perspective, for those of us who want "to round up all of them bad boys," Paul should be in a Roman jail at the end of Acts. Paul's grace is a criminal deviation from justice.

In one respect, the arch-villain in *The Fifth Element* is even more horrifying, and more like Paul, than Kahn is. In this science-fiction film by Luc Besson, aliens protect Earth from unspeakable evil with a defensive weapon known as the Fifth

Element. When the threat of war on twentieth-century Earth threatens the weapon, the aliens remove it but promise the priest who is their liaison that they will return the weapon before Earth needs it. Three hundred years later, a dark, pulsating, mysterious evil force that grows exponentially when attacked by conventional weapons approaches Earth. The aliens return the weapon, but evil dog-people destroy their ship en route. Gradually, it becomes clear that the bumbling dogs are in the service of Jean-Baptiste Emmanuel, the ironically named arch-villain who is himself in the employ of the approaching evil force known to him as Mr. Shadow. Failing to acquire the stones that arm the defensive weapon, Jean-Baptiste kidnaps the priest charged with keeping the alien tradition in order to ascertain the stones' location.

Their subsequent conversation is the intriguing moment in this campy film. When the priest wonders how anyone could act as callously as Jean-Baptiste has, Jean-Baptiste, paraphrasing Nietzsche in a Southern accent, justifies his actions with a pastiche of religious imagery reminiscent of Paul's destructive grace. In short, Jean-Baptiste asserts that one has to destroy a little in order to create. Unfortunately, while telling the priest that life comes from chaos, describing the lovely ballet of that destruction as the chain of life, and claiming that he and the priest are actually in the same religious, life-giving business, he chokes on a cherry. Before saving the villain with an abrupt slap to the back, the priest speaks rather dryly and quite slowly about the interconnectedness of life and of our need for other people.

Jean-Baptiste's flirtation with anarchy is only a plot device postponing the ultimate deliverance of Earth by the priest, the hero, and the super-girl brought from above by the aliens and engineered into existence by Earth's scientists. In fact, the plot reiterates the priest's message, because the super-girl and the hero's redeeming love for her constitute the necessary fifth element that ultimately stops evil. As always at the movies, romantic love saves the day, because Earth's good-enough order only needs a little more love to stop our dangerous, destructive tendencies. The priest, then, protects and oversees human order. Jean-Baptiste Emmanuel with two, not one, prophetic names is the more dangerous advocate of apocalypse and, thereby, the figure more reminiscent of Paul.

Although Nietzsche despised Paul as the arch-priest of resentment,[56] Paul's anarchic grace resembles the message of Nietzsche's famous madman. Nietzsche's madman announces the murder of God, while Paul announces the death and resurrection of his God-Christ. Both signify the apocalyptic end of the world that is, the transvaluation of all values. Both imagine themselves inaugurating an entirely new world. What Nietzsche's madman predicts, Paul has already done.

How shall we comfort ourselves, the murderers of all murderers? What was holiest and mightiest of all that the world has yet owned has bled to death under our knives: who will wipe this blood off us? What water is there for us to clean ourselves? What festivals of atonement, what sacred games shall we have to invent? Is not the greatness of this deed too great for us? Must we ourselves not become gods simply to appear worthy of it? There has never been a greater deed; and whoever is born after us—for the sake of this deed he will belong to a higher history than all history hitherto.[57]

Paul is simply further along the road to godhead than Nietzsche's madman. Paul already has the cleansing waters of baptism and a hierophanic view of himself.[58]

I wish to be clear. I am not associating Paul with Nietzsche's madman in order to Christianize Nietzsche as "death of God" theologians have often done.[59] I associate the two in order to highlight Paul's anarchic, apocalyptic, destructive grace.[60] Perhaps I can make my point clearer simply by remarking that this Nietzschean Paul is not at all unlike the Paul of Scorsese's *Last Temptation of Christ*. That Paul, too, will kill (both Lazarus and Jesus) for his invented Christ. Of course, the apocalyptic Paul retains a transcendence that Nietzsche eschews, and that Paul is not necessarily as mendacious as Scorsese's Paul. Nonetheless, all these constructs have one important feature in common. They eschew existing orders. Only gods, madmen, and criminals do so. No wonder they need to "light lamps in the morning."[61]

Offensive Grace: Those Dirty Gentiles

Paul's anarchic grace does not restructure the world at a subatomic level. Instead, it erases all the recognizable social boundaries of the previous world.

> There is no longer Jew or Greek, there is no longer slave or free, there is no longer male and female; for all of you are one in Christ Jesus. (Gal 3:28)

Paul erases these common human distinctions in favor of the new, apocalyptic world of "in Christ." More accurately, Paul transgresses all previous boundaries by crossing them out through the cross of Christ. Paul's cross—and/or its metaphorical replacement, baptism—separates this world from "in Christ," which signifies both Paul's sectarian followers and the world to come.[62] Standing "in Christ" marks out previous distinctions like Jew or Greek, slave or free, male or female.

Of course, Paul is notoriously flexible on the last two of these three boundaries. It is not only the post-Paulines that conserve the boundaries between slave and free and between male and female. Neither I Cor 7 nor Philemon, for example, challenges the institution of slavery, although the latter certainly encourages one Christian slave owner to rethink the Christian status of one Christian slave. Similarly, neither I Cor 11:2–16 nor 14:33b–36 challenges the patriarchal order of the first century. The post-Paulines, of course, reinforce the boundaries between slave and free, male and female, with a vengeance. Thus, while Colossians repeats some of the erasures of Gal 3:28, it omits the male-female distinction. Similarly, the various household codes assume not only the submission of wives to husbands, but also the hierarchical submission of Christian slaves to their Christian or non-Christian masters (for example, Col 3:22–24). While Paul exhorts Philemon to consider Onesimus as his Christian brother, Colossians demands that Christian masters treat their slaves "justly" (Col 4:1).[63] As we have seen, justice is a far cry from world-destroying, boundary-erasing grace.

Given these inconsistencies, some scholars describe Paul's "grace" simply as the acceptance of the Gentiles, that is, the erasure of the boundary between Jews and Gentiles. Paul never equivocates here. On this point, Paul's grace is entirely revolutionary. Certainly, it is something far wilder than the domestic acceptance that gives a drunken derelict a second chance at small-town family life. This grace destroys, at least, the Jewish "world." It depicts social chaos as good, if not divine.

While Paul considers himself a Jew, he also radically departs from the Judaism of his day. Using claims to divine revelation and a theology of grace, Paul opens the floodgates and allows Gentiles into God's kingdom without first becoming Jews.[64] Colossians remembers Paul's erasure and expands Galatians' "neither Jew nor Greek" to dispense with the distinction between circumcised and uncircumcised as well (Col 3:11). Similarly, Ephesians erases the wall that separated Gentiles from the temple's Court of Israel (Eph 2:14).

Ephesians, like Acts, speaks from the standpoint of a triumphant, inclusive gentile Christianity. Perhaps this perspective explains why Ephesians imagines so sanguinely that the hostilities between Gentiles and Jews have vanished. Galatians is more aware of hostilities. It remembers that Jews other than Paul reacted violently against his boundary erasures. In Galatians, even the conciliatory Peter draws back in horror from Paul's social improprieties (see Gal 2:11–14). Even Acts is more conciliatory than Paul is. It uses the device of the apostolic letter from certain Jerusalem leaders to demand that the gentile faithful respect Jewish sensibilities by observing certain "essentials" (Acts 15:23–29). The anarchic Paul never mentions such a letter in any of his correspondence and occasionally acts in a way that may deliberately flout it. Instead, Paul claims that the Jewish leaders added nothing to his grace, to his boundary-erasing gospel, but that he, and his gentile converts, remember the Jewish poor (Gal 2:10). Paul, then, makes no attempt to mitigate the offense of the admission of the Gentiles.[65]

We ignore the offensiveness of Paul's grace by reading it sacramentally and individually. Further, we are quite happy with passages like Gal 3:28 because we blithely consider ourselves an egalitarian society. After all, modern society is far more "open" than the closed societies of traditional eras, including that of Paul.[66] Modern, liberal society emphasizes individualism, an emphasis like Paul's emphasis on grace and faith that leaves no rational basis for the hierarchical distinctions that Paul mentions in Gal 3:28. Like Paul, however, we have not always spoken or acted consistently on these points. The Holocaust still haunts us. Marxists and feminists still prick our consciences. Racial, ethnic, and national conflicts particularly bedevil us. More importantly, for my purposes, distinctions, divisions, and boundaries of some type remain important to us.[67] Of course, we want these boundaries to be "just," but, once again, justice is a far cry from and is offended by Paul's grace.

Reading *Places in the Heart* with Paul·registers the offensive boundary crossings of grace more clearly. The movie opens with a family at church and then segues to the family's Sunday lunch. An unexpected disaster disturbs that lunch when a deputy arrives to alert the man of the family, the town sheriff, that a young black man is drunk and armed. Unalarmed, because he knows the young man, the sheriff leaves to handle this problem. As he tries to talk the young man into custody, the young man accidentally shoots and kills the sheriff. Thereafter, townspeople lay the sheriff out on the same dining table that he had too recently left. During the sheriff's funeral, the local KKK drags the lynched young man past the house.

For Edna, the sheriff's wife, life comes undone. Matters worsen when the local banker informs her that she is seriously behind on the mortgage. Eventually, the banker even foists his blind, sullen brother-in-law, Mr. Will, on her. Meanwhile, Moze, a wandering black man, stops by for food and steals her silver. Surprisingly, however, when the deputy catches and returns him, Edna lies on his behalf and takes him on as a "hand." The inclusion of Mr. Will and Moze, along with Edna's two children, forms Edna's new, unusual family. The movie ultimately traces the reformation of these two additional characters and the formation of family feeling among all of the main characters. This characterization centers on a plot in which Moze convinces Edna to plant cotton, teaches her to do so, and, despite all manner of opposition, leads the family to salvation: the money to pay the mortgage.

Despite the economic triumph, trouble soon returns. The local KKK comes to call on Moze. The blind Mr. Will saves Moze from abuse and possibly death, not by violence, but because he recognizes the voices of the local men and threatens to expose them. Neither Mr. Will nor Edna, however, can ultimately save Moze from the racial hostilities of 1930s Texas, so Moze leaves the family. Before he departs, Edna pays tribute to him by telling him that he saved them all, that he's the farmer, whether he's colored or white. The tribute, of course, is not unlike the boundary erasures of Gal 3:28. The movie, however, works far more realistically than Gal 3:28. The tribute is simply Edna's perspective. Moze may belong, regardless of race, to the new family, but that family and Moze still live in a racially hostile world. The movie never imagines, as does Ephesians, that racial hostilities are over. Instead, the movie simply salves our anxieties about race issues in our society and suggests that such hostilities may be partially overcome by individuals or small groups.[68] Of course, these liberal individuals and groups are powerless vis-à-vis the boundaries of the larger world.[69]

The movie's final scene, in the same church in which the movie begins, reinforces the inclusive family's fragility. The preacher reads 1 Cor 13 and leads the church in communion. Fantastically, Edna's whole family is there, including Moze, her dead husband, and the young black boy who killed her husband. The fantasy, of course, disrupts the movie's realism. The dead and the departed are not present, even in the movie, outside that fantastic church. Forsaking realism, the movie's love feast portends an apocalyptic communion or a mythic remembrance that restores the inclusive family. The presence of murdered, murderer, and exiled underscores the fantastic inclusiveness of this vision. In the divisive present of the movie, only ritual and fantasy suggest such inclusiveness. The world remains unchanged and is still violently demarcated.

Paul's sectarian communities are just as fragile and fantastic. Galatians 3:28 and Col 3:11 are likely baptismal formulae. That is, they depict the erasure of social boundaries only "in Christ," in a sect's worship and in an anticipated apocalyptic denouement resembling that in the fantasy that ends *Places in the Heart*. As we have seen, even Paul equivocates on boundaries. Certainly, outside the sect those boundaries remain in the surrounding culture, and they remain today. Where in 1930s Texas, or today, do blacks and whites sit together in church or elsewhere? Where do murderers and victims take communion together?

The Violence of Grace

In a famous book-length essay, Camus claims that modern individuals have a choice between two possible worlds, the world of grace and the world of revolt. For Camus, the world of grace is a world of dependence upon and determination by transcendent power(s). The world of revolt is the world of existential freedom. It rejects all essentialisms, all blueprints for human life, in the name of individual freedom.[70] Given Camus' place in post-Nietzschean Europe, his perspective is reasonable and somewhat compelling. Reconsidering Paul's offensive, anarchic grace brings us to another place. There, Paul's grace also seems revolutionary, a rejection of the social, if not metaphysical, essentialisms of his society. At least considering Paul as revolutionary nicely suggests the violence inherent in Paul's grace. It is violent because, as we have seen, it destroys world and offensively effaces boundaries. It is also violent because it invites violence.

In an intriguing criticism of the recent neoliberal lives of Jesus, Jeff Staley argues that such approaches fail to consider the danger inherent in the flouting of the boundaries of convention. Staley makes this point by reading one of those lives in conversation with *Patch Adams*. Following his conversation partners, Staley concerns himself with the way that lives of compassion transgress various boundaries (which he calls "purity codes") and with the "danger" and "political ramifications" of these transgressions. While Patch does not die in the movie, his "sufferings" suggest the violence that did befall Jesus and may befall anyone serious about living beyond social norms.[71]

Paul, according to both Acts and the genuine epistles, had an arduous, difficult life in an increasingly hostile world. The church and the academy train readers to see this as heroic devotion to a cause. Film trains us to see this as the individual's heroic assertion of himself/herself against corrupt institutions. From another perspective, Paul's transgressions look like criminal disturbance of the peace and demand response from the ruling authorities.

James Sanders once noted that we could read scripture constitutively or prophetically. In the first case, we would read scripture as myth, as the foundation of our world and our ideological perspective. From this perspective, Jesus and Paul are our heroes and mythic icons for our liberal selves. If we read scripture prophetically, however, we arrive at less sanguine perspectives. Sanders, for example, invites us to read Luke 4:16–30 and to identify with the good people of Nazareth who wished to do away with Jesus.[72] The result reconfigures Jesus, not as messiah, but as a criminal deviant. Paul's grace invites us to configure Paul similarly. He, too, was a troublemaker par excellence.

If we return to Luke 4:16–30 with this perspective, we will notice that it is Jesus who raises the hostility in the situation until it escalates to violence. He pronounces scripture fulfilled (Luke 4:21). All speak well of him (4:22), but he assumes they require proof (4:23). He then assumes their unbelief (4:24) and launches into a diatribe about the inclusion of the Gentiles (4:25–27) that finally incites their rage and attempted violence (4:28–29). In short, Jesus deliberately incites violence. From this perspective, Jesus has a death wish that he plays out against his initially receptive audience.[73]

That it is the inclusion of the Gentiles in God's salvific program that incites violence, of course, returns us nicely to Paul's apocalyptic grace. Paul's anomic, anarchic grace can hardly expect nonviolent acquiescence from the world whose boundaries it erases. Accordingly, Paul's grace gospel includes warnings to his followers to expect hostility from the world (see, for example, both 1 and 2 Thessalonians). Here, then, is another reason for Paul to state his gospel in terms of his own death wish, his followers' crucifixion (Gal 2:19–20), a martyrdom that some of his followers, like Ignatius, desired all too devoutly. Is it any wonder, then, that some "good people" resisted Paul and his followers violently?[74]

Conclusion: Saving Paul?

My phrase "saving Paul" characterizes various attempts in antiquity and modernity to appropriate Paul for particular cultural moments. In each case, someone redeems Paul from antiquity and from irrelevance and makes him speak for a particular ideological perspective. In each case, someone domesticates Paul. Over against this salvage project, I have alienated Paul. I have questioned Paul's attractiveness for our world. In particular, I have suggested that Paul's grace is not the domestic matter that a conversation with *Tender Mercies* might suggest. Instead, Paul's grace is anarchic, criminal, anomic, offensive, and violent. Perhaps, then, we do not want to be too close to Paul. Perhaps watching Paul(s) is preferable to saving Paul. Ironically, this watchful alienation may save Paul from us. Modernization invariably leaves Paul in the service of an ideological project foreign to him. It conscripts and enslaves Paul for its own purposes. My watchfulness has its own ideological agenda, but it does not require nor conscript Paul's authority.

Notes

1. Peter L. Berger's phrase for the limited transcendence available in modernity is "a rumor of angels." See his *A Rumor of Angels: Modern Society and the Rediscovery of the Supernatural* (New York: Anchor, 1990), 55–85. Outside the academy and the established churches, transcendence is less rare. See Peter Williams, *Symbolic Change and the Modernization Process in Historical Perspective* (Englewood Cliffs, N.J.: Prentice-Hall, 1980). Further, at the movies, fantasy, science fiction, and religious horror approximate traditional notions of transcendence. For discussion of films in these genres, see chapter 2. For a discussion of the portrayal of the sacred in various film genres, see Thomas M. Martin, *Images and the Imageless: A Study in Religious Consciousness and Film*, 2nd ed. (London: Associated University Presses, 1991), 59–111.

2. In *The Tao of Steve*, for example, while disparaging his friends' marriage, the hero complains that romantic love is the American religion. Naturally, the movie traces this hero's move from detachment, which he justifies with references to Eastern religions, to his own romantic (American?) commitments.

3. Some scholars believe that a cultic official offered an oracle of salvation, which sparked the move from complaint to praise, during the ritual use of lament psalms.

4. Gerhard von Rad, *Old Testament Theology*, trans. D. M. G. Stalker (New York: Harper & Row, 1962), 1:355–56, nicely describes the Psalms as "Israel's answer" to God. Despite their canonical status, the Psalms clearly have a different, and more human, narrative voice than biblical history, law, or prophecy.

5. The phrase comes from Ps 130:1. Bernhard Anderson uses the phrase as the title of a small but helpful book on the psalms (*Out of the Depths* [New York: Board of Missions, United Methodist Church, 1970]).

6. Here, the lament psalms and *Tender Mercies* differ dramatically from the miraculously answered lament of Job (see Job 38–41).

7. The banal realism of this film separates it from most film romances that tend to privilege the dramatic, spectacular onset of romance rather than the business of living with such outbursts thereafter. *Tender Mercies* eschews this glamour and glitz for the stark Texas scenery and middle-aged, "washed-out" characters.

8. "Wings of a Dove" suggests a more ritualistic and religious response, but the important rendition of this song accompanies Mac's final "rest" in the arms of his loving family.

9. Jewett, *Saint Paul at the Movies*, 55.

10. Richard Blake, cited in ibid., 58.

11. Ibid., 63.

12. Ibid., 64.

13. Resurrection grows out of apocalyptic worldviews in Judaism (see Dan 12:2).

14. For other theological readings of divine absence, see Samuel L. Terrien, *The Elusive Presence: Toward a New Biblical Theology* (San Francisco: Harper & Row, 1978); Jack Miles, *God: A Biography* (New York: Vintage, 1996); and Richard Elliott Friedman, *The Hidden Face of God* (New York: HarperSanFrancisco, 1997).

15. If Mel Gibson's *The Passion of the Christ* marks the return of the biblical epic, it is one that differs from those of the Cold War. Gibson focuses on suffering, not miracle. For a theological critique rejecting the "miracle" of the biblical spectaculars in favor of mystery, although his word is "transcendence," see Paul Schrader, *Transcendental Style in Film* (Berkeley, Calif.: University of California Press, 1972).

16. Mircea Eliade, *The Sacred and the Profane: The Nature of Religion*, trans. Willard R. Trask (New York: Harcourt, Brace & World, 1959), 11–12.

17. Jesus' interlocutors in the Gospel of John, like Nicodemus, the Samaritan woman, and the Jews, make this "mistake." They interpret matters materially while the Johannine community interprets them

spiritually, that is, in light of the world above. John's narrator hardly explains the reason for these different perspectives. He simply damns the unenlightened and/or makes them victims of his irony.

18. In Laurence Cossé, *A Corner of the Veil* (New York: Scribner's, 1999), the divine absence is serendipitous not only for religion but also for secular modernity. Modernity simply could not exist simultaneously with the presence of God.

19. For the parable and other viewpoints, see John H. Hick, *Philosophy of Religion*, 2nd ed. (Englewood Cliffs, N.J.: Prentice-Hall, 1973), 84–96. Hick's own solution is "eschatological verification," which he explains with a parable about two men walking down a road. One claims it leads to the Celestial City. The other claims it leads nowhere. According to Hick, the end of the journey will prove one of them right, the other wrong. Clearly, Hick's parable is more similar to Paul's apocalyptic perspective than Wisdom's parable is. Long ago, William James (*The Will to Believe and Other Essays in Popular Philosophy* [New York: Dover, 1956], 27) chose a religious interpretation of life far more cautiously: "Dupery for dupery, what proof is there that dupery through hope is so much worse than dupery through fear?" He concludes, thereafter, that we choose, act, and hope "for the best" and "take what comes" (ibid., 31).

20. Told from Rosa Lee's standpoint, *Tender Mercies* would have some similarity to *Babette's Feast*, the story of an exiled French chef's provision of an extravagant French meal for an austere religious sect (and one visiting, cultured military man). Babette's feast is simultaneously an act of self-expression and self-sacrifice. Unlike *Tender Mercies*, which focuses on one character's response to life's serendipity, *Babette's Feast* focuses on the varied responses to Babette's largess.

21. Jonathan Z. Smith, *Map Is Not Territory* (Leiden, the Netherlands: E. J. Brill, 1978), 289–309, has a more postmodern view of religion in which interpretation becomes a conscious part—if not the whole—of the religious enterprise. Interpretation is already part of Eliade's notion of hierophany; however, his phenomenological approach, in which a hierophany is that in which various groups hear the sacred speak, obscures the matter of interpretation by marginalizing questions of truth and by essentializing the abstract hierophany pattern.

22. Compare Hosea (2:19–20; 6:6) for a rendering of "faith" in terms of marital fidelity.

23. On Paul's request for definitive public acts of faith, see Norman R. Petersen, *Rediscovering Paul* (Philadelphia: Fortress, 1985), 141–49.

24. See, e.g., Rodney Stark, *The Rise of Christianity: A Sociologist Reconsiders History* (Princeton, N.J.: Princeton University Press, 1996), 3–27.

25. I have used exclusive language deliberately in order to highlight the essentializing or universalizing tendency in this interpretation of the individual.

26. See Krister Stendahl, "The Apostle Paul and the Introspective Conscience of the West," in Krister Stendahl, *Paul among the Jews and Gentiles, and Other Essays* (Philadelphia: Fortress, 1976), 78–96. For Stendahl, the forerunner of this modern Protestant interpretation is Augustine, "the first modern man." Of course, Luther was an Augustinian monk and Bultmann was a Lutheran.

27. See Burton L. Mack, *Who Wrote the New Testament? The Making of the Christian Myth* (New York: HarperSanFrancisco, 1995), 75–106, for an argument that the whole Christ myth (1 Cor 15:3–5; Rom 3:21–26; Phil 2:6–11) arose from the need to justify the inclusion of the Gentiles. For Mack, Paul's gospel simply builds upon this Christ myth.

28. I have used the marginal reading of the NRSV in this passage because "in me" or "by means of me" seems a better translation of the Greek *en mē* than the NRSV's text, "to me."

29. "Apocalypse" roots appear throughout Romans as well. See, particularly, Rom 1:17–18; 2:5; 8:18–19; 16:25.

30. Paul's notion of death and resurrection may owe as much to Hellenistic mystery cults, with their stories of dying and rising gods, as it does to apocalyptic. Certainly, Paul's Gentiles would have seen comparable features. See David Seeley, *The Noble Death: Graeco-Roman Martyrology and Paul's Concept of Salvation* (Sheffield: Sheffield Academic Press, 1990), for an argument that Paul understands Jesus' death in terms

of the noble death of the martyrs. Seeley builds on the earlier work of Sam K. Williams, *Jesus' Death as Saving Event: The Background and Origin of a Concept* (Missoula, Mont.: Scholars, 1975). Both argue for the obedience of Jesus' death and his similarity to the martyrs in 4 Maccabees, but Seeley is clearer that these deaths are part of an apocalyptic context (*The Noble Death*, 101–10).

31. Jewett discusses these two passages in dialogue with *Tender Mercies*; nevertheless, they are quite dramatic. Romans 12:1–2 is Paul's demand for a public display of faith. Romans 13:1–7 suggests that Paul saw no immediate conflict with Rome in this demand, but later readers may wonder how far Rom 12:1–2 is from the "death-wish" discipleship of Mark 8:34–38 or that of Ignatius's letters. Whenever Rome saw Christianity as an "illegal religion," Christianity became intensely dramatic. Romans 4 is equally dramatic. It compares the life of Paul's followers to Abraham's heroic faith in God's ability to give life beyond human possibilities. Commenting on Gen 22, rather than Rom 4, Søren Kierkegaard (*Fear and Trembling*, trans. Alastair Hannay [New York: Penguin, 1985], 54, 77–82) sees Abraham as an indication that faith is belief in the absurd, an overwhelming passion beyond human comprehension. Kierkegaard's Abraham sounds more Pauline, more a matter of ex nihilo, than Mac does.

32. Peter L. Berger, *The Sacred Canopy: Elements of a Sociological Theory of Religion* (Garden City, N.Y.: Anchor, 1969), 27–28, defines religion so. One wonders if this tendency is fundamentally human or pathologically narcissistic.

33. For Eliade (*The Sacred and the Profane*, 20–47), a hierophany founds a world and becomes its axis.

34. For Eliade (*Myth and Reality*, trans. Willard R. Trask [New York: Harper & Row, 1963], 18–19), myth is a report of a cosmogony or of a hierophany that founds a world.

35. Mythically, the historical Paul is analogous to the historical Jesus. On the later figure as a modern hero, see Richard Walsh, "Three Versions of ~~Judas~~ Jesus," in George Aichele and Richard Walsh, eds., *Those Outside: Noncanonical Readings of Canonical Gospels* (New York and London: T & T Clark International, 2005), 161–65. On the historical critical method as an adaptive, religious response to modernity, see Richard Walsh, *Reading the Gospels in the Dark*, 121–46.

36. Modern "alienation" is inevitable because modern persons have subjective, private selves, which differ from their public selves.

37. See Stephen Moore, "Ugly Thoughts on the Face and Physique of the Historical Jesus," in J. Cheryl Exum and Stephen Moore, eds., *Biblical Studies and Cultural Studies: The Third Sheffield Colloquium* (Sheffield: Sheffield Academic, 1998), 376–99.

38. Jewett, *Paul the Apostle to America*, 1–69. Cf. the project in Neil Elliott, *Liberating Paul: The Justice of God and the Politics of the Apostle* (Maryknoll, N.Y.: Orbis Books, 1994), 3–90.

39. Jewett, *Paul the Apostle to America*, 112–27.

40. Ibid., 73–127.

41. "The Domesticated Apostle," in Meeks, *The Writings of St. Paul*, 207–8.

42. The reductions are actually more severe. In order to arrive at a sexually liberated Paul, for example, Jewett also eliminates 1 Cor 14:33b–36, claiming that it is not authentically Pauline. The manuscript evidence does not support this elimination. The NRSV, notably concerned for political correctness, includes the verses but places them in parentheses. John Gager, *Reinventing Paul* (Oxford: Oxford University Press, 2000), 4–10, takes a similar approach to save Paul from the charge of anti-Semitism. He finds pro-Israel and anti-Israel passages in Paul and privileges the former.

43. Jewett, *Saint Paul Returns to the Movies*, 3–20, 179–89. For a very different reading of Paul as an ancient person, see Bruce J. Malina and Jerome H. Neyrey, *Portraits of Paul: An Archaeology of Ancient Personality* (Louisville: Westminster John Knox, 1996). Their Paul does engage in "honor" contests.

44. Richard B. Hays, *Echoes of Scripture in the Letters of Paul* (New Haven: Yale University Press, 1989), also constructs a Paul who supports present communities of character.

45. Frank Kermode, *The Genesis of Secrecy: On the Interpretation of Narrative* (Cambridge: Harvard University Press, 1979), 123.

46. Alan Segal, *Paul the Convert: The Apostolate and Apostasy of Saul the Pharisee* (New Haven: Yale University Press, 1990), 278–81, 130–33, also argues that this now-palatable position was not the historical Paul's position. John Dominic Crossan and Jonathan L. Reed, *In Search of Paul: How Jesus' Apostle Opposed Rome's Empire with God's Kingdom* (New York: HarperSanFrancisco, 2004), xiv, 110, 233–34, 391, are quite refreshing in their refusal to identify their politics with Paul's. With respect to the "two covenants," they observe, "We now say what Paul never imagined. *There are twin covenants, one Jewish and one Christian, both free gifts of divine grace, both accepted initially and lived fully by faith*" (ibid., 391). See N. T. Wright, *The Climax of the Covenant: Christ and the Law in Pauline Theology* (Minneapolis: Fortress, 1993), 231–57, for a critique of the modernism and deism implicit in the two-covenant position. Ironically, given the motivation of the two-covenant interpreters, he also contends that Paul would see that position as anti-Semitic.

47. Barthes, *Mythologies*, 109–59. See also Elisabeth Schüssler Fiorenza, "Paul and the Politics of Interpretation," in Horsley, *Paul and Politics*, 40–57.

48. See, particularly, Jewett, *Saint Paul Returns to the Movies*, 52–67, where he critiques *Forrest Gump* for reducing the boundary-busting Gal 3:28 to acceptance in the nuclear family.

49. It provides a "fantasy" of acceptance for the alienated individual. While the family that accepts Mac is not quite the ideal nuclear unit of the idealized 1950s, it does not raise troublesome questions about divorced, absent, or same-sex parents. The movie altogether skirts troubling issues like sex, violence, and race. Its ethic, like those of the Deutero-Paulines and that of the focus on the individual in modernity, is quite conservative.

50. While Acts admits this accusation only to dispute it, recent interpreters who focus on Paul and politics have constructed a Paul that this accusation fits exactly. See, for example, Horsley, *Paul and Politics*; Elliott, *Liberating Paul*; Crossan and Reed, *In Search of Paul*; Slavoj Žižek, *The Puppet and the Dwarf: The Perverse Core of Christianity* (Cambridge, Mass.: MIT Press, 2003); Badiou, *Saint Paul*; and Jacob Taubes, *The Political Theology of Paul*, ed. Aleida Assmann and Jan Assmann in conjunction with Horst Folkers, Wolf-Daniel Hartwich, and Christopher Schulte, trans. Dana Hollander (Stanford: Stanford University Press, 2004). In fact, this feature of Paul is particularly attractive to the "radical" or "materialist" philosophers. They seek a perspective from which to launch an attack on global capitalism. Thus, Taubes, *The Political Theology of Paul*, 10, celebrates Paul's transvaluation of the values of Judaism and the Roman Empire. Badiou, *Saint Paul*, 40–54, gleefully observes Paul's rejection of the discourse (i.e., the social and linguistic world) of both Jews and Greeks. Žižek, *The Puppet and the Dwarf*, 112, marvels at Paul's ability to find an uncanny interpellation beyond ideological interpellation. Žižek ends his *On Belief* (London and New York: Routledge, 2001), 148–51, with similar reflections, not on Paul, but on Kierkegaard's religious suspension of the ethical (typified by Abraham).

51. The weak Paul is equivalent to the offensive gospel. In 2 Cor 4:1–5:20; 10–13, Paul sets up a more elaborate contrast between the weak, suffering Paul and his gospel and the self-glorifying "super apostles" who have some other—never described—gospel (especially 2 Cor 11:4–5). What we may fail to notice is that Paul's rhetoric also associates himself with nothing less than the divine glory (2 Cor 3:4–18). As a result, Paul's self-effacing rhetoric is ultimately quite aggrandizing.

52. Petersen, *Rediscovering Paul*, is an intriguing treatment of Paul's letters as demands for Paul's followers to embrace and live according to the social world of Paul's gospel rather than the Greco-Roman social world. Jewett, *Saint Paul Returns to the Movies*, 38–87, repeatedly calls attention to the fact that Paul's letters to the Corinthians call them to eschew the contest for honor, their cultural myth, in favor of Paul's shameful gospel. See also Richard A. Horsley, "Rhetoric and Empire—and 1 Corinthians," in Horsley, *Paul and Politics*, 72–102. Recent interpreters have read Paul's gospel and demands vis-à-vis and in conflict with the Roman Empire or with the new world order. See the references in n. 50.

53. Desiderius Erasmus, *The Praise of Folly and Other Writings: A New Translation and Commentary*, trans. Robert Adams Martin (New York: W. W. Norton, 1989), also uses Paul's foolish gospel as an ironic perspective from which to condemn his world.

54. Jacob Taubes, *The Political Theology of Paul*, 97–105, describes himself as having no investment in the world as it is. Accordingly, Paul's "transvaluation of all values," his critique of the law, and his call to life in the world "as not"—or what Taubes calls Paul's "negative political theology"—attracts Taubes. The appeal may be lost on those who profit from the current world order. Elliott, *Liberating Paul*, 84–89, 227–30, claims that Pauline scholars are frequently among those who profit.

55. While *The Wrath of Khan* does acknowledge the aging of its heroes and their mortality, later episodes in the series fail to continue this theme. As every Trekkie knows, the next episode picks up intimations in this movie and resurrects Spock. As a result, the movie never really moves past the simulation of death with which it began. It, too, never "faces death."

56. See *The Antichrist*, 41–45; idem., *Daybreak: Thoughts on the Prejudices of Morality*, trans. R. J. Hollingdale (Cambridge: Cambridge University Press, 1982), 68.

57. Friedrich Nietzsche, *The Gay Science*, trans. Walter Kaufmann (New York: Vintage, 1974), 125.

58. In addition to the Paul as hierophany language of Gal 1:16, see also the discussion of Paul's usurpation of divine authority in the "imitate me" passages in Elizabeth A. Castelli, *Imitating Paul: A Discourse of Power* (Louisville: Westminster John Knox, 1991).

59. James Morrow's trilogy of novels, taking a literal death of God as its fantastic assumption, translates Nietzsche in this "Christian" or liberal fashion. Important characters ultimately opine that God died so that humans could mature. Nietzsche's murder of God is an altogether different matter. The trilogy includes *Towing Jehovah, Blameless in Abaddon*, and *The Eternal Footman*.

60. Both Taubes, *The Political Theology of Paul*, 76–88, and Badiou, *Saint Paul*, 61–62, 72–73, compare Paul to Nietzsche at several points. Taubes, *The Political Theology of Paul*, 79, describes Nietzsche (particularly *Daybreak*, 68, 84) as his best teacher on Paul. Badiou, *Saint Paul*, 61, says that Nietzsche treated Paul violently because he saw Paul as his rival.

61. Nietzsche, *The Gay Science*, 125.

62. See, for example, Rudolf Bultmann's famous existentialist restatement of Paul's apocalyptic ethical dualism—man prior to faith and man under faith—in his *Theology of the New Testament*, trans. Kendrick Grobel (New York: Charles Scribner's Sons, 1955). Petersen, *Rediscovering Paul*, handles the dualism in terms of a social sectarianism.

63. Elisabeth Schüssler Fiorenza, *In Memory of Her: A Feminist Theological Reconstruction of Christian Origins* (New York: Crossroad, 1987), describes these trajectories as a fall from grace, a move from revolutionary equality into cultural patriarchy and hierarchy.

64. Terence L. Donaldson, *Paul and the Gentiles: Remapping the Apostle's Convictional World* (Minneapolis: Fortress, 1997), 51–78, 235, 247, surveys Jewish attitudes to Gentiles in Paul's day and argues that Paul expects Gentiles to become proselytes before the apocalypse. Significantly, however, they become proselytes to Christ, not Torah.

65. No attempt, that is, unless we consider the division of missionary territory to be a concession (see Gal 2:7–9) or unless we read "the weak" and "the strong" in 1 Cor 8–10 and Rom 14:1–15:3 respectively as Jews and Gentiles. Acts also reports that Paul publicly fulfilled certain Jewish religious customs as an ameliorative tactic (Acts 16:3; 21:17–26). The Paul of Acts is more Torah observant than the Paul of the genuine letters (but see 1 Cor 9:20; 10:32). In Acts, the question is Jewish behavior. In Galatians, the question is gentile status "in Christ." The vagaries, however, lead some scholars to conclude that Paul imagined distinct Jewish and Gentile "paths to salvation." See, for example, Gager, *Reinventing Paul*.

66. See Bruce J. Malina, *Christian Origins and Cultural Anthropology: Practical Models for Biblical Interpretation* (Atlanta: John Knox, 1986).

67. For the human need for order, see Richard Walsh, *Mapping Myths of Biblical Interpretation* (Sheffield: Sheffield Academic, 2001), 13–53.

68. Various movies massage our racial concerns. See, for example, *To Kill a Mockingbird*, *Grand Canyon*, and *Pleasantville*. Despite its fantastic conclusion, *Places in the Heart* handles the matter more realistically than these others. For a far less sanguine and more apocalyptic look at racial conflict, see *Strange Days*.

69. Various movies deal with the theme of the small, idyllic group's inability to escape a larger hostile world. See, for example, *Dances with Wolves*, *The Gods Must Be Crazy*, *Pale Rider*, and *Witness*.

70. Albert Camus, *The Rebel: An Essay on Man in Revolt*, trans. Anthony Bower (New York: Vintage, 1956), 21.

71. Jeffrey L. Staley, "Meeting Patch Again for the First Time: Purity and Compassion in Marcus Borg, the Gospel of Mark, and *Patch Adams*," in Aichele and Walsh, *Screening Scripture*, 213–28.

72. See James Sanders, "Hermeneutics," in Keith Crim, ed., *The Interpreter's Dictionary of the Bible*, Supplementary Volume (Nashville: Abingdon, 1976), 404–7. I follow his invitation in "Three Versions of ~~Judas~~ Jesus."

73. See Fred Burnett, "The Characterization of Martin Riggs in *Lethal Weapon 1*: An Archetypal Hero," in Aichele and Walsh, *Screening Scripture*, 251–78.

74. See n. 50. Certainly, the Roman Empire was an oppressive force. In fact, the New Testament mentions Augustus only with reference to taxation (Luke 2:1). Nonetheless, Crossan and Reed, *In Search of Paul*, 412, judiciously observe that the Roman Empire was not an evil empire—it was simply the "normalcy of civilization"—and that it was precisely that normalcy which Paul opposed. In an amusing scene in *Monty Python's Life of Brian*, a revolutionary meeting comes undone when one revolutionary begins to question the wisdom of attacking the empire. After all, empire has brought roads, aqueducts, and so on. Imperial benefits are, of course, beside the point at a revolutionary rally and in Paul's "in Christ" communities. Incidentally, the Roman Empire was incredibly tolerant on religious issues. It treated as "legal" the religions of peoples incorporated into the empire. This status changed only as it was necessary to preserve the peace and justice of the empire. New religions, like emerging Christianity, were a different matter and were "illegal" as unnecessary sources of potential trouble.

Chapter 2

One Scary Rabbit: Messianic Superheroes and Apocalyptic "Nuts"

For I want you to know, brothers and sisters, that the gospel that was proclaimed by me is not of human origin; for I did not receive it from a human source, nor was I taught it, but I received it through a revelation of Jesus Christ. . . . But when God, who had set me apart before I was born and called me through his grace, was pleased to reveal his Son to me, so that I might proclaim him among the Gentiles, I did not confer with any human being. (Gal 1:11–12, 15–16)

Inasmuch then as I am an apostle to the Gentiles, I glorify my ministry in order to make my own people jealous, and thus save some of them. For if their rejection is the reconciliation of the world, what will their acceptance be but life from the dead! . . . I want you to understand this mystery: a hardening has come upon part of Israel, until the full number of the Gentiles has come in. And so all Israel will be saved. (Rom 11:13–15, 25–26)

We're on a mission from God. (The Blues Brothers)

Myths and Madmen

According to Paul's account of his missionary career in Gal 1–2, an apocalypse began gentile Christianity. The living Christ called him to take a gospel to the Gentiles.[1] In the even more miraculous Acts 9:1–22, a light from heaven leaves Paul (called Saul at this point in Acts) blind on the ground but privy to a heavenly voice (see also Acts 22:4–16; 26:9–18). When Paul follows the voice's instructions to Damascus, another Christian visionary lays hands on him so that Paul receives the Spirit as his sight is restored. Thereafter, an enthused Paul preaches Jesus as Christ even though doing so places him in dire jeopardy (9:23–30).[2]

According to both Acts and Paul's letters, Paul pursued this heavenly mandate despite great personal risks for the rest of his life. In Rom 15:14–33, written near the end of his career, Paul sees his task as almost complete. Having preached to the "edge" of Rome, he proposes to use Rome as a stepping stone to Spain. The breathless account of his career sounds like the report of a race. Coupled with Rom 9:4–5, Rom 15:29 may suggest that Paul saw his work as the fulfillment of the promise to Abraham that all the earth would be blessed in him (Gen 12:3).[3] At any rate, Rom 15:9–12 is replete with scriptures, now fulfilled in Paul's work, that prophesy the eschatological salvation of the Gentiles (Ps 18:49; Deut 32:43; Ps 117:1; Isa 11:10) and another scripture that justifies Paul's pioneering style in missionary work (Isa 52:15, cited in Rom 15:21).

Various Hebrew prophets had imagined a future in which God's judgment of the nations and Israel's salvation would follow the divine judgment on Israel. In fact, that is the structure of some of the prophetic books.[4] Certainly, Paul was familiar with that expectation. Postexilic Jewish history, however, had left these hopes unfulfilled. If God judged the nations, he did so one nation at a time and replaced that nation with yet another nation, not Israel (see Dan 2; 7). Not surprisingly, apocalyptic expectations and hopes for vengeance grew more and more dramatic. In that context, the message of Jesus' death and resurrection seemed to inaugurate the awaited end, but once again, the end did not come. Even worse, Gentiles, not Jews, responded to the message of the Christ.

Paul was left, then, with a difficult hermeneutical problem. Paul had already learned, however, to elongate the apocalypse. His "in Christ" communities participated in Christ's death and resurrection in an interim period between the end's beginning—the Christ event—and its end, the new age. In Paul's revision of the prophetic future, the end begins with Christ's death and resurrection and the conversion of the Gentiles in Paul's mission, not the judgment of the Gentiles. Paul, that is, writes himself and his gentile communities into the prophets. The salvation of the Gentiles, not their judgment, will bring about the salvation of Israel (Rom 9–11).[5] With and after Christ, Paul becomes the crucial eschatological figure. He joins with Christ in turning the ages. Paul becomes the savior of the Gentiles and his own people. No wonder, then, that Paul expects his followers to imitate him as well as Christ.[6] No wonder, then, that Paul races. The world, God, and the end wait upon him.

For Paul, this scenario—Christ, Paul and the Gentiles, Israel's salvation, the end—begins with apocalypse, the revelation of this program and future to Paul. If the curious, allusive comments in 2 Cor 12:1–4 refer to Paul, as the continuation in 12:5–10 suggests and as most scholars believe, Paul was prone to visions (see Gal 2:2; Acts 16:9; 18:9–10; 22:17–21; 23:11; 27:23–24). In 2 Cor 12:1–4, however, Paul describes an otherworldly visit, not the apocalyptic end.[7] Paul states twice that he does not know whether this experience was an out-of-body experience or not. He does know that "this man" heard "unspeakably sacred words" (*arrēta rēmata*). Surely such a numinous, ineffable experience deserves the label "ecstatic." In fact, on another occasion, Paul refers to himself as being "ecstatic" (2 Cor 5:13; see Acts 22:17).

In 2 Cor 5:13, Paul admits that "we [he and his cohorts] are beside [*eksēstemen*] our-selves." If that is the case, Paul contends that "it is for God." Previously in the pas-sage, Paul has discussed things observable only to spiritual sight and the possibility of being out of the body and with the Lord. All of this, of course, fits nicely with *ekstasis*, or "standing outside oneself," a state preparatory to or coterminous with pos-session (enthusiasm), and corresponds well enough to 2 Cor 12:1–4. What is reveal-ing about 2 Cor 5:13 for our discussion, however, is that Paul there places "beside ourselves" in contrasting parallel with "if we are in our right mind." In other words, ecstasy and apocalyptic visions raise uncomfortable associations with lunacy.

Generally, however, ancients treated seers and "miracle men" as either divine or demonic. At least, passages like Mark 3:20–35 suggest that is the case.[8] When we confront those who hear voices, have messianic complexes, and exhibit paranoia today, we are more likely to ask for a psychological workup. We exempt Paul from the ranks of the insane, of course, because he is the apostolic hierophany that founds gentile/Western Christianity. In this scenario, his apocalyptic visions do not por-tend the end. Instead, they stand at the beginning of and help found the Christian myth. As such, Paul's visions do not trouble us. They are unassailably, canonically true. As Paul's heirs, of course, we have gradually learned to read Paul's apocalypse, as Augustine taught us, as a revelation of the superiority of the spirit to the body. With Augustine's Paul, we have longed for ecstasy, to be absent from the body and present with the Lord (see 2 Cor 5:1–10; Phil 1:21–24). Even after the neo-Platonic medieval world in which this dichotomy made sense ended,[9] we still read Paul as the model of religious transformation, of the ever-new possibilities available to the expressive individual. We read Paul, that is, as Mac Sledge's precursor.

In chapter 1, we moved beyond Paul as the precursor of this modern liberalism to Paul as a world-troubling, violent revolutionary. Here, with the help of Roland Boer, I would like to pause and consider Paul's sanity.[10] As far as we know from Paul's letters and Acts, Paul never wavered in his grasp on his apocalypse. Recently, we have seen increasingly dangerous servants of transcendence, people willing to forgo common decency and to shed countless lives in the name of some higher cause.[11] Perhaps, then, we should waver. Perhaps we should ask whether Paul is mes-sianic hero, villain, or insane, or whether he or we need divine authority for our very human programs.[12] With the help of various films, I will explore those options and look for a way beyond them.[13]

Superhero Dreams

As Paul Verhoeven's *Total Recall* opens, Douglas Quaid wakes from a troubling dream in which he is dying in the arms of a brunette woman on Mars. His blonde wife com-forts him, but she also complains about his obsession with Mars. As a lowly construc-tion worker, he cannot afford to visit Mars, so he decides to visit Recall, a company

Caravaggio's first painting of The Conversion of St. Paul *(above) clearly identifies the supernatural agents. The second (facing page) leaves the revelation's source unspecified. This chapter similarly challenges Paul's apocalypse.*

that implants vacation memories. There, a salesman offers him the delightful possibility of a vacation from himself, an "ego trip" as a secret agent with a woman who looks like his brunette dream. As the technicians implant this memory, they break open a memory cap and learn that Quaid has already been to Mars and that someone, probably the Agency, has erased his memory.

Quaid's life as a lowly construction worker comes undone. Almost everyone—his coworkers, his wife, and agents led by the villain Richter—tries to kill him, but he remembers unexplained, violent skills that allow him to escape. A plot by the evil administrator of Mars, Cohaagen, rounds out Quaid's new life. Cohaagen does not want Quaid killed. He has "plans" for him. Meanwhile, Quaid learns about his (new) identity through a computer message from his old self, Hauser. Hauser tells Quaid, "You are not you. You are me. I met a woman that convinced me that I was on the wrong team. It's all up to you."

Following Hauser's instructions, Quaid removes the monitoring device in his head and makes his way to Mars to stop Cohaagen's plans. On Mars, Quaid follows more messages from Hauser to Melina, the brunette girl of his dreams, in Venusville. While she knows him as Hauser, he claims to be Quaid. Believing that he still works for Cohaagen, she will not help him, so he returns to his hotel disappointed.

There, a psychiatrist—whom we have already seen as a huckster for Recall—visits him, with Quaid's wife in tow, to talk Quaid out of the dangerous delusion that he is a secret agent. He is not on Mars. He is a lowly construction worker strapped in a chair in Recall in the midst of a "bad trip." If he does not come to terms with this reality, he risks permanent mental damage. Quaid almost believes this story until he sees the psychiatrist sweating as Quaid threatens his life. For Quaid, the sweat is a marker of reality, a sign that the psychiatrist knows his physical jeopardy, and he kills the psychiatrist.

In the battle that ensues, Melina helps Quaid escape Richter's agents. They flee to Venusville, so Cohaagen shuts off the air to that part of the colony. Melina then takes Quaid to Kuato, the rebel leader. As the psychic Kuato reads Quaid's future, agents arrive. Before a traitor kills him, Kuato manages to tell Quaid to start the alien reactor he has seen in Quaid's future and free Mars. Richter catches Quaid and Melina and delivers them to Cohaagen. A smug Cohaagen thanks Quaid for helping him defeat the rebels. Cohaagen has been using Quaid from the beginning. He is only a pawn, the perfect mole who allowed Cohaagen to bypass Kuato's psychic defenses. Worse, his old self, Hauser, was in cahoots with Cohaagen. Another computer message from Hauser verifies this story. Cohaagen then sends Quaid and Melina to "memory machines" like those at Recall so that Quaid can return to his Hauser self and Melina can become his willing consort.

Quaid escapes these evil designs and saves Melina. In the climax, Quaid kills the bad guys and starts the alien reactor. He does this, however, only after Cohaagen sets off an explosion rupturing the colony's protective shell. Sucked out onto the surface of Mars, Quaid and Melina die; however, as they die, the reactor creates an atmosphere, and they are saved (resurrected?) for new life on Mars. Their death scene is a version of the dream with which the movie began. While we may have thought understandably that Quaid's opening dream was a buried memory, the course of the movie ultimately makes the dream into Quaid's future. In short, Quaid lives his dream. Troubled by this coincidence, Quaid asks Melina, "What if this is a dream?" Melina responds practically, "Kiss me quick before you wake up."

Total Recall makes an excellent conversation partner for Paul because Quaid's story is unsettlingly similar to Paul's own apocalyptic identity.[14] Both Paul and Quaid have disturbing visions. As they give in to these visions, they enter into dangerous, or paranoid, lives in which they become the central messianic figure in a world conflict. Both have otherworldly journeys whose "reality" (in the body or not?) is questionable. Finally, both heroes reduce an old world to chaos and bring a new world into existence.

Read with Paul, *Total Recall* transforms Paul into an action hero. Science fiction, implanted memories, computer messages, psychic mutants, and special effects take the place of Paul's apocalyptic visions. More importantly, the movie overcomes the disturbing "already, not yet" quality of Paul's apocalypse. Paul never realizes his apocalypse. He follows his "ego trip" dream and becomes a gentile missionary establishing scattered "in Christ" communities, but Israel is not saved and the new age does not arrive. Even if, as a later follower says, he fought the good fight, Paul lives "the dream" rather incompletely. By contrast, Quaid's ego trip is much more complete. The movie starts with a dream that it realizes in a satisfying action-hero fashion. *Total Recall* succeeds in bringing in the Martian new age.

Moreover, the movie depends upon a death-resurrection pattern that is quite similar to Paul's gospel. In the opening dream, Quaid dies. In the dream's realization, Quaid lives, or is resurrected to a new life complete with a new woman and a new, Martian Eden. Even if, in action-hero fashion, this finale is an escape from death in the nick of time rather than an actual death-resurrection, Quaid dies to his old self not once, but twice.

First, he dies to the sham identity of an ordinary guy. Cohaagen, of course, provided Quaid with this false identity. Quaid gradually dies to this self as he learns that his true identity is that of a secret agent embroiled in an ongoing conflict with Cohaagen. He receives this gnosis when Recall disrupts his memory cap and when he receives computer messages from his past, secret agent self (Hauser). Despite the science-fiction aura of the whole, this enlightenment and dual identity is quite Gnostic. Like Neo in *The Matrix* and Paul en route to Damascus, Quaid awakens from an illusory stupor to find his true heroic calling.

Second, as Quaid plumbs the depths of the plot in which Cohaagen and Hauser have embroiled him, he dies to his former "asshole" self.[15] Despite the promise of wealth and a docile Melina, he refuses to be Hauser any longer. His new role as world savior is too compelling. He dies to Hauser to bring a free Quaid— a self-created self, not one determined by Cohaagen and Hauser—into existence.

The parallels to Paul's gospel, to Galatians in particular, are intriguing. After describing his apocalyptic career (Gal 1:11–2:10), Paul describes his Christ-gospel. This message involves the death and resurrection of both Christ and Paul.

For through the law I died to the law, so that I might live to God. I have been crucified with Christ; and it is no longer I who live, but it is Christ who lives in me. And the life I now live in the flesh I live by faith in the Son of God, who loved me and gave himself for me. (Gal 2:19–20)

Hauser dies in order that Quaid might live. Paul dies with Christ to live in Christ. Old selves go and new selves arrive. Moreover, the new selves are heroic. In fact, Paul's new self is divine. For Paul, those in Christ are sons of God, not servants to Torah or Cohaagen's evil plans (Gal 3:15–5:1). Moreover, they, like the newly created Quaid, are free (Gal 5:1). Of course, Quaid, as befits a modern action hero, is far more self-created than Paul. Paul relies on Christ for his new self, but that Christ may not be terribly different from *Total Recall*'s dreams and computer messages. After all, Paul knows Christ only through apocalyptic visions and internal voices (Gal 4:6).

Quaid's freedom is escape from the machinations of Cohaagen and Hauser. Paul's freedom is escape from former bondage, but it is also a freedom to serve others "in Christ" (Gal 5:2–26). Nonetheless, Quaid's freedom also has an ethical quality. He chooses a better self. Like Paul, he knows the evil character of his former "asshole" life only after he has found a new, enlightened self. Thus, now that he has a new life in Christ, Paul regards what once seemed excellence as "rubbish" (Phil 3:4–11). Similarly, Quaid forgoes Hauser's former goals—wealth and a docile woman—for his new freedom. Paul's description of sinful humanity in Rom 1:18–3:20 is probably more apposite. Even though this passage is the opening movement in Romans, Paul knew the depths of sin only after he came to the new life in Christ.[16]

Quaid's two deaths to self are, of course, somewhat metaphoric. They are real deaths in about the same way that Paul's baptism is. Without air on the Martian surface, however, Quaid comes much closer to "real" death. There, without hope and dying, he lives only through the rather miraculous, last-second intervention of the alien reactor. As befits science fiction, this miracle is an alien, not a deus ex machina. If the computer messages do resemble Paul's apocalyptic visions and "the word of the Lord" (1 Thess 4:15), the movie's climax resembles Paul's fantasy of the new age. At the last moment, beyond all human possibility, the divine new age arrives.

> But we do not want you to be uninformed, brothers and sisters, about those who have died, so that you may not grieve as others do who have no hope. For since we believe that Jesus died and rose again, even so, through Jesus, God will bring with him those who have died. For this we declare to you by the word of the Lord, that we who are alive, who are left until the coming of the Lord, will by no means precede those who have died. For the Lord himself, with a cry of command, with the archangel's call and with the sound of God's trumpet, will descend from heaven, and the dead in Christ will rise first. Then we who are alive, who are left, will be caught up in the clouds together with them to meet the Lord in the air; and so we will be with the Lord forever. (1 Thess 4:13–17)

Or an alien reactor will start in the nick of time. At any rate, life will triumph over death.

Total Recall reprises a short story by Philip Dick, "We Can Remember It for You Wholesale." Like the movie, the story opens with a dream.

> He awoke—and wanted Mars. . . . The dream grew as he became fully conscious, the dream and the yearning. He could almost feel the enveloping presence of the other world, which only Government agents and high officials had seen. A clerk like himself? Not likely.[17]

Here is an even stronger dichotomy between the protagonist's ordinary self and his heroic dreams than that in the movie. Fittingly, the name of this frightened, timid character is Quail, not Quaid.[18] Quail's Martian obsession is also more intense than Quaid's. It is a desire, not a memory; therefore, memory erasure and implants are ineffective against it. Like Paul's "Christ" and "spirit," it becomes "the enveloping presence of the other world." In fact, that phrase makes an excellent, succinct description of the "in Christ" fantasy or myth that Paul desperately tries to create for his followers. He wants them to live as if they were in Christ, in "the enveloping presence of the other world," not in this evil age.

As in the movie, Quail decides to go to Rekal, Incorporated (the spelling differs from that in the movie), for a memory of a Martian trip. He is, if anything, even more skeptical than Quaid. The salesman finally convinces him by saying,

> "As you explained in your letter to us, you have no chance, no possibility in the slightest, of ever actually getting to Mars; you can't afford it, and what is much more important, you could never qualify as an undercover agent for Interplan or anybody else. This is the only way you can achieve your, ahem, life-long dream; am I not correct, sir? You can't be this; you can't actually do this." He chuckled. "But you can *have been* and *have done*. We see to that. And our fee is reasonable; no hidden charges."[19]

Another Pauline element surfaces here in the short story's play with time. Quail cannot have the present or the future he desires, but he can have any past. Paul faces similar difficulties with his apocalypse and reaches a similar solution. He cannot bring about the new age. He really have that life. He can, however, have death and resurrection in baptism and in Christ. He can *have been* crucified with Christ and *have done* with this evil age and his former, impotent self. Thereafter, of course, he must elide any differences between that projected past and the anticipated future. Paul did that so successfully that some of his followers came to believe that they already lived in the new age. In response, Paul repeatedly insists on the partial— should we say illusory?—quality of the new life in Christ.

Already you have all you want! Already you have become rich! Quite apart from us you have become kings! Indeed, I wish that you had become kings, so that we might be kings with you! For I think that God has exhibited us apostles as last of all, as though sentenced to death, because we have become a spectacle to the world, to angels and to mortals. We are fools for the sake of Christ, but you are wise in Christ. We are weak, but you are strong. You are held in honor, but we in disrepute. To the present hour we are hungry and thirsty, we are poorly clothed and beaten and homeless, and we grow weary from the work of our own hands. When reviled, we bless; when persecuted, we endure; when slandered, we speak kindly. We have become like the rubbish of the world, the dregs of all things, to this very day. (I Cor 4:8–13; see also 2 Cor 4–5)

If that is the present and the future tarries, the past is the safest place for messianic heroism.

The salesman's description of Quail's meager possibilities convinces him, and he undergoes the memory implant. As in the movie, the technicians discover that someone (Interplan) has covered up Quail's actual memories of Mars. After that revelation, the movie handles Quaid's dual life through the device of visual computer messages from Hauser. The short story struggles with the issue of Quail's own mental state, or psychosis, more seriously.[20] Quail fears insanity because he struggles with rival memories: he has memories of Mars and memories of never having been to Mars.

Ironically, Interplan comes to the rescue. Fearing that he will remember and reveal his work for them as an assassin on Mars, they send agents to kill him. They know what he thinks because he has a telepathic transmitter inside his head. He flees, but he eventually makes a compromise with them by talking it out with them in his own head (Gal 4:6?). He suggests that they overcome the problems that his deep desires cause for his memory by discovering a deeper desire, his most expansive, ultimate fantasy, and making it real for him. Their psychiatrists discover an apparently childish fantasy in which he once met invading space aliens with kindness. The aliens were so moved that they agreed not to invade Earth as long as he lived. Simply by existing, he is the most important person on Earth, the messiah who staves off world destruction.

Incidentally, this fantasy may also be rather Pauline. In 2 Thessalonians, Paul, or a later follower, describes the final, terrible days before the apocalypse. Those days will begin with the apocalypse of the lawless one (2 Thess 2:3).

He opposes and exalts himself above every so-called god or object of worship, so that he takes his seat in the temple of God, declaring himself to be God. . . . And you know what is now restraining him, so that he may be revealed when his time comes. For the mystery of lawlessness is already at work, but only until the one who now restrains it is removed. And then the lawless one will be revealed, whom the Lord Jesus will destroy with the breath of his mouth, annihilating him by the manifestation of his coming. (2:4, 6–8)

The mysterious lawless one is a fairly common apocalyptic trope. We might trace it to the abomination of desolation in Daniel (Dan 8:13; 9:27; 11:29–31; 12:11), a motif that recurs in each of the synoptic apocalypses (Mark 13:14; Matt 24:15; Luke 21:20). The more unusual feature is the "one who restrains" (*ho katechōn*), the man who keeps the apocalypse at bay. Not surprisingly, some argue that Paul is that definitive, central figure.[21] Even if that is not the case, we have already seen that Paul saw his gentile mission as the last act in history leading to the eschatological salvation of Israel. Like Quail, Paul is the world savior. At least he is in his own mind.

Even though various characters express revulsion at Quail's arrogant, grandiose fantasy, Interplan asks Rekal to implant this memory. At this point, the short story abandons its play with multiple memories, paranoia, and psychosis. The short story ends surprisingly. As Rekal tries to implant the memory, they find out that it is quite true. Quail has saved the earth. He is the "one who restrains" the alien invasion. Upon his death, the apocalypse will begin.

Paul is hardly such a figure, although if the author of 2 Thessalonians is post-Pauline, that author may be trying to configure Paul so. Nonetheless, when Paul died, the apocalypse did not arrive. *Total Recall* helps us recover this Pauline ambiguity more easily than the short story does. The movie's ending is far more ambiguous. The penultimate line, and the hero's last words, asks the question with which Verhoeven bookends the entire movie: "What if this is a dream?" Quaid entertains a possibility that Paul does not. He may not be the messianic hero. He may simply be on an ego trip, living a Recall-implanted fantasy. The salesman's pitch also raises this possibility, for that pitch predicts the movie uncannily: you are a secret agent in deep cover; everyone is trying to kill you; you meet a girl; but by the end of the trip, you get the girl, kill the bad guys, and save the entire planet.

As the opening dream predicts the movie's future, not Quaid's past (at least not a past that we ever see), Quaid has good reason to worry about his grip on reality. Paul simply will not tolerate such indecisiveness.

Now if Christ is proclaimed as raised from the dead, how can some of you say there is no resurrection of the dead? If there is no resurrection of the dead, then Christ has not been raised; and if Christ has not been raised, then our proclamation has been in vain and your faith has been in vain. We are even found to be misrepresenting God, because we testified of God that he raised Christ—whom he did not raise if it is true that the dead are not raised. For if the dead are not raised, then Christ has not been raised. If Christ has not been raised, your faith is futile and you are still in your sins. Then those also who have died in Christ have perished. If for this life only we have hoped in Christ, we are of all people most to be pitied. (1 Cor 15:12–19)

Paul does not entertain this non-apocalyptic possibility. He suggests it in order to dismiss it as absurdly unthinkable. Either Paul's gospel/dream is true or Christ is not raised. Further, Paul is a liar; the Corinthians' faith is in vain; the Corinthians are trapped in their old, pitiful lives (in sin); the dead are dead; and we are pitiful (the KJV has "most miserable").

This rhetoric works in a fashion similar to Hume's argument against miracle: miracle is a violation of natural law; natural law rests on the accumulated experience of humans; it is easier to believe that one who testifies to a miracle is mistaken or lying than it is to believe universal human testimony, that is, natural law, mistaken or lying. In short, one "proves" the desired case—the resurrection or the absence of miracle—by offering it as the preferable option. One simply needs to put material on the other side—for example, we are pitiful and the dead are dead—that one does not want to accept. Interestingly, the Recall psychiatrist tries the same rhetorical ploy with Quaid but far less effectively. He asks a troubled Quaid, "What's bullshit? That you are having a paranoid episode triggered by acute neurochemical trauma or that you are really an invincible secret agent from Mars, victim of an interplanetary conspiracy to make him think that he's a lowly construction worker?" Unfortunately for the psychiatrist, Quaid chooses the latter option.

Norman Petersen has shown that Paul was quite adept at this rhetoric of preference and, thereby, at imposing his worldview on others. Examining the rhetoric of Philemon, Petersen contends that Paul asks Philemon to make a public choice (the letter is addressed to the whole church) between the Pauline worldview (Onesimus is my brother) or the Greco-Roman worldview (Onesimus is my slave). In other words, Paul stacks the deck in his favor. Petersen contends that Paul uses the same tactics in other places as well (for example, 2 Cor 8–9 asks publicly for financial support for the collection for the poor). In short, Paul repeatedly asks people to live as if they are in Christ rather than within the evil age or the larger realities of the Roman Empire. As they live Paul's dream, his apocalypse takes over their mundane lives.[22] To realize this (non-) end, the sect meets frequently and revitalizes themselves as an identifiable group through ritual activities. They are baptized, they eat the supper, they worship together, and they frequently greet one another with a holy kiss (Rom 16:16; 1 Cor 16:20; 2 Cor 13:12; 1 Thess 5:26). Incidentally, Melina deals with Quaid's worries similarly by saying, "Kiss me quick." Visionaries, dreamers, and sectarians must enact the dream continually in order to live the dream against anomalous evidence. Intriguingly, Kuato tells Quaid something similar. Kuato dismisses Quaid's troubling, diverse memories and asserts that a man is what he does, not what he remembers. One wonders if the Recall psychiatrist would agree.

Even though we have previously seen the psychiatrist as a huckster in Recall advertisements, he is the greatest threat to the movie's surface reality. He picks up several claims in the movie that Quaid is the victim of a schizoid embolism or of paranoid delusions. Neither Quaid nor the movie resolves this issue with "evidence." Quaid simply acts. Admittedly, he sees the psychiatrist sweat in apparent fear for his life, but the movie never explains why this "sweat" is real and not itself part of an ego trip or a delusion.[23] Quaid simply acts in a fashion consistent with his preferred reality, dream, ego trip, or delusion. The hotel shoot-out furthers the movie's action-hero plot. It brings Melina and Quaid together and to the rebel leader. Like Paul, Quaid enacts the dream. In fact, Quaid even admits it. Battling with the psychiatrist, Quaid contends that Melina is real because he dreamed her before visiting Recall. The dumbfounded psychiatrist queries, "She's real because you dreamed her?" Quaid responds decisively, "That's right."

Paul and Quaid live the dream of the preferable option. Roland Boer has succeeded, however, in questioning that option in an essay on *Total Recall* and Paul. He contends that the deep structure of both the movie and the apostle is psychosis. To make his argument, Boer explores the texts of three "nuts," Philip Dick, Daniel Schreber, and Paul, in light of the psychological theories of Freud and Lacan. Boer contends that all three exhibit paranoia, the crucial element in which is "the belief by the psychotic subject that he is in some way a redeemer figure and undergoing a process of emasculation in order to become God's female partner."[24] According to both Freud and Lacan, this psychosis results from a failure to negotiate the Oedipal conflict. For Freud, the castration anxiety remains so dominant that the subject cannot move from narcissism to "object-love." Instead of recognizing the latent homosexuality here, the subject disavows it through fantasies of persecution and of becoming a woman.[25] For Lacan, the refusal of the Oedipus complex means that the psychotic subject

is unable to move by the usual means into the Symbolic, the realm of signification and therefore of language and the law. The subject does not experience the quilting point of the Oedipus conflict, so signifier and signified do not connect, do not provide the link so that meaning and thereby language might operate. Instead, signifiers relate directly to other signifiers and not to signifieds. In order to deal with and find another path into the Symbolic, the subject generates an alternative language, the "non-sense" of psychotic speech and writing. In doing so, the subject senses that the Real— that which is inaccessible yet constitutes the very ground of the subject's existence—has crashed in, quite specifically in the figure of God as Other. But this Real becomes a substitute, that which takes the place of the Real.[26]

The breaking in of an alternative real is nonsense. Meaning collapses as the imaginary and the real collapse into one other and as God becomes intensely present as the Other.[27]

Although its theological form does not occur, this problem dominates *Total Recall*. In fact, Dick's stories often explore reality as a construct that eventually shows flaws or "cracks in the real." That which cracks the real, however, is not necessarily more "real" (or the "really real"). In Dick's later works, the "crack in the real" becomes a religious vision.[28] We have, of course, returned to Paul's apocalypse. Now, however, that hierophany does not look like the unimpeachably divine foundation of gentile Christianity. Now it looks like psychosis:

> It is as if Paul in particular becomes part of a psychotic brotherhood, a coterie of crazy religious types who all believed that God had spoken to them and therefore they were, of course, the most important individuals in human history.[29]

Maybe the rhetoric of 1 Cor 15:12–19 is no more convincing than *Total Recall*'s sweating psychiatrist. Maybe Quaid and Paul have both lost their grip on reality. Maybe they are on vacations from the real, on terribly expensive ego trips.

Does it matter? After all, *Total Recall* is only an entertainment. As Margaret Miles observes, however, we are what we see repeatedly.[30] She bases this claim on Roland Barthes's notion that myth transubstantiates history into nature. He claims, that is, that myth makes us forget that we (or our culture) have made choices and constructed worldviews (reality) with our social arrangements. Instead, we see those choices as given, natural, or divine, rather than human and political. As it inhibits change, myth also invests a society with incredible authority.[31]

In this way, *Total Recall* reinforces our myth of individualism, an individualism that often borders on narcissism and on apocalypse.[32] Krister Stendahl has, as we have seen, famously argued that Augustine and the Protestant Reformation made Paul the precursor of the modern, introspective individual.[33] Using *Total Recall*, Boer takes the case a step further. Boer's Paul is the precursor of psychosis, and the Christianity he founds is psychotic. It is not merely that Quaid is on an ego trip, a victim of paranoid delusions. The modern individuals formed by Western Christianity are as well. Following Paul, we, too, are "a coterie of crazy religious types who all believed [*sic*] that God had spoken to them and therefore they were, of course, the most important individuals in human history."[34] The bellicose history of Western culture and religion makes this assertion inescapable. We are dangerous servants of a transcendence that places us at the divine center of history.

Transmitted Visions, Shared Delusions

Apocalypse threatens the world. We do not see Paul as threatening, because the Pauline apocalypse is safely in our mythic past. *Total Recall* and Quaid obscure the apocalyptic threat because the movie presents Quaid heroically and Cohaagen villainously. Quaid saves Mars from Cohaagen's evil designs. Quaid does, however, bring the colony on Mars to the brink of destruction. Only the deus ex machina alien reactor averts the catastrophe. How different, then, is the heroic Quaid from *Star Trek*'s villainous Khan? Disenchanted with the world, Quaid, Khan, and Paul risk everyone and everything to aggrandize themselves, to make themselves the center of history. Paul's own proximity to apocalyptic villainy is even clearer when we read Paul alongside *Frailty*, a movie about a visionary serial killer, the God's Hand Killer.

As the movie opens, Fenton Meiks arrives at the Dallas FBI office to inform on his brother, Adam. Fenton claims that Adam is the God's Hand Killer. As Fenton tells the FBI agent, Doyle, his tale, we see Adam commit suicide. Adam's last words are, "Demons are taking over the world. I can't destroy them all. They're everywhere. I can't take it anymore. It's over. Whatever happens you have to take me to the rose garden. You promised." Doyle does not believe Fenton, so Fenton tells a far more complicated story, the story of the origins of the God's Hand Killer, and claims to know the location of the bodies. Thereafter, the movie moves back and forth between the trip to the rose garden burial ground and flashbacks to the story Fenton tells about the youth of the two brothers.

Their dad raised them after the death of their mother. One night, their normal life ended when Dad had a vision. Like Paul on the road to Damascus, Dad saw a blinding heavenly light and received a heavenly mandate. While we see the light in the flashback story and Dad's beatific face, we hear no words. According to Dad, however, God's angel announced the eschatological release of demons and called Dad and his sons to destroy these demons, as God's Hand. The angel also provided Dad a special divine sight allowing him to know these demons who masquerade as normal people. Fenton resists this apocalyptic message, but Adam gleefully concludes that they are superheroes who will save the world. Thereafter, the movie seductively educates us in apocalypse. We share Dad's visions revealing the magical weapons necessary for the demon destruction: an axe, gloves, and a pipe.[35] Only Fenton resists this crazy nightmare.

Well aware of Fenton's unbelief, Dad promises that Fenton will soon see the truth. While Fenton does not see it, we do. When Dad receives his first list of demons, we see a flaming angel with a sword descend from an oil pan (Dad is a mechanic). The movie further legitimates Dad's visionary world when Dad refuses Adam's list of demons as self-manufactured. Dad's moral code is simple: "You can't just make stuff like that [Adam's list] up. We destroy demons. If we were to use your list, we wouldn't be destroying demons. We'd be killing people. We can never do that. Destroying demons is a good thing. Killing people is bad." Further, before Dad kills a demon, we see him touch the "person" and shake uncontrollably. A sure sign, of course, that one is in the presence of a demon. Dad may see the demons' sins when he touches them, but we do not. Not surprisingly, Adam claims that he shares his Dad's visions.

Increasingly worried about his family's murderous fantasies, Fenton warns Dad that he will alert the proper authorities. A worried Dad tells Fenton that if he betrays their cause, someone will die. Scared to death, Fenton relents and assists Dad's demon-destruction. Dad knows, however, that Fenton still does not believe. One night, an anxious Dad, troubled by another message from the angel, wakes Fenton to tell him that the two of them have to work harder on Fenton's faith. Dad's educational program requires Fenton to pray as he digs a huge hole in the backyard.

The finished hole becomes a dungeon under the backyard shed, the arena where Dad expects Fenton to prove his faith by destroying a demon trapped for the purpose. Still unbelieving, Fenton runs to the sheriff for help. The sheriff hardly believes Fenton's wild tale, but he takes Fenton home to check out the story anyway. Dad, of course, kills the sheriff and then blames Fenton for making him a murderer. Up to now, Dad has destroyed only demons. Afraid that Fenton is himself a demon, as the angel has said, Dad shuts a screaming Fenton in the dungeon, telling him to pray for a saving vision. After seven days without food, Fenton rebelliously claims, "There's no God." Shut in again, Fenton lapses into what he reports as insanity and claims that he sees God. Interestingly, we do not participate in his vision. We see only Fenton's disembodied face.

Adam and Dad remove a devastated, apologetic Fenton from the dungeon and nurse him back to health. When he is well, the happy family goes demon-hunting again. Fenton turns the tables on Dad, however, and kills Dad instead of the trapped demon. Fenton, that is, responds murderously to his Dad's apocalyptic vision. Adam kills the demon, and the two boys bury the bodies.

We then come quickly to the present, as Fenton says that the boys went to separate orphanages when the authorities could not find their missing father. Meanwhile, Fenton and Doyle have arrived at the rose garden. Fenton has mentioned that he needs to keep a promise that he made to his brother, and Doyle asks Fenton about that promise. As Fenton talks about the promise, we see the young Fenton ask Adam to bury him in the rose garden if Adam ever destroys him. Doyle is confused, for the promise makes sense only if he whom we have known as Fenton is actually Adam, the true believer. Realizing this, Doyle asks, "So you killed all those people?" Adam replies, "I never killed anyone in my life. Fenton was the killer. . . . You'll understand soon. Just let me show you where I buried Fenton." There are, in fact, multiple graves, the demons that Adam has destroyed over the years, not the humans killed by Fenton. Finally, Adam tells Doyle that God put Fenton on Adam's list, and Adam stopped

Fenton, the serial killer. Suddenly, we see Adam's suicide again, but now as Adam's destruction of the demon Fenton.

While Doyle thinks Adam insane, we see flashbacks of the destruction of some earlier demons. For the first time, we see their sins as Dad and Adam did. Adam's apocalyptic perspective has become ours. Back in the present, Adam accuses Doyle of matricide. When he lashes out at Adam, Adam grabs him and we see his "sin" as well. Adam then kills Doyle.

Eerily, as the movie ends, no one discovers Adam. The agent who saw him in Doyle's office cannot remember what he looked like. The surveillance tapes are fuzzy. Finally, agents follow clues to Fenton's house and find bodies and Doyle's bloody wallet in the basement. When the agent who has met Adam before goes to tell him about his brother, he still does not recognize him. As the agent leaves, the camera lingers on Adam and his pregnant wife. Adam's final words are "God's will has been served." His wife replies, "Praise God."

Total Recall ends ambiguously. Is Quaid "really" a secret agent, or is he simply an ordinary guy on an ego trip? The dream possibility connects the story and the audience nicely. After all, most of the viewers of *Total Recall* are ordinary guys voyeuristically enjoying the movie's ego trip. *Frailty* ends far more disconcertingly, as befits the horror genre. At the end, only Adam's apocalyptic vision remains. Do we believe?

Frailty educates us visually in apocalypse. The dream becomes a crazy nightmare and then reality. First, we see heavenly light, and then we see the apocalyptic angel himself as Dad describes his holy visions. More important, we participate in Dad's relentless conversion of his unbelieving son. Except for the early visuals supporting Dad's audacious claims, we share young Fenton's viewpoint for most of the movie. As the nightmare becomes real for him, it does for us as well. The quotidian setting of the most horrific conversations at the family's kitchen table further "realizes" the horror. In the movie's final twist, when we abandon Fenton's perspective for Adam's, we see the "sins" of the destroyed demons with Adam. Further, we also share Adam's perspective on Fenton as a crazed serial killer seeking his own apocalyptic peace in the valley without a divine commission. With Adam, we can discriminate between the hand of God and murder.

The finale underlines this perspective emphatically. As Adam kills Doyle, he predicts that God will blind those who seek him. Here, the movie's rhetoric is quite like that of the Gospel of Mark. Mark "proves" Jesus' apocalyptic predictions by presenting minor details of the passion narrative as fulfillments of Jesus' predictions. His prophetic correctness suggests that he will be right again, about apocalypse. *Frailty* uses this same rhetoric to enforce Adam's apocalyptic vision. His correct predictions lend force to his claim to be God's hand. That Adam is the last man standing in the movie, the alternate perspectives having been violently dispatched, is simply the final rhetorical straw. Surely, at least in the movie theater, the horror takes over. Our education is complete. The crazy nightmare becomes the only reality left.

Apocalyptic texts work similarly. A seer has visions, but he transmits those visions to his followers as a written text. Read in sectarian worship, however, the text's visions become the sect's alternative, and defining, reality. Outside the sect's worship, some evil empire continues to rule. But apocalypse realizes the anticipated end and the arrival of heavenly sovereignty in and for the worshiping community.[36] The repeated injunctions to prayer in *Frailty* are, then, hardly incidental. *Frailty*'s primary means of realizing the apocalyptic God's sovereignty is, however, the unquestioning obedience of the Hand of God killers.

Similarly, Paul's mission and letters transmit Paul's apocalypse to his followers. They do so in order to control his mission. Outside his communities, the reality is the Roman Empire. Inside, reality is Paul's apocalyptic "in Christ." Paul expects his followers to realize that reality in worship, in which they also read Paul's texts, and to be obedient to that reality rather than the reality of the Roman Empire. As we have seen, that is the basis for Paul's "requests" to Philemon and the Corinthians. Beyond Paul's texts, the post-Pauline literature unabashedly demands the same obedience to Paul's visionary reality.

> I am reminded of your [Timothy's] sincere faith, a faith that lived first in your grandmother Lois and your mother Eunice and now, I am sure, lives in you. For this reason I remind you to rekindle the gift of God that is within you through the laying on of my hands. . . .
>
> You then, my child, be strong in the grace that is in Christ Jesus; and what you have heard from me through many witnesses entrust to faithful people who will be able to teach others as well. (2 Tim 1:5–6; 2:1–2)

The canon renders Paul indisputable. We do not have to wonder whether to believe or not. The apostle(s) is the last reality standing. He is our mythic past.

In one regard, however, *Frailty* has a huge advantage over Paul. Paul's visions are ultimately ineffable (2 Cor 12:1–4). In place of blinding vision, Paul's followers have only his word and text. Ultimately, Paul can speak only of things unseen, of faith, spirit, the heart, and the inner man (2 Cor 3:7–5:21). By contrast, *Frailty*'s visions appear in brilliant "Technicolor" glory. Accordingly, the movie constantly associates sight and belief. Dad does not say that Fenton will believe. He says that Fenton will see. The palpable vision is undeniable.

Perhaps because of its greater visual powers, *Frailty* also seems to dare to do something that Paul does not. It portrays a real-life unbeliever, conversing with and struggling against Dad's apocalypse. We never hear from any Pauline unbelievers in such a direct fashion. Of course, the final twist that reveals that "Fenton" is Adam also reveals that we do not hear from an unbeliever in *Frailty* either. Adam has spoken for Fenton. The parallel to Paul is quite precise. In Romans, for example, a Jew often raises questions for Paul to answer, but scholars describe this format as a diatribe. An author states his case by answering the objections of a hypothetical interlocutor. Not surprisingly, Paul can answer the questions he puts in the Jew's mouth. In other letters, Paul attacks opponents (for example, in Galatians and 2 Corinthians), but he describes those opponents, states their position, and destroys them. His opponents are his malleable creations. In fact, Paul so dominates his texts that we cannot confidently identify his opponents today. Similarly, we are not sure about the outcome of Paul's tumultuous relations with communities like Corinth, for his communities do not speak in his letters either.[37] For us, both Paul's opponents and his communities are Pauline fictions.

Frailty's education is quite horrific. Dad uses torture and brain-washing tactics to induce Fenton's belief. Ultimately, it all fails, and Fenton pays a horrible price. If his words, reported as Adam's suicide message, are truly his, then he has become a crazed serial killer. Denied Dad and Adam's serene confidence in their divine election, he also loses touch with anything like the "normal" reality of the rest of us. For him, demons are everywhere. Adam presents Adam/Fenton's death as a suicide. In a sense, it was. According to Adam, Fenton left notes at the murders for Adam, not the police. He wanted Adam to kill him. He could no longer bear life in his crazed, demonic world. In short, Fenton lives in a world where death is good news.

Doyle also receives an apocalyptic education. While Fenton is Dad's trainee, Doyle is Adam's. Dad tried to bring Fenton into the elect fold, but Adam teaches Doyle only to lure him to his destruction. Dad repeatedly denies that Fenton is a demon and refuses to destroy him, but Adam has no such qualms about dispatching Doyle. Like Paul, he is absolutely obedient to his vision. Fenton is a murderer. Doyle is a matricide. Adam is the vengeful hand of God.

In his review, Roger Ebert opines, "Heaven protect us from people who believe they can impose their will on us in this world because of what they think they know about the next." For Ebert, Dad is deluded, and his obsession warps his children's lives.[38] Unfortunately, the movie leaves us little room to dissent from Dad and Adam. It leaves us little room to claim that Dad's vision is a delusion. The horrible education is too complete. The visuals support Dad's visionary claim. Admittedly, Fenton and Doyle dissent, but the movie vilifies and dispatches them. The movie leaves Adam in canonical authority. Like Paul, only Adam speaks.

Ebert is right, however, that this vision is horrific. It is so because Adam speaks for an apocalyptic, vengeful God. If we follow the visuals and the movie's apocalyptic education, it is not Adam who is the villain:

God is the villain, God with his lists and his angels whispering inside your head. God who, in his infinite wisdom, knows when to pass the axe. Good and evil are flip sides, of course, but sometimes God forgets to change the record.

That's a challenging enough thesis for "Thought for the Day" Britain. Down in the Bible Belt, USA, as Saddam slips on to the list, it is positively incendiary. But Hanley [the scriptwriter] never ducks or weaves. He sticks it to us, time and again.[39]

Here is an incredibly dark vision. *Frailty*'s God is the God of apocalyptic vengeance. He is also a God who demands awful obedience. Here is a God, as Adam mentions, far less merciful than Abraham's.

He [Fenton] was [a demon]. That's why he couldn't see the truth. Dad knew it too. He just couldn't accept it. You see, God asked Dad to destroy his son much like he asked Abraham to sacrifice his son Isaac. But Dad couldn't do it. And God didn't take pity on Dad like he did Abraham. So he handed down the duty to me.

Is Paul's God as villainous? Paul himself wonders. Romans is a tendentious, unsuccessful theodicy. It strives to reveal God's justice despite his (apparent) abandonment of Israel (Rom 1:17; 3:1–8; 9:6, 14; 11:1). On one hand, Romans is typical apocalyptic; the elect's suffering will soon give way to triumph. On the other hand, as we have seen, Romans differs from apocalyptic. The Gentiles, who in traditional apocalyptic "cause" Israel's suffering, avoid apocalyptic judgment. Instead, they find grace in Paul's Christ. No wonder, then, that Paul's fictional Jew asks where this leaves God's justice, his promises, and his covenant (Rom 9–11). The fictional Jew, of course, is Paul himself. Clearly, Paul is striving to convince himself that his God is not a villain.[40]

Perhaps we should wonder, too. For Paul, like Fenton, life is so apocalyptically bad that his gospel fixates on death, the death of Paul's Christ and the subsequent death of Paul's followers "in Christ" or their complete submersion "in Christ." Paul justifies both God's grace to the Gentiles and his death-gospel by the ubiquity of human sin (Rom 1:18–3:20). In short, to justify a villainous God and gospel, Paul vilifies humans.[41]

Frailty's humans—at least some of them—seem even more villainous. They are demons.[42] In Paul's death-gospel, however, all fall short of God (Rom 3:23). No one has grounds for boasting (Rom 3:27–31). Ultimately, the difference between Paul's sin and *Frailty*'s demons is minor, for the Pauline wages of sin is also death (Rom 6:23). When the good news includes failed divine promises, the death of the cult hero, ineffable esoteric visions, internalized divine voices, and the ubiquity of human sin, what will one not do in the name of God? *Frailty* takes us to the frightening edge.

Perhaps only a first-time director, an actor who does not depend on directing for his next job, would have had the nerve to make this movie. It is uncompromised. It follows its logic right down into hell. We love movies that play and toy with the supernatural, but are we prepared for one that is an unblinking look at where the logic of the true believer can lead? There was just a glimpse of this mentality on the day after 9/11, when certain TV preachers described it as God's punishment for our sins, before backpedaling when they found such frankness eroded their popularity base.[43]

We should not backpedal. We should stare this horror in the face. Paul is the precursor of the apocalyptic fanaticism of 9/11 and of those TV preachers who wax eloquent about human sin and its "just" punishment. While Paul is no serial killer, he is not as benign as Christians generally assume. Ask a Jew. Or listen to the murderous vengeance that occasionally peeks around the corners of his texts:

> For you, brothers and sisters, became imitators of the churches of God in Christ Jesus that are in Judea, for you suffered the same things from your own compatriots as they did from the Jews, who killed both the Lord Jesus and the prophets, and drove us out; they displease God and oppose everyone by hindering us from speaking to the Gentiles so that they may be saved. Thus they have constantly been filling up the measure of their sins; but God's wrath has overtaken them at last. (1 Thess 2:14–16)[44]

Those outside Paul and Adam's apocalyptic certitude face the wrath of God (Rom 1:18; 5:1; see 2 Thess 1:5–10). Outside the canon, Paul is a scary, apocalyptic visionary. He may not ask us to kill others, but he asks us to do violence to ourselves, to lose ourselves "in Christ." He is, at least, the partial founder of death-wish (martyr) and anti-Semitic Christianity.

It is difficult to resist apocalyptic visions. No one in *Frailty* does. Two discordant elements in the movie provide, however, some hope. First, the movie offers two different visuals of Fenton's death. Further, on the first occasion, we think the one dying is Adam, not Fenton. In short, the visuals are not unimpeachable, not necessarily real. Therein is the possibility of an alternate footing for the viewer. Second, after the first destruction of a demon, young Adam and Fenton watch an episode of *Davey and Goliath* on TV ("The Silver Mine"). Davey has a broken arm and complains that God is responsible. Davey's father differs wisely: "Don't blame God, Davey. It wasn't his fault. . . . What God lets you do is decide for yourself what you will do. You're not a puppet with strings tied to you. . . . So God doesn't make you do anything. He wants you to decide for yourself." Ironically, in *Frailty*'s apocalyptic world, only Claymation figures (puppets) stand up for free will and human responsibility, and we depend upon TV for a non-apocalyptic revelation.

Except for those breaks, the God of *Frailty* is far too apocalyptically certain. He knows the hearts of humans too clearly. Perhaps he, or we, should listen to the old Amish grandfather in Peter Weir's *Witness*. In that intriguing film, a Philadelphia detective, John Book, runs afoul of corrupt policemen. Wounded, he returns

Rachel Lapp, an Amish woman, and her son, Samuel, to their home. The Amish nurse him back to health, but Book has unwittingly brought guns and violence to their peaceful farms. When the young boy finds Book's gun, his grandfather, Eli Lapp, educates him non-apocalyptically.

> Grandfather: This gun of the hand is for the taking of human life. We believe it is wrong to take life. That is only for God. Many times wars have come. And people have said to us, "You must fight. You must kill. It is the only way to preserve the good." But, Samuel, there is never only one way. Remember that. Would you kill another man?
> Samuel: I would only kill a bad man.
> Grandfather: Only the bad man. I see. And you know these bad men by sight? You are able to look into their hearts and see this badness?
> Samuel: I can see what they do. I have seen it.
> Grandfather: And having seen, you become one of them. Don't you understand? What you take into your hands you take into your heart. "Wherefore come out from among them and be ye separate," saith the Lord. "And touch not the unclean thing." Go and finish your chores now.

The end of *Witness* realizes another, non-apocalyptic way. Although the evil forces arrive at the Amish farm and a battle ensues between them and Book, the climax adopts Amish nonresistance. When the Amish answer the alarm bell, the final bad man cannot kill them all. Their sheer number or perhaps the criminal's awakening shame in the face of his vile actions overcomes him, and justice and peace arrive in this valley without the need of an apocalypse.

To arrive at the grandfather's alternative to apocalyptic violence, *Witness* has to dare to live in a world without Adam and Paul's apocalyptic certitude. In the world of *Witness*, humans cannot distinguish between the good and the evil as easily as Paul and Adam. If we are to live with such frail, human realities,[45] we, too, will have to quarantine apocalyptic certitude.

Schizophrenic Isolation: Narcissistic Worlds

In *Total Recall*, the visionary is a messianic hero. In *Frailty*, the visionaries are serial killers whose horrible reality overtakes us all. *Donnie Darko*'s visionary is a far more isolated figure. Richard Kelly, the director, has said of his film, "It's the story of Holden Caulfield resurrected in 1988 by the spirit of Philip K. Dick."[46] To his description, we must also add elements of horror and dark comedy, but Kelly succinctly describes Donnie Darko as an adolescent, self-destructive schizophrenic.[47] Donnie feels that the world simply "doesn't get him." As the movie plays out, we see why.

The frighteningly smart Donnie has problems. He has burnt down a house. He takes, and sometimes does not take, medications for his emotional problems. He has an expensive therapist, Dr. Thurman, who eventually diagnoses him as a paranoid schizophrenic. He sleepwalks. He has typical problems with his siblings. He quarrels increasingly with his mother. Essentially, he is lost in the midst of a loving, but distant, wealthy 1980s Republican family.

The supporting cast caricatures that affluent, suburban stratum of 1980s America. Most of the characters are comically ineffectual. Mrs. Farmer, a gym teacher who supervises the school's dance squad, has an obsession with the mindless, fear-conquering therapy of Jim Cunningham. She expects her students to be able to reduce all of life's complexities to a plot on Cunningham's "love or fear" lifeline. She is a dolt who thinks Graham Greene is the star of *Bonanza*. The more intelligent characters mislead others. At least Donnie pastes their unconnected insights together into a destructive mix that he refuses to accept as coincidence. A mildly rebellious English teacher leads Donnie to Graham Greene's "The Destructors" and the idea that destruction is creation. A nervous, religiously obsessed physics teacher points Donnie to Grandma Death's book on time travel. Gretchen Ross, a new girl in town hiding under an assumed name, is the "visionary" who wishes wistfully that one might travel back in time and replace bad stuff with beautiful images. Combined, this bricolage forms Donnie's apocalyptic worldview.

Alienated in this stultifying environment, smart Donnie wanders through most of the movie with a sardonic grin on his face. Soon, troubled Donnie starts having visions of a six-foot, macabre rabbit that leaves the safe, amusing world of *Harvey* far behind. Donnie's visions, and Donnie, are one scary rabbit. The allusion to *Harvey*, however, leaves a comic undertone. The macabre rabbit, whom we also hear and see, calls Donnie from his room on the evening of October 2 to announce the end of the world in 28 days, 6 hours, 42 minutes, and 12 seconds.[48] Donnie wakes the next morning on a posh golf course with this number scrawled on his arm. Returning home, he finds that a mysterious jet engine has crashed into his bedroom in his absence. The rabbit, which Donnie calls Frank, has saved him.

At first, Donnie recognizes that Frank is imaginary, but he falls increasingly under Frank's thrall because Donnie refuses to admit coincidence and because he fears being alone. Following Frank's orders, Donnie floods the school, leaves an axe in a statue of the school's bulldog mascot ("The Mongrels"), and scrawls, "They made me do it," on the school grounds. Later, Donnie follows Frank through a portal during a Halloween Frightmare Double Feature to burn down Jim Cunningham's house. An apocalyptic event itself, the arson reveals Cunningham as a child pornographer and disrupts the town's serenity.

Meanwhile, Donnie sees time lines emerging from people—time lines anticipating their imminent future. Donnie's own time line leads him to his father's gun. A conversation about time travel with his physics teacher leads back to Grandma Death, who has already told Donnie secretly that everyone dies alone. Coming to believe that everything is Frank's will, Donnie tries to stay in "God's channel" in order to learn the master plan and to avoid dying alone even though he knows Frank is going to kill someone. The macabre, imaginary Frank has become Donnie's God. Dr. Thurman vainly tries to "save" the frightened, hypnotized Donnie who sees Frank throughout her sermon: "If the sky were to suddenly open up, there would be no law. There would be no rule. There would only be you and your memories. The choices you've made. And the people you've touched. If this world were to end, there would only be you and him and no one else." In short, Donnie's apocalypse swallows everything but the narcissistic individual.

In the climax, Donnie, Gretchen, and others leave a party celebrating Donnie's sister's acceptance to Harvard on the eve of Halloween. In an allusion to *E.T.*, they all bicycle to Grandma Death's home. When they surprise the town hoodlums in her cellar, a squabble leaves Donnie helpless as Frank, a young man dressed in a scary rabbit costume and accompanied by a clown, runs over and kills Gretchen. Donnie shoots Frank in the head and takes Gretchen to the mountain lookout where the movie began. With wormholes or storm clouds swirling on the horizon, Donnie says, "Going home" (another allusion to *E.T.*). The movie's scenes rewind as Donnie reads his letter to Grandma Death: "Sometimes, I'm afraid that you will tell me that this is not a work of fiction [her book on time travel]. I can only hope that the answers will come to me in my sleep. I hope that when the world comes to an end, I can breathe a sigh of relief because there will be so much to look forward to." Donnie laughs on his bed as the jet engine drops through the roof. We have come back to October 2. As men wheel Donnie out on a covered stretcher, "Mad World" plays in the background: "No one knew me. Hello, teacher, tell me what's my lesson. Look right through me. Look right through me. And I find it kinda funny, I find it kinda sad. The dreams in which I'm dying are the best I've ever had. I find it hard to tell you. I find it hard to take. The people run in circles. It's a very, very mad world. . . ." While the family cries, the rest of the world, including Gretchen, who now does not even know Donnie, continues as if untouched by Donnie.

Once again, this troubled visionary has eerie resemblances to Paul. Apocalyptic visions portend the end, and the hero's dream takes over his "normal" life. Unlike Paul, Donnie fails to communicate his apocalyptic visions effectively to anyone else. He leaves behind no community. Donnie dies alone.

Undelivered messages and secrets recur throughout the movie. While no references mention such myths, this motif recalls numerous myths in which some human narrowly misses or misunderstands a divine message and thereby brings death to the human race. Certainly, the movie's double plot, in which two different futures—Donnie the murderer and Donnie the suicide—emerge from October 2, suggests that Donnie could have avoided his own death in some other future.[49] What we learn about the secrets in *Donnie Darko* is that they do not really communicate. Some of these secrets are banal and some are mere plot devices. Thus, Grandma Death whispers to Donnie that everyone dies alone. While Donnie long resists divulging this information, it is hardly a revelation. It is banal. Other secrets, for example, that Donnie has his father's gun, simply further the plot. No authority can know this secret if the movie is to reach its appointed end.

The truly revelatory secrecy scene is the amusing conversation between Donnie and his father en route to the therapist. They talk about the mysterious jet engine, Donnie's therapist, and the government's demand that they not talk about the accident. The punch line, delivered by Donnie, is that his parents have signed a form saying that they will not reveal what they do not know. This punch line reveals the dark hollow at the heart of *Donnie Darko*. No one has anything worth saying to anyone else. It is as Thoreau once caustically remarked about the telegraph: "Maine and Texas are now connected, but they have nothing to say." Fittingly, Donnie writes about and draws pictures of Frank that no one comprehends. Fittingly, we hear what Donnie wrote to Grandma Death only after Donnie's fate is sealed.

This hollowness should give us pause before Paul's apocalyptic secrets as well. All our apocalyptic seers, including Paul, have two revelations: (1) I am God's appointed representative at the end of this evil age. (2) This age is so vile that life, or hope, lies in death, either that of others or that of the self.[50] Given this context, Donnie's reading Graham Greene's "The Destructors" is hauntingly appropriate. Donnie summarizes Greene's story: "Destruction is a form of creation. So the fact that they burn the money is ironic. They just want to see what happens when they tear the world apart. They want to change things." The story narrates a teenage gang's unmotivated destruction of Old Misery's house. As their leader says, the boys are "like worms, don't you see, in an apple."[51] They hollow the house from within until it falls into a pile of rubble. They negate what is, but they offer only ironic imaginations in its place.

Paul and Donnie have ample reasons to be disenchanted with the Roman Empire and 1980s America, respectively. Their alternatives, however, offer little help. In their nightmarish worlds, escape is all.[52] What *Donnie Darko* illustrates more clearly than Paul, *Total Recall*, or *Frailty* is the fundamental narcissism, the hollowness, at the heart of these visionary escapes. Despite a joking claim to Gretchen that he is a superhero, because his name sounds like such, Donnie's revelations are for him alone and he dies to save himself (and his love, Gretchen). He chooses narcissistic isolation and death over meaningful, painful interaction with the world. He chooses apocalyptic fantasy.[53]

Another intertextual connection clarifies this point. Donnie is at a Halloween Frightmare Doublefeature when Frank shows him the portal that leads to Donnie's arson. The double feature includes *The Evil Dead* and *The Last Temptation of Christ*. The latter film has a hero and a double ending not unlike those of *Donnie Darko*. Like Donnie, the troubled visionary Jesus of that film is unable to escape the God who haunts him. He, too, chooses suicide by enlisting the murderous Judas. On the cross, however, Jesus faces doubts. A young girl (Satan) tempts him to leave the cross for a "normal" family life with various wives. As that pleasant vision unfolds, Judas, reeking of the smoke of burning Jerusalem, arrives at Jesus' home claiming that Jesus is responsible for this disaster. As a result, Jesus returns to the cross to die smiling. Facing options like Donnie's, a life responsible for the death of others or suicide, he makes the same choice.

As in *Donnie Darko*, this Jesus' revelation is solipsistic. Only he knows what he does, and his death is, accordingly, for him alone. Nonetheless, Scorsese's Jesus' fate differs at one point from Donnie's. He finds a visionary successor. As we have already seen, during his fantastic vision, Jesus meets a crazed Paul who travels preaching the death and resurrection of Christ. Scorsese's Jesus argues with Paul. It did not happen that way. Scorsese's Paul could not care less. His gospel is the way it should have been. His preaching is more important than truth and reality. Not incidentally, Scorsese's Paul is also responsible for the murder of the resurrected Lazarus. Unlike Donnie and Jesus, Scorsese's Paul chooses murder as an accompaniment of his apocalyptic fantasy. He is a lying version of *Frailty*'s Adam.

Our visionaries twist and turn around the options of murder (or at least responsibility for the death of others) and suicide.[54] They arrive at these decisive, calamitous moments because they refuse to admit coincidence. They refuse to admit

Donnie, Gretchen, and Frank at the Halloween Frightmare Doublefeature. The viewer sees Frank, as Donnie does, throughout the movie.

that matters may simply happen in some chaotic fashion. Instead, they assume some larger meaning. Their visions bring together the bricolage of their life as the will of a transcendent, manipulative deity. Thereafter, there is no escape. Thus, Donnie has conversations with his physics teacher and his therapist in which he effectively denies his free will. He "must" stay in "God's channel" and must obey Frank.

Such obedience is deadly, so resistance seems required. Albert Camus once wrote that there were only two possible worlds, the world of grace and the world of rebellion.[55] His rejection of the former was part of a long essay (*The Rebel*) in which he considered the ethical merit of murder and found it wanting. He had previously considered the ethical merit of suicide (*The Myth of Sisyphus*) and found it equally wanting. The rejection of transcendence, that is, grace, and death led him to a difficult freedom:

Outside of that single fatality of death, everything, joy or happiness, is liberty. A world remains of which man is the sole master. What bound him was the illusion of another world. The outcome of his thought, ceasing to be renunciatory, flowers in images. It frolics—in myths, to be sure, but myths with no other depth than that of human suffering and, like it, inexhaustible. Not the divine fable that amuses and blinds, but the terrestrial face, gesture, and drama in which are summed up a difficult wisdom and an ephemeral passion.[56]

Instead of the apocalyptic irony, negation, and transcendence of Donnie Darko and Paul, Camus calls humans to patience and lucidity, to creation:

It [creation] is also the staggering evidence of man's sole dignity: the dogged revolt against his condition, perseverance in an effort considered sterile. It calls for a daily effort, self-mastery, a precise estimate of the limits of truth, measure, and strength. It constitutes an ascesis.[57]

Donnie is not up to such effort. Paul considers it and names it misery (I Cor 15:19 KJV). Camus imagines, instead, persistent Sisyphus, a mythic icon that we should consider "happy."[58] Such happiness requires the affirmation of coincidence, chaos, and nonelection.

When the Blues Brothers claim, "We're on a mission from God,"[59] we laugh. Such laughter forgoes the apocalyptic fantasies that render us destructive superheroes. This laughter is not the smiling suicide of Donnie, Scorsese's Jesus, or the Jericho Cane of *End of Days*. It is more akin to the laughter of Donnie and his father when they realize they have vowed not to reveal what they do not know. Such laughter reveals the essential hollowness of apocalyptic visions.[60] It resembles the laughter of the truck driver at the end of Greene's short story, as he sees that in place of

Old Misery's house "there wasn't anything left anywhere."[61] He also apologetically remarks to Old Misery that his laughter is not "personal." While that must strike Old Misery as insensitive, it provides a healthy counterpoint to our narcissistic visionaries who think themselves the very center of God's world.

Laughing at Paul

Our trajectory of apocalyptic visionaries has moved from the sublime to the ridiculous, from the heroic to the comic. I do not wish to be insensitive to the problem of teenage schizophrenia, but *Donnie Darko* is, in one sense, simply a retelling of *Harvey* as horror, a transformation of Elwood P. Dowd's relatively harmless bunny into one scary rabbit.

Elwood P. Dowd has dropped out of life—he tears up his mail unread—and spends his afternoons drinking at local taverns in the company of his friend, Harvey, a six-foot rabbit. While Dowd is congenitally pleasant and seemingly harmless, he embarrasses his sister, Veta Louise Simmons. Veta needs to present a better facade in order to procure her daughter, Myrtle Mae, a husband. When Elwood, with Harvey in tow, spoils the party introducing Myrtle Mae to society, Veta Louise decides to have him committed to Dr. Chumley's Rest. As *Harvey* is a comedy, matters go awry. When Veta admits to Dr. Lyman Sanderson that she, too, has seen Harvey, she finds herself committed and Elwood released. Elwood, however, nobly refuses to sign commitment papers for Veta.

When Dr. Chumley's wife, who has had a conversation with Elwood about his pooka on the institution grounds, reports this to Dr. Chumley, Dr. Chumley fires Dr. Sanderson, releases Veta, and institutes a search for Elwood. Dr. Sanderson and his nurse-assistant, Miss Kelly, eventually track Elwood down at a local tavern. There, Sanderson argues, "We all must face reality, sooner or later." Elwood responds, "Well, I've wrestled with reality for thirty-five years, Doctor, and I'm happy to state that I finally won out over it." Elwood also tells Sanderson that Harvey and Dr. Chumley have left together. Under Elwood's influence, Sanderson and Kelly remember their lost romance. As they dance, Elwood slips into the alley. When they catch him again, Elwood describes his life.

> Harvey and I sit in the bars. Have a drink or two. Play the jukebox. And soon the faces of all the other people, they turn toward mine and they smile. And they're saying, "We don't know your name, mister, but you're a very nice fellow." Harvey and I warm ourselves in all these golden moments. We've entered as strangers. Soon we have friends. They come over and they sit with us. They drink with us. They talk to us. They tell about the big, terrible things they've done. And the big, wonderful things they'll do. Their hopes, their regrets, their loves, their hates. All very large, because nobody ever brings

anything small into a bar. And then I introduce them to Harvey, and he's bigger and grander than anything they offer me. And when they leave, they leave impressed. The same people seldom come back, but that's envy, my dear. There's a little bit of envy in the best of us. That's too bad, isn't it?

Although impressed with Elwood's wisdom, Sanderson returns Elwood to the institution. There, Elwood talks privately with Dr. Chumley, who has arrived with Harvey before them. As *Donnie Darko's* precursor, the most important part of this conversation is Elwood's revelation that Harvey can stop clocks and allow people to go anywhere for any length of time and return to the same time that the clock stopped. While Chumley wants to be elsewhere, Elwood has never been able to think of anywhere else he would rather be. He is happy, like Sisyphus, where he is. When Chumley reveals that Veta has plotted his incarceration, Elwood simply marvels at her industry. Perplexed, Chumley says, "Haven't you have any righteous indignation?" Elwood replies, "Oh, Doctor, years ago, my mother used to say to me, 'In this world, Elwood, you must be oh so smart or oh so pleasant.' For years I was smart. I recommend pleasant. You may quote me."

Veta arrives to institutionalize Elwood, and Sanderson recommends Formula 977, which will shock Elwood back to reality. Elwood agrees to take the formula in order to please Vera. As Sanderson prepares to administer the formula, their taxi driver tells Veta that the formula changes happy people into crabby, hurried, faithless people. Frightened, Veta stops the injection. She chooses Elwood's eccentric vision without succumbing to its reality. The typical comic denouement—reunited couples—follows.

Despite the shadow of Harvey that appears on VHS and DVD covers, we never see Harvey in the course of the movie, except for the very bad painting of Harvey and Elwood that Elwood hangs over Veta's fireplace. Instead, we see Elwood act as if Harvey is there.[62] As the movie progresses, other characters, including Veta and Dr. Chumley, see Harvey as well. Finally, we also begin to see evidence of Harvey: a hat with rabbit-ear holes, an encyclopedia entry about pookas personalized for Mr. Wilson, mysteriously opening doors, and missing coin purses. We are left with the impression that Harvey is there, or, even better, we are left to decide for ourselves whether he is there. Surprisingly, these tactics create a more communal imagination among the characters than the special effects of *Frailty* and *Donnie Darko*. By the end of the movie, most of the characters have agreed to tolerate Elwood and Harvey whether they believe or not. The movie ends with couples everywhere, not suicides and murders.

This feel-good movie, like its main character, is pleasant rather than smart. Elwood and Harvey, the pooka,[63] stand in the tradition of quixotic saint-idiots and trickster figures that appeal to and affirm our better nature. In films like *Monty Python's Life of Brian*, *Being There*, and *Forrest Gump*, some critics have seen these saintly

Except for this painting, the viewer never sees Harvey, except for his "effects," in the movie.

idiots as Jesus figures.[64] Indeed, Elwood, like the Jesus of the Gospel of Luke in particular, invites the riffraff home for dinner to create new communities. While Paul lets the riffraff, in the form of the Gentiles, in for dinner as well, we seldom think of Paul as a benign, harmless figure like Elwood P. Dowd, Brian, Chauncey, or Forrest. He is far too authoritative and authoritarian for this pose.

The liberal salvation program of recent historical criticism tries to rewrite Paul in the "accepting" mode. It never quite rises to a Paul like Elwood P. Dowd or Joliet Jake Blues; however, if we have no desire to save Paul and to make him legitimate liberal modernity, we can insist on the comedy. Surely, an "Elwood P. Dowd" Paul is preferable to a "Donnie Darko" Paul. We would be better off laughing at human foibles than killing ourselves in despair or murdering others with whom we do not agree in a fit of divine election. We could do worse than Elwood's pleasantness.

Nonetheless, *Harvey* is problematic in its own right. It embraces modern society and liberalism far too glibly. Its "subversive protest against conformity and the then-nascent rat race"[65] is too subtle. Here, *Donnie Darko* is right. There is something that needs destroying or, better, contending with in 1980s suburban America and in modern liberalism. On reflection, perhaps it is not so surprising that "radical" philosophers have turned to Paul. We might simply say that postmodern projects are never satisfied with one story. They celebrate pluralism and often have their own pooka-quality. We can have both *Donnie Darko* and *Harvey*. If we keep both,

Donnie Darko—or the world-rejecting Paul—may remind us that even Harvey or Saint Paul—or the new world order—can be one scary rabbit if they are the only story in town.

Harvey, however, does allow us to forgo apocalypse for comedy. Comedy's view askew, its wry look at the world we have, is preferable to violent, murderous, and suicidal visions that long for new worlds. Comedy does not dispense with death, but it does not vainly feel that it can overcome death through death either. Comedy is neither a happy ending nor a life after death; rather, it is an ability to see life differently: "If the same life or world or reality can be judged by some as tragic and others as comic, then the latter has clearly won because it is already comic that the same events could be interpreted in such diametric opposition. Tragedy is swallowed up eventually in comedy."[66] Comedy laughs at our incongruities; it does not resolve them with death's finality.

If comedy sees the world "as it is" with all its pains and troubles, it also sees the world "as if"—or "as not"—through a looking glass. It is a play that "transubstantiates the world—in which actually, after all, things are not quite as real or permanent, terrible, important, or logical as they seem."[67] Apocalyptic figures—Douglas Quaid, Adam Meiks, and Donnie Darko—are deadly serious. Elwood P. Dowd and Jake Blues are not. Of course, it is very difficult to render the apocalyptic and apostolic Paul comic. He is too deadly serious.[68] Perhaps that is the very reason that we need to see Paul "as if" he were Elwood P. Dowd and Jake Blues. Generally, and specifically in the case of Paul, we need both "as is" and "as if" if we are going to live well. Both totalitarian systems and apocalyptic nuts are destructive alone and in tandem. We need escapes that do not imagine there is any other place to go. We need to live in our worlds lightly. We need comic relief.

If we keep Paul alongside *Harvey* and *The Blues Brothers*, as well as *Total Recall*, *Frailty*, and *Donnie Darko*, he ceases to be Saint Paul, the sole authority, the only voice speaking. He becomes one among other conversation partners rather than the apostle demanding obedience.[69] Such conversation eschews apocalyptic certainty for human frailty.

To handle diverse Pauls, particularly deadly ones, we might need to adopt the solution of John Nash in Ron Howard's *A Beautiful Mind*. Nash, a brilliant mathematician, sees things and patterns that others do not see. This sight enables him to develop "governing dynamics," a revision of Adam Smith's overly selfish economic theory, for which Nash ultimately wins the Nobel Prize. The sight also involves him in delusions, in which he has imaginary friends to ease his loneliness and in which he is doing work vital to the Cold War, to ease his frustration at the banality of his research. The delusions finally take over, and he winds up institutionalized for schizophrenia.

Gradually, painfully, Nash emerges from his delusions through the help of a kindly psychiatrist, his loving wife, Alicia, and a renewed commitment to his work.

In essence, he decides to treat his schizophrenic delusions as a problem, which, like his mathematics problems, has several possible solutions. John's solution is to "ignore" his delusions. They continue to accompany him, but he manages gradually to move them into a corner of his life and to live a "normal" life of work and family. The triumphant, albeit sentimental, conclusion has him twisting Alicia's handkerchief as he confesses in his Nobel speech: "I have made the most important discovery of my career, the most important discovery of my life. It is only in the mysterious equations of love that any logic or reasons can be found. I'm only here tonight because of you [Alicia]. You are the reason I am. You are all my reasons."

While critics rightly acknowledge its sentimentalizing of the problems of schizophrenia, *A Beautiful Mind* can teach us to cope with dangerous apocalyptic visionaries like Paul. *A Beautiful Mind* immerses us in Nash's delusions. Like Nash, we think his imaginary friends and his crucial Cold War job are "real" at the start. As Nash learns they are delusions, we do, too. *A Beautiful Mind*, then, is not an education in apocalypse or schizophrenic delusion. It is an education in reality. Nash goes on with life and his delusions by relegating his delusions to a corner. We could do the same with Paul by leaving multiple interpretations and stories in the field—some of the dangerous ones in the corner—as we have suggested above.

Above all, *A Beautiful Mind* teaches us to overcome apocalyptic, narcissistic delusions with humor and love. Like John Nash, we need a sense of humor. At one crucial moment, Nash teases a concerned friend by telling him not to sit on Harvey. To calm the friend's exasperation, Nash opines that there is no point in being "nuts" if you cannot have a little fun. Later, when another friend sees him after a long absence and exclaims, "Jesus Christ," Nash responds wryly that his savior complex does not take that particular form. That self-mockery underlines Nash's awareness of his relative unimportance. He is not the apocalyptic center of the world. These same friends, and Alicia, also help him avoid narcissistic isolation. Nash simply has better friends than Quaid, Adam, Donnie, and Paul. Like Elwood P. Dowd, he has to learn, however, to seek them out. Like Paul, he has to learn that love surpasses agonistic conflict (see I Cor 11–14).

Notes

1. On Paul as apocalyptic seer, see Segal, *Paul the Convert*. On the apocalyptic nature of Paul's gospel, see J. Christiaan Beker, *Paul the Apostle: The Triumph of God in Life and Thought*, 2nd ed. (Philadelphia: Fortress, 1984).

2. As we saw in chapter 1, Acts doubles and repeats this hierophanic foundation of gentile Christianity. Both Paul (Acts 9) and Peter (Acts 10) have visionary experiences that lead them to the Gentiles, and Acts has both characters repeat the story of these hierophanies: Peter in 11:1–18; Paul in 22:4–16; 26:9–18. The three versions of Paul's conversion in Acts gradually make Paul the more immediate recipient of a personal contact with the risen Christ (cf. Gal 2). Generally, the artistic tradition of this experience includes divine figures. See, e.g., Caravaggio's first painting of the conversion on page 48. Ironically, Caravaggio's second painting (on page 49) is more faithful to the account in Acts 9. Brueghel's version (on page 8) also lacks visible supernatural authority for Paul's experience.

3. Abraham is an important figure in Paul's worldview (e.g., Gal 3:1–5:1; Rom 4). Galatians 3:8, 14 allude to the Genesis passage in question. N. T. Wright, *The Climax of the Covenant*, argues that Paul saw Christ as completing and making possible the blessings to the nations in the Abrahamic covenant.

4. See Richard Walsh, *Reading the Bible: An Introduction* (Notre Dame: Cross Cultural Publications, 1997), 258–60.

5. See Johannes Munck, *Paul and the Salvation of Mankind*, trans. Frank Clarke (Atlanta: John Knox, 1977), 36–68, 275–79. On Paul's interpretive technique here, see Hays, *Echoes of Scripture*, 34–83. Donaldson, *Paul and the Gentiles*, 69–74, 187–214, rejects the notion of an eschatological pilgrimage of Gentiles as the background for Paul's mission to the Gentiles. Instead, he argues that Paul was making proselytes to Christ, rather than Torah, as the new boundary marker of Israel.

6. Luke-Acts presents the life of Jesus as a blueprint that later figures like Stephen, Peter, and Paul follow. See Charles H. Talbert, *Literary Patterns, Theological Themes, and the Genre of Luke-Acts* (Missoula, Mont.: Scholars, 1974). Paul also sees Christ as a blueprint to follow. Thus, while Phil 2:5–11 describes the kenotic mind of Christ, Phil 3:4–16 describes the similarly kenotic life of Paul. Not surprisingly, Paul asks his followers to have the same mind (2:5; 3:15) and to imitate him (3:17). For a discussion of the "imitate me" passages (1 Thess 1:6; Phil 3:17; 1 Cor 4:16; 11:1), see Castelli, *Imitating Paul*.

7. Scholars identify two types of apocalypses: (1) those that predict the imminent end and (2) those that feature otherworldly journeys.

8. Although it is the only gospel to mention the possibility that Jesus is "beside himself" (*ekstē*), Mark quickly leaves that possibility behind to engage in a debate over Jesus' supernatural empowerment. See Walsh, "Three Versions of ~~Judas~~ Jesus."

9. The popularity of C. S. Lewis among many Christian groups indicates that Neoplatonism remains ensconced in Christianity. According to Nietzsche, Christianity is simply Platonism for the masses. See the preface to *Beyond Good and Evil: Prelude to a Philosophy of the Future*, trans. Walter A. Kaufmann (New York: Vintage, 1966).

10. Roland Boer, "Non-Sense," claims that Paul's religious language is the basis of psychotic language in the West.

11. Jewett, *Paul the Apostle to America*, 112–27, describes Ollie North as such a lawless superhero. We might add the terrorists of September 11 and subsequent American foreign policy to this list of dangerous servants of transcendence as well. One wonders if some first-century Jews might have seen Paul similarly. Jewett, of course, does not.

12. See Žižek, *The Puppet and the Dwarf*, 169–71.

13. Margaret Miles, *Seeing and Believing: Religion and Values in the Movies* (Boston: Beacon, 1996), 12–21, argues that films in the 1980s began to treat religious leaders as fraudulent or neurotic. We could add horrific and mysterious to the list, but her notion certainly suggests that film will help us distance Paul.

14. I rely on Boer, "Non-Sense," for this connection with *Total Recall* and for much of the analysis.

15. Here, of course, Quaid battles his memory of himself, a memory aided by computer messages. In *The Sixth Day*, the main character battles himself—again, an evil self—in a plot dependent on cloning.

16. See chapter 3. If, as some think, Rom 7:7–23 describes life prior to that "in Christ," that description would also depend upon the later "in Christ" perspective.

17. Philip K. Dick, "We Can Remember It for You Wholesale," in *The Philip K. Dick Reader* (New York: Citadel, 1997), 305.

18. Quaid is portrayed on-screen by Arnold Schwarzenegger, who hardly projects such an image. Does that account for the change in name from short story to film?

19. Dick, "We Can Remember It for You Wholesale," 307–8.

20. See Boer, "Non-Sense," for a detailed discussion of psychosis in Dick's life and work.

21. Is Rev 11:1–13 another version of this trope of the restraining figure(s)?

22. Petersen, *Rediscovering Paul*, sees Paul's "in Christ" as a new, sectarian social reality.

23. See Boer, "Non-Sense," 123.

24. Ibid., 132.

25. Ibid., 133. Boer lists and traces other key elements in paranoia in the movie and in Paul (ibid., 132).

26. Ibid., 134.

27. Ibid., 142.

28. Ibid., 125–31, 134–35.

29. Ibid., 136.

30. Miles, *Seeing and Believing*, 190–93.

31. Barthes, *Mythologies*, 109–59.

32. See Walsh, *Reading the Gospels in the Dark*, 173–85.

33. Stendahl, "The Apostle Paul and the Introspective Conscience of the West," 78–96.

34. Boer, "Non-Sense," 136. See also ibid., 153–54. See Žižek, *The Puppet and the Dwarf*, for a discussion of whether Christianity and psychoanalysis are fundamentally opposed; that is, whether Christianity itself needs psychoanalysis.

35. At least we see a heavenly light that directs Dad to a barn and the axe gleaming "Excalibur-like" in a stump. See Xan Brooks, *"Frailty."*

36. See Richard Walsh, "On Finding a Non-American Revelation: *End of Days* and the Book of Revelation," in Aichele and Walsh, *Screening Scripture*, 15–20.

37. Some scholars take some of the "quotations" in I Corinthians as excerpts from a letter from Corinth to Paul. If so, they remain Paul's quotations.

38. Roger Ebert, *"Frailty,"* http://www.suntimes.com/cgi-bin/print.cgi (accessed May 28, 2004).

39. Peter Preston, "God and the Father," http://film.guardian.co.uk/News_Story/Critic_Review/Observer_Film_of_the_week/0,426.html (accessed May 28, 2004). Preston's review originally appeared on September 8, 2002.

40. Although he does not discuss Romans, Jack Miles, *Christ: A Crisis in the Life of God* (New York: Alfred A. Knopf, 2001), also takes on the issue of God's covenant faithfulness. He portrays Christ's passion as God's payment for his own sins, for his own failure to live up to his violent promises to deliver Israel from her enemies.

41. Philippians 3:4–7 indicates how far this revelation of "sinful" humanity takes Paul from his own earlier inclinations.

42. *Seven* also features a serial killer acting on behalf of God. His view of his victims is closer to that of Paul's view of humans than *Frailty* is. His victims are sinners, not demons. *Seven* presents this serial killer at a distance. We do not share his apocalyptic vision of the world. Our vantage point is that of the two detectives who pursue him.

43. Ebert, *"Frailty."*

44. Some scholars claim that this passage is a non-Pauline interpolation, but there is little textual support for this claim. These scholars often also suggest that the last part of 1 Thess 2:16 suggests a post-70 CE date. For references to the argument that it is an interpolation, see Elliott, *Liberating Paul*, 234 nn. 4–5.

45. Does the title of *Frailty* suggest the uncertainty of the human grasp on reality? If so, it would be another element questioning Adam's final apocalyptic certitude.

46. Cited in Philip French, "Into the Heart of Darko," http://film.guardian.co.uk/News_Story/Critic_Review/Observer_Film_of_the_week/0,4267,820029,00.html (accessed June 1, 2004).

47. As schizophrenia is a rising problem among teenage males, *Donnie Darko* is certainly as horrific as *Frailty*. Nonetheless, elements of dark comedy, issuing particularly from the supporting cast, characterize the movie.

48. Like *High Noon* and *Seven*, the rest of the movie counts down time ominously. Countdowns to the end are, of course, also common in apocalyptic texts.

49. French, "Into the Heart of Darko," intuits a sense throughout the movie that Donnie has cheated death.

50. Similarly, Bultmann, *Theology of the New Testament*, 2:66, claims that all that the Jesus of John ever reveals is that he is the revealer.

51. Graham Greene, "The Destructors," http://www.gmtech.com/rocktheband/the_destructors.html (accessed June 1, 2004).

52. Stanley Cohen and Laurie Taylor, *Escape Attempts: The Theory and Practice of Resistance to Everyday Life*, 2nd ed. (London: Routledge, 1992), claim that such failed "escape" is the defining characteristic of modern individualism. Once again, Paul is precursor.

53. MaryAnn Johanson's review is appropriately titled "Choose Your Own Psychotic Breakdown: *Donnie Darko*," http://www.flickfilosopher.com/flickfilos/archive/014q/donniedarko.shtml (accessed June 2, 2004). She suggests the possibility that both post-October 2 stories are psychotic fantasies; that there is no reality outside Donnie's mind after the first warning. Before the movie begins on my DVD copy, Donnie and Frank's faces morph into one another, suggesting that they are one character or that Frank is a voice in Donnie's head. If so, Johanson's suggestion has even more merit.

54. Incidentally, the same option defines another apocalyptic film, *End of Days*. See Walsh, "On Finding a Non-American Apocalypse."

55. Camus, *The Rebel*, 21.

56. Albert Camus, *The Myth of Sisyphus and Other Essays*, trans. Justin O'Brien (New York: Vintage International, 1991), 117–18.

57. Ibid., 115.

58. Ibid., 123.

59. Elwood claims that the authorities will not catch them because they're on a mission from God. This stands in comic counterpoint to Adam's claims in *Frailty*. We might also place Jake's vision of the light in the black Baptist church in counterpoint to the far darker visions of *Frailty* and *Donnie Darko*.

60. We might also think of the revelation of the wizard at the end of *The Wizard of Oz*. I admit that I cannot think of Hick's notion of eschatological verification and his story of the celestial road without thinking of that yellow-brick road. See chapter 1, n. 19.

61. Greene, "The Destructors."

62. Does this "as if" resemble Paul's apocalyptic "as not" (1 Cor 7:29–31)? Taubes, *The Political Theology of Paul*, 53–54, 72, sees "as not" as a key component of Paul's apocalyptic rejection of the world. This "negative political theology" refuses to legitimate any earthly order. Elwood's "as if" is a non-apocalyptic rejection of the finality of the world. That stance may be more akin to that which Crossan and Reed, *In Search of Paul*, 409–12, associate with activists like Václav Havel, who having seen the system crush revolution, reject violent resistance in favor of small, immediate changes in daily life. Unlike apocalyptic visionaries, such activists are aware that revolutionary violence may lead to its own

unforeseen evil consequences. Crossan and Reed want to read Jesus and Paul in light of such figures. Obviously, I am reading a different Paul at this point.

63. The movie defines *pooka* as a fairy in the form of a large animal, a benign, mischievous figure beloved of rumpots and crackpots. The *Oxford English Dictionary* refers to it as an animal spirit, a hobgoblin, or a malignant spirit often thought responsible for minor accidents. *Pooka* or *phooka* is Irish. The Middle English form is *pouke*, from whence comes the famous Shakespearean Puck.

64. Jesus as idiot appears famously in Dostoevsky, *The Idiot*; and Nietzsche, *The Antichrist*. See Walsh, "Three Versions of ~~Judas~~ Jesus," 177–80.

65. Pam Grady, *"Harvey,"* http://www.reel.com/movie.asp?MID=536&buy=closed&PID=10090203&Tab=reviews&CID=18 (accessed June 3, 2004).

66. John Dominic Crossan, *Raid on the Articulate: Comic Eschatology in Jesus and Borges* (San Francisco: Harper & Row, 1976), 21. Crossan (146–49) contends that Jesus' teachings are fundamentally comic, not apocalyptic. See also Walsh, *Reading the Gospels in the Dark*, 69–93.

67. Joseph Campbell, *The Masks of God* (New York: Penguin, 1969), 1:29.

68. See chapter 3.

69. See Schüssler Fiorenza, "Paul and the Politics of Interpretation," 40–57. She points out that in the historical context of his own churches, Paul was not a canonical authority. He was engaged in a rhetorical-political fight for authority.

Chapter 3

Gospels of Death

It was before your eyes that Jesus Christ was publicly exhibited as crucified! (Gal 3:1b)

I have been crucified with Christ; and it is no longer I who live, but it is Christ who lives in me. And the life I now live in the flesh I live by faith in the Son of God, who loved me and gave himself for me. (Gal 2:19b–20)

May I never boast of anything except the cross of our Lord Jesus Christ, by which the world has been crucified to me, and I to the world. (Gal 6:14)

Mesmerizing Death-Gods

"Death is beautiful. What a bunch of crap." So concludes Rachel Mannis near the end of *Flatliners*. Like Paul, the cast of *Flatliners* flirts with death. Near-death experiences of light and peace fascinate Rachel. Her father committed suicide when she was a small child, and she desperately wants some peaceful resolution of that trauma. Nelson, whom the other characters call "Dr. Death," desires the renown and worship that scientific exploration of "the other side" will bring. As the movie opens, he sets the tone by intoning, "Today is a good day to die." The rest of the cast, all fellow medical students, are simply caught up in Nelson's obsession. He assembles them as a team to induce his death and resuscitate him.

At first, they are triumphant. Nelson's death-resurrection—they refer to both Jesus Christ and Lazarus after Nelson's return—and his new zest for life intrigue them, and they soon vie for the opportunity to flatline themselves. Except for Randy Steckle, they all do so. As competitive medical students, they bid for the opportunity to go first by daring to stay dead longer than the others. Accordingly, the resulting resuscitations become more and more dramatic.

Nelson, however, has not told them everything, and horror soon engulfs them. The resuscitated bring their sins—people they harmed in the past in some way—

back with them as haunting, seemingly physical, visions. Death is not sweet, and despite near-death reports, nothing beautiful is out there.

Finally, David Lobraccio discovers that restitution, or "atonement" as Nelson calls it, can stop the horror. He and Joe Hurley apologize to those they have wronged. Rachel's reconciliation with her dead father is more difficult, but she finally meets him successfully in her dreams. Nelson's atonement is the most difficult. As a child, he was involved in a taunting incident that led to Billy Mahoney's death. To escape this nemesis, who inflicts physical suffering upon him, Nelson decides to flatline alone. After all, he "deserves" to die. On the other side, he trades places with his victim and "dies." Meanwhile, the team arrives and tries to revive him. As they do so, David, the token atheist, rails at God and denies that Nelson, or anyone, deserves to die. Finally, David asks God to forgive them for trifling in his territory (death), but that admission is not enough, and Nelson does not revive. After all seems lost, however, Nelson makes his peace with Billy on the other side and returns. Waking, he mumbles to David that today was not a good day to die after all.

Early on, Nelson contends that religion and philosophy have failed vis-à-vis death and that science must take their place. David's foxhole conversion, however, belies this presumption. Like Gen 3, *Frankenstein*, and hundreds of movies, *Flatliners* chastises scientific arrogance. Thus, the movie's tagline opines, "Some lines shouldn't be crossed," and the atheist angrily apologizes to God for having "stepped on your fucking territory." Two contrasting scenes visually underline the movie's conservative point. Near the opening of the movie, Nelson walks through a rotunda, the paintings in which are obscured by restoration work. At the end of the movie, Nelson walks through the same rotunda, and we see a wrathful, Michelangelo-like deity towering over cowering humans. A forgotten deity—or maybe it is just death—reasserts its power over mere mortals.

In addition to this traditional religious message, the movie also espouses a liberal ethic of love and toleration. At first blush, this message is trite.

> The sum profundity of tackling such an epic issue as life after death is for William Baldwin to say sorry for secretly making videotapes of the women he beds, for Kevin Bacon to apologize to a Black girl he was mean to growing up, and for Julia Roberts to come to terms with her father who committed suicide. The film operates on the infuriatingly banal presentiment that all the problems of the past can be solved by warm fuzzy feelgood clichés. It's sad to think when it comes to taking on the great challenge of what lies after death all that *Flatliners* can end up doing is to resolve everything on a figurative group hug.[1]

Perhaps atonement does come too easily, but the point of *Flatliners* is not necessarily trite. Like *The Sixth Sense*, *Flatliners* affirms this life, not the next. From that perspective, it is hardly trite to reduce death to ethical lessons about this present life.[2]

Like *Flatliners*, Paul also opposes human arrogance. Like Nelson, Paul is also fascinated by death. But Paul does not affirm this world.[3] Instead, Paul crucifies the world (Gal 6:14). For Paul, the cross undoes the world's wisdom and power, because the crucified, rejected Christ is God's wisdom and power (I Cor 1:18–25). Paul's crucified becomes the world's crux, its ironic, apocalyptic reversal, the transvaluation of all values.[4] In this apocalypse, death becomes the sacred source of meaning and power, if it does not become god. Not surprisingly, then, the sacred symbol of Western Christianity, adorning its churches, is the cross (or crucifix).

In fact, the death fascinating apocalyptic visionaries is more macabre and deadly than that in *Flatliners*. Apocalyptic visionaries find themselves drawn to dispatch the wicked to bring about God's new age (Adam Meiks) or see suicide as an escape from the evil times in which they live (Fenton Meiks, Donnie Darko). Mere near-death does not mesmerize them, for they wish to die to live in another world. They do not want to merely glimpse the other side. They have already done that in their visions. They want to live on the other side. Death itself, then, is their good, their gospel, and their god.

While we may think of such apocalyptic visionaries as weaklings unfit for life, Paul hardly fits such a description. He is as authoritarian and authoritative as any medical student. Supremely confident of himself and his goals and demanding of others, a surprising "crack in his real" disrupts his life. Paul's vision of the "cursed," crucified Christ undoes the whole world (Gal 3:13–14). This world and all human effort become as naught. Humanity's best is folly, weakness (I Cor 1:18–25), and refuse (Phil 3:7–9). All humans are sinners (Rom 1:18–3:20). The world is dead (Gal 6:14).

Christ's death alone leads out of this evil age (Rom 3:21–26). As Paul and his followers die to their nothingness in Christ, they become superheroes. The cult superhero himself lives in them, replacing their puny selves, their bodies of death (Rom 7:24–25). Paul's good news, then, is no call to restitution, nor is it an affirmation of this life. It is a call to, at least, metaphorical suicide. Like Douglas Quaid, Paul and his followers die to their old weak, or evil, selves (Hauser) in order to be reborn as new superhero selves.

For Paul, this rebirth requires the transcendent invasion of the resurrected Christ (Gal 2:19–20) or the spirit. Accordingly, Paul's formulaic summaries of his preaching often include the resurrection and sometimes even focus on it (for example, I Cor 15).[5] Nevertheless, the crucifixion always remains the fundamental datum (see I Cor 15:3). Thus, Paul becomes quite indignant with his followers when they so stress the triumph of the spirit or of the resurrection that they forget the suffering and weakness of the cross (see 1–2 Corinthians). Neither the resurrection nor the spirit delivers Paul and his followers from this present evil age. Their lives are not now triumphal. Instead, they participate fully in Christ's sufferings in the present evil age. As a result, present triumph is highly suspect. Now, suffering portends their future glory (Rom 8:17–18). Their resurrection depends now upon apocalyptic visions (I Cor 15:5–8; Gal 1:11–12), upon the spirit, and upon hope.

> If the Spirit of him who raised Jesus from the dead dwells in you, he who raised Christ from the dead will give life to your mortal bodies also through his Spirit that dwells in you. . . .
>
> For all who are led by the Spirit of God are children of God . . . and if children, then heirs, heirs of God and joint heirs with Christ—if, in fact, we suffer with him so that we may also be glorified with him.
>
> I consider that the sufferings of this present time are not worth comparing with the glory about to be revealed [*apokaluphthēnai*] to us. For the creation waits with eager longing for the revealing [*apokalupsin*] of the children of God. . . . We know that the whole creation has been groaning in labor pains until now; and not only the creation, but we ourselves, who have the first fruits of the Spirit, groan inwardly while we wait for adoption, the redemption of our bodies. For in hope we were saved. Now hope that is seen is not hope. For who hopes for what is seen? But if we hope for what we do not see, we wait for it with patience. (Rom 8:11, 14, 17–19, 22–25)

In short, death is the empirical reality now.

Paul's transcendent invasion, that is, does not now completely replace the world. Like the memories of *Flatliners*, the resurrection and the spirit only haunt Paul and his followers. Life "in Christ" is beset with tensions. The new age of which Christ and the spirit are forerunners tarries. Caught between this age and the next, Paul desires to be done with present suffering, to end the tension between this world and "in Christ." No wonder, then, that Paul desires death for himself (Phil 1:21–24) and for his followers (2 Cor 5:1–10). Death is better than life. At least it is better than the partial, riven life that Paul and his followers have, like Fenton and Donnie. No wonder, then, that Paul determines to know, to preach, and to become nothing other than Christ crucified (1 Cor 2:2; 2 Cor 4:10–12).

It is the message of suffering that makes the gospel relevant and understandable to those who live in horrible times. Paul's followers live in such times. They are without resources, apart from transcendent intervention. There is not one cross in their world, but many. Their hero comes to them, then, where they live, as "empty" as they are (Phil 2:5–11). He dies as they do.

The Public Display of the Crucified

Like Paul, Mel Gibson's *The Passion of the Christ* publicly displays Christ crucified. Like Paul, Gibson cares little for Jesus' teaching or ministry,[6] and Christ's suffering unto death fascinates him. Where Paul merely announces the crucifixion, however, Gibson films a passion narrative, filtered through Catholic mysticism (the visions of two nuns, Mary of Agreda and Anne Catherine Emmerich) and Catholic ritual (the stations of the cross and the Eucharist).

The result focuses on Christ's physical suffering far more than Paul does. Gibson's movie starts with Gethsemane's sweated blood, dramatizes the beatings of the police and the Jewish trial, and adds a striking visual of Jesus hung, like a side of beef (or a lamb), from a bridge. The scourging is the most vicious, emotional moment in the movie. In fact, thereafter, the subsequent crucifixion is somewhat anticlimactic. Throughout, terrible physical anguish dominates the screen. Roger Ebert estimates that one hundred of the film's one hundred twenty-six minutes depict Christ's suffering, and he claims that *The Passion of the Christ* is the most violent film he has ever seen.[7] Everything is sweat and blood, flayed body, and grim anguish.

By contrast, the ancient world seldom describes crucifixion in detail. In fact, most authors pass over everything but the brute fact of crucifixion in silence.[8] Paul himself certainly never luxuriates in the details of Christ's suffering as Gibson does.[9] When Paul details physical sufferings, it is his own suffering that is in view (for example, I Cor 4:9–13; 2 Cor 4:7–12; 6:4–10; 11:23–33; 12:7–10). Christian mysticism began to focus on the physical sufferings of Christ in something like Gibson's manner only in the thirteenth century, the era of the stigmata of St. Francis and the rise to popularity of the stations of the cross. Previous medieval mysticism was more Neoplatonic, an eschewing of the body in favor of the spirit. While Paul is hardly Neoplatonic, Paul's cross is not so much physical suffering as it is a descent into shame, a loss of status, a humiliation:[10]

> who, though he [Christ Jesus] was in the form of God, did not regard equal-
> ity with God as something to be exploited, but emptied himself, taking the
> form of a slave, being born in human likeness. And being found in human
> form, he humbled himself and became obedient to the point of death—
> even death on a cross. (Phil 2:6–8; see also 2 Cor 8:9)

This emptying indicates Christ's solidarity with humans who suffer in an evil age. In short, in Paul, Christ's suffering "for us" is a suffering "with us."[11]

Gibson's heroic Christ suffers far more uniquely. The horrible scourging is crucial. After a whipping that would have killed a "normal man," Gibson's Christ catches Mary's eye and rises slowly from the ground to endure more suffering. This figure is not a fellow apocalyptic sufferer. This suffering is not the apocalyptic prelude to glory. This Christ is already triumphant in his suffering, in this slow rise. After this, the brief, stigmatic resurrection visual at the movie's end is anticlimactic and unnecessary. This Christ becomes heroic as he endures suffering. He is the Hollywood passion-action hero.[12] As a result, Gibson's cross has little about it of

Mark's God-forsakenness (Mark 15:34) or of Paul's weakness and folly (1 Cor 1:18–2:5). Instead, it resembles the Johannine passion hero's triumph.[13] Gibson's Christ is "a tough dude who can take a licking and keep on ticking."[14]

Such suffering is beyond us. If we are more than mere voyeurs, it is because the suffering extends grace to us. Accordingly, the most important flashback in the movie is to the institution of the Eucharist. This flashback from the cross merges the crucifixion and the Eucharist into one ritual moment (compare John 6) re-realizing this mythic-founding time.[15] Gibson's movie visually breaks the body and sheds the blood for us. If only the bell would tinkle during this reel sacrament, for the movie aspires to transubstantiate the crucifixion. As it does so, Gibson's heroic Christ becomes even less human. He becomes the religious objects of the sacrament. He becomes the body eaten and the blood drunk (John 6:53–58).

Paul can speak similarly of the supernatural power of the supper (1 Cor 11:23–32). Nonetheless, for Paul, baptism better symbolizes the believer's participation in Christ's death and sufferings in this evil age.

> Do you not know that all of us who have been baptized into Christ Jesus were baptized into his death? Therefore we have been buried with him by baptism into death, so that, just as Christ was raised from the dead by the glory of the Father, so we too might walk in newness of life.
>
> For if we have been united with him in a death like his, we will certainly be united with him in a resurrection like his. (Rom 6:3–5)

Baptism, that is, marks the interim quality of the new life "in Christ." Baptism and present suffering look forward to apocalypse. Of course, in Paul's hands, even the supper "proclaim[s] the Lord's death *until he comes*" (1 Cor 11:26, emphasis added). It, too, involves Paul's followers in Christ's ongoing sufferings. Their lives become like Christ's life and death. They, too, are "for others." When they eat, even the strong are to be mindful of the weak, and all are to aspire to love (see 1 Cor 8–14).

Gibson's Christ does not suffer with us in this way. His suffering is heroically before and beyond us. His suffering is always "for us." Accordingly, Gibson interprets the passion with two "headlines." First, the movie sets Isa 53 as a title over the entire passion. This headline reads Christ's suffering as for us and because of our sins. In short, we watch Christ suffer what we reprehensible creatures deserve. The ritual aspects of the movie—the Eucharist and the stations of the cross— also contribute to this interpretation. Second, the opening scene in Gethsemane frames the passion as a conflict between a heroic Christ and an androgynous Satan. Christ resists Satan's temptations; he decides to bear what Satan says "no man" can bear; and he crushes a hissing snake under his heel (see Gen 3:15). These motifs, of course, present Christ's suffering as a triumph over Satan. Thereafter, there is no real conflict. Instead, the rest of the movie stretches its viewers on an emotional rack in order to provide them a visceral sense of the suffering on their behalf. If the suffering is sacrifice and conflict, it is also a public proclamation, a public display of the crucified.

While not developing a sophisticated theory of the atonement, Gibson flirts with the three major theological views: substitution, ransom, and moral influence. In the former case, Christ appeases a wrathful God by dying in place of sinful humans. The ransom theory imagines humans in thrall to Satan, and Christ's death as breaking Satan's hold. The moral influence theory asserts that Christ's death on the cross shows errant humans that God still loves them. The ransom motif fits the pattern of the Hollywood passion hero most neatly, but Gibson visualizes such notions only in Gethsemane. It remains in the background, however, in Christ's heroic endurance. Most of the movie's rhetoric endeavors to display the depths of Christ's suffering to a human audience; nevertheless, that suffering is clearly "for us." As a result, the spectacle's deepest logic is the substitution theory. The opening title from Isa 53 is quite clear on this point. The use of Catholic ritual and mystic devotion focusing on Christ's suffering also contributes to this interpretation. We see what we deserve and what Christ bore for us as the mythic foundation of our faith, not in apocalyptic suffering with us.

Paul, standing as he does near the beginning of speculation about the meaning of the cross, never offers a sophisticated theory either.[16] He, too, flirts with various metaphors to explain what happened at the cross.

> But now, apart from law, the righteousness [*dikaiosunē*] of God has been disclosed, and is attested by the law and the prophets, the righteousness [*dikaiosunē*] of God through faith in Jesus Christ for all who believe. For there is no distinction, since all have sinned and fall short of the glory of God; they are now justified [*dikaioumenoi*] by his grace as a gift, through the redemption that is in Christ Jesus, whom God put forward as a sacrifice of atonement by his blood, effective through faith. He did this to show his righteousness [*dikaiosunēs*], because in his divine forbearance he had passed over the sins previously committed; it was to prove at the present time that he himself is righteous [*dikaiov*] and that he justifies [*dikaiounta*] the one who has faith in Jesus. (Rom 3:21–26)

These metaphors are less clearly related to any of the theories of the atonement than Gibson's spectacle. Paul gestures at the meaning of the cross with images drawn from the law court (justification), economics (redemption), and religious sacrifice (sacrifice of atonement). *Dikaio* words, which English translations generally render with forms of "just" or "righteous," dominate this passage. The Greek words designate a person, action, or thing that adheres to some standard, as in the justified margins of computer word-processing. In the context of the law court, the

words designate the innocent, with respect to a particular charge, or a person acting appropriately with respect to his/her function. A judge, for example, is righteous when he absolves the innocent and punishes the guilty.[17]

Given this passage's prominent location in Romans (after Paul's indictment of
sinners and before his description of the life in Christ), the importance of Romans
in Paul's extant texts, and the dominant interpretation of Romans, scholars have
long thought justification by faith the center of Paul's thought. Present scholars are
less certain.[18] After all, "justification" language is important only in Galatians and
Romans. Further, many are suspicious of the anti-Semitism lurking in the traditional statement of justification by faith by Protestant scholars. More important,
influenced heavily by Stendahl, they also suspect that the traditional "justification
by faith" reading of Paul interprets Paul far too individualistically. As we have seen,
Rom 3:21–26 ceases to be the crux of Romans in Stendahl's reading. The crux
shifts to Rom 9–11, and Romans becomes a theodicy in which Paul defends God
against the charge that he has rejected Israel.

Gibson needs no such theodicy. He is far more certain about justice than Paul
because he is the heir of a long-standing, legalistic reflection that begins with
Tertullian and proceeds through the development of medieval penance and Anselm's
feudalistic reflections on the atonement. This Western Christianity is relentlessly
about the forgiveness of an individual's sins, a religious matter whose "justice" has
come in the West to rely upon some macabre transaction taking place at the cross
or in its ritual reenactment.[19] This legal, sinful fascination is written so deeply
into the Western imagination that it seems a fact, not merely an interpretation.[20]
Gibson's exorbitant spectacle relies upon this "fact" and succeeded financially.
Evangelical Protestants and Catholics lined up together to watch Gibson's public
display of Christ's suffering. Clearly, Gibson nicely captures the West's cruciform,
sinful imagination, with its crucifixes, stigmata, bleeding hearts, stations of the
cross, and Eucharist.

With such at its imaginative center, it is no wonder that Western Christianity
has also sponsored Crusades, Inquisitions, Colonizing Missions, Empires, Hell,
and, at the movies, religious horror like *The Passion of the Christ* and *Flatliners*. The crucified imagination, so vividly captured by Gibson, makes us insensitive to suffering.
In fact, the crucified imagination makes sinners of us all. Similarly, Paul knows
human sinfulness only after the apocalypse of Christ. The order of Romans is mis-
leading, for its discussion of sin precedes Paul's discussion of the cross and life "in
Christ." Romans, however, is a theodicy for the inclusion of the Gentiles, a mission
that Paul was committed to long before writing Romans. In fact, he wrote Romans
to extend that mission (Rom 1:13–15; 15:23–29). The declaration of human sinfulness that opens Romans, then, actually follows Paul's apocalypse and gentile mission.[21] In Romans, the assertion of the ubiquity of sin is merely the opening vol-
ley in Paul's attempt to extend his gentile mission. That is, he concludes that humans

are sinful only after his apocalypse. Later readers, like Augustine, Luther, and Gibson, forgot Romans's place in Paul's apocalyptic imagination and made the declaration of human sinfulness the foundational datum to which the cross responded. Thereby, Westerners became sinners deserving death. No wonder Nelson (in *Flatliners*) guiltily decides he deserves to die. Only the atheist David demurs. Maybe we should reply with David and Will Munny in *Unforgiven* that "deserve's got nothing to do with it."

Will Munny is the protagonist of Clint Eastwood's *Unforgiven*. He is a "known thief and murderer," not a hero. When he married, however, Munny quit drinking and gave up his life of crime. As the movie opens, his wife has died, and Munny is left with a farm and two children. A hopelessly bad farmer, he returns to his outlaw life when the Schofield Kid arrives to recruit Munny to help him kill two cowboys. One of the cowboys has badly cut a whore, and Little Bill, the sheriff in Big Whiskey, has considered a fine a sufficient restoration of "justice." The angry whores, led by Strawberry Alice, have put up a bounty on the cowboys in retaliation. They have done so secretly because Little Bill rules Big Whiskey with an iron fist, ruthlessly destroying all who oppose his order.

Will enlists his old partner, Ned Logan, and starts after the cowboys. When they arrive in Big Whiskey, Little Bill beats Munny badly. After this ritual humiliation, the whores nurse Will back to health, and he begins his journey back to his old criminal self. Unlike his partners, he can kill without thought and without remorse. After they kill the first cowboy, Ned, no longer "cut out" for this life, starts home to his wife. After Will and the Schofield Kid kill the second cowboy and wait for the bounty, they both reflect on the horror of killing. The Schofield Kid tearfully tries to justify his killing by the cowboy's own wicked actions against the whores: "Well, I guess, they had it coming." Will replies, "We all have it coming, Kid." The "it," of course, is death, not justice.

When one of the whores arrives with the bounty, she tells Will that Little Bill caught Ned on his way home and killed him, after torturing him. Ominously, Will begins to drink. Returning to the saloon where Little Bill beat him, Will shoots the owner for displaying Ned out front and then shoots five other men, including Little Bill. As Will drinks at the bar afterwards, the wounded Little Bill reaches for his pistol, which Will knocks away. Dying, Little Bill says, "I don't deserve this. To die like this. I was building a house." Will replies, "Deserve's got nothing to do with it." Angrily, Little Bill retorts, "I'll see you in hell, William Munny." Will laconically agrees and fires.

In *Unforgiven*, Eastwood shares a bleak view of human nature with Paul and Gibson. Unlike Gibson, however, Eastwood provides no heroes. Unlike Paul, Eastwood does not show new creations. Instead, he dramatizes a failed conversion and Munny's return to his old, despicable life. Nonetheless, Eastwood refuses to damn humans as universally as Paul and Gibson do. Ned and the Schofield Kid are not killers like Little Bill and Will. In fact, almost everyone has to drink excessively in order to live with killing. More important, *Unforgiven* resists a melodramatic view of life. People do not "get what they deserve" in death. People simply die. To put it in *Unforgiven's* most memorable line, "Deserve's got nothing to do with it."

In fact, there is little justice in this movie. At least no one thinks themselves treated justly. The whores think that Little Bill lets the cowboys off too easily. They respond to this travesty with their own travesty of justice. They hire vengeance. The only salvific element in the movie is Will's refusal to ennoble his role. He is no divine instrument, not even a hero. He is only a mercenary. He has to drink to carry out his role. As he does not lionize himself, he does not need to demonize his enemies. Thus, he refuses to say that his victims deserve their deaths or that his actions restore justice. If Will has any nobility, it is in his attempt to soldier on, in his attempt to please his wife, to care for his children, and to remain loyal to his friends. These are mundane matters, and matters remain on this level.[22] Will and everyone else in the movie are unforgiven, for there is no one, no larger power anyway, to forgive them and no hero to save them.[23]

The movie never explains its title; therefore, the title sits rather loosely on the film. So far, I have suggested an interpretation that sets it in counterpoint to Paul and to *The Passion of the Christ*. On this view, the movie refuses forgiveness as it refuses to imagine a deity who stands behind just deaths (and public crucifixions). Another interpretation, however, might assay another altogether different way, a way that might appeal to Eli Lapp, the grandfather in *Witness*. On this reading, the characters are "unforgiven" because they refuse to forgive. They refuse to walk away from slights and pay for murder or accept pay for murder. These characters refuse, that is, to find forgiveness on a simply human level. To do so, the whores would have to refuse vengeance. To do so, Will would have to walk away from his mercenary solution to his financial problems.

Perhaps that way, like that of the Amish in *Witness*, is mere fancy. Even so, *Unforgiven* still stands as a question mark against the Western sinful, cruciform imagination. Maybe if we did not insist on deserved deaths, on the bestial nature of humans, on vengeful Gods, we would not have public crucifixions and ritual humiliations. Public death is the price of forgiveness in the Western imagination. Neither Paul nor Gibson will let us forget it with their public displays. What if we refused to assert that people deserve to die?

Dark, Fractured (?) Gods

Paul and Gibson's dark gospels and public displays avoid the charge of a sadistic or masochistic delight in suffering by condemning humans. Paul's justification of God, and the resulting imagination of Western Christianity, requires humans to be sinful.[24] Gibson's leering, sadistic Roman soldiers who scourge Christ mercilessly are the logical consequence of this imagination. As such, they represent all (at least Western) humans.

> There is such naked, unfettered cruelty in the way Jesus is treated that it makes one ponder the nature of man. And the dark reality is that worse torments have been visited upon others throughout history. Over the centuries, our civilizations and technology have evolved, but that aspect of our essential nature has not changed. Given the chance, we easily revert to the bestial barbarians who derived sadistic enjoyment from the torture of Jesus. It's a sickness that cannot be expunged.[25]

Appropriately, Peter Travers says, "The film seems like the greatest story ever told by the Marquis de Sade."[26]

The world is an unforgiving, vengeful place in the visions of Gibson and Paul. Not just Christ, but also those who reject him pay (Rom 6:23; 1 Thess 2:15–16). Thus, in *The Passion of the Christ*, demonic children harry Judas to his death. Immediately after the bad thief reviles Christ, a bird descends from heaven to peck at his eye. When a single raindrop falls from heaven, supernatural events begin that climax in an earthquake that destroys the temple. Certainly, anti-Semitism lurks in Gibson's horrific expansion of Matthew's torn temple veil (see Matt 27:51–54), but an even deeper misanthropy troubles the entire movie. Behind it stands a wrathful, vengeful God. The sinful—and we are all sinful—pay.

Gibson's public spectacle reveals the vicious God at the heart of legalistic, imperial Western Christianity. At the cross, God is sadistic executioner. He is not on-screen in Gibson's film. God does not need to be because the headlines, Isa 53 and Gen 3:15, identify him as the prime mover behind the scenes. The bird and teardrop from heaven are suspicious clues as to the real culprit as well. Gibson's public spectacle names God as complicit in the suffering of innocents. Unlike Paul's Christ, he does not share the suffering. He causes it. This God resembles the monster deities of Gen 22, Exodus, and Job. This God, like the gods of Isaac and Job, brings humans to the point of death for no human reason. Human death simply displays this monstrous God's status, his reputation, and his power (thus, the refrain that punctuates the horrors of the Exodus narrative is "they/you shall know that I am the Lord").[27]

Paul's tortured theodicy in Romans suggests that he had doubts himself about the character of his God. In Paul's desperate defense of his God against the charges of unjustly betraying Israel, abandoning Torah, and declaring the guilty innocent, Christ's death is the universal panacea restoring God's righteousness. Paul's cross is a means to a good end. No one else in antiquity saw crucifixion so. Paul himself needed apocalyptic visions, or psychotic breaks, to come to this point.

In this process, Paul foists his fractured, visionary self onto God. If we follow Paul's apocalypse, Paul's God becomes the psychotic who suffers a crack in the real.[28] The crucifixion, of course, is a massive, divine cover-up. God sacrifices Christ "to show his righteousness, because in his divine forbearance he had passed over the sins previously committed" (Rom 3:25b). In Paul's law court imagery, God is the divine judge. Further, he is a judge who lets his son take the fall for his judicial malfeasance. He commits murder to clear himself for passing over sins. He does what he finally did not demand of Abraham and what Dad Meiks could not bring himself to do. Afterward, this divine judge declares innocent the guilty who align themselves with his crucified (Rom 3:26). That is, the judge absolves those who put themselves completely at his disposal by joining him in his colossal cover-up. No wonder they cannot "boast" thereafter (Rom 3:27–31). It is hardly a matter to speak of publicly. Only Paul has the audacity to publicize this sordid tale of a judge who maintains his justness, loudly and murderously, as he clears the guilty who refuse to protest his murder. Such characters belong to a Coppola or Scorsese mobster movie, not to a gospel.

Psychosis is, however, written deeply into religious images of the gods. As gods personify the holy or sacred center of religion, they symbolize both creative and destructive power. In Jack Miles's creative reading of the Hebrew Bible, this psychosis ultimately renders God inactive and silent.[29] In Miles's equally creative reading of the Gospel of John, Christ overcomes this inactive silence with a suicidal mission. This suicide responds to the Edenic curses, to the fact that the human condition and the world are a divine punishment, by taking these curses (death) upon God himself.[30] In this act, God also admits and responds to his inability or unwillingness to keep his covenant promises to Israel. To acknowledge his failure to reenact the Exodus, he elects to share Jerusalem's fate and entices Jerusalem to deliver him to the Romans. Thereby, the Lord of Hosts becomes the Lamb of God, a repentance that constitutes the argument of the Christian Bible.[31]

> The Gospel story, a story in which the Jewish God is condemned, tortured, and executed by the foreign oppressor of the Jews, is a particularly violent and dramatic way to announce that that God is no longer a warrior prepared to rescue the Jews from foreign oppression but, rather, a savior who has chosen to rescue all mankind from death. The New Testament story as a whole—combining the Gospel story with the story of the early church—is a particularly radical and disruptive way to announce that God has exchanged warfare on behalf of the Jews for missionary teaching through the Jews.[32]

More clearly than Paul, the Gospels, and Gibson, Miles presents the cross as a rejection of the infliction of death on others, for, thereby, Christ replaces vengeance with nonretaliation; and death, vengeance, and violence become the enemies, not other humans. The New Testament is hardly so kind. For John—Miles's precursor—the

Jews are the enemies. The Synoptics associate the fall of Jerusalem with the crucifix-ion, and Paul's gospel asserts that everyone deserves to die.

Miles extends this "dessert" to God and reveals suicide to be the foundation of Christianity.[33] James Morrow's similar story, *Towing Jehovah*, is a less solipsistic ver-sion of the same tale. In his novel, when God dies, various characters struggle with the meaning of God's death and with the problem of disposing of God's body. Thomas Wyclif Ockham, Jesuit priest and scientist, finally decides that God com-mitted suicide to clear the way for humans, so that they might finally mature. While this "Nietzsche-like" explanation is only one interpretation of the events in *Towing Jehovah*, it resembles Miles's story and that of *Donnie Darko*. It differs, however, in nar-rative perspective. Morrow silences God in favor of the humans who struggle with life without the hope of divine deliverance. At their best, they resemble Will Munny and Camus' Sisyphus, carrying on in frustrating, desperate situations without despair and without making a pact with death. Camus' characters even rise to acts of creation.[34]

Perhaps we can glimpse the difference between suicide and mundane creation more clearly by returning to Scorsese's *The Last Temptation of Christ*. Basing the movie on Kazantzakis's novel of the same name, Scorsese's interest is the conflict between the spirit and the flesh. As we have seen, his troubled Christ makes Roman crosses and helps crucify messianic claimants in order to distance himself from the God who torments him. Ultimately, however, Christ chooses a monastic life over Mary Magdalene and makes a pact with death, with a God who wants him to suffer. On the cross, Christ has second thoughts inspired by a satanic temptation, a vision in which he leaves the cross for a life with wives and family. As he lies dying in old age, Judas arrives from the burning Jerusalem and castigates Jesus for rejecting his messianic destiny and for being responsible for the destruction of Jerusalem. Thereupon, Jesus returns to the cross as Christ, prays for forgiveness, tells God that he wants to be the messiah, and dies smiling. Once again, Christianity begins with a suicide, but now we see more clearly what the cost is. Jesus trades a normal life for messianic status. He trades the flesh for the spirit. He trades life for suicide. Out of his torment, he manufactures a higher destiny for himself. Perhaps we should say that Jesus dies that Christ might live.

If Jesus dies that Christ might live, we have returned to Paul (Gal 2:19–20). Of course, we have also returned to Scorsese's rather sleazy, murderous Paul. As we have seen, that Paul rejects Jesus for his resurrected Christ, the powerful gospel "truth" that people really need. While this scene may simply be typical Hollywood bashing of religious institutions, it may also speak more deeply about death-gospels. Obviously, when Scorsese's Jesus returns to the cross to die to become the messiah, the savior of the world, he no longer has any legitimate quarrel with Scorsese's Paul of Tarsus.

Dying (to Be) Gods/Heroes

Leaving the death of this Donnie Darko Jesus aside for a moment, Scorsese's Christ also resembles the popular superheroes of the comic book, who pass undetected as ordinary people, even nerds, until they slip into a phone booth, the wilderness, baptism "in Christ," or Recall Incorporated to emerge as a Superman. When these superheroes die, it is only to their weaker or evil selves. This "death" reveals them as the superheroes they truly are. The fantasy they offer us is patent. These superheroes represent our deeper, true selves.[35] Our normality or mediocrity is also only a guise. Of course, as we saw with *Total Recall*'s Douglas Quaid, this fantasy may only be an ego trip, a vacation from self.

This possibility does not trouble Scorsese's Paul. His Christ is far more important than a Jesus indistinguishable from ordinary people. It is Christ, not Jesus, who elevates Paul and his followers to their own superhero status. When Paul dies and Christ lives through him, Paul has died to become his own god (Gal 2:19–20), to conquer all of his weaknesses and inadequacies (Rom 8:35–37).

M. Night Shyamalan's *Unbreakable* reflects this comic book world. The film's two protagonists are diametric opposites. Elijah Price is the victim of a disease that makes him terribly susceptible to broken bones. Children call him Mr. Glass. His mother enticed him beyond his pain and fears by providing him comic books as a reward for his ventures into the world. These comic books are the adult Elijah's livelihood (he sells them as art) and articulate his worldview. Given the dualistic dance between hero and villain in the comics, Elijah searches for his opposite, someone who does not get hurt, someone whom the comics are about, someone who does not really know he has this "gift," someone "put here" to protect the rest of us.

David Dunn is that someone. David is a college security guard who has grown apart from his wife, Audrey, because of his desperate sadness and his inability to communicate with her. Much of the story, like Shyamalan's earlier *The Sixth Sense*, centers on a child's perspective on all this. David's young son, Joseph, lionizes his father and wants him to be the hero whom Elijah suspects him to be.

David comes to Elijah's attention when he alone survives a train wreck. At first, Elijah doubts that David is the one because David's football career ended in an injury sustained in a car crash. Nonetheless, Elijah pursues David, and we gradually discover David's "superpowers." He has incredible strength, and, more important, he has the ability to see people's lives (past and future) by simply touching them.[36] Elijah's explanations interest David, but he is frightened away from his "call" when Joseph threatens to shoot him to prove once and for all that David is "no ordinary man."[37] Scared, David tells Elijah to "stop messing" with his life, but Elijah retorts that he knows that David faked the car injury for Audrey. David shatters Elijah's dreams, however, when he tells him that he almost drowned as a child.

Soon, however, Elijah has an epiphany in a comic book store: all superheroes have a weakness. David's is water. Meanwhile, David struggles to overcome his sadness so that he can keep his family together. Finally, he calls Elijah and asks him what he is "supposed to do." Elijah tells him to go to a public place so that he can sense the dangers people face. David does and saves two children from a man who has invaded their house, held their family hostage, and killed their mother and father. To do so, of course, he has to overcome his fear of water.[38] When he returns home as the triumphant hero, he connects with Audrey for the first time in ages and begins to re-create his happy family. The next morning, a surprised Joseph finds happy parents at breakfast. While Audrey insists that the family avoid Elijah, David points surreptitiously to a newspaper headline, "Saved," to let Joseph know that his father is a hero, "no ordinary man."

To this point, the movie is a comic book gospel. Elijah identifies David as the messiah who "saves" people and, in a nice updating for our times, his fractured family as well. In typical comic book fashion, his "ordinary guy" appearance is only a disguise for his true superhero identity. Only his young son and Elijah know his true identity.[39]

The movie's denouement, however, deconstructs this story. David visits Elijah's art gallery to confirm Elijah's hopes and to thank him. When they shake hands, David "sees" that Elijah has caused several terrible accidents to make his messiah. Elijah confesses:

Do you know what the scariest thing is? To not know your place in this world. To not know why you're here. That's . . . that's just an awful feeling. ("What have you done?") I almost gave up hope. There were so many times I questioned myself. ("Killed all those people?") But I found you. So many sacrifices . . . just to find you. ("Jesus Christ.") Now that we know who you are, I know who I am. I'm not a mistake. It all makes sense. In a comic, you know how you can tell who the arch-villain is going to be? He's the exact opposite of the hero, and most times they're friends like you and me.

Appropriately, Elijah talks over David's whispered interjections to this horror (in parentheses above). Nonetheless, end titles tell us that David reported Elijah to the authorities and that Elijah is now in a hospital for the criminally insane.

The denouement centers on the question, "Who makes a messiah?" In this regard, the film resembles both *Monty Python's Life of Brian* and Hal Ashby's *Being There*.[40] The movie explores more clearly than those films, however, the narcissism that generates the creation of messiahs. It suggests that we, like Elijah, create messiahs to find our own place in the center of the universe, to lionize, if not deify, ourselves. David was right, then, when he accused Elijah, in their very first meeting, of trying to take advantage of him. Here, Shyamalan's Elijah resembles Scorsese's Paul. Both create messiahs in order to position themselves at the center of the world.

This messiah-making process also sheds light on Gibson's public crucifixion. From this perspective, that strange break in perspective, when the camera abandons the terrestrial frame to look down on the cross from heaven, is not so strange after all. That break testifies to the movie's fundamental transubstantiation, our transformation into divine voyeurs untroubled by and not responsible for human passion.[41] That Christ dies horribly and that other Jews do, too, in the temple earthquake matters little. We, like gods and Shyamalan's Elijah, consume the images of rubble, broken bodies, and flowing blood in order to live.[42]

Leaving Ourselves Behind

Dying to be gods allows us to leave the weaknesses and fragmentation of human life behind. Paul speaks eloquently of this human fragmentation in Rom 7:7–25:[43]

> I do not understand my own actions. For I do not do what I want, but I do the very thing I hate. . . . I can will what is right, but I cannot do it. For I do not do the good I want, but the evil I do not want is what I do. (Rom 7:15, 18b–19)

At least according to the interpretation of Augustine, Luther, and Bultmann, he speaks of this human fragmentation. Their interpretation makes Paul the precursor of modern consciousness and modern humans' desperate, futile desires to find wholeness by overcoming themselves.[44] Paul's answer to this fragmentation is openness to transcendence, a loss of self in the powerful other.

> Wretched man that I am! Who will rescue me from this body of death? Thanks be to God through Jesus Christ our Lord! . . .
> There is therefore now no condemnation for those who are in Christ Jesus. For the law of the Spirit of life in Christ Jesus has set you free from the law of sin and of death. (Rom 7:24–25a; 8:1–2)

Even if it is unlikely that Paul experiences modern self-doubt, his "already, not yet," "in Christ" gospel fragments himself and his followers socially, if not psychologically.[45] Paul's "in Christ" did not end the world. "In Christ" became an enclave of the new age in the world, and Christ and the spirit became enclaves of the colonizing God within the believer. "In Christ," then, creates dichotomies between the world and the age to come, the world and Paul's sectarian "in Christ" communities, the self and Christ, the flesh and the spirit, and so forth. In every case, despite the overwhelming material evidence in favor of the former, Paul privileges the latter.

This privileging becomes an ethical demand that creates its own dichotomies between the ideal and the actual, between the "ought" and the "is." Thus, Paul's descriptions of the life "in Christ" are always also ethical demands to leave the world, the self, and the flesh behind (see Rom 5–8; 2 Cor 3–5).[46] As the new age is only tenuously present, Paul's followers must consciously, deliberately realize it: for example, they have been justified, they should live justly; they have been delivered from the world, they should not conform to it; and they have been set free, they should not live as slaves (see Rom 5:1; 12:1–2; Gal 5:1, 16). Of course, the most succinct versions of the ideal are Christ, Paul, and the spirit, ideals that the followers can never fully actualize.[47] As they realize their religious goals, however, there is less and less of the followers and more and more of Christ (Phil 2:5–11; 3:4–11). The result is an ethically and socially schizoid life, lived uncomfortably between ideal and actual, between the apocalypse and the suffering present. At best, Paul and his followers are out of place.[48]

Paul's death-gospel creates this tension and resolves it by providing the fantasy that we can become superheroes if only we find the right phone booth. *Being John Malkovich* imagines another, similar portal, but its "ride" into celebrity scans the dark side of death-wish gospels. Craig Schwartz is a puppeteer whose most basic routine is Craig's Dance of Despair and Disillusionment. Significantly, the Craig puppet performs this destructive dance after the puppet looks into a mirror, for Craig desperately wants to be anyone else. Puppetry allows him a temporary escape into someone else's skin, but he fails as a puppeteer and takes a job at Lestercorp, housed mysteriously on floor 7½. There, he meets and becomes enthralled with the seductive but aloof Maxine. He also finds a mysterious half-door behind a filing cabinet that leads him down a dark tunnel into the mind of John Malkovich for fifteen minutes, after which he falls unceremoniously from the sky into a ditch alongside the New Jersey Turnpike.[49]

Thereafter, Craig's art becomes his new life. Although Craig is now the ultimate puppeteer and voyeur, the "metaphysical can of worms" of the Malkovich "ride" troubles him. By contrast, when Maxine and Lotte, Craig's wife, find out about the Malkovich ride, they simply plunge ahead. Knowing that everyone wants to be someone else, Maxine markets the ride for two hundred dollars a trip. Lotte uses the ride to realize a new transsexual (or lesbian) life in which she inhabits Malkovich's body while he has sex with Maxine.

Facing the loss of Maxine (and Lotte), Craig flexes his puppetry muscles. He locks Lotte in a cage with her pet chimp and forces her to schedule trysts with Maxine and Malkovich so that he can inhabit Malkovich and finally enjoy sex with Maxine. Using his puppetry skills, Craig completely takes over Malkovich, marries

Maxine, and launches a successful puppetry career. Intriguingly, Malkovich now dresses and looks like the old Craig Schwartz.[50]

Meanwhile, Lotte learns from Dr. Lester that the portal was his device and Malkovich his chosen "vessel." Dr. Lester has been cheating death for some time by entering new "vessels" on their forty-fourth birthday. This time, he intends to take a whole committee of old folk with him. If they miss the deadline, however, they risk being trapped in the subconscious of a younger vessel, forced forever to see life through someone else's eyes. Desperate, this cadre kidnaps Maxine and threatens to kill her if Craig will not leave Malkovich. Craig, however, refuses to leave Malkovich because he would be only Craig Schwartz if he did so.

Ever angrier, Lotte decides to kill Maxine for betraying her with Craig, but Maxine escapes into Malkovich. Lotte pursues her, and they are disgorged after the requisite fifteen minutes. Craig, too, leaves Malkovich in a desperate bid to keep Maxine. All three wind up beside the turnpike, where, unfortunately for Craig, Maxine and Lotte declare their love for one another and leave Craig standing in the rain. Meanwhile, the Lester committee takes over the hapless Malkovich.

In the denouement, seven years later, an older Malkovich, who now looks and dresses like Dr. Lester, explains his immortality plan to Charlie Sheen. The new vessel is Emily, the love child of Lotte/Malkovich and Maxine. As the movie closes, we see this child playing with her two mothers at a pool. Then, suddenly, we see the world through her eyes and hear Craig's trapped, Maxine-obsessed voice issuing seemingly from within Emily's head.

This end is nicely ambiguous. Is Craig lying in wait to manipulate yet another puppet? Or has he, as Dr. Lester's fears suggest, been trapped as a helpless voyeur in someone else's life? Read with *Being John Malkovich*, Paul's gospel poses the same ambiguities. On one hand, his death-gospel may lead us beyond our weak selves to the superhero's conquest of death. On the other hand, this death trip may simply render us voyeurs who have abandoned responsibility for our lives and who have become trapped in fantastic ego trips, unable to relate to others or to the world. Or this gospel may simply render us hopeless vessels for colonizing forces like Christ, the spirit, Paul, Dr. Lester, or even the stories and ideologies of the movies.

Paul's gospel is constructive, that is, if we are Douglas Quaid. It is not if we are Donnie Darko. Moreover, in both cases, the death-wish gospel devalues everyday, banal life. As we leave the weaknesses and fragmentation of human life behind, we leave our humanity behind. Craig becomes a monster and still does not overcome his fear of his insignificance nor connect meaningfully with Maxine. He loses himself as we all do when we die to become someone else. *Being John Malkovich* allows us to see more completely these different aspects of becoming other than ourselves. Paul never really shows us Christ or his followers. Paul's solipsistic letters completely colonize them. In *Being John Malkovich*, however, we see both Craig's banal, frustrated life and his colonizing of Malkovich. We see both his loss of self in this process and what his death wish costs others. We see Malkovich "die" so that Craig and Lester can cheat banal frustration and death. Horribly, despite the sunny light and bright colors of the end, we are left with dark fears for Emily at the hands of either Craig or Lester.

It is difficult to tell whether Malkovich and Emily represent Paul's Christ or Paul and his followers. I am not sure, that is, who is ultimately puppet and puppeteer either in Paul or in *Being John Malkovich*. That, however, is precisely the point. As in *Donnie Darko*, the world collapses in this narcissistic gospel. We are John Malkovich. We are Paul's Christ. Lotte worries at one point: "What is this strange power that Malkovich exudes? All I think about is wanting to be him." We could say the same thing of Paul's Christ. Like Paul's Christ, Malkovich exudes promises of power and immortality. *Being John Malkovich* warns that the price of such immortality is narcissistic self-annihilation.

Interestingly, Lotte asks Dr. Lester the question quoted above. In response, he tells his tale of immortality and offers her a place in Malkovich, but her pursuit of Maxine—through the bizarre, amusing world of Malkovich's subconscious—leads her away from this opportunity (or catastrophe). Instead, in the denouement, she winds up happy in a lesbian, we suppose, relationship with Maxine. She also winds up more herself. As the movies teach us so frequently, perhaps our banal lives are not so bad after all. Perhaps we should consider Lotte, if not Craig, happy. That would take us beyond Paul. He would have us crucify the whole world (Gal 6:14) for our own salvation. If we consider Craig, not Craig/Malkovich, happy, that would take us beyond the movies, too.

Bearing Jesus' Death in the Body

According to his letters, Paul strives to turn his life and his ministry into a proclamation of his gospel. Accordingly, he boasts not of his success and "powers" but of his sufferings on behalf of Christ (2 Cor 3:7–6:10; 11:1–12:10). He and his associates are "always carrying in the body the death of Jesus" (2 Cor 4:10). Paul's life and the lives of his associates and followers are themselves public displays of the crucified. Probably neither 2 Cor 4:10 nor 2 Cor 12:7–9 indicates that Paul was stigmatic. Paul's idea of bearing the cross is more metaphorical. As he puts it at another point, his followers should be a "living sacrifice" (Rom 12:1).

The stigmata, of course, have been far more literal for mystics like Saint Francis. The movie *Stigmata* imagines a rather unconventional modern occurrence of these wounds of Christ. The movie begins with the separate stories of Frankie Paige, a young hairdresser, and Father Andrew Kiernan, scientific debunker of miracles for the Vatican. When Frankie receives a rosary originally belonging to Father Alameida, a deceased South American priest, from her mother, she begins to have frightening stigmatic attacks (nail holes in her wrists). Meanwhile, Father Andrew visits Father

Alameida's parish and finds an inexplicably bleeding statue of the Virgin Mary.[51] At the Vatican, Cardinal Houseman rejects Andrew's findings, saying that faith is based on the church, not on miracles.

Frankie and Andrew's stories come together when the cardinal sends Andrew to Pittsburgh to investigate Frankie after receiving a video from a local priest of her second stigmatic attack (the scourging). When Andrew meets Frankie, he rejects the possibility that she is a stigmatic because she is an atheist. After all, only the most devout have the stigmata, the five wounds of Jesus, a gift of God representing a battle with evil in the body. The nail holes in her wrists and a note written in a language unknown to her perplex him, however, and he continues to meet with Frankie, who has more stigmatic attacks (wounds from the crown of thorns, nail holes in her feet).

When she investigates the stigmata herself, she takes comfort from Christian art displaying the wounds in Christ's palms. In her mind, her wrist wounds prove that she is not really a stigmatic. Unfortunately, Andrew explains that Christian art is devotional, not accurate. In fact, the crucified Christ would likely himself have been nailed through the wrists. Then Father Delmonico, a scholarly friend of Andrew's at the Vatican, reports that Frankie's mysterious language is Aramaic. Furthermore, her words resemble a recently discovered first-century Aramaic gospel, which Delmonico believes may come from Jesus himself. Ominously, Delmonico warns Andrew that Cardinal Houseman has squelched work on this gospel. The cardinal wants to keep the gospel a secret because its message supports a mystic, personal religion—its kingdom is within the individual—not the institutional religion of Roman Catholicism.[52]

The tension heightens when this evil cardinal arrives to take over Frankie's case. While Andrew prays alone in a church, a mysterious visitor arrives who tells Andrew that he, Delmonico, and Alameida were the translators of the suppressed Gospel of Thomas and that Alameida was a stigmatic. Concluding that Alameida, not Christ, has possessed Frankie, Andrew rushes to save her. He arrives in time to stop Cardinal Houseman's murderous exorcism. He then proves his faith by walking through a supernatural fire and taking on Alameida's gospel mission. Satisfied, Alameida leaves Frankie after a final stigmatic attack. Andrew then carries Frankie into the garden past a statue of Saint Francis. As she recovers, birds land upon her so that she mirrors the statue. In the denouement, Andrew returns to Alameida's South American church and recovers the hidden Gospel of Thomas.

Stigmata is a stereotypical Hollywood treatment of religion. It focuses on individual religion while disparaging institutional religion as hopelessly corrupt and submerges traditional religion beneath modern heroism and romance. In short, *Stigmata* celebrates modern individualism. It does, however, strive to span the gap between secular modernity and tradition. Accordingly, its atheist has the stigmata and eventually "saves" a doubting priest. In short, modernity redeems that which is valuable in traditional religion.[53]

In light of Paul's gospel of death, however, the intriguing element in this movie is another common Hollywood device, that is, the relegation of religion to the genre of horror. In the hands of *Stigmata*, "carrying in the body the death of Jesus" becomes demonic possession and a death sentence.[54] Not incidentally, Scorsese's treatment of Jesus' relationship with God as a torment and Gibson's treatment of Christ's passion in *The Passion of the Christ* are also horrific. For these movies, the cross is a horror. It negates the world (Gal 6:14). Only Gibson suggests, like Paul, that it is somehow salvific for anyone else, and Gibson does so only by abandoning the cross for Catholic ritual (the flashbacks to the Eucharist).

Stigmata ultimately abandons the cross and apocalyptic death-gospels in a different way. *Stigmata* eschews the horror of possession and death for an affirmation of this life in the stereotypical Hollywood form of the romance. Instead of the death-cross, Andrew carries the recovering Frankie into a garden. *Stigmata* offers romance-love-sex as an attractive option to stigmata and death. Neither Paul, who thinks marriage an unfortunate encumbrance (1 Cor 7), nor Gibson explores this option. Perhaps this is why, even though all historians agree that Jesus was crucified nude, Gibson does not explore this aspect of his hero's humiliation. His Christ, like the Christ of most Christian art and almost all movies, remains strategically clothed.[55] Despite his sadistically in-depth exploration of Christ's suffering, Gibson's passion hero does not plumb the depths of shame involved in sexual humiliation.

I wonder, in fact, if Gibson's financial success and the failure of Scorsese's Jesus movie are not linked at precisely this point. Although he strategically avoids full frontal nudity, Scorsese films Christ nude on the cross. More daringly, he visualizes Christ's temptation to depart from the cross for a "normal" life of marriage and children. That climax threatens both the ascetic, crucified Western imagination and the model of the Hollywood passion hero. By contrast, Gibson is far too savvy to offer us a nude, sexual Christ.

Of course, Scorsese imagines this normal life only as a temptation. In fact, his Satan is an angelic young girl, typically the height of innocence in American and Hollywood mythology. By contrast, *Stigmata* affirms "normal" romance. Instead of death and evil ages, *Stigmata* offers us life in an idyllic garden. The traditional religious figures have become mere statues in the background.

This espousal of modern liberalism resembles imaginations like those in movies such as *Tender Mercies*. I am now using something like what I challenged in chapter 1 to counter Paul's apocalyptic gospel of death; nevertheless, I am not quite ready to extol the liberal Paul. What I would like to do is to leave various Pauls, including liberal and apocalyptic Pauls, in play against one another. If we can use an apocalyptic Paul to challenge liberal ideology, we can use liberal Pauls to counter apocalyptic death wishes. If we affirm only one, we are left unable to dispute either present culture or attempts to escape said culture. We need both liberal Pauls and apocalyptic Pauls to thwart that dilemma. Multiple Pauls, or the constant attempt to recognize that we interpret and construct, might be the best path toward whatever freedom from determinism, domination, and death is humanly possible.

Perhaps we simply choose life instead of death gospels (see Deut 30:15–20).[56] *The Big Lebowski* is a humorous expression of this point. In the midst of determinism (at least mysterious forces) and death, it manages to affirm life. A mysterious narrator tells the story of the Dude, Jeff Lebowski, who becomes embroiled in and gradually escapes various insane plots involving a millionaire, a kidnapping, and a nymphomaniac. In the midst of these absurd, chaotic plottings, Donny, one of the Dude's friends, dies in an inane conflict with a roving band of German nihilists. The hero of *The Big Lebowski* simply accepts this death as he does the rest of life. He does not expect to conquer, to escape, or to find some larger meaning. He is far too inept and too lazy. He simply "takes it easy" at his neighborhood bowling alley. The rambling narrator's last words[57] affirm his approach to life:

> The Dude abides. I don't know about you, but I take comfort in that. It's good knowing he's out there. The Dude. Taking her easy for all us sinners. Shush. I sure hope he makes the [bowling] finals. Well, that about does her. Wraps her all up. Things seemed to have worked out pretty good for the Dude and Walter. And it was a pretty good story. Don't you think? Made me laugh to beat the band. Parts anyway. I didn't like seeing Donny go. But then, I happen to know that there's a little Lebowski on the way. I guess that's the way the whole durn human comedy keeps perpetuating itself down through the generations.

Life goes on. This human comedy is the alternative to the determinism and death of apocalyptic gospels.

Of course, if we are going to live such lives, we will have to accept our own deaths, not that of Christ. *Barabbas* is quite instructive on this point. The protagonist lives while Jesus dies in his place. Barabbas is hardly thankful. He is angrily perplexed. He does not understand this event or his girlfriend's fascination with Jesus. Finally, after various debaucheries, he returns to his outlaw life only to be captured by the Romans again. Pilate, who represents the law, cannot condemn him to death. He has been "redeemed," so Pilate sentences Barabbas instead to the living death of the sulfur mines. Barabbas then descends into hell because, as he angrily observes, Christ has "taken his death." In fact, despite various near escapes and cruel Roman punishments, Barabbas lives while everyone around him dies. Christ has taken his death. His hellish life goes on and on. Eventually, as a gladiator in Rome, he is surrounded by Christians. He cannot escape them or the silent God who will not reveal himself clearly to Barabbas. Finally, Barabbas tries to set fire to Rome in order to bring in the apocalypse. All that he does is to bring himself and various Christians to their own deaths. As the movie ends, he finally dies *on his own cross*, entrusting himself to and embracing the dark, as God has never made himself known to Barabbas as light. In short, Barabbas is an object lesson in the folly of living someone else's life. He would be, and is, better off dying his own death rather than accepting someone else's (Christ's) voyeuristically and vicariously. To do so is to cheat oneself of all the life that is.

Notes

1. Richard Schreib, *"Flatliners,"* http://www.moria.co.nz/sf/flatliners.htm (accessed June 7, 2004).

2. Incidentally, *The Epic of Gilgamesh*, one of the oldest extant pieces of literature, makes the same point vis-à-vis death.

3. Materialist philosophers either reject Paul on this point, as Nietzsche did (*The Antichrist*, 42–43, 47), or construct a Paul that does not reject the world and does not obsessively concentrate on death, as Badiou does (*Saint Paul*, 65–74). For the politicians, the useful Paul opposes sociopolitical structures, not cosmological or biological ones. See Taubes, *The Political Theology of Paul*, 58–60. It is not so easy to compartmentalize ancient apocalyptic. There, the entire cosmos comes undone before, or if, it is remade. The whole of creation, not just the social world, needs redemption (compare Rom 8:18–39). See chapter 1.

4. Martin Hengel, *Crucifixion: In the Ancient World and the Folly of the Cross*, trans. John Bowden (Philadelphia: Fortress, 1977), has an extremely helpful review of ancient attitudes about the shameful slave death of crucifixion. In fact, he contends that a gospel proclaiming "the utterly vile death of the cross" is closer to madness (*mania*) than to folly (*mōria*) in antiquity (ibid., xi–xii, 83).

5. We have discussed the resurrection or, at least, Paul's apocalyptic and visionary quality in chapters 1–2. If we take Paul at his word, apocalypse also precedes (the understanding of) the cross for him.

6. Gibson borrows from all the canonical gospels, but he relies most heavily on John. Beyond the passion narrative, Gibson offers a few flashbacks to the ministry and a brief, stigmatic resurrection scene.

7. Roger Ebert, *"The Passion of the Christ"* (February 24, 2004), http://www.suntimes.com/ebert/ebert_reviews/2004/02/022401.html (accessed May 17, 2004). Other reviewers agree. David Edelstein calls the movie "The Jesus Chain Saw Massacre" (quoted in Deborah Hornblow, "The Cash-In of the Christ," *The Fayetteville Observer*, April 2, 2004, E1); and John Petrakis labels it "the *Kill Bill* of Jesus movies ("*The Passion of the Christ*," *The Christian Century* 121.6 [March 23, 2004]: 40). Peter Travers says that Caviezel, the actor playing Christ, "doesn't so much give a performance as offer himself up as raw meat" ("*The Passion of the Christ*," *Rolling Stone* [February 23, 2004], http://www.rollingstone.com/reviews/movie?id=5949551&pageid=rs.ReviewsMovieArchive&pageregion=mainRegion [accessed May 17, 2004]). Not surprisingly, many reviewers cautioned parents about taking their children to the movie.

8. Hengel, *Crucifixion*, 25, observes that the gospel passion narratives have more details than other ancient references to such deaths.

9. The crucifixion entered Christian art late. There is a mocking second-century graffito that shows an ass-headed man on a cross with the inscription "Alexander worships God." See Crossan and Reed, *In Search of Paul*, 367–68. Otherwise, the oldest portrayal of Christ on the cross comes from the fourth century (after Constantine's vision), and such depictions were not popular until the sixth century. Artists began portraying dead Christs on the cross only in the twelfth century. See Roland H. Bainton, *Behold the Christ: A Portrayal in Words and Pictures* (New York: Harper & Row, 1976), 144–57.

10. Hengel, *Crucifixion*, 51–63, says ancients saw it primarily as the "slave's punishment." Robert Jewett, *Saint Paul Returns to the Movies*, 123–35, nicely articulates the "shameful" qualities of the cross.

11. See Hengel, *Crucifixion*, 88. Paul frequently joins his sufferings with those of Christ both as part of the end of this apocalyptic age and as ethical example. For example, see the parallel structure of humiliation/glorification in Christ's life in Phil 2:5–11 and in Paul's life in Phil 3:4–16. There is, of course, a long-standing debate in Pauline interpretation about Christ's death. Does Paul think it saves as a sacrifice on our behalf (Rom 3:21–26), or does it save as we participate in it (Rom 6:1–4)? See David G. Horrell, *An Introduction to the Study of Paul* (London: T & T Clark, 2000), 57–59. For Žižek, *The Puppet and the Dwarf*, 98–115, the distinction is a false choice. Death appears as sacrifice under the "horizon of the law" and as participation from the perspective of love.

12. Gibson made his acting career writing suffering upon his body from the hero of *Mad Max* and *Lethal Weapon* to that of *Braveheart*. As a reviewer for the *New York Times* wittily remarked, Gibson prepared

for the role of the heroically suffering Christ his entire career. Unfortunately, the role came too late, and he was too old. As a result, Jim Caviezel stands in for Mel Gibson who is standing in as Wallace, a latter-day Christ.

13. Like John's passion, the suffering in *The Passion of the Christ* "lifts" its hero "up," exalts him, and glorifies him.

14. Petrakis, "*The Passion of the Christ*," 40.

15. Gibson is not documenting a real crucifixion. He visualizes the Western imagination of the crucifixion, so he nails his Christ through the palms, not the wrists. When the female stigmatic in *Stigmata* wonders why Christian art is "wrong" on this point, her mentor priest instructs her on the power of art on Christian imagination.

16. Martin Hengel, *The Atonement: The Origins of the Doctrine in the New Testament*, trans. John Bowden (Philadelphia: Fortress, 1981), 54, 65, claims that Paul does not explain the atonement because it is not a controversial datum in early Christianity. As already mentioned, the main debate in Pauline interpretation is between sacrificial and participatory ideas. See n. 11. Wright, *The Climax of the Covenant*, 18–40, argues, relying on Rom 5:12–21, that Paul sees the cross primarily in terms of an obedience that fulfills the covenant, a matter that disobedient Adam and Israel did not realize. Seeley, *The Noble Death*, 13–17, 83–112, also argues for obedience—but the obedience of the martyrs—as the background for Paul's understanding of the cross. Broadly speaking, both of their views are participatory.

17. Given the apocalyptic character of Paul's letters, many recent scholars interpret the righteousness of God in apocalyptic terms (see *pephanerotai* in Rom 3:21) rather than in forensic categories, or in terms of his faithfulness to his covenant (see Rom 9–11). These ideas have been popular since Ernst Käsemann, *New Testament Questions of Today*, trans. W. J. Montague (Philadelphia: Fortress, 1969), 168–82. Despite the legal imagery in Rom 3:21–26, the covenant and the apocalyptic categories are a more likely background for Paul's apocalyptic cross. I am concerned here, however, with Paul's dominant interpretation in the legalistic West and with Gibson's film.

18. Recent scholars have suggested other centers of Pauline thought. Given the occasional nature of Paul's letters, others doubt that we can talk meaningfully about the center of Paul's thought at all. See Victor Paul Furnish, "Pauline Studies," in Epp and MacRae, eds., *The New Testament and Its Modern Interpreters*, 333–36.

19. Žižek, *The Puppet and the Dwarf*, 15, refers to such sin and redemption ideas as "the perverse core of Christianity."

20. In Barthes's terminology (*Mythologies*, 109–59), this "fact" is a Western myth, neither a fact nor a politicized interpretation. We can politicize it by observing that the crucifixion needs to be "just" only for the "legal" form that Western imperial Christianity took. Tertullian, the first great Latin Christian writer, was a lawyer. The first Christian churches in the West were basilicas, renovations of or replicas of Roman law courts. Accordingly, scholars often characterize Latin or Roman Christianity as moral or legalistic when comparing it to other early Christianities. Perhaps this tone built upon the Stoicism that was so popular in the Roman Empire. In this connection, the popularity of Pelagius in Rome is worth remembering. Eastern Christianity follows different paths. Moreover, the New Testament documents themselves hardly speak uniformly on this point. Paul never uses the notion of "forgiveness," although he does speak about "reconciliation" (e.g., Rom 5:1–11; 2 Cor 5:18–21). Paul's notion of the cross lies somewhere between apocalypse (the death of the obedient martyrs belongs here as well) and the mystery cults. Mark's cross opens the apocalypse. Luke's is the Jewish murder of the innocent one. Matthew's has to do with sin, forgiveness, obedience, and law (read "Torah"). John's cross is the passion hero's triumph, his glorification, an overcoming of death, not unlike the understanding of salvation in Orthodox Christianities. John's understanding of the cross is most similar to Hollywood versions of the passion hero.

21. This "solution precedes plight" interpretation has been common in Pauline studies since E. P. Sanders, *Paul and Palestinian Judaism: A Comparison of Patterns of Religion* (Philadelphia: Fortress, 1977),

474–511. See chapter 4 for more discussion. Those disputing Sanders's notion do so by moving even further than he does from individualistic and legalistic interpretations. Wright, *The Climax of the Covenant*, 258–67, rejects this formulation in favor of understanding exile as the deep background (or plight) behind Paul's thought. Roetzel, *Paul*, 65–67, thinks that Hellenistic religious alienation is the deep background.

22. Eastwood's role in *Unforgiven* contrasts dramatically with his similar roles in *High Plains Drifter* and *Pale Rider*. While all three movies set an "outlaw" over against corrupt orders and lawmen, *Unforgiven* abandons the heroic presentation of just, violent vengeance (but see Jewett, *Saint Paul Returns to the Movies*, 147–62, for a completely different reading). In fact, one of the most intriguing features of *Unforgiven* is its play with the Western myth. On one hand, a dime novelist character transforms outlaws into mythic figures throughout the movie, but the movie relentlessly unmasks these heroes. Little Bill's triumph over English Bob is crucial to this aspect of the movie. On the other hand, Will, who constantly denies that he is anything but an ordinary fellow, finally rises to a legendary level beyond even the rumors about him. Nevertheless, he hardly becomes heroic even here. He remains a villain.

23. Interestingly, Žižek, *The Puppet and the Dwarf*, 6, 169–71, thinks that a materialist approach reveals the core of Christianity to be the loss of hope in the Big Other (which is, not incidentally, the goal of psychoanalysis).

24. Berger, *The Sacred Canopy*, 72–75, observes that the notion of sin takes God "off the hook" by putting humans "on the hook." Anthropodicy replaces theodicy.

25. James Berardinelli, "*The Passion of the Christ*," http://movie-reviews.colossus.net/movies/p/passion_christ.html (accessed May 17, 2004). By the way, Gibson includes himself in this indictment. In the movie, his hands hold the nails that are hammered into Christ's hands at the crucifixion.

26. Travers, "*The Passion of the Christ*."

27. Stephen D. Moore, *God's Gym: Divine Male Bodies of the Bible* (New York: Routledge, 1996), inspired by Foucault, provides a helpful critique of this divine quest for power and the spectacles that ensue. Anselm's *Cur Deus Homo* makes horrific reading on this point as well.

28. This transfers Boer's claims in "Non-Sense" from Paul to Paul's God. Of course, Paul's God is his own religious, aesthetic creation. Boer also claims that psychosis is the center of Christianity (ibid., 154).

29. Miles, *God: A Biography*, 325–29, 402–6.

30. Miles discusses Christ's death as "suicidal" at length (*Christ*, 160–78). His Christ deliberately provokes murderous hostility against himself. Compare Luke 4:16–30.

31. Ibid., 244, 313 n. 247.

32. Ibid., 207.

33. See Nietzsche, *The Gay Science*, 131. Camus, *The Myth of Sisyphus*, 28–50, famously describes religion as philosophical suicide, the deification of the absurd.

34. Camus, *The Myth of Sisyphus*, 93–118. Camus' absurd creator ultimately abandons "divine fables" for the "terrestrial face," for "myths with no other depth than that of human suffering" (ibid., 117–18). Although Žižek critiques Camus as "outdated," his own materialist reinterpretation of Christianity sounds like Camus at this point. See his *On Belief*, 148–51. A later book by Morrow, the third of what became a trilogy dealing with the death of God, *The Eternal Footman*, commits itself to human creation even more decisively. Its story focuses on the artist chosen to create God's sepulcher.

35. Joseph Campbell's studies of myth generally came to this point. The myths, or his modernizing interpretation of them, awaken us to the hero within us all. See, for example, *The Hero with a Thousand Faces* (Princeton: Princeton University Press, 1972).

36. This supernatural "sight" provides another parallel to Shyamalan's *The Sixth Sense*.

37. Reportedly, Shyamalan considered this phrase as a title for the film.

38. Submerged in a pool, he rises to superhero status. The similarity to Paul's "phone-booth baptism" is surely coincidental.

39. Incidentally, that his name is David and his son's name is Joseph only reinforces these messianic allusions.

40. See Walsh, *Reading the Gospels in the Dark*, 38–39.

41. The abandonment of responsibility is the issue that *Monty Python's Life of Brian* explores with its messiah-making theme.

42. One could, of course, explore a rather unholy connection to the Dracula movies here. See Tina Pippin, "Of Gods and Demons: Blood Sacrifice and Eternal Life in *Dracula* and the Apocalypse of John," in Aichele and Walsh, *Screening Scripture*, 24–41. Larry Kreitzer, "The Scandal of the Cross: Crucifixion Imagery and Bram Stoker's *Dracula*," in George Aichele and Tina Pippin, eds., *The Monstrous and the Unspeakable: The Bible as Fantastic Literature* (Sheffield: Sheffield Academic, 1997), 181–219, connects *Dracula* and Paul's cross specifically.

43. This passage presents several famous exegetical problems. Does Paul speak of himself, of humans generally, of Adam, or of some combination of these? Does Paul speak of his or humanity's pre-Christian or Christian experience? How does this passage relate to the robust, confident attitude that Paul expresses toward the law in Phil 3:4–7?

44. See Stendahl, "The Apostle Paul and the Introspective Conscience of the West," 78–96. While I used Stendahl's work in chapter 1 to critique the modern, liberal Paul, I am now concerned with Paul as precursor of modern individualism, not as an apocalyptic stranger to modernity. Stendahl's Paul may be more historically compelling than the Augustine-Luther-Bultmann Paul, but the Paul of Augustine-Luther-Bultmann is arguably more historically significant than that of Stendahl. More importantly, both Pauls are only interpretative constructs, and such constructs—not some hypothetical, historical Paul— are my concern here.

45. I have carefully extracted the quotes from Rom 7 above to avoid reference to "the law" (at least the "law" as Torah). The role of Torah in light of Paul's "in Christ" gospel is Paul's major concern in Rom 7, as Stendahl has shown. Paul turns Torah into an advance guard for his "in Christ" apocalypse as he also does in Gal 3:1–5:1. In the modern individualism of which Paul is forerunner, "law" becomes a guilty conscience. Larry Kreitzer, *The New Testament in Fiction and Film: On Reversing the Hermeneutical Flow* (Sheffield: Sheffield Academic, 1993), 88–126, nicely relates Rom 7:7–25 to modern moral dilemmas by comparing the passage to Stevenson's *Strange Case of Dr. Jekyll and Mr. Hyde* and to various film versions of that story. I have compared Paul's fragmentation to superhero stories, but Kreitzer's essay pushes the comparison toward horror films. In that case, the "normal guy" guise covers an evil monster, serial killer, and so on. Superhero films also flirt with the darkness within as well. The hero frequently likes the power or the darkness that his alias provides him. The Batman comics and films are among the best examples of this trope.

46. It is curiously appropriate, then, that scholars are not sure whether Rom 5:1 should read "we have peace with God" or "let us have peace with God."

47. See Castelli, *Imitating Paul*.

48. Here, Paul becomes precursor of almost every modern novel and film. Their protagonists are almost always "out of place" and looking for acceptance or self-realization. Peter Weir films are excellent examples of movies that deal with such out-of-place individuals. Roetzel, *Paul*, 1–3, describes Paul's own life as caught between various cultural commitments. That tension is, of course, not quite the modern split between private selves and public personas.

49. The time limit creates interesting and amusing plot situations, and it also suggests Andy Warhol's dictum that in the future everyone will have fifteen minutes of fame.

50. The movie plays in amusing ways with the notion of personal identity. As Craig takes over, Malkovich fears that he is going insane. He then stalks Maxine to find out what is going on and discovers their "Being John Malkovich" enterprise. Craig tells him that it is only a simulation, but Malkovich learns the truth when he takes the trip himself. Inside his own head, he discovers a solipsistic world composed entirely of Malkoviches.

51. The movie suggests with music and images that Frankie is a new Mary. When we first see Frankie, as she goes out for a night on the town, the background music is "Whatever Happened to Mary?" Soon after her first stigmatic attack, she has a vision of a woman in blue carrying a baby in red that she drops in traffic. Religious art often shows Mary, of course, in a blue cloak. Not surprisingly, Frankie rushes into traffic to save the baby (Jesus). After her second attack, Frankie arrives at work in her own blue cloak. Later, we find out that Frankie does indeed bear the gospel, if not Jesus.

52. *Stigmata* quotes passages from the Gospel of Thomas, a Coptic gospel variously dated by scholars from the mid-first to the late second century. The church has not suppressed it. It is widely available, even online.

53. Frankie's rushing into traffic to rescue the baby (Jesus) is emblematic of the movie's thrust. For complaints about the movie's treatment of Catholicism, see Roger Ebert, "*Stigmata*," http://www.suntimes.com/cgi-bin/print.cig (accessed June 21, 2004). By contrast, James Berardinelli finds the movie "almost relevant." See "*Stigmata*," http://movie-reviews.colossus.net/movies/s/stigmata.html (accessed June 21, 2004).

54. To the contrary, Ebert, "*Stigmata*," contends, "It is not a dark and fearsome thing to be bathed in the blood of the lamb." Given his comments on *The Passion of the Christ*, he may have changed his mind.

55. The crucifixion that is part of the passion facade of Gaudi's *La Sagrada Familia* in Barcelona is a notable exception. There is already some discussion about what the Roman Catholic Church will do with this nude Christ when the completed church becomes its property. For photos, see http://www.photoguide.to/barcelona/sagradafamilia.html.

56. If this suggestion comes too close to an uncritical endorsement of modernity, we need only return to apocalyptic rebels or watch a movie like *Trainspotting*. Opening and closing narrations in that movie assert that the hero and we should "choose [middle-class] life." The hero is hardly convinced, however, and the narration and the movie ultimately compare the addictions of drug use and middle-class life. By the end of the movie, neither lifestyle seems a choice for life.

57. Comically, the narrator loses his place on occasion. This ineffectuality raises questions about any overarching providence. James Berardinelli, "*The Big Lebowski*," http://movie-reviews.colossus.net/movies/b/big_lebowski.html (accessed June 21, 2004), cites this mockery of the voiceover as one of the most entertaining features of the film.

Chapter 4

The Problem with Grace: Anti-Semites and Paul, the Jew

Just as you were once disobedient to God but have now received mercy because of their disobedience, so they have now been disobedient in order that, by the mercy shown to you, they too may now receive mercy. For God has imprisoned all in disobedience so that he may be merciful to all.

O the depth of the riches and wisdom and knowledge of God! How unsearchable are his judgments and how inscrutable his ways!

"For who has known the mind of the Lord? Or who has been his counselor?"

"Or who has given a gift to him, to receive a gift in return?" (Rom 11:30–35)

For Christ is the end of the law so that there may be righteousness for everyone who believes. (Rom 10:4)

For the whole law is summed up in a single commandment, "You shall love your neighbor as yourself." . . . *Bear one another's burdens, and in this way you will fulfill the law of Christ.* (Gal 5:14; 6:2)

The Problem(s) of Grace

In chapter 1, we considered grace as both the inclusion of the Gentiles and the apocalyptic disruption of the world. Grace, then, is an abandonment of social norms or the law in its broadest sense, as discourse or world.[1] As such, grace presents two insurmountable problems. It is indefensible intellectually by any standard of justice, and it is useless in terms of establishing the norms for a community. These two difficulties are evident in Paul's inability to provide a theodicy for grace and in his abandonment of grace so that he might rule his "in Christ" communities. Furthermore,

109

as has become uncomfortably public in post-Holocaust interpretation, previous interpreters of Paul have often used the notion of grace to vent their anti-Semitic spleen. Given these problems, it might be salutary to reconsider the Judaizers whom Paul vilifies, to recover Paul's own Jewishness, or, at the very least, to affirm the human need for order.

Justifying Grace

Religion begins with hierophany, or with myth if one is an outsider. Religion sustains itself by inculcating a tradition. Religion defends itself against anomalies, data that contradict the tradition, through theodicy. Most often, these anomalies are experiences of evil. Accordingly, various intellectual and practical attempts to deal with the problem of evil litter the history of religion. Milton and Dostoevsky wrote voluminously on the topic. Voltaire wrote a memorable satire against the most popular theodicy of his day. The Holocaust has generated a plethora of theodicies in recent times. In the West, however, Job remains the classic theodicy.

As the story goes, Job, a righteous man, has all the goods of life. Unbeknownst to Job, however, an adversary in a heavenly court makes him a pawn in a cosmic game with God, a game played to determine whether disinterested righteousness exists, whether anyone, that is, "fear[s] God for nought" (Job 1:9 KJV). In the game, Job loses everything but his life. As he remains faithful to God, cursing his life but never his God, he appears to be disinterestedly righteous. In short, Job suffers in order to prove God's point that at least one man "fear[s] God for nought." Thereafter, the adversary vanishes from the story.

Job's friends sit with him in silence for a week. After Job's curse, a prayer for the release of death, his friends beg him repeatedly to repent of some sin, perhaps even one unknown to him, so that his "punishments" may cease. Job refuses and demands an audience with the judge of the whole earth. Instead, he receives a terrifying audience with the creator.[2] Refusing to trifle with Job's petty life and complaints, this creator bellows out his sovereign claims. Facing this inscrutable, cantankerous creator, and in fear for his life, Job repents. Thereafter, the creator returns the goods of Job's life.

Unfortunately, this repentance and the return of Job's "goods" leave the adversary's original question about disinterested righteousness in doubt. More important, Job's pursuit of justice also goes unanswered. In the face of the whirlwind, Job drops his questions to preserve his life. This is a sensible course of action to be sure, as the creator clearly does not deign to answer his questions. The result is a blatant assertion of divine sovereignty. Accordingly, Job never learns what the readers of Job know from the beginning, that he is a mere pawn in a game of cosmic chess. At the story's end, Job remains ignorant both of the creator's secret ways and of the powers that rule his life. If the whirlwind is a theophany, it reveals little.

Job leaves many modern readers aghast. To deal with its affront, modern schol-ars often claim that Job's repentance is ironic or that the book is about piety, not theodicy.[3] Certainly, the book's statement of its own question—"Doth Job fear God for nought?" (Job 1:9 KJV)—supports the latter interpretation; nevertheless, an exclusive focus on piety or faith obscures the fact that such faith, that is, the submis-sion to God evident in Job's repentance, is itself Job's theodicy. Repentance enables Job to live despite the overwhelming presence of inscrutable, wrathful sovereignty.

In Peter Berger's sociological analysis of theodicies, Job's submission reveals an element fundamental to all theodicies and, in fact, to all social orders.[4]

> There is a fundamental attitude, in itself quite irrational, that underlies all of them [theodicies]. This attitude is the surrender of self to the ordering power of society. Put differently, every nomos [a socially constructed, mean-ingful order] entails a transcendence of individuality and thus, *ipso facto*, implies a theodicy.[5]

Berger describes this masochistic attitude as "the intoxication of surrender to an other."[6] Therein, the self becomes nothing, the other becomes everything, and the self finds its bliss in this sadomasochistic pact. True to form, then, Job becomes nothing, or of "small account" (Job 40:4), as he recognizes the transcendent other as the Almighty (Job 40:2). Job's repentance—"Wherefore I abhor myself, and repent in dust and ashes" (Job 42:6 KJV)—condenses and internalizes this masochism.[7] As the masochistic theodicy par excellence,[8] Job abandons reason and ultimately aban-dons the intellectual question of theodicy altogether:

> In other words, the problem of theodicy is solved by an *argumentum ad hominem* in the most drastic sense—more accurately, an *argumentum contra hominem*. The implicit accusation against God is turned around to become an explicit accu-sation against man. In this curious reversal the problem of theodicy is made to disappear and in its turn appears a problem of anthropodicy (or *iustifica-tio*, to use a later Christian term). The question of human sin replaces the question of divine justice.[9]

What Job repents of, then, is of little moment. What is important is that the focus shifts from the possible injustice of God to human culpability. The linchpin in this move is, of course, the overwhelming whirlwind. That overwhelming brutality moves Job from a quest for justice to whimpering repentance.[10]

Paul has a similar transformation via apocalypse (see Gal 1:11–17). While we have looked at the implications of Paul's apocalypse before, Job reminds us of apocalypse's reduction of humans to "small account." Paul's point in Gal 1–2 is the divine origin of this gospel and mission, but that origin derogates the human.

> For I want you to know, brothers and sisters, that the gospel that was pro-claimed by me *is not of human origin*; for I *did not receive it from a human source*, nor was I taught it, but I received it through a revelation of Jesus Christ. (Gal 1:11–12, emphasis added; see also Gal 1:16–17)

As Paul says, he is clearly not trying to please people (see Gal 1:10). The apocalyptic vision overwhelms and trumps the human. Paul returns again and again to this apocalyptic belittling of the human. He sounds the same themes in another defensive description of his mission.

> From now on, therefore, we *regard no one from a human point of view*; even though we once knew Christ from a human point of view, we know him no longer in that way. So if anyone is in Christ, there is a new creation: everything old has passed away; see, everything has become new! *All this is from God*, who reconciled us to himself through Christ, and has given us the ministry of reconciliation; that is, in Christ God was reconciling the world to himself, not counting their trespasses against them, and entrusting the message of reconciliation to us. So we are ambassadors for Christ, since God is making his appeal through us; we entreat you on behalf of Christ, be reconciled to God. For our sake he made him to be sin who knew no sin, so that in him we might become the righteousness of God. (2 Cor 5:16–21, emphasis added)

The apocalypse, or "new creation," arrives at the expense of the human, even the human Christ.

Moreover, this passage makes it inescapably clear that the cost of God's righteousness here, as it was in Job's whirlwind, is the loss of innocence. The book of Job is quite clear on Job's innocence. He is just an unlucky pawn. Further, no one ever successfully disputes his claim to innocence. All anyone ever does is assert God's sovereignty against Job's protests. Paul is more concise on the innocence of the sacrificed Christ: he knew no sin. But God "made him to be sin" (2 Cor 5:21). According to Berger, the suffering, incarnate Christ mitigates Job's masochism somewhat because Christ intercedes between the sovereign God and the suffering human (for example, Job). Nonetheless, as Christ suffers for sinners, not for the innocent, the masochism remains:

> Again, the problem of theodicy is translated into the problem of anthropodicy. . . . God suffers in Christ. But Christ's suffering does not justify God, but man. Through Christ the terrible otherness of the Yahweh of the thunderstorms is mellowed. At the same time, because the contemplation of Christ's suffering deepens the conviction of man's unworthiness, the old masochistic surrender is allowed to repeat itself in a more refined, not to say sophisti-

cated, manner. We would contend that the fundamental religious motorics of Christianity cannot be understood if one does not understand this and that, furthermore, the plausibility of Christianity (at least in its major orthodox forms) stands or falls with the plausibility of this theodicy.[11]

All of this is implicit in 2 Cor 5:16–21, but Paul makes the same move in excruciating detail in Rom 1–3. To open Romans, Paul describes his gospel as the revelation of God's righteousness (Rom 1:16–17). Paul then makes the standard monotheistic move from theodicy to anthropodicy by embarking upon a discussion of human sinfulness (1:18–3:20).[12] To take God off the hook, like the author of Job, he puts humans on the hook. Compared to God's glory, then, humans fall short (Rom 3:20). To save their miserable lives from the all-embracing wrath of God (Rom 1:18; 5:9), they must submit or have faith, the Pauline equivalent of Job's repentance. No wonder, then, that the saved have no grounds for boasting (Rom 3:27–31). Once again, humans are of small account and God is almighty.

While Paul begins his theodicy in Romans with a declaration of the ubiquity of human sinfulness and then moves to Christ's obedient sacrifice as the gracious divine response to that problem, Paul's own report of his apocalyptic transformation suggests that the vision of the crucified antedates his awareness of human sinfulness (Gal 1–2).[13] One thinks also of the robust conscience that Paul claims he had before he knew Christ (Phil 3:4–11). In short, Paul knows God's act in Christ before he knows the human predicament. As a result, God's act—whirlwind, apocalypse, or grace—makes humans sinful. Grace does not respond to some human predicament other than helplessness before an inscrutable, irascible deity. In short, grace is the problem, not the solution. It is chaotic and world-disruptive (see chapter 1). It wreaks havoc with reason and with justice.

Like the book of Job, Paul departs dramatically from reason. He leaves reason behind as he moves from theodicy, his stated topic, to anthropodicy. Not surprisingly, readers, like C. H. Dodd, have found Romans's logic tortured. Dodd disagrees with Paul frequently, but his main problem with Paul's argument is Paul's attempt to hold on to what Dodd sees as the incompatible ideas of (1) the privileged status of Israel and (2) monotheism. Most of Rom 1–2 does not trouble him. Dodd becomes alarmed by Paul's lack of logic first in his discussion of Rom 3:1–8, a passage that he calls obscure and feeble.[14] Others have been even less confident about the successfulness of Paul's argument about the ubiquity of sin. In particular, Rom 2:10, 14–15, 26 undercuts Rom 3:20 significantly. Paul, then, does not reasonably prove the ubiquity of human sinfulness. He merely assumes it in light of an apocalypse not unlike Job's whirlwind. He needs to deprave humans, as all theodicies do, in order to advance his gospel of divine righteousness.

Paul's theodicy has been dramatically effective. It has successfully convinced most Western Christians of their inherent sinfulness. In fact, that guilt is a cornerstone of the traditional Protestant reading of Romans as the theological statement of the individual's salvation by grace. Of course, Stendahl has nicely shown that Romans is not about individual salvation, but about God's righteousness vis-à-vis Israel.[15] What is becoming clearer as we read Paul with Job is that the basic problem of theodicy for Paul in Romans is grace, not evil. Romans is not about the justification of the individual. It is about the justification of grace, that is, the inclusion of the Gentiles and the resulting betrayal of Israel.

Like a tax cut, grace is a delightful idea as long as you are its beneficiary. If someone else is the beneficiary, you may worry that their largess comes at your expense. Moreover, as we saw in the analysis of the ending of *Places in the Heart*, we do not want those who have offended or victimized us to "get off scot-free." As recent international events have shown, we are more likely to kill the innocent in righteous anger than we are to forbear vengeance. Jonah, various psalms crying out for vengeance, and the parable of the vineyard workers (Matt 20:1–16) all testify to the problem that grace presents for those outside its beneficence.

Accordingly, Berger's analysis of theodicies deals with theodicies of happiness as well as of suffering.

> One of the very important social functions of theodicies is, indeed, their explanation of the socially prevailing inequalities of power and privilege. In this function, of course, theodicies directly legitimate the particular institutional order in question. It is important to stress in this connection that such theodices may serve as legitimations *both* for the powerful *and* the powerless, for the privileged *and* for the deprived. For the latter, of course, they may serve as "opiates" to make their situation less intolerable, and by the same token to prevent them from rebelling against it. For the former, however, they may serve as subjectively quite important justifications of their enjoyment of the power and privilege of their social position. Put simply, theodicies provide the poor with a meaning for their poverty, but may also provide the rich with a meaning for their wealth. . . . It is, of course, another question whether the *same* theodicy can serve both groups in this way. If so, the theodicy constitutes an essentially sado-masochistic collusion, on the level of meaning, between oppressors and victims—a phenomenon that is far from rare in history.[16]

Job responds to the problem of suffering. Paul and his Protestant interpreters respond to the problem of grace. Like Job, Paul turns from theodicy to anthropodicy to answer the question. As a result, Paul's grace is as masochistic as Job's tormented repentance. It is masochistic, that is, if we consider how the notion belittles humans before God. It is sadistic if we consider how it has belittled some (for example, the Jews) so that others might be elevated.[17]

In short, someone profits from the transactions taking place in Job and in Romans. Of course, if such grace ensures our position of privilege, we are unlikely to complain. If we leave God's reputation aside, the clear winners are Job, Paul, and his followers. God returns Job's goods. Paul and his followers share God's righteousness. The losers are Job's family; Christ, whose loss is obscured by Paul's resurrection of him as a totem; and the Jews. Accordingly, in Romans, Paul struggles with the problem of God's justice vis-à-vis Israel. We should be clear. It is not human sin or Christ's death that causes this problem. The real culprit is grace.[18] In particular, the problem is the inclusion of the Gentiles at the expense of the Jews. In Romans, that is, Paul desperately explains the privilege of the Gentiles "in Christ."

To deal with the question, Paul interweaves several points in Rom 9–11. He redefines Israel as the chosen, even if this means a remnant within Israel (Rom 9:6–13).[19] He asserts that the sovereign God has the right to choose whom he will, even Gentiles (9:14–29). He claims disobedient Israel deserves her exclusion (Rom 9:30–10:21). He observes that the chosen, however, always includes a remnant from among Israel (Rom 11:1–10). Finally, in a dramatic rewriting of prophecy, Paul claims that the fall of Israel is part of God's plan of salvation (Rom 11:11–32).[20] The prophets often assumed that Israel's fall (judgment) would bring about the judgment of the nations that would usher in Israel's salvation. Instead, Paul avers that the salvation of the nations precedes and instigates the salvation of Israel.

Paul thinks that he plays a major role in this plan and, thus, the salvation of Israel. So far, of course, he has not been proven right unless one redefines Israel yet again (in increasingly spiritual terms so that it becomes Christianity) or accepts the formation of the modern state of Israel as the denouement of Paul's hopes. What has happened, of course, is that Israel has paid for Paul's doxology (Rom 11:33–36, which includes, by the way, references to Job). First, Paul abandons reason and redefines Israel in a bewildering number of ways. He also unhelpfully resorts to "mystery" at a crucial moment (Rom 11:25) and to the inscrutable wisdom of God at another (Rom 11:33–34). No wonder, then, that scholars cannot agree on who and what the "all Israel" saved in Rom 11:26 is. Second, Paul stands in for Job's whirlwind and tells Israel to shut up and repent and hope that God will work it out better in the future. No wonder, then, that Paul does so much whining about his people (Rom 9:2–3; 10:1). He has betrayed them. He has decided that they should take Job's place on the dung heap.[21]

If we can sing doxologies in the face of that, then there is "by no means" any "injustice on God's part" (Rom 9:14). If we accept that, of course, we have accepted Paul's Jobian call for sadomasochistic submission to the sovereignty of God. We are all sinful and of small account (Rom 11:32, Paul's most concise statement of his theodicy), and God is almighty (Rom 11:33–36). We have also accepted, of course, the exclusion of Israel. Whatever Paul's own intentions about the salvation of Israel, Israel's exclusion is one of the consequences of the success of Romans as a theodicy.[22] We accept its God and the privileged place provided by that God's grace, at the cost of innocents.[23]

Forsaking the Evils of Theodicy

At this cost, maybe we should simply forgo theodicy altogether. As Tilley observes, theodicy "disguises real evils while those evils continue to afflict people."[24] Most importantly, theodicies obscure the structural evil of the societies they serve.[25] In the case of Romans, its theodicy obscures the privileged position that Paul's Christians hold at the expense of Israel or that the graced hold at the expense of Christ and the excluded. Moreover, it attributes that privilege and exclusion to the mysterious sovereignty of God (Rom 9:14–29). In the process, their status becomes unimpeachable. Perhaps we should imagine other stories, stories that deal with evil less triumphantly. After all, "victory over Evil may be impossible for us."[26] *Jakob the Liar* is such a story.

Like the protagonist of *Life is Beautiful*, Jakob deals with the horrors of the Holocaust through his sense of humor. In an opening voiceover, Jakob tells a joke:

Hitler goes to a fortune-teller and asks, "When will I die?" And the fortune-teller replies: "On a Jewish holiday." Hitler then asks, "How do you know that?" And she replies, "Any day you die will be a Jewish holiday."

Then, as we see Jakob sitting in the ghetto, he says,

So you ask me as a Jew, "How could you tell a joke like that at a time like that?" That's how we survived. And those were some of the things that kept us going. Everything else the Germans had taken. They built high walls covered in barbed wire to shut us in the ghetto. We were isolated from the rest of the world for years without any news. So we relied on the little things. A dark joke. A sunny day. A hopeful rumor.[27]

This dark joke, however, is largely on Jakob. A newspaper drifts by on the wind, and, desperate for news, he chases it until a disembodied voice tells him to report to the Commandant for breaking curfew, even though curfew has not yet begun. In the Commandant's office, as Jakob explains the joke the guard must be playing on him, he hears a radio broadcast about a Russian victory a mere 400 kilometers away. After curfew, the Commandant sends him home without a pass, in effect, a death sentence. Jakob makes it home safely, however, and along the way picks up a young girl, Lina, whose family spirited her off one of the trains en route to the camps.

The next day, on the work gang, Jakob tells his friend Mischa about the radio broadcast in order to stop him from trying to escape. Thereafter, word spreads through the ghetto that Jakob has a radio, and he makes up stories to satisfy those who press him for news. Unfortunately, one of Jakob's friends is shot when he tries to spread Jakob's "news" to people on a train to the camps. Distressed, Jakob tells an old man the truth. When the old man dies in despair, Jakob faces a dilemma that we hear as a voiceover: "Fine. Truth can kill. Samuel died because I told him the truth. And that crazy Herschel died because he believed the news from a radio that doesn't exist. So that's dangerous too. Whatever I do, I'm wrong. Hunger for hope may be worse than hunger for food." Thereafter, Jakob reluctantly lies about Russian artillery, American jazz bands, soccer games, and so forth in order to bring hope to the ghetto.

The lies bring new troubles because everyone from Lina to the gang led by Max Frankfurter wants to see the radio. Max is Jakob's nemesis. In contrast to Jakob's dark humor, Max, an actor, is somberly fatalistic. Accordingly, his favorite role is Lear, and early in the movie he appropriately quotes (badly) with help from his daughter: "As flies to wanton boys are we to the gods. They kill us for their sport." Max, who actually has a radio, destroys it when news spreads about Jakob. Not surprisingly, Max wants to stop Jakob and comes to Jakob's room with his gang one evening to destroy the radio. The gang finds Jakob and Professor Kirschbaum, who has come to tend to the sick Lina. Kirschbaum, an intelligent man, knows that Jakob is lying—the jazz band was a bit too much—but he admires what Jakob has done with his lies. Therefore, Professor Kirschbaum stops the gang simply by observing that no one has committed suicide in the ghetto since Jakob's "news reports" began. At that point, a series of comic escapes begin that keep the illusion of the radio alive. Jakob mockingly calls them "miracles." The most important elements in preserving the illusion are, of course, Jakob's quick thinking, ready lies, and ability to distract searchers. In one particularly amusing (and important) scene, Jakob keeps the radio illusion alive for Lina by playing a record of "Beer Barrel Polka" that he pretends is a radio broadcast, as they dance in his ruined restaurant.

Finally, the gang, the professor, and events conspire to make Jakob the leader of the resistance. At the organizational meeting at Kirschbaum's, Jakob puts off suicidal resistance by telling his followers to wait for a signal that he never reveals to them! The Gestapo arrives during the meeting and takes Kirschbaum, a famous cardiologist before the war, to the Commandant's office. A new general has arrived to liquidate the ghetto, but he has a serious heart condition. To avoid helping the man who will kill his people, Kirschbaum commits suicide. Enraged, the general decides to find the radio. He threatens to kill ten hostages unless the ghetto turns over the man with the radio.

Trapped, Jakob has no choice but to turn himself in. When Lina observes that he has no radio to turn over, Jakob grimly states that he hopes the Germans will see the joke. As the Germans round up the ghetto for deportation, the Commandant tortures Jakob. Finally, Jakob tells the Commandant that he will show him the radio and points at the radio in the Commandant's office. To break the ghetto's hopes about this illusory radio, the Commandant decides that Jakob will confess his lies before the assembled ghetto. The Commandant promises that he will not shoot him if Jakob complies.

As Jakob stands on the gallows before the assembled ghetto, however, he cannot dispel their illusions. He cannot take away their hope. As he smilingly looks at his friends, his restaurant, and flying birds, the general shoots him. As the Germans herd the ghetto onto the train, we hear Jakob's voiceover:

> So that's how it ended. I never got a chance to be the big hero and make my big speech. I swear I had a speech all prepared about freedom and never giving in. But somehow . . . yes, that's how it ended. And they all went off to the camps and were never seen again. But maybe it wasn't like that at all. Because, you know, as Frankfurter says, "Until the last line has been spoken, the curtain cannot come down." About 50 kilometers out of town, the train was stopped by Russian troops. . . .

The visuals that accompany this voiceover move from Jakob lying dead on the gallows to the Russian liberation of the train. As Lina watches a Russian tank with an American jazz band atop, we also see Lina's memory of dancing with Jakob as "Beer Barrel Polka" plays again.

Most critics panned this conclusion.[28] Some even claimed it had nothing to do with the rest of the movie. It fits quite nicely, however, with the opening joke. From beginning to end, *Jakob the Liar* jokes and dances in the face of overwhelming, unthinkable evil. Its everyman hero is reluctant and nonheroic. Instead of fighting against the Germans, he puts off suicidal resistance with a sign he never reveals. Despite the last eerie voiceover, Jakob is dead at the movie's end. Instead of a heroic triumph over evil, *Jakob the Liar* imagines a banal human story in which Jakob simply struggles to survive as long as possible in the midst of evil. To this end, he uses humor, music, friends, lies, and, most important, hope.[29] Instead of weapons and violent resistance, Jakob simply laughs and dances as much as he can.

By the way, this answer to evil is not unlike the end of Voltaire's *Candide*. That short novel tells the tale of the terrible sufferings and journeys of Candide and his friends. It is a riotous, satirical attack on Leibniz's "best of all possible worlds" theodicy. Instead of reaching an alternative theodicy, Candide forgoes theodicy for life with the no-longer-fair Cunegonde in a garden. The alternative end of *Jakob the Liar* is similar. Over against cruel deaths and final solutions, it offers another story, delightfully featuring a jazz band on a tank. Like the opening joke, this extravagant imagination changes nothing on any grand scale. Evil does not fall, nor is it explained. Good does not triumph. People simply live, the best they can, as long as they can.

The ending of *Jakob the Liar* is hardly rational. It is a pure flight of fantasy that bemuses some and affronts others. But if neither grace nor evil—or the world itself—is "rational," why should we add the pain and evil of theodicy to life?[30] *Jakob the Liar*, like Voltaire's *Candide*, *Sullivan's Travels*, and the comedies of Charlie Chaplin, suggest that we should simply live.

Forsaking God's Grace

Jakob the Liar's comic near escapes and dominating voiceover (from a dead narrator!) suggest a superintending providence. Of course, all orderly plots and overt narration do, so *Jakob the Liar* is not particularly religious here. In fact, the movie has an ironic attitude toward matters religious most obvious in Jakob's dismissal of the near escapes as "miracles."[31] In the movie's most religious scene, a Shabbat celebration prepared by Lina, she observes that Jakob is not a very good Jew and asks why he does not believe. Jakob responds, "I believe we are the chosen people. But I wish the Almighty had chosen somebody else. . . . In the eyes of the Gestapo, I'm the biggest Yid they've ever seen." Unlike Job and Paul, Jakob refuses to submit to the dark forces—whether Gestapo or God—that rule his life.[32] In fact, as the quote nicely suggests, Jakob is willing to forsake the grace of God's election.

After all, if God is in the ghetto, God—or structural evil—is indefensible. Camus refers to this irrational situation as absurd.

> I said that the world is absurd, but I was too hasty. This world in itself is not reasonable, that is all that can be said. But what is absurd is the confrontation of this irrational and the wild longing for clarity whose call echoes in the human heart.[33]

Job's response to a world that will not comply with human reason is the humiliation of humans. For Camus, that quintessentially religious move masochistically deifies that which crushes humans. It is a philosophical suicide that renders the absurd divine.[34]

Camus rejects suicide, actual or philosophical (and he is more concerned with the former), in favor of revolt, an act that refuses to deny the irrationality either of the world or of the human desire for meaning. Only such revolt gives meaning to life: "Thus I draw from the absurd three consequences, which are my revolt, my freedom, and my passion. By the mere activity of consciousness I transform into a rule of life what was an invitation to death—and I refuse suicide."[35] In short, the only answer to the problem of life is living. Camus sees his own literary work in this vein and calls aesthetic creation "the staggering evidence of man's sole dignity: the dogged revolt against his condition, perseverance in an effort considered sterile."[36]

The key to revolt or creation is to live as much as possible in the moment and to hope as little as possible for any outcome or result.

> It [absurd creation] frolics—in myths, to be sure, but myths with no other depth than that of human suffering and, like it, inexhaustible. Not the divine fable that amuses and blinds, but the terrestrial face, gesture, and drama in which are summed up a difficult wisdom and an ephemeral passion.[37]

What it must never do is to forget or forsake its mere humanity. Such rebels, of course, always forgo the divine.

> The rebel is a man who is on the point of accepting or rejecting the sacred and determined on laying claim to a human situation in which all the answers are human—in other words, formulated in reasonable terms. From this moment every question, every word, is an act of rebellion while in the sacred world every word is an act of grace. It would be possible to demonstrate in this manner that only two possible worlds can exist for the human mind: the sacred (or, to speak in Christian terms, the world of grace) and the world of rebellion.[38]

Dostoevsky would complain, of course, that such nihilism (primarily the end of belief in God) leads inevitably to moral chaos. If we forgo God, will we reap the whirlwind? Woody Allen, who has made a career in movies by directing and starring in movies featuring the juxtaposition of the tortured, anguished conscience of the little man with his fantasies of success, struggles with precisely this problem in *Crimes and Misdemeanors*.

The movie weaves together the stories of two different men, Judah Rosenthal and Cliff Stern, through the connections of friends and families and through old movie clips. Quite often, Allen cuts from a scene in Judah's life to Cliff, an unsuccessful documentary filmmaker, watching movies that parallel the action in Judah's life. As a result, Judah becomes a "celebrity," while Cliff's story is the familiar Allen tale of an anguished intellectual who wonders why he does not get the girl and why he does not succeed. Allen tells this story by bringing Cliff into interaction with his brother-in-law, Lester, a pompous, successful TV producer. Cliff's wife convinces Lester to give the unemployed Cliff a job directing Lester's biography for a PBS series on the creative mind. Cliff has no respect for Lester, but he takes the job in order to acquire money to support his documentary about an unknown philosopher. Along the way, Cliff falls for the assistant producer of Lester's biography, Halley, but loses her in the end to the successful Lester.

Judah's story is more unusual fare for an Allen movie. The movie opens with a dinner honoring this ophthalmologist for his philanthropy; however, there is a worm at the core of this happiness. Judah has been having an affair, and his neu-rotic mistress, Dolores, threatens his family life more and more persistently. Judah's acceptance speech suggests the possibility of an even deeper problem.

> That the new ophthalmology wing has become a reality is not just a tribute to me but to a spirit of community, generosity, of mutual caring, and answered prayers. Now, it's funny I use the term "answered prayers." You see, I'm a man of science. I've always been a skeptic, but I was raised quite reli-giously. And while I challenged it even as a child, some of that feeling must have stuck with me. I remember my father telling me, "The eyes of God are on us always." The eyes of God. What a phrase to a young boy. And what were God's eyes like? Unimaginably penetrating, intense eyes I assumed. And I wonder if it was just a coincidence that I made my specialty ophthalmology.

The issues of community and the watchful, judging deity hover in the background of Judah's relentless focus on his happiness. Troubled by guilt, he turns to Ben, a rabbi who is, quite ironically, losing his sight. Although Ben urges Judah to confess his sin to his wife and to ask for forgiveness, Judas refuses. He knows that his wife will not forgive him, and he cannot bear to risk his life of prestige and privilege.

When Dolores threatens to expose Judah's embezzlement of philanthropic funds as well as his adultery, matters become more serious. Judah seeks the help of his crim-inal brother, Jack, who offers to have Dolores killed so that Judah can go on with his "country-club life." Despite his inability even to say the word "murder," Judah decides to follow Jack's advice.[39] As he puts it later, he opts for Jack's real world, not Ben's kingdom of heaven. God is a luxury that he cannot afford.

The eyes of God remain, however, to haunt Judah. After the hit, he spins per-ilously close to a breakdown and to a religious conversion. He worries about divine forgiveness and comes to believe in God; otherwise the world is a cesspool. He does not confess, however, because his brother threatens to kill him if he does. Finally, Judah's religious interlude passes.

The movie ends four months later with the wedding of Ben's daughter, and the stories of Cliff and Judah finally come together as they meet at the reception. Cliff is angry because he has learned that Lester and Halley are together, and he jokingly tells Judah that he is plotting the perfect murder. When Judah asks him if this is a movie project, Cliff claims that he does not do such movies (a humorous comment on the movie, of course). Judah, however, offers a murder story with a strange twist:

> Judah: Let's say there's this man who is very successful. He has everything [the story pauses and the camera cuts to the successful Lester]. And after the awful deed is done, he . . . he finds that he is plagued by deep-rooted guilt. Little sparks of his religious background which he had rejected are

suddenly stirred up. He hears his father's voice. He imagines that God is watching his every move. Suddenly, it's not an empty universe at all, but a just and moral one. And he's violated it. Now he's panic stricken. He's on the verge of a mental collapse, an inch away from confessing the whole thing to the police. And then one morning he awakens. The sun is shining and his family is around him. Mysteriously, the crisis is lifted. He takes his family on a vacation to Europe. And as the months pass, he finds he's not punished. In fact, he prospers. The killing gets attributed to another person, a drifter who has a number of other murders to his credit. So what the hell, one more—what does it even matter? Now he's scot-free. His life is completely back to normal, back to his protected world of wealth and privilege.

Cliff: Yes, but can he really ever go back?

Judah: Well, people carry sins around. I mean, oh, maybe once in a while he has a bad moment, but it passes. In time, it all fades.

Cliff: Yeah, but, so then, you know, then his worst beliefs are realized.[40]

Judah: Well, I said it was a chilling story, didn't I?

Cliff: I don't know. I think it would be tough for somebody to live with that. Very few guys could live actually with that on their conscience.

Judah: People carry awful deeds around. What do you expect them to do? Turn themselves in? This is reality. In reality, we rationalize. We deny or we couldn't go on living.

Cliff: Here's what I would do. I would have him turn himself in. 'Cause then, you see, then your story assumes tragic proportions. Because in the absence of a god or something, he is forced to assume that responsibility himself. Then you have tragedy.

Judah: But that's fiction, that's movies. I mean, you've seen too many movies. I'm talking about reality. If you want a happy ending, you should go see a Hollywood movie.

Judah's story is chilling. Camus, for one, would be happier with Cliff's suggested ending. Camus never intended revolt (read "self-assertion") to lead to murder. In fact, just as *The Myth of Sisyphus* denies suicide, the later *The Rebel* denies the legitimacy of murder. In particular, *The Rebel* rejects the murderous, totalitarian ideologies that often result when humans revolt against their metaphysical condition.

The important thing, therefore, is not, as yet, to go to the root of things, but, the world being what it is, to know how to live in it. In the age of negation, it was of some avail to examine one's position concerning suicide. In the age of ideologies, we must examine our position in relation to murder. . . . It is incumbent upon us, at all events, to give a definite answer to the question implicit in the blood and strife of this century. For we are being put to the rack. Thirty years ago, before reaching a decision to kill, people denied many things, to the point of denying themselves by suicide. God is deceitful; the whole world (myself included) is deceitful; therefore I choose to die: suicide was the problem then. Ideology today is concerned only with the denial of other human beings, who alone bear the responsibility of deceit. It is then that we kill. Each day at dawn, assassins in judges' obes slip into some cell: murder is the problem today.[41]

In *The Rebel*, Camus rejects the nihilism of his earlier work for the human solidarity of rebellion.

Man's solidarity is founded upon rebellion, and rebellion, in its turn, can only find its justification in this solidarity. We have, then, the right to say that any rebellion which claims the right to deny or destroy this solidarity loses simultaneously its right to be called rebellion and becomes in reality an acquiescence in murder. . . . In order to exist, man must rebel, but rebellion must respect the limit it discovers in itself—a limit where minds meet and, in meeting, begin to exist. . . .

In absurdist experience, suffering is individual. But from the moment when a movement of rebellion begins, suffering is seen as a collective experience. Therefore the first progressive step for a mind overwhelmed by the strangeness of things is to realize that this feeling of strangeness is shared with all men and that human reality, in its entirety, suffers from the distance which separates it from the rest of the universe. The malady experienced by a single man becomes a mass plague. In our daily trials rebellion plays the same role as does the "*cogito*" in the realm of thought: it is the first piece of evidence. But this evidence lures the individual from his solitude. It founds its first value on the whole human race. I rebel—therefore we exist.[42]

Rebellion eliminates the legitimacy of murder and founds a new social contract. Nihilism remains only in a negative sense, in the constant denial that we become gods, that we become certain, in revolt.[43]

The emphasis on community, on human solidarity, is what escapes Judah. Solidarity, however, is not uniformity, as long as we are willing to eschew divinity and totalitarianism. That is, without some imperial institution, there is not one answer after the denial of God's justice/grace, but many. *Crimes and Misdemeanors* does not say that the world is a cold, harsh, unforgiving place. Instead, the ensemble cast offers several different worldviews and lifestyles. As his conversation with Cliff and the movie end, Judah walks away with his wife planning their daughter's wedding. Cliff sits alone in a bar. Lester and Halley have already left. And the blind rabbi dances happily with his newly married daughter. Whose life is the right choice? *Crimes and*

Misdemeanors does not say. It simply offers the different worldviews of Judah, Ben, and others, as well as the different film styles of Cliff and Lester.

Perhaps the material results are in favor of Judah and Lester, but they are hardly the most appealing characters. We have not yet considered, however, Cliff's philosopher. That philosopher extols love, both in our conceptions of God[44] and in our relationships with others, as the secret of life. Surprisingly, he commits suicide during the course of the movie. Cliff and Halley (and we) are bemused, because the philosopher embraced life so fully. Despite his suicide, he has the final voiceover in the movie as we watch flashbacks of the movie's action:

> We are all faced throughout our lives with agonizing decisions. Moral choices. Some are on a grand scale. Most of these choices are on lesser points. But we define ourselves by the choices we have made. We are, in fact, the sum total of choices. Events unfold so unpredictably, so unfairly. Human happiness does not seem to have been included in the design of creation. It is only we with our capacity to love that give meaning to the indifferent universe. And yet most human beings seem to have the ability to keep trying and even to find joy from simple things like their family, their work, and from the hope that future generations might understand more.

Like the hopes of the blind rabbi, these words significantly challenge Judah's cynicism. While Judah's two speeches—at the award dinner and at Ben's daughter's wedding—bookend his story and interpretation of life, Allen undercuts that story by turning the last speech into a dialogue with an unconvinced interlocutor (Cliff) and with the philosopher's final voiceover. *Crimes and Misdemeanors* is realistic enough, however, not to say that life turns out well for the hopeful or the humane. Ben goes blind. Cliff loses the girl. The Camus-like philosopher commits suicide.

Not incidentally, Judah's story cynically rewrites the story of Job.[45] Unlike Job, this successful man "with everything" is rotten to the core. He becomes the pawn, not of God or the adversary, but of a neurotic mistress. Further, in some sense, he deserves his problems, as he has clearly led Dolores to believe that she has a future with him. Like Job, he talks to his friends and family as he struggles with what to do. Instead of appealing to God and ultimately repenting, however, he takes matters vigorously into his own hands. Actually, he does not even have the courage to do it himself. He passes the murder off to his criminal brother. Nonetheless, like Job, he gets his life back.

Left alone, Judah's story undoes Job, Shakespeare's *Macbeth*, Dostoevsky's *Crime and Punishment*, and a host of lesser melodramatic fiction that contends that murder will out. Left alone, his chilling story suggests that we live in a cold, harsh world. As we have seen, however, Judah's story does not stand alone. It stands as one story among many. Thus, the end of God's justice/grace does not necessarily mean moral chaos. Human responsibility may not be impossible even if it is the fiction the cynical Judah says it is. Camus and Cliff are right. Without God, we make our lives by our choices. What kind of character do we wish to create? Do we want to be Judah, Cliff, Ben, Jakob, or Camus? We should also consider that Judah's fear that God was watching did not change Judah's decision to murder Dolores. Apparently, belief in God is itself no guarantee of moral order (see Jas 2:14–26).[46] Even a cursory reading of the Bible would impress that fact upon us. Maybe, then, it is character, not murder, that will out.

Costly Forgiveness[47]

David Hugh Jones's *The Confession* plays out what might happen if we took responsibility for our character. The movie begins with and cuts back and forth between the stories of two men, Harry Fertig and Roy Bleakie. The film's dilemmas begin when Harry's son Stevie dies because a hospital staff does not deal with his appendicitis quickly enough. Six weeks after his son's death, Harry kills the three hospital employees he holds responsible and then turns himself into the police. Harry, an observant Jew, takes ethical issues quite seriously. Meanwhile, Roy, a lawyer, uses intimidation and dirty tricks to win politically sensitive cases and to advance his own ambition to become a district attorney. His success brings him to the attention of the wealthy and powerful Jack Renoble, for whom Harry worked as CFO. Renoble hires Roy to free Harry on an insanity plea.

Unfortunately for Roy, Harry sees a guilty plea as necessary to give meaning to his actions, to honor his son's memory, to make amends, and to make atonement with God, whose commandments he has violated. Unlike Job, Harry has taken justice into his own hands, but he now feels culpable before God. By contrast, Roy wishes to dismiss God from the matter or to assume that God is the providence guiding him to success. Bemused that Harry is unhappy when the DA elects not to pursue the death penalty, Roy complains that Harry is complex. Harry demurs:

> Harry: I'm a very simple man, Mr. Bleakie. It's the world that's complex. And because we live in a complex world, we're forced to make choices. And sometimes the choices . . . the choices. . . . I wanted to avenge my son's death. I did not . . . want to . . .
> Roy: Kill the three people responsible?
> Harry: [*Nodding yes*] Sometimes I think the world is nothing but sorrow. The district attorney is surprised I feel remorse. Of course I feel remorse. Why wouldn't I feel remorse? I'm sorry for you.
> Roy: You're sorry for me? Why?
> Harry: You really want to do what's right, don't you? You really want to do the right thing. People think it's hard to do the right thing. It's not hard

to do the right thing, Mr. Bleakie. It's hard to know what the right thing is. Once you know, once you know what's right, it's hard not to do it.

Roy: When you shot those people, you knew? Murder two, the death penalty. You knew? You knew?

Harry: I knew.

Roy: I get it. They killed your son; you killed them; the state kills you; except the state won't kill you, so the state's more merciful than you. Is that it?

Harry: Please go.

Roy: Is that it? You want to be martyr?

Harry: I want to be a good man.

Roy: You murdered three people.

Harry: A good man is not without sin. He admits and expiates his sin.

In short, Harry feels compelled to pay with his life for his sins. Employing all his guile, Roy eventually convinces Harry that God wants him to plead guilty (to avoid the death penalty). Meanwhile, however, Roy undergoes his own "conversion." He decides that Harry was right after all. While various factors contribute to Roy's "conversion," the major factor is his discovery that Renoble needs Harry to plead insane so that Harry cannot testify against Renoble in another case. Renoble has deliberately polluted the New York City water supply so that he can receive the eight-billion-dollar contract for a water filtration plant. Roy's conversion begins, however, when he confesses to Harry that he has committed adultery with Harry's wife. Harry, who already knows, reiterates his basic position: "A good man is not without sin. He admits and expiates his sin."[48]

In court, Roy helps Harry enter a guilty plea. Harry offers an anguished statement: "I killed them . . . because they would not help my son. They were too busy. They didn't care. I killed them to show the world that they must care. I know what I did was a crime. No, worse than a crime. It was a sin against God, against God's law." Falling on his knees, he asks his wife for forgiveness and quotes the commandments out of order, climaxing with the prohibition against killing. After officers take him ranting from the courtroom and the judge calls a recess, Renoble congratulates Roy on demonstrating Harry's insanity. When court resumes, however, Roy declares his commitment to God's law (instead of that of the state of New York) and exposes Renoble's dirty dealings. As a result, of course, Harry goes to jail (twenty-five years to life), and Roy loses his opportunity to be a district attorney.

Grace, transcendent salvation, is in short supply in *The Confession*. Those who find salvation find that it comes with a heavy price. One has to pay for forgiveness, by making restitution, in *The Confession*. One is culpable for one's choices. To be a good person, one has to assess one's own acts and atone for one's sins.[49]

In essence, then, *The Confession* rejects the two "gains" of the theodicy of Romans. First, it rejects the anguished, guilty conscience that Paul's interpreters have passed on to the West. It rejects, that is, the depiction of the human condition as so mired in sin that only divine grace can deliver it. Instead, it says repeatedly that a good person can live well before God. It is not that one will not sin but that one may find forgiveness through confession and expiation if one does sin. As Harry is an observant Jew, *The Confession* reminds us nicely that there was no shortage of forgiveness of sins in pre-Pauline Judaism. The process therein for an individual to find forgiveness is quite similar to Harry's confession, amends, and atonement.[50] Whether that forgiveness would actually extend to Harry's deliberate sin (a sin of the high hand) is, of course, another matter.

> And the priest shall make atonement before the LORD for the one who commits an error, when it is unintentional, to make atonement for the person, who then shall be forgiven. For both the native among the Israelites and the alien residing among them—you shall have the same law for anyone who acts in error. But whoever acts high-handedly, whether a native or an alien, affronts the LORD, and shall be cut off from among the people. Because of having despised the word of the LORD and broken his commandment, such a person shall be utterly cut off and bear the guilt. (Num 15:28–31; see also Lev 4:2)

While the movie does not explore this technicality, perhaps the intentional nature of Harry's sin is what leads him to desire the death penalty ("to be cut off"), to despair when the DA chooses not to seek the death penalty, and to attempt suicide.

If that is the case, Harry may be following a pattern similar to that of Matthew's Judas. According to William Klassen, after the betrayal of Jesus, Matthew's Judas also follows Jewish patterns of repentance: he repents, he makes restitution, and he confesses (Matt 27:3–4). When the priests deny Judas's quest for absolution, he is left alone and does the noble thing; that is, he takes his own life as an act of restitution.[51] The dominance of Christian attitudes about suicide as itself a sin may make it difficult, however, for audiences to think of Harry (or Judas) as noble at this point.[52] Nonetheless, the movie presents Harry as sympathetically as possible. Its dynamics strive to convert the audience, as well as Roy Bleakie, to Harry's perspective. It struggles to make a murderer and attempted suicide the ethical standard in what Harry calls a complex world. Of course, the gospel and Paul face similar difficulties in making Jesus, a condemned criminal (and suicide?), into their audience's ethical standard.

Second, *The Confession* revises Paul's salvation history hopes. The movie does not imagine that the salvation of the Gentile(s) will lead to the salvation of the Jew(s) as Paul does in Rom 9–11. Instead, the suffering of an observant Jew leads to the salvation of a lapsed Presbyterian (with an assist from an Irish Catholic private detective).[53] Of course, even in Rom 9–11, the Jews' suffering (their being "cut off") leads to the inclusion of the Gentiles.[54] More important, Paul and the Gospels also argue that the suffering of another Jew leads to the salvation of the world. That Jew is, of course, not Harry. By giving us Harry, *The Confession* helps us remember that the suffering of a Jew—or better, Jews—stands at the center of the religious, if not the moral, conscience of the West.

The Torah Saves

Paul makes numerous negative statements about the law (Torah), particularly in Galatians and Romans.[55] Galatians, for example, inveighs against circumcision (although this is the entry to the whole law as Paul puts it in Gal 5:3), social dietary practices that would prevent inclusive communion in Christ (Gal 2:11–14), and special calendar observances (Gal 4:10). Clearly, Paul's apocalypse revised his thinking on the law (see Phil 3:4–11). The vision of the crucified, accursed by the standards of the law (Gal 3:13) but God's fulfillment of the promise to Abraham that he would bless the nations through him (Gal 3:6–14), re-centers Paul's thought on God's salvation of the Gentiles, not Israel's elect position of difference.[56] Thereafter, Paul moves away from observances—like dietary regulations and circumcision—that distinguish Israel for his gentile converts, at least.[57]

Even at his most negative, Paul sees the law as pointing toward salvation. Even if it enslaves (negative), it also leads toward God's promises (positive).

> Now before faith came, we were imprisoned and guarded under the law until faith would be revealed [*apokaluphthēnai*]. Therefore the law was our disciplinarian [*paidagōgos*] until Christ came, so that we might be justified by faith. But now that faith has come, we are no longer subject to a disciplinarian, for in Christ Jesus you are all children of God through faith. (Gal 3:23–26)

The *paidagōgos*, of course, is a slave who leads children to their education. Similarly, in Rom 10:4, Christ is the end (*telos*) of the law. Certainly, like Gal 3–4, this passage asserts the law's temporal and prophetic nature, but Hays is probably also correct when he argues that Christ is the "goal," not the termination, of the law.[58] At least that interpretation certainly coheres with the "guiding" of the *paidagōgos*. We should also observe, however, that Paul states that Christ is the *telos* of the law "so that there may be righteousness for everyone who believes." In short, Paul's discourse on the law is about the inclusion of all, that is, the Gentiles, as the Jews are already God's people (Rom 3:1–2; 9–11).

For *The Confession*, too, the law, or an observant Jew, points toward salvation. *The Confession*, however, lacks the supercessionism implicit in Paul's language. No one in the movie ever says anything remotely negative about the law. The law is holy (Rom 7:12), complete, and effectual for salvation. Thus, in Roy's final speech, clever attorneys may circumvent human law, but they cannot prevail against God's law (Torah). Its neglect leads to destruction. Most important, the law does not lead to Christ. For *The Confession*, if you neglect God's law, Christ is of no more help than an attorney. Clearly, *The Confession* reads the law more optimistically than Paul does.[59] The law saves, illuming a simple path in a dark, complex world (Ps 119:105).[60]

Despite his numerous negative comments, Paul never left the law behind. In fact, he apparently could not quit talking about it.[61] Thus, despite the logical problems it causes him in Romans, Paul never gives up the special place of Israel, a place that Israel has only because of the covenant. In fact, as we have seen, the special problem of the Jews, given Paul's successful gentile mission, is the specific topic of Romans. Further, the Jews are the light of the world and the promises belong to them (Rom 3:1–2; 9:1–5). Even the disobedience of Israel is the salvation of the world (Rom 11:11–12). Paul reads Israel according to patterns in the Hebrew Bible and according to his death-resurrection gospel. It is difficult, then, to find a difference in the suffering-rising pattern between Paul's Christ, Paul's life, and Paul's Israel.

Paul's "negative" attitude toward the law depends entirely on his apocalyptic perspective. The law is not bad; it is simply ineffectual against the evil powers now ruling this wicked world.[62] That much, at least, seems clear in Rom 7, whatever else Paul is saying. The law is a good thing in a bad time. Given the inevitably ironic mind of an apocalyptic seer like Paul, however, it is precisely the law's goodness that makes it ineffectual. In bad, apocalyptic times, life comes from death (Christ's and the believer's), and the cursed one actualizes the blessing to the nations. Further, and perhaps most important, the law is the special possession of Israel, and Paul's apocalypse calls him to the Gentiles. For Paul, the law is not necessary or even effectual in terms of their entry into Christ.

Paul's Rowdy Communities

Paul's expected end did not arrive. Does that mean we should rethink the importance of the law?[63] In fact, after Paul forms his gentile communities, he himself sounds more and more pro-law. According to E. P. Sanders, while Paul does not see the law as a possible means for entering Paul's "in Christ" communities, he does see the law as an important factor in staying within the communities.[64] In fact, as Rom 8:2 puts it, entry into Christ simply moves a believer from one law, that of sin and death, to another, that of the spirit of life in Christ (compare Gal 6:2).

Accordingly, as Sanders observes, Paul's "pattern" of religion is in harmony with
Judaism's view that election and salvation are by God's grace, while reward and punishment correspond to one's deeds.[65] If Paul's apocalyptic mind requires a transcendent act of salvation, a bestowal of grace, his communities require ethos, character
formation, and discipline. It is difficult to imagine communities existing without
some rules and norms.[66] Despite his emphasis on grace, then, Paul's letters are
highly invested in order and ethos.[67]

Paul's ethic depends primarily on the death-resurrection of the believer or on the
resulting indwelling of Christ/Spirit. While these motifs internalize and universal-
ize the law, they also mean that this law is no longer Torah, the specific contours of
Israel's covenant relationship with God. Instead, Christ, or even the law of Christ
(Gal 6:2), replaces the law among Paul's gentile followers in the present evil age and
for all in the new age.[68] For the Gentiles, however, Christ in the interim between this
age and the next is quite comparable to Torah (Rom 8:2). Thus, Paul can succinctly tell his followers to fulfill the law of Christ (Gal 6:2) in the same letter in
which he stresses their freedom from the law without any apparent sense of contradiction. Similarly, he can say that even when he is outside the law, he is under Christ's
law, not free from God's law (1 Cor 9:21). In both cases, Paul's "law of Christ" condenses an ethic of service to others that he elsewhere describes as "the mind of
Christ" (Phil 2:5–8). Neither condensation differs—at least in part[69]—from
Torah's own self-condensations, as Paul specifically remarks (Gal 5:14; see also
Rom 13:8–10). While Paul may not be trying to inculcate Jewish behavior, he calls
for a decent life that is quite similar ethically to his Jewish heritage.[70]

Paul's commitment to a law of Christ or of the spirit or of love, rather than
chaotic grace, becomes most obvious when his congregations fail to understand his
apocalyptic gospel and fail to live according to his "in Christ" ethos. Paul's followers concluded, for example, that the gospel justified antinomian and licentious lives
(Rom 3:8; 6; Gal 5:13—26) or that life in the spirit meant that the body, both
physical and corporate, was of little concern (1–2 Corinthians). Paul's letters point
out these errors and enforce Paul's norms (read "law"). Paul's letters correct, cajole,
and threaten the errant with divine (read "Pauline") judgments. When the letters
fail, Paul sends fellow workers to bring the rowdy communities to heel. When that
fails, Paul threatens to come himself. While Paul's apocalyptic worldview anticipates
the delivering and judging arrival of the resurrected Christ (1 Thessalonians), that
end tarries. In the interim, Paul's parousia takes the place of that of Christ. In the
absence of Christ, Paul dispenses judgments.

This pattern is most complete in the Corinthian correspondence. Paul's first visit
to Corinth, founding an "in Christ" community there, was in lowliness and humility.
That demeanor was in keeping with his death-gospel and in striking contrast to
the Corinthians' own falsely placed spiritual pride (1 Cor 1:26–2:5). Paul expects
his followers to imitate his humble lifestyle, castigates them when they do not (1 Cor

1–4), and sends Timothy to them to remind them of his ways (1 Cor 4:14–21). Paul warns the arrogant, in particular, to take heed, because he will not tarry: "What would you prefer? Am I to come to you with a stick, or with love in a spirit of gentleness?" Apparently, at Corinth, judgment begins with those in the community.

By the time of the writing of 2 Corinthians, a composite of several letters, matters had deteriorated. Paul had paid Corinth another unsuccessful visit, and part of the community was in open revolt against him. Instead of another painful visit, he wrote to them again (2 Cor 1:15–2:11).

> I wrote for this reason: to test you and to know whether you are obedient in everything. Anyone whom you forgive, I also forgive. What I have forgiven, if I have forgiven anything, has been for your sake in the presence of Christ. (2 Cor 2:9–10)

Even this forgiveness inculcates Paul's authority, for he stands for their sake "in the presence of Christ," and, not surprisingly, forgiveness is only for those who comply with the Pauline norms, by obedience or repentance (compare 2 Cor 7:8–13).

Similar patterns and warnings dominate 2 Cor 10–13, likely once a separate letter to Corinth. When Paul's opponents make much of Paul's humble person and bold letters, Paul promises a third, powerful visit (2 Cor 10:1–11; 12:14–13:10). Unless they correct their behavior and live according to Paul's gospel, he will come in judgment.

> I warned those who sinned previously and all the others, and I warn them now while absent, as I did when present on my second visit, that if I come again, I will not be lenient. . . .
>
> Examine yourselves to see whether you are living in the faith. Test yourselves. Do you not realize that Jesus Christ is in you?—unless, indeed, you fail to meet the test! (2 Cor 13:2, 5)

If they do not agree with Paul—that is, if they sin—they stand to lose the indwelling Christ. Grace figures little here. The model for this judgment is the Lord's apocalypse. Here, Paul is the Lord, standing in for Christ. Grace may bring one into Paul's communities, but justice—Paul's measurement of his followers' adherence to his norms or law—determines one's continuance or one's exclusion.

Paul's communities are new creations, and some of these new Adams have already failed to keep Paul's gospel or, more precisely, Paul's commandments. As a result, Paul's communities stand in need of law and justice, not grace. Similarly, while the American mythology of Hollywood movies idealizes small communities as Edenic, even these Edens sometimes need cleansing. On those occasions, an apostolic stranger brings justice to town (compare *Shane*, *Bad Day at Blackrock*, *High Plains Drifter*, and *Pale Rider*).

Thus, in *Bad Day at Blackrock*,[71] a one-armed stranger, whom we eventually come to know as John J. Macreedy, arrives at Blackrock on a sunny day in 1945. The Streamliner's unscheduled stop surprises the locals, who do not welcome him. They deny him a room, take his room when he commandeers one, and refuse to help him find Adobe Flat, the last known home of a Japanese-American named Komono. Why Macreedy wants to find Komono remains a mystery, as does the reason for the town's hostility, until fairly late in the film.

The town, led by Reno Smith, and Macreedy try to solve these respective mysteries. Smith hires a private detective in Los Angles to find out who Macreedy is. He is unsuccessful. Meanwhile, Macreedy hires a jeep from Liz Wirth and drives to Adobe Flat to find a burned-out house, an abandoned well, and a field of wildflowers (as if they were adorning a grave). In his absence, Smith whips up the town bullies, claiming that Macreedy is a smallpox destroying the town and causing the cowardly townspeople to dispute Smith's control. His head ruffian, Coley Trimble, sets out to kill Macreedy and runs Macreedy off the road as he returns from Adobe Flat.

In town, Macreedy makes his intentions to leave known, but there is no transportation and no communications with the outside world. Macreedy is trapped in a place where "the rule of law has left and the gorillas have taken over." That evening in the café, Coley picks a fight with Macreedy, but the one-armed man beats Coley senseless. Macreedy then accuses Smith of murder and warns him that his gang will ultimately turn against him. For the present, however, Smith remains firmly in control of the town.

Justice asserts itself when the town doctor, the hotel clerk, Pete Wirth, and Macreedy pool their knowledge and solve the mysteries. Macreedy is there to give Komono the Medal of Honor that Komono's son, who saved Macreedy's life, won posthumously. Pete confesses that he was with Smith and three other drunks when they burned Komono out the day after Pearl Harbor. Smith killed Komono when he fled the burning building. To make restitution, Pete asks his sister Liz to spirit Macreedy away, but she takes him into Smith's trap. Smith kills her before Macreedy can make a Molatov cocktail that sets Smith, with a bit of poetic justice, afire. Macreedy takes Smith back to town to jail, where the sheriff has rounded up the rest of the gang. In the denouement, the police cart off the outlaws, the sheriff represents law and order once again, and the doc asks Macreedy for the medal so that the town can start anew, building upon it.

The similarity to Paul's threatened and actual parousias is uncanny. The apostolic stranger brings justice and law back to the corrupt community. No one is more committed to justice, discipline, and community formation than Paul, unless it is Macreedy. Obviously, in terms of ongoing communities, grace is a failure. Unless, of course, one finds grace—that is, transcendent salvation—in the stranger, the mysterious figure who appears and then disappears. Macreedy never offers grace or himself as a divine savior. He simply offers people a second chance at law and order. By contrast, Paul embodies divine grace. At least he offers all the grace ever available to his errant communities who find "salvation" by first agreeing with Paul. Thereafter, Paul becomes the norm or law by which they live.[72]

The Interplay of Order and Freedom

Paul's grace does apocalyptically disrupt alien orders, but in the name of Christ and of the spirit, Paul's grace also reimposes order. In short, Paul's new creation obliterates difference and malcontents. Grace is a problem even for Paul. He likes to use it as a critical device. He does not want it—or the spirit—used against his own order. Over against Paul, then, we need a new experience of grace/escape.[73]

The Coen brothers' films nicely express the necessary human dance between order and freedom. Their films slide back and forth between melodrama and dark comedy. On occasions, that is, their characters "get what they deserve," and on other occasions, they receive far better. Characters in *Blood Simple, Fargo,* and *The Man Who Wasn't There,* for example, stray beyond cultural norms of law and decency and pay for their indiscretions. By contrast, the grotesque, comic characters of *Raising Arizona* and *O Brother, Where Art Thou?* fare far better than they deserve as they escape stultifying orders. Some characters seek to establish codes to live by in the face of chaos (*Miller's Crossing*), while others circumvent social norms by sheer luck (*The Hudsucker Proxy, O Brother, Where Art Thou?*) and solicited (*O Brother, Where Art Thou?*) or unsolicited divine help (*The Hudsucker Proxy*).[74]

Of course, the Coen brothers have a clear preference for grotesque, abnormal characters. They delight in focusing on someone just outside the norm. They also like deus ex machina deliverances of hopelessly entangled heroes (*Barton Fink, The Hudsucker Proxy, O Brother, Where Art Thou?*) and strange, fantastic departures from the reality they have painstakingly established (*Barton Fink, The Man Who Wasn't There*). At the same time, they are fascinated with the tradition of movies and painstakingly re-create the look and feel of earlier movies. They like voiceovers that supply, along with melodramatic plots, a sense of overarching order and providence. In fact, they spend so much time on highly ordered sets and visuals that some critics have decried their lack of human feeling. In short, while their films are filled with whimsy and humor, the Coen brothers are as much servants of order as tricksters.

Nonetheless, they advocate sitting lightly in that larger order. Their most memorable characters (Marge in *Fargo* is an exception) sit lightly in life. The Dude, who takes it easy for us all, in *The Big Lebowski* is the quintessential character here, but Ulysses Everett McGill (*O Brother, Where Art Thou?*) and Ed Crane (*The Man Who Wasn't There*) have some of the same qualities.[75] At the same time, the characters who pay the highest price are those who go too far and try to bend life completely to their will (the entire cast of *Blood Simple,* Sidney J. Mussburger in *The Hudsucker Proxy,* Ed Crane in *The Man Who Wasn't There*).

With these tensions, the Coens have revamped Sophocles for a modern day. There is a fate or luck or divinity—some unknown, overarching order—that rough-hews human life. The response to that fate is what creates character and either a comedy or a melodrama. The result is a collection of films that simultaneously affirms grace (luck and unexpected deliverances) and justice (order, social norms, law).

In *O Brother, Where Art Thou?* for example, three misfit, escaped convicts find themselves on the road to a treasure. Ultimately, they are the victims of, and the beneficiaries of, larger forces: the capitalization of old-timey music and political maneuverings. They become the Soggy Bottom Boys, whose signature song, "I Am a Man of Constant Sorrow," encapsulates their difficult circumstances in depression-era Mississippi. On the road, they find themselves tossed to and fro between divine and demonic forces. Delmar and Pete find salvation in a revival river. Ulysses Everett McGill eschews the baptismal opportunity and mocks Delmar's naive belief that divine forgiveness equals forgiveness from the state of Mississippi. They are victims, he thinks, of ridiculous superstition. Immediately thereafter, they pick up Tommy Johnson, a young black man who has sold his soul to the devil (delightfully, the devil is a white man in Tommy's report) for the ability to play the guitar. Given the religious choices recently made, Everett wryly delights in the fact that he is the only one "unaffiliated." Like the Dude's lazy ease in *The Big Lebowski*, Everett's lack of affiliation centers the film and is the Coens' (seeming) recommendation. Everett is a sly trickster figure like the Odysseus who is his precursor.

Of course, matters are hardly so simple. As the film nears its end, we find out that Everett is, in fact, quite affiliated. He broke out of jail to stop his wife from remarrying. He told Pete and Delmar that there was a treasure only in order to get them to go along. After all, they were all chained together. Despite the absence of treasure and their pursuit by a lawman in sunglasses (the successor of the prison guard in *Cool Hand Luke*), they eventually find a double salvation. Having saved Tommy from a KKK hanging, they attend a political rally in disguise so that Everett can speak to Penny, his wife. As they sing their signature song, Homer Stokes, the leading candidate for governor and the head of the local KKK, recognizes them and rails against them. When the crowd turns against him because of its fondness for the "ole-timey" music, the boys save the career of Pappy O'Daniel, the incumbent governor, and he returns the favor by pardoning them. Then Penny agrees to take Everett back, but she demands that he retrieve her ring from their cabin. There, the sunglasses-wearing lawman apprehends them and refuses to recognize the governor's pardon. Abandoning the law, which he describes as a mere human institution, he prepares to hang them. After their graves are dug, Everett begins to pray, asking for forgiveness and deliverance. Immediately, a flood, created by the new hydroelectric dam, does just that. Floating on a wooden coffin, Delmar calls their deliverance a miracle, Pete calls it answered prayer, and Everett regales their superstition once again. When they criticize his change of tone, Everett defends himself by saying that a man will say anything in distress.

Everett tries to remain an unaffiliated trickster, but the film's denouement undercuts this stance once again. Claiming that his adventures are over, Everett walks submissively behind Penny down the road to their renewed marriage. Further, Penny makes him "toe the line" to the very end. The ring he has recovered is not hers, and he must return to the cabin at the bottom of the lake to retrieve her ring. She has spoken.[76]

O Brother, Where Art Thou? is a paean to the human need for comic escape. The title alone signals this perspective. The Coens took the title from the tragic film about the Depression that Sullivan is making at the beginning of *Sullivan's Travels*. While the studio heads worry that this film departs from Sullivan's typical, highly successful comedies, Sullivan sets out on various journeys in order to understand the plight of the common person. On the last trip, Sullivan is falsely accused of (his own) murder and is incarcerated. While imprisoned, he makes a trek through the swamps one evening with his other inmates and arrives at a rural black church. The prisoners, whom the pastor welcomes as fellow sufferers, find temporary escape as they watch cartoons on a makeshift screen at the front of the church. As Sullivan laughs with his fellows, he has the epiphany that recommits him to comedy. Ordinary people need temporary release. Incidentally, the Coens even re-create this scene in *O Brother, Where Art Thou?* by having prisoners marched into a theater for a matinee. The original is more effective; nonetheless, the Coens are as clearly committed as Sullivan to the temporary release that comedy can bring. Further, they are more aware of its temporary nature.

The interplay between order and freedom is even closer to Paul's grace and his problems with it in *Intolerable Cruelty*.[77] Here, Miles Massey plays a cold-hearted, greedy divorce attorney. His specialty, which has made him rich and the president of NOMAN, the National Organization of Matrimonial Lawyers Nationwide, is the impregnable, never-breached Massey Prenuptial Agreement. Paradoxically, various characters say (1) where the Massey Prenup is there is no romance; and (2) only love is in mind when the Massey Prenup is signed. This seeming contradiction is the heart of the film and an implicit recognition of the human need for both order (marriage) and freedom (romance, love).

Miles, bored because of the ease of his success, meets his match in Marilyn Rexroth. Marilyn has married the millionaire Rex Rexroth in order to divorce him and to gain wealth, independence, and freedom. Her private detective, Gus Petch, has captured Rex's marital indiscretions on film. Miles, however, is Rex's attorney and is captivated by Rex's unwillingness and inability to compromise at all with Marilyn even though he is as "guilty as sin." This piques Miles's interest because his philosophy is that compromise/marriage is death and that life is the annihilation of your opponent. Even though he falls for Marilyn at first sight, he wins the case for Rex anyway.

Marilyn immediately plots her revenge. She finds Donovan Donaly, a TV producer, reduced to a bum's life on the street because his unfaithful wife hired Miles to conduct her divorce proceedings. Donovan supplies an actor who can play the part of a rich Texas oilman, Howard. Marilyn brings Howard to Miles and asks Miles to prepare a Massey Prenup for Howard as her wedding gift to him. At the wedding, Howard eats the Massey Prenup, claiming that he wants nothing but love and trust between them. Of course, Miles is hopelessly intrigued.

Six months later in Las Vegas, Miles meets Marilyn again. She has divorced Howard. After a series of lies and deceptions, they wind up at a wedding chapel. Before they marry, however, Miles's trusty associate prepares a Massey Prenup that they sign. In the hotel, Marilyn stops Miles's advances, asking him if he loves her and if she can trust him. Satisfied with his answers, she tears up the prenup.

The next morning, a happy Miles resigns his position as president of NOMAN. He makes a speech at their annual conference, dismissing the technicalities of the law and extolling the naked vulnerability of love. Extolling love in a manner reminiscent of I Cor 13, Miles calls on his colleagues to counsel trust rather than fear and cynicism. He for one has made the leap of love. Drinking at the bar with his trusty associate thereafter, they recognize Howard as an actor on a TV soap opera. Marilyn has duped them, and Miles's wealth is exposed to her designs.

Back home, the octogenarian head of the law firm upbraids Miles. This is not a time for the servants of the law to obey the law. Accordingly, Miles hires a hit man, Wheezy Joe, to kill Marilyn. When Rex Rexroth dies suddenly without a will, however, Marilyn becomes far richer than Miles, so Miles and his associate set out to stop the hit man. Marilyn, of course, buys off the hit man, and Miles escapes death only when Wheezy mistakes his gun for his asthma inhaler.

The movie ends fittingly with a divorce conference. Still enamored with Marilyn, he asks to reconcile with her. After they discuss trust, he signs the Massey Prenup (she does not), and they kiss. Meanwhile, in the background, their lawyers fight over the prenup. In the denouement, Miles and Marilyn become joint owners of Donovan's new TV show, *Funniest Divorce Videos*, starring Gus Petch as its host.

On one hand, *Intolerable Cruelty* is a typical American, screwball romantic comedy. In keeping with the American myth of the supreme value of individual self-expression, it extols love and romance at the price of the order/norm/law of marriage, a norm unsuccessfully protected by various legalities. On the other hand, neither law nor love ever clearly wins in this movie. Instead, the two are locked in a swirling, changing dance that nicely reflects the human need for both order and freedom. The conflicting statements that the Massey Prenup banishes romance and that it means true love are a sign of this continuing dance.

This dance makes the movie a nice foil for Paul. The movie reminds us vis-à-vis Paul that grace (here, miraculous, romantic love) alone is a serious problem. Humans need norms for communal life. If we do not accept that need, we may find ourselves saddled with Paul's spirit instead, a surreptitious establishment of an authority figure (Paul) or of his universals, losing any hope of equality, freedom, and difference. In short, if we abandon the law for grace, we will not long have grace. We will have new, even more inescapable norms. In the face of this problem, we need Paul's Judaizers, the emphasis on and the possibility of difference, to offer us a new possibility of grace in the face of Paul's colonizing, imperial grace.

Notes

1. Compare the use of *nomos* to indicate a social world. Badiou, *Saint Paul*, 40–54, uses "discourse" in this way and argues that Paul rejects the possible discourses of his day. On occasion, Paul seems to use "law" in the broad sense of aeon or world order. See, for example, Rom 8:2. Of course, in Torah itself, God's gift of the Torah to Israel at Sinai is that which creates Israel and provides the world or biosphere in which she lives.

2. It is possible, I suppose, that this creator is not the same deity who made Job a pawn in his game.

3. For a discussion of various interpretations, see Walsh, *Reading the Bible*, 336–41, 354–55. Miles, *God: A Biography*, 303–28, has one of the most intriguing recent interpretations.

4. Peter Berger, *The Sacred Canopy*, 74. Berger relies on Max Weber's earlier analysis of theodicy. See Weber, *The Sociology of Religion*, 4th ed., trans. Ephraim Fischoff (Boston: Beacon, 1963), 138–50.

5. Berger, *The Sacred Canopy*, 54.

6. Ibid., 55–56.

7. Ibid., 74.

8. Berger provides the following taxonomy of theodicies: (1) at the irrational end of the spectrum is self-transcending participation in a collectivity or sacred force/beings; (2) at the rational end of the spectrum is karma-samsara; (3) in the intermediate region lie (a) future this-worldly recompense, (b) otherworldly recompense, and (c) dualism. Monotheism faces the most difficult problems with theodicy and therefore develops the masochistic attitude, as in Job, par excellence (ibid., 60–74).

9. Ibid., 74.

10. One can read Job as the move from a death wish (Job 3) to awe before the creation/creator that leads to life-grasping repentance. After the struggle with his friends, however, Job has already moved from despair to a quest for justice/answers (Job 29–31). Job's friends, not the creator, save him from his death wish. The whirlwind refuses his quest for justice and "puts him in his place."

11. Berger, *The Sacred Canopy*, 78.

12. See Hays, *Echoes of Scripture*, 34–83, for a reading of Romans as a successful theodicy. His argument hinges on the claim that Paul is working with the same judgment/grace paradigm that underlies the Hebrew Bible. Hays finds the key expression of this paradigm in Deut 32 (ibid., 47, 74, 164). I, of course, am indicting the "judgment" phase of this pattern as an equivocation on the question of theodicy.

13. As mentioned previously, the "solution precedes plight" interpretation has been common in Pauline studies since Sanders, *Paul and Palestinian Judaism*, 474–511. See also E. P. Sanders, *Paul, the Law, and the Jewish People* (Philadelphia: Fortress, 1983), 35, 81–82, 125.

14. C. H. Dodd, *The Epistle of Paul to the Romans*, Moffatt New Testament Commentary (New York: Harper & Brothers, 1932), 42–46, 63. See also Heikki Räisänen, *The Torah and Christ: Essays in German and English on the Problem of Law in Early Christianity* (Helsinki: Finish Exegetical Society, 1986), on Paul's inconsistencies on the law.

15. See Stendahl, "The Apostle Paul and the Introspective Gospel of the West."

16. Berger, *The Sacred Canopy*, 59.

17. The new perspective on Paul labors to save its Paul from this anti-Semitic charge. After their work, Romans seems a Pauline attack on gentile arrogance. Nonetheless, that does not save those hypothetical Gentiles or earlier Pauline constructs like that of the Protestant Reformation from the sado-masochistic mechanisms I discuss here.

18. See Hyam Maccoby, *The Mythmaker: Paul and the Invention of Christianity* (New York: Harper & Row, 1986).

19. Of course, defining and redefining Israel is fully at home in, and a fundamental part of, Jewish discourse.

20. See Hays, *Echoes of Scripture*, 63–70, 74–75.

21. Taubes, *The Political Theology of Paul*, 3, 27–40, observes that Paul accepted the idea of God's creation of a new people in him but that Moses would not. He contrasts Rom 9–11 with Exod 32.

22. Paul, the apocalyptic seer of chapter 2, is comparable to Jonah, another reluctant prophet to the Gentiles. Paul's apocalyptic worldview envisions a salvation for Israel beyond the salvation of the Gentiles (a salvation occurring at the end of Jonah). As the apocalypse did not arrive, Jonah's anger, which sees God's salvation of the Gentiles as a betrayal of Israel, fits subsequent history more realistically than Paul's hope of Israel's salvation.

23. I have not dealt here at any length with the other innocent lost in 2 Cor 5:16–21, the human Christ. We looked at that issue in chapter 3. In light of this discussion, however, we should mention that Jesus is the Jew who dies for Paul's Gentiles. See the discussion of *The Confession* below. Unfortunately, under the hegemony of subsequent Christianity, a precarious slip between that individual Jew's suffering and the subsequent suffering of Jews has often taken place. That history makes the similar slips between the individual and the collective in Isaiah's servant songs haunting reading.

24. Terrence W. Tilley, *The Evils of Theodicy* (Washington, D.C.: Georgetown University Press, 1991), 3.

25. Ibid., 241–42. Tilley exempts Job from this critique. For Tilley, theodicy proper begins with the Enlightenment, and Job is a warning "never to write theodicies" (ibid., 245; see chapter 4 of his book as well).

26. Ibid., 250.

27. In fact, dark jokes punctuate the movie. At several tense moments, Mischa arrives, knocking and calling out, "Gestapo." On one such occasion, Jakob responds, "May you die laughing."

28. See, for example, Roger Ebert, "*Jakob the Liar*," http://www.suntimes.com/cgi-bin/print.cgi (accessed July 8, 2004); and Peter Matthews, "*Jakob the Liar*," http://www.bfi.org.uk/sightandsound /reviews/details.php?id=269 (accessed July 8, 2004). They find the conclusion a gimmicky effort, unrelated to the rest of the movie, to find a happy ending. Other critics also feel that the film treats the Holocaust too lightly. James Berardinelli calls the film "distasteful" and "almost an affront" ("*Jakob the Liar*," http://movie-reviews.colossus.net/movies/j/jakob.html [accessed July 8, 2004]). Interestingly, *Train of Life* reverses the reality-fantasy order and proportion of *Jakob the Liar*. It begins with a village purchasing their own train in order to escape the approaching Germans. They intend to take the train to Palestine. After a series of comic escapades, the villagers and their train find themselves at the Russian border between fronts with rockets racing overhead. At this point, the "reality" of the film turns surreal. Then, suddenly, we see Shlomo, the village idiot whose idea the "train of life" was, in the garb of and behind the wires of a concentration camp. What we thought was reality has become fantasy, and we are left with a grim shot of the village's true reality. Berardinalli, "*Train of Life*," http://movie-reviews.colossus. net/movies/t/train_life.html (accessed August 23, 2004), found this ending "tremendous" and the early part of the film "mediocre." Once again, the issue seems to be whether or not we can laugh in the face of events like the Holocaust.

29. The much more somber *The Pianist* also uses music to cope with the same horrors. It has a clearer individual triumph over evil as the hero survives to become a pianist again.

30. Jewett, *Saint Paul at the Movies*, 31–42, has an excellent discussion of the irrationality of sin in the movies and Paul. To his discussion, we could add some of the Coen brothers' early films, particularly *Blood Simple* and *Fargo*. Jewett does not, however, discuss the irrationality of grace or of theodicy. If sin is irrational, the claim of the ubiquity of sin, or the claim that people are necessarily bad, is in some doubt. *Fargo*, in particular, seems to express a sense that humans are fundamentally decent. At least this sense underlies Marge's speech to Gaear in the prowler: "And those three people [dead] in Brainerd. And for what? For a little bit of money. There's more to life than a little money, you know? Don't you know that? And here you are, and it's a beautiful day. Well . . . I just don't understand it."

31. As the movie embraces incongruity, it is religious in J. Z. Smith's postmodern sense of religion. See his *Map Is Not Territory*, 289–309.

32. Elie Wiesel has repeatedly asserted that protest is the proper religious response to God when God appears to be unjust. See, for example, *The Trial of God* (New York: Random House, 1979).

33. Camus, *Myth of Sisyphus*, 21.

34. Ibid., 31–32, 41–42. Later, Camus, 106–11, calls attention to Dostoevsky's Kirilov (in *The Possessed*). Kirilov claims that humans invented God to prevent suicide (a criticism akin to Camus' philosophical suicide), but he then decides to commit suicide in the absence of God in order to become God. Camus describes Dostoevsky's response to Kirilov in *The Brothers Karamazov* as philosophical suicide.

35. Ibid., 64.

36. Ibid., 115.

37. Ibid., 117–18.

38. Camus, *The Rebel*, 21. Nietzsche, *Beyond Good and Evil*, 265, asserts similarly: "The concept 'grace' has no meaning or good odor *inter pares*; there may be a sublime way of letting presents from above happen to one . . . but for this art and gesture the noble soul has no aptitude."

39. There are suggestions in the film that Judah's character is thoroughly despicable. Jack, for example, refers to other times that Judah has needed dirty work done. Most damningly, Judah justifies his breaking of the law on the grounds that the law did not provide him justice—protection from his neurotic mistress.

40. I have omitted pauses, silent and verbal, from Cliff's part of the dialogue.

41. Camus, *The Rebel*, 4–5. Frederick A. Olafson, "Camus, Albert," *The Encyclopedia of Philosophy*, ed. Paul Edwards (New York: Macmillan, 1967), 2:15–18, concisely traces the development of Camus' thought in both his philosophical essays and his novels.

42. Camus, *The Rebel*, 22.

43. Ibid., 302–6. See also Camus' Nobel Prize acceptance speech, http://www.nobel.se/laureates/literature-1957-acceptance.html (accessed November 1, 1999).

44. He does not demand love of God. He extols love as a part of our construction of God, that is, of our ideal.

45. *Bruce Almighty* rewrites Job far less cynically. Bruce's complaints convince God to give Bruce the divine job temporarily. Like Job, Bruce learns that he cannot handle this position. Of course, this lesson handles human arrogance far more gently than the original. The kindness is part of the modernizing of Job in *Bruce Almighty*. Thus, the story does not end with repentance but with Bruce's commitment to social responsibility.

46. In *Commandments*, Seth Warner loses everything, but unlike Job, he proceeds to break the commandments in order to provoke God to action.

47. The title of this section gestures at Dietrich Bonhoeffer's critique of cheap grace (see *The Cost of Discipleship*, rev. ed., trans. R. H. Fuller (New York: Macmillan, 1963).

48. Manuel Jordan, the protagonist of *Levity*, is another guilty murderer seeking redemption. His rejection of a belief in God allows the matter to proceed on an altogether human level. Whether he finds any redemption depends on one's interpretation of the final scene. Manuel boards a subway and leaves the ghost of Abner, his victim who has attended him periodically throughout the movie, on the landing. Has Manuel left his burdens behind? The movie's title may support the optimistic reading of the ending (or does it simply denote Manuel's search for freedom?). No character ever discusses levity, but Manuel and Abner do discuss gravity. Are we, in an Augustinian manner, meant to read gravity as the weight of sin and levity as redemption? Regardless, like *The Confession*, *Levity* testifies to the costliness of redemption. The costly forgiveness in these two movies stands in dramatic contrast to the cheap, voyeuristic redemption offered by movies like *The Passion of the Christ*.

49. Nietzsche, *The Gay Science*, 289, rejects forgiveness and pity altogether in favor of the necessity of justice.

50. While the temple stood, as the citation from Num 15 indicates, animal sacrifices would also play a role. As many recent Pauline scholars have observed, the death of Jesus is hardly necessary in that context as a sacrifice for individual sins. For this reason, Wright, *The Climax of the Covenant*, reads Paul's notion of Jesus' death as a response to exile, not to individual sin. The idea of Williams (*Jesus' Death as Saving Event*) and Seeley (*The Noble Death*) that Paul understood Jesus' death in terms of those of the martyrs who helped end the oppression of Antiochus is similar. See Taubes, *The Political Theology of Paul*, 28–47, for an interesting argument that Paul and Yom Kippur—still the Jewish method for dealing with collective and individual sins—are essentially different readings of Exod 32.

51. See William Klassen, *Judas: Betrayer or Friend of Jesus?* (Minneapolis: Fortress, 1996), 28–40, 96–115, 160–76.

52. Suicide became an ignoble event only with the rise of Christianity. Augustine, for example, is largely responsible for the idea that Judas's suicide removed him from the possibility of salvation. See Arthur J. Droege and James D. Tabor, *A Noble Death: Suicide and Martyrdom among Christians and Jews in Antiquity* (New York: HarperSanFrancisco, 1992).

53. *The Confession* recognizes that Roman Catholicism, as well as Judaism, expects one to acknowledge responsibility for one's sins. In an amusing scene, Mel, Roy's Irish Catholic private detective, baptizes Roy with bourbon in a bar after Roy has spent the night with Sara Fertig. He seduces Roy by asking him if he wants to go to heaven. After the baptism, Mel confesses that he did not tell Roy one important thing: he can go to hell now, too. This scene is another element in Roy's conversion. Adele Reinhartz, *Scripture on the Silver Screen*, 39–53, has an excellent discussion of *Dead Man Walking* in which she argues that Sister Helen leads Matthew, a rapist and murderer, to redemption by leading him to take responsibility for his acts.

54. Should we read *The Confession* and Rom 9–11 in light of Isa 53 and the other suffering servant songs of 2 Isaiah, focusing on the corporate nature of that servant Israel? See n. 23. Hays, *Echoes of Scripture*, 61–63, argues that Isa 53 is in the background throughout Rom 9–11.

55. See Gager, *Reinventing Paul*, 5–7. Gager feels that Paul makes negative and positive statements about the law, so he decides, against most scholars, to privilege the positive. He and others, as we have seen before, argue that Paul may have even imagined—at least temporarily—two gospels, one for Jews through Torah and one for Gentiles through Christ (see Gal 2:7–8; Rom 2:6–29) (*Reinventing Paul*, 43–75). More scholars contend that the negative comments on the law (Torah) should not be read as criticisms of Judaism but as defenses of Paul's mission and of the Gentiles' place in Christ. Scholars have reached these positions, at least in part, because of a growing post-Holocaust sensitivity to Judaism and because of scholarly commitments to toleration in a pluralist society. They have also come to these positions because of the hopelessly tangled logic of Rom 1–3 (and 9–11) and because of Paul's incredibly ambiguous statements about the law. For a review of recent positions on Paul and the law, see Segal, *Paul the Convert*, 129–36, 281–84; Jewett, *Paul the Apostle to America*, 32–44; and Gager, *Reinventing Paul*.

56. See Daniel Boyarin, *A Radical Jew: Paul and the Politics of Identity* (Berkeley: University of California Press, 1994), for a discussion of Paul's place in the Jewish discourse about universalism and Jewish cultural difference. Boyarin contends that Paul's emphasis on the spirit is a move toward universalism that reduces Jews and Judaism to erasable signs. He does, however, also conclude that Paul's emphasis on universalism and the rabbis' emphasis on cultural difference are helpful correctives of one another.

57. See Sanders, *Paul, the Law, and the Jewish People*, 101–3.

58. See Hays, *Echoes of Scripture*, 75–79.

59. While the movie shows several Jewish rituals, it focuses on ethical issues. In this, the movie reads the law more modernly than Paul does.

60. Ben, the blind rabbi in *Crimes and Misdemeanors*, tells Judah that without the law it is all darkness. Jewett, *Saint Paul Returns to the Movies*, 136–46, finds a similarly positive attitude to the law in *The Firm*, although this law is the American legal system. Hopelessly embroiled in a legal firm with connections

to the mob, Mitch and his wife extricate themselves from a life-threatening situation after Mitch observes, "I know it's weird, but if we follow the law, it might just save us." Thereafter, Mitch collects evidence of mail fraud against the firm. As Mitch puts it later, "I won my life back. . . . I discovered the law again. You actually made me think about it." Jewett, however, argues that romantic love, an analogue of grace and not the law, is the real salvific impetus in the movie (ibid., 141–42). This interpretation resembles his interpretation of *Tender Mercies*. See chapter 1.

61. He also remained a Jew (at least in his own mind) to the end of his days. Several Jewish interpreters have made this point of late. See Segal, *Paul the Convert*, and Boyarin, *A Radical Jew*.

62. Wright, *The Climax of the Covenant*, finds the problem in disobedience, not in the law. For him, the exile (read "this evil age" of apocalyptic) continues until Christ's obedience unto death.

63. Paul's apocalyptic grace and Jewish obedience to law respectively resemble William James's famous two forms of religion: the sick-souled, which requires transcendent help in impossible circumstances, and the healthy-minded, which believes that humans can live religiously and ethically without special divine aid. See his *Varieties of Religious Experience: A Study in Human Nature* (Glasgow: William Collins Sons, 1960).

64. See Sanders, *Paul and Palestinian Judaism*; idem, *Paul, the Law, and the Jewish People*.

65. Sanders, *Paul, the Law, and the Jewish People*, 105–6. Sanders does also find significant differences between Paul's "new creation" and Judaism's covenantal nomism (ibid., 207–9). Paul starts a move toward a new covenantal nomism, particularly in the Corinthian correspondence, that Christianity eventually actualized (Sanders, *Paul and Palestinian Judaism*, 512–15).

66. Given the failure of apocalyptic hopes, I consider Badiou quite helpful on this point. On one hand, Badiou, *Saint Paul*, 40–54, sees law under the guise of "discourse" negatively and celebrates Paul's attempt to escape it. On the other hand, Badiou realistically realizes that law, as discourse, cannot be left behind. Accordingly, he reads Paul's apocalyptic tension, which he calls the "not, but" (instead of the more common "already, not yet"), as meaning not law, but grace (ibid., 63–64). In short, the human is constituted by both law and grace, or grace relies on and spins off of law. We could compare the relationship of postmodernism to modernism.

67. See Petersen, *Rediscovering Paul*, and Hays, *Echoes of Scripture in Paul*, on Paul's attempts to form communities of character.

68. As Sanders observes, that which is wrong with Torah is simply that it does let the Gentiles in as freely as Paul's revelation demands (*Paul, the Law, and the Jewish People*, 147).

69. The "in part" seems necessary because—as Taubes, *The Political Theology of Paul*, 52–60, observes—Paul reduces the double command—to love God and the neighbor—to its second part.

70. Sanders, *Paul, the Law, and the Jewish People*, 94–95.

71. For a very complete plot summary, see Tim Dirks, "*Bad Day at Blackrock*," http://www.filmsite.org/badd.html (accessed July 16, 2004).

72. I will not explore it here, but Paul's spirit is his attempt to install an internal monitor in his followers. Cf. Castelli, *Imitating Paul*, who helpfully brings Foucault into this discussion. On Paul's spiritualizing, see Boyarin, *A Radical Jew*, and George Aichele, *The Control of Biblical Meaning: Canon as Semiotic Mechanism* (Harrisburg, Pa.: Trinity Press International, 2001).

73. Not surprisingly, Boyarin finds it in Torah, read as the foundation of diaspora identity. Boyarin's fundamental insight is correct. We need the interplay. The interplay is, in fact, in Paul. It simply gets lost in the post-Reformation, anti-Semitic reading of Paul as well as in Paul's own attempts to rule unruly spiritual communities. Grace alone is a problem. Given that, we should remember Paul's own Jewishness, a matter that Paul does with some difficulty in Romans. Perhaps, then, it is Paul's lack of logic in Romans that redeems his humanity.

74. While the Coen brothers employ the same actors again and again, these actors are subject to the same interplay. In some films, then, Frances McDormand plays a cheating wife (*Blood Simple, The Man Who Wasn't There*), and in another she incarnates the rule of common decency and of law and order (*Fargo*).

Michael Badalucco plays a small businessman in one film (*The Man Who Wasn't There*) and a murderous, manic-depressive outlaw in another (*O Brother, Where Art Thou?*).

75. The mockery of the voiceover technique in *The Big Lebowski* is an excellent example of the Coens' inability simply to affirm order at the expense of grace, freedom, or escape. The narrator loses his place, bumbles, and ultimately recommends "takin' her easy." If *Fargo* is their most unflinching affirmation of order, *The Big Lebowski* takes freedom's revenge on *Fargo* as it replays, on drugs, the plot of *Fargo* without the representative of law and order (Marge in *Fargo*). *The Big Lebowski* also reduces common decency by parody to a bowling alley. The voiceover that begins *Blood Simple* eschews order in another way. That narrator says that something always goes wrong; there is no guarantee. The plot that follows eloquently affirms him. In this film, there is no overarching, monotheistic providence. Instead, multiple plotters create a maze that destroys almost everyone.

76. The old, blind black prophet who predicted their adventures near the beginning of the movie also rides by on a handcar. This element also bespeaks a higher sense of order beyond the trickster Everett.

77. This movie was the first made by the Coens in which they were not the scriptwriters as well.

Chapter 5
Playing God:
Canonical Saints
and Mere Humans

The saying is sure and worthy of full acceptance, that Christ Jesus came into the world to save sinners—of whom I am the foremost. But for that very reason I received mercy, so that in me, as the foremost, Jesus Christ might display the utmost patience, making me an example to those who would come to believe in him for eternal life. (I Tim 1:15–16)

Let those of us then who are mature be of the same mind; and if you think differently about anything, this too God will reveal to you. Only let us hold fast to what we have attained.

Brothers and sisters, join in imitating me, and observe those who live according to the example you have in us. For many live as enemies of the cross of Christ; I have often told you of them, and now I tell you even with tears. Their end is destruction; their god is the belly; and their glory is in their shame; their minds are set on earthly things. But our citizenship is in heaven, and it is from there that we are expecting a Savior, the Lord Jesus Christ. He will transform the body of our humiliation that it may be conformed to the body of his glory, by the power that also enables him to make all things subject to himself. (Phil 3:15–21)

Playing God

Phone Booth begins with a montage about the ubiquity of phones. Intriguingly, the camera takes us from a satellite in outer space to the streets of New York. This sequence provides a visual metaphor for the entire film, for we move in the film from above—from some divine eye?—to the intimate details of an individual life. Oversight and voice, if not God, impinge upon one cavalierly chosen character and, therefore, through the ever-present miracle of satellite communications, potentially upon all of us.

The chosen one is Stuart Shepard, a conniving, lying publicist. We first see him as he walks the streets of New York City talking on several cell phones. An unpaid,

145

adoring assistant juggles these phones for Stu in the hopes that he, too, may some-
day become a successful publicist. Leaving his assistant with various tasks, Stu steps
into the only remaining phone booth in the city in order to call an aspiring young
actress, Pamela McFadden. He is attempting to bed Pam without letting her know
that he has a wife. With an interesting display of conscience, Stu takes off his wedding ring before making the call that betrays his marriage. He, of course, has no
intention of leaving his wife, and he calls from the phone booth so that there will
be no trace of the call. In short, Stu treats both women dishonestly.

Unsuccessful again in arranging a tryst with Pam, he hangs up the phone, but
it rings again. The caller, whom I will call the Voice, quickly turns Stu into his
hostage in the phone booth. The mysterious Voice has a rifle with a telescopic lens
trained on Stu. He convinces Stu of his intentions by destroying a toy robot outside the booth, by playing a red laser sight upon Stu's chest, and by shooting Stu in
the ear when he tries to use his cell phone to call help. The Voice also tells Stu that
he has done this before. He is responsible for the death of a pornographer and a
CEO who used inside knowledge to sell his company stock before it plummeted.
The Voice, then, is a self-appointed moral enforcer, an external conscience for those
in need of reform. The Voice wants Stu to confess his sins, in particular, his deceitful treatment of Pam and his wife, Kelly.

While Stu struggles to make sense of this anguished situation, enduring difficult phone calls with Pam and Kelly, local prostitutes begin to harass him. They
need the phone booth that he has taken over. When they cannot roust him, they
bring in their pimp, who beats the phone booth with a baseball bat and ultimately
throttles Stu. When the choking Stu acquiesces to the Voice's offer of help, the
Voice kills the pimp.

Soon, the police and SWAT surround Stu's phone booth. They think him the
shooter and demand that he surrender his weapon. The Voice, of course, will not
allow Stu to enlighten the police, and it seems that Stu will quickly become a victim of the police. Fortunately for Stu, Captain Ramey takes charge of the scene
and refuses to allow Stu to become another "suicide by cop."

Seeing Stu's plight on local TV, Kelly and Pam show up and provide more fod-
der for the Voice's sadistic manipulations. The Voice promises not to kill Kelly and
to let Stu go if Stu confesses his affair with Pam to Kelly. When he does so, the
Voice refuses to release him. Angrily, Stu slams the phone down and steps outside
the booth. Ramey stops the police, who still think Stu is armed, from shooting.
The phone rings again. If Stu does not answer, he knows the Voice will shoot Kelly,
so he returns to his cage. The return, of course, is an epiphany for Ramey. He
knows then that Stu is held captive by the caller, so he sets the police in motion to
discover the Voice's location.

Meanwhile, the Voice has told Stu that a pistol is lodged in the roof of the
phone booth and tries to entice Stu to fire at him by moving curtains in a window,

exposing his position. Of course, if Stu takes the gun, the police will shoot him. When that temptation fails, the Voice threatens to kill either Kelly or Pam. Stu must choose which one. Acting overwhelmed, Stu falls to his knees in order to call his wife on his cell phone so that Ramey can hear the Voice's demands. Ramey defuses the situation by approaching the booth.

After the Voice makes Stu send Ramey away, the Voice demands Stu's full public confession. Stu complies:

> I've never done anything for anybody who couldn't do something for me. I string along an eager kid with promises that I'll pay him money. I only keep him around because he looks up to me. Adam, if you're watching, don't be a publicist. You're too good for it. I lie in person and on the phone. I lie to my friends. I lie to newspapers and magazines who sell my lies to more and more people. I'm just a part of a big cycle of lies. I should be fucking president. I wear all this Italian shit because underneath I still feel like the Bronx. I think I need these clothes and this watch. My $2,000 dollar watch is a fake, and so am I. I neglected the things I should have valued most. I valued this shit. I take off my wedding ring to call Pam. Kelly, that's Pam. Don't blame her. I never told her I was married. If I did, she would have told me to go home. Kelly, looking at you now, I'm ashamed of myself. I mean . . . I worked so hard on this image of Stu Shepard the asshole who refers to himself in the third person that I only proved I should be alone. I've been dressing up as something I'm not for so long that I'm so afraid you won't like what's underneath. But here I am. Just flesh and blood and weakness. I love you so fucking much. I take off this ring because it only reminds me of how I've failed you. I don't want to give you up. I want to make things better. But it may not be my choice anymore. You deserve better.

Stu is no murderer or great criminal. He is only an everyman sinner.

Duplicitous to the end, the Voice still intends to kill Stu; however, the police serendipitously discover the Voice's location. As Stu taunts the Voice about the police's imminent arrival, the Voice threatens Kelly yet again, so Stu grabs the pistol in the phone booth and races into the street, yelling, "Take me." He falls shot. Meanwhile, the police break into a room and find a man with a slit throat.

In the denouement, Ramey approaches Stu, who has been shot with a rubber bullet by the police in order to save him from the Voice. Kelly embraces Stu and declares her undying love for him. He pledges a commitment to honesty with her. Chillingly, however, we learn that the dead man was not the Voice. In fact, as a drugged Stu sits in the back of an ambulance, the Voice approaches him and threatens to return if Stu does not continue his new, honest life. As the movie ends, a voiceover from the Voice says, "Isn't it funny. You hear a phone ring, and it could be anybody. But a ringing phone has to be answered, doesn't it? Doesn't it?" As a phone rings, we ascend rapidly from the world to the satellite view with which the movie began.

In *Phone Booth*, the Voice plays God.[1] The Voice provides an external conscience or norm and imposes that norm on Stu (and us?) through the ever-present phone. Murderously, the Voice forces Stu toward a new life. Faced with death, Stu confesses his everyman sins and finds a new life. As the movie ends, the Voice threatens a judgmental return if its norms are not fully followed. This open ending, the ever-present phones in our lives, and the everyman quality of Stu's sins embroil us in the story as well. We, too, may face transcendent calls, forced conversions, and judgmental parousias.

So described, the Voice differs little from Paul. Sans electronic devices, Paul impinges upon and interrupts the lives of his listeners with an apocalyptic message. The message threatens them with divine wrath and death if they do not comply. If Paul successfully manipulates their conversion, they die to their old selves and find a new life. This new life, of course, is according to Pauline norms, and Paul uses emissaries, personal visits, and letters to enforce obedience to his norms. In short, Paul's followers must comply with his gospel. To reach complete compliance, as we saw in the last chapter, he endeavors to turn the external norms of Paul, Christ, and gospel into internal norms, an indwelling Christ or spirit. Finally, Paul threatens his communities with various judgmental parousias—both apostolic and divine—if they do not comply with these new norms. Like *Phone Booth*'s Voice, Paul, Christ, and God are watching.

Of course, we normally think of Paul as a more benign figure than the Voice. In our culture, Paul has sacred trappings and a cultural centrality that the Voice simply does not have. He is, after all, Saint Paul the Apostle. The post-Pauline letters, Acts, the canonical New Testament, and years of interpretation have enthroned Saint Paul's virtually unassailable authority. If Paul did not have this sacred status, however, we might see Paul as something quite akin to *Phone Booth*'s Voice. We might see him, as his opponents apparently did, as someone desperately striving to garner authority for himself. We might see Paul, like the Voice, as playing God.

In a movie by that name, a young man, Eugene Sands, walks down a dark street to a sleazy bar to buy drugs. His voiceover reflects on his life:

> Sometimes, we all wonder how things come to be. A chain of events. A leads to B leads to C leads to Z. Each life is made up of big decisions, and each day is made up of a million little decisions. . . . All these seemingly inconsequential choices might change your life forever. But who can handle that kind of responsibility? It would paralyze you to think about it. So you have to trust your instinct. What the Greeks might call your character. You had better pray to whatever God you believe in that your character knows what

the hell it's doing. I thought I was a man of character. Good character. Until I made a mistake. A bad one that changed everything. That's why I found myself walking into a lousy LA bar to buy . . . synthetic heroin. My personal favorite. You see, when I got high, the chain of events disappeared. No past, no future, just the sweet, sticky now. But before I could get home that night with my bag of goodies, something happened. I did a good thing. One good deed that started another chain I wasn't ready for. And a ride I had no business taking.

His mistake was his decision to operate on a young lady while under the influence of drugs. Arrogantly, he thought that no one else could do the job and that he could rise above the influence of drugs. She died. In the course of the flashback in which we learn this history, we see him report one prayer and pray another: (1) "When I pray to God, I don't ask him to eradicate disease. I pray that he send me something that I haven't seen," and (2) "My God, I'm sorry." The move from the first prayer to the second nicely describes his fall from grace.

His good deed is his rescue of a man shot in the sleazy bar with quick-thinking medical improvisation. Unfortunately, that good deed so impresses a young lady there, Claire, that she relates the story to her lover, Raymond Blossom. This criminal has two of his thugs kidnap Eugene. When they bring Eugene to Raymond's house, Raymond insists that they be "friends" and gives Eugene ten thousand dollars for his help. Raymond sees Eugene as "off-the-books" medical assistance for his various criminal associates. Eugene sees Raymond as the opportunity to practice medicine again, so he is quickly seduced into Raymond's criminal enterprises.

An ambitious FBI agent, Gage, who sees Raymond and his international criminal associates as a leg up in his career, traps Eugene further and forces him into working undercover. Matters come to a climax when Raymond's enemies break into his home and shoot Claire. As Eugene tries to help her, he finds a "wire." She, too, is working for the FBI. In order to save her, he drugs her so that she will appear dead and spirits her away from Raymond. Stopping at a motorcycle bar, Eugene operates on her and saves her life.

When Raymond discovers Eugene's ruse, Claire and Eugene run for their lives. On the run, Claire saves Eugene by shaming him into abandoning his drugs and into taking responsibility for his life. After a dark night of the soul, he starts his recovery by talking about his fall from grace.

When you come from a long line of doctors, it's not good enough to be a doctor. You have to be the doctor. . . . It wasn't about being a surgeon anymore. It was about me. When you're a surgeon, people come to you and they say, "You can save my life. You can save the life of my child." They look at you with these eyes, full of hope. And you want to do it. You think, "If I go to sleep, who's going to save all these people?" That's the way God feels, right? But I needed help to stay up though. Start taking drugs. I'm a doctor; I can handle it. . . . Then one day, I found myself up and down at the same time. And I realized that I wasn't God. I wasn't even an angel. And all those lives that I saved didn't add up to the one life that I lost. That's what I've been thinking about anyway, all night.

In short, Eugene quits playing God.

They call the FBI, not knowing that Gage has made a private deal with Raymond. Gage sends Claire back to Raymond and puts Eugene in a safe house. After Raymond's thugs fail to kill Eugene, Eugene disrupts the sting engineered by Gage and Raymond. In a shoot-out, Raymond flees with Claire with Eugene in pursuit. As the FBI falls behind, Raymond stops to kill Eugene. Eugene, however, winds up with the weapon and the girl. When Raymond goes into traffic for his lost weapon, he is struck by a passing car. Eugene, ever the doctor, goes to help him, but Raymond winds up holding a gun on the doctor. Unless Eugene helps him, however, Raymond will die, so he lowers the gun, saying, "Are you going to save me?" Eugene responds, "I can't do that, Ray. I'm only a doctor."

The movie ends with Eugene's voiceover detailing the fates of the various characters. His final words indicate a wry humor unlike the depressed fatalism of the opening voiceover and underline his new humility: "I made her [Claire] take out insurance so she can get a really good doctor. I can't be everywhere, you know. I may get my license back; I may not. We'll see. In any case, I guess I learned that if you're in the business of saving lives, you better start with your own. And, of course, always call 911."

On one level, this movie simply updates Gen 3.[2] On this view, Eugene plays the role of Adam. Of course, he is already outside the garden when the movie starts. Only gradually do the audience and Eugene learn that he was playing God and that he must eschew this role to save himself. Eugene-Adam's temptations, however, are not over after his fall. Standing in for the snake, Raymond seduces Eugene even more deeply into evil. Fortunately, in a standard Hollywood pattern, there is also a damsel in distress whose plight leads the hero back to himself. Instead of a fall, then, this movie is about the hero's redemption. Left safely within Christian discourse, it is a 'paradise regained' story.

It is, even on this reading, quite a secular story. A transcendent God is noticeably absent, but there are prayers. The whole story may be either a fulfillment of Eugene's initial prayer to bring him something new or a response to his prayer of repentance after the death of the young girl. There is a God, too, in the sense of a fate governing events, that mysterious something that governs the chain of events— or the chain of events itself—that Eugene speaks about in the opening voiceover.

The most obvious God in the story, however, is clearly Eugene. Not only does he play God, but he is also the voice that reveals the movie's "lesson." Not incidentally, Eugene's final voiceover takes place as the camera pulls back from the highway bridge where Eugene saved Raymond's life. As a result, we look down upon the Los Angeles skyline as Eugene's voiceover finally ends. The camera work and the voiceover suggest that Eugene is the God of this movie. The words of the voiceover, however, deny his divine status.

Clearly, Eugene is not the dominant God of Gen 3 or Job. He is also not the elusive, effective Voice of *Phone Booth*. This God is more like the ineffectual, threatened deity that some critical readers see behind Gen 3 and the Tower of Babel story. Such readers envision those deities as comic figures, vainly trying to defend a vanishing order. Those deities are quite similar to the TV repairman in *Pleasantville*. That TV repairman magically translates two 1990s teenagers, David and Jennifer, into the world of the 1950s sitcom "Pleasantville" as Bud and Mary Sue. For some reason, the repairman needs someone new to follow the 1950s script. He chooses David, an expert in the trivia of that sitcom world. In that world, however, Bud and Mary Sue prove insidious influences. They bring the values of the 1990s to the 1950s and change the sitcom world forever. The TV repairman has not repaired the script. Instead, he has introduced a fatal flaw and ruined that world. Not surprisingly, David/Bud simply uses a TV remote—now in his control, not the repairman's—to silence the repairman's comic threats. The world has escaped this God's control.

By contrast, Eugene is a dramatic, not a comic, figure; nonetheless, he, too, learns that the world is beyond his control. As he eschews arrogant dominance, he repents of his godhood and gradually becomes a human. He becomes "just" a doctor, a person who can help others but not save them. Of course, as we have seen, his words sit in some tension with the camera angle and the voiceover device that end the movie.

In striking contrast to Eugene's humility, Paul plays God. Like the Voice in *Phone Booth*, he intends to save people, regardless of the cost to them. A transcendent God, however, is actually no more evident in Paul than it is in *Playing God*. Paul speaks about and for God/Christ constantly. God and Christ do not, however, figure in his letters as story actors. They are warrants for Paul's actions, particularly the action of evangelizing the Gentiles. They are warrants, that is, for Paul's life and authority. According to Paul's voiceover, God and Christ have acted before and will act after Paul's story. In the meantime, if they act, they act in Paul's words. Paul is the Voice of his letters. He claims to have had an apocalypse of Christ and to share that vision with his followers, but he does so, in his letters, only as the Voice. For Paul's audience, Paul plays God.

On this point, Paul is unrepentant. He never learns Eugene's humility. Even when Paul speaks of his human weakness or his sufferings, he does so in order to cement his authority over others. His suffering marks him as a vehicle of the divine glory.

> *But we have this treasure* [the glory of God] in clay jars, so that it may be made
> clear that this extraordinary power belongs to God and does not come from
> us. We are afflicted in every way, but not crushed; perplexed, but not driven
> to despair; persecuted, but not forsaken; struck down, but not destroyed;
> always carrying in the body the death of Jesus, so that the life of Jesus may
> also be made visible in our bodies. For while we live, we are always being
> given up to death for Jesus' sake, *so that the life of Jesus may be made visible in our
> mortal flesh.* (2 Cor 4:7–11, emphasis added)

While mere humans fall short of this divine glory (Rom 3:20), Paul and his associates have the divine glory. In Paul, the divine glory does not fade as it does in other ministers, even the revered Moses (2 Cor 3:13). That divine glory, the "real Paul" if you will, heroically survives all afflictions, confusions, persecutions, and blows (compare Rom 8:18–39). No wonder, then, that Paul expects to be present with the Lord when absent from the body (2 Cor 5:1–8). In fact, Paul is always looking for the apocalyptic phone booth (the sufferings) that will reveal his true, glorious superhero self. Later, Paul returns to boasting about his suffering in order to assert his authority over other ministers and the community (see 2 Cor 11:21–12:10). His sufferings glorify him and elevate him above mere human authorities—his competition. In his sufferings, Paul plays the apocalyptic Christ (2 Cor 12:9).

When humans claim such divine authority—when a voice speaks as the Voice—we usually demure, run for cover, or call 911. We should. At the very least, we should place such Voices in competition with other voices. The resulting cacophony would reveal various gods wrangling for power, all desiring to establish their own monotheistic imperialism. Paul's apocalypse cements Paul's authority, but an apocalypse of wrangling voices might be truly liberating. At least such an apocalypse would reveal the political economy at work behind the Voice and the rage therein for order, sameness, and hierarchy.

Saint Paul the Apostle

When his followers and the canon transformed him into Saint Paul, Paul passed beyond all hope of repentance. In fact, he passed beyond human limitation altogether. The canon enshrines Paul's hubris at the same time that it ensconces his divine authority.

New Testament documents, generally judged late by New Testament scholars, treat the apostles as a group in this mythic fashion. The apostles found and guarantee the one holy apostolic tradition and church.[3]

> So then you are no longer strangers and aliens, but you are citizens with the
> saints and also members of the household of God, built upon the founda-

tion of the apostles and prophets, with Christ Jesus himself as the corner-stone. In him the whole structure is joined together and grows into a holy temple in the Lord; in whom you also are built together spiritually into a dwelling place for God. (Eph 2:19–22; compare 2 Pet 3:2; Jude)

The reification (stones in a building) and spiritualization of humans is, once again, blatant. Here, however, we are primarily concerned with the nonhuman or mythic apostles. In the documents in the Pauline orbit, Paul plays the premier apostolic role. If the "mystery" has been revealed to apostles and prophets (Eph 3:4–5), Paul is its primary spokesperson (Eph 3:3, 9–10), because the mystery concerns the inclusion of the Gentiles (Eph 3:4–6), and Paul, of course, is the apostle to the Gentiles par excellence.[4] Paul also takes a premier place because of the magnitude of his "conversion" (I Cor 15:8–10; Eph 3:8; I Tim 1:15–16).

The saying is sure and worthy of full acceptance, that Christ Jesus came into the world to save sinners—of whom I am the foremost. But for that very reason I received mercy, so that in me, as the foremost, Jesus Christ might display the utmost patience, *making me an example* to those who would come to believe in him for eternal life. (I Tim 1:15–16, emphasis added)

This rhetoric resembles Paul's rhetoric about suffering. As Paul's suffering proves his authority, his abject sinfulness proves his gospel of grace. Paul, then, incarnates the gospel of grace/mercy, the gospel of transcendent transformation. He is the example par excellence, not only for leadership, but for the very nature of Christian life.

Contemporary scholars, who search for the historical Paul, do not like to speak of Paul's conversion. They prefer to speak of Paul's call.[5] Their hesitation is understandable. After all, Paul hardly moves from one religion (Judaism) to another (Christianity). That is hardly a historical possibility. My concern here, however, is not historical. It is about claims to divine authority. The canonical New Testament makes Saint Paul the mythic basis of gentile Christianity. He originates Christianity. Of course, he does not do this alone: the myth of the church needs the foundation of all the apostles. Mythically speaking, he is far more important than even Jesus is. After all, the Christ of Christian discourse almost wholly obscures Jesus.[6] Saint Paul, the incarnation of grace, the exemplar of Christian living, and the apostle to the Gentiles, is far more visible. Within Christian discourse, Paul is the prototype of the "before-after" story of evangelical revivals and testimonials and the precursor of Augustine and Luther, among other notable, dramatic Christian converts.

In Acts, Peter is Paul's equal in the drama of his "conversion." In Luke's passion narrative, Peter is a craven coward unable to withstand the queries of menials (Luke 22:54–62). After the empowerment of the resurrection/spirit, however, Peter speaks boldly before the rulers of the people and refuses to be silenced despite their deadly threats (Acts 3–5; 12). Surely, that transformation is as dramatic as Paul's, but Paul is the centerpiece of the tale of the move of "the church" from Jerusalem to Rome. In this story, Peter is Paul's precursor. Therefore, Acts narrates the tale of Paul's transformation on three separate occasions, each of which stresses, in different ways, the miraculous nature of Paul's "conversion" (9:1–22; 22:4–16; 26:9–18).[7] Despite the wealth of visions and "pentecosts" in Acts, Paul's conversion is the central hierophany, the mythic foundation of the move to the Gentiles of the Greco-Roman world.

Not surprisingly, in the canon, Paul's voice becomes the Voice, indistinguishable from scripture.

> So also our beloved brother Paul wrote to you according to the wisdom given him, speaking of this as he does in all his letters. There are some things in them hard to understand, which the ignorant and unstable twist to their own destruction, as they do the other scriptures. You therefore, beloved, since you are forewarned, beware that you are not carried away with the error of the lawless and lose your own stability. (2 Pet 3:15b–17)

He is the conduit of the divine revelation (Titus 1:1–3). Any other teaching abandons his divine instruction. Other teaching is mere myth and vain speculation (1 Tim 1:3–7). While Paul's teaching leads to life and peace, even in the Roman Empire (1 Tim 2:1–2), other teaching leads to destruction (1 Tim 6:3–5).

As the Voice, Paul is the very source of divine grace/mercy (2 Tim 1:6; 2:10). In the story of Acts, Paul is a divine man who trails miracles wherever he goes and who is constantly in visionary touch with the spiritual world. Accordingly, his followers (all later Christians after Paul becomes canonical authority) must align themselves as closely as possible with Paul (2 Tim 1:8). They should hold and teach the Pauline tradition, not think about it (1 Tim 6:20–21). Those who deviate from Paul, the mythic example of grace and the apostolic Voice, do so at their peril. While Paul may wish them no personal harm, God will repay them. At its simplest, God is with Paul, not others (2 Tim 4:9–18).

No wonder, then, that many mistook Paul for a god (Acts 14:18; 28:3–6). The canonical New Testament does its best to blur the distinction, to efface the human Paul with sainthood, glory, and divine authority. In the late New Testament documents, which we have been looking at here, Paul plays a role similar to that of YHWH in the Psalms and Jesus in the gospels. Paul is the sacred source of power and meaning. To be with him is to live. To depart from him is to die. Outside Paul, there is no salvation (see Acts 27:24).[8] If Paul is only a vehicle for a transcendent God, that God is absent apart from his Pauline conduit. As a result, in the canonical New Testament, Paul plays God.[9]

The canon also makes Paul unassailable by relegating him to the golden mythic age.

> And now I know that none of you, among whom I have gone about proclaiming the kingdom, will ever see my face again. . . . Keep watch over yourselves and over all the flock, of which the Holy Spirit has made you overseers [*episkopous*, "bishops"], to shepherd the church of God that he obtained with the blood of his own Son. I know that after I have gone, savage flocks will come in among you, not sparing the flock. Some even from your own group will come distorting the truth in order to entice the disciples to follow them. Therefore be alert, remembering that for three years I did not cease night or day to warn everyone with tears. (Acts 20:25, 28–31)

Acts 20 does not specify the point, but, likely, we are to think of these "bishops" as Pauline men. After all, Paul was the conduit by which the Holy Spirit came to Ephesus (Acts 19:5–6). In the economy of Acts, the apostles follow Jesus, Paul follows the apostles, and the gentile bishops follow Paul. In fact, as various scholars have observed, Luke-Acts presents the major characters of its story—Jesus, Peter, and Paul—as if cut from the same prophetic pattern. They hardly seem "real" characters; they are one character, all of whom are conduits for the one Voice.[10] Thus, the sermons in Acts are remarkably similar. The point in Acts 20, as in other passages, like 2 Pet 3 and Jude, is that this one apostolic truth precedes variation, difference, and heresy. Accordingly, the "keep watch" and "be alert" of Acts 20 differ noticeably from apocalyptic watchfulness. Divergence from the one apostolic truth—not wars and rumors of wars, and other messianic woes—now marks the "last days."

> But you, beloved, must remember the predictions of the apostles of our Lord Jesus Christ; for they said to you, "In the last time there will be scoffers, indulging their own ungodly lusts." It is these worldly people, devoid of the Spirit, who are causing divisions. But you, beloved, build yourselves up on your most holy faith; pray in the Holy Spirit. (Jude 1:17–20; compare 2 Pet 3:1–4; I Tim 4:1–5; 2 Tim 3)

The overriding commitments here are to oneness and sameness, to the elimination of choice (heresy) and difference (compare Eph 4).[11] An apostolic and episcopal hierarchy oversees this unity. This mythic perspective commits followers forever to the mythic past, not to the apocalyptic future. The mythic perspective also founds an ongoing institution in the world struggling to find its place amid other powers. Not surprisingly, then, this institution diverges from the larger, more powerful world only when necessary.[12]

First of all, then, I urge that supplications, prayers, intercessions, and thanks-givings be made for everyone, for kings and all who are in high positions, so that we may lead a quiet and peaceable life in all godliness and dignity. This is right and acceptable in the sight of God our Savior, who desires everyone to be saved and to come to the knowledge of the truth. (I Tim 2:1–4; com-pare Rom 13:1–7)

No wonder, then, that the household codes in Colossians and Ephesians and the community codes in the Pastorals differ so little from the general ethical advice in other ancient texts of that culture.

Vive la Différence[13]

As the Western world has moved away from tradition and hierarchy toward innova-tion and equality, the politics and ethics of the canonical institution(s) have become increasingly suspect. In a day of expressive individualism (a myth fundamentally necessary to consumer capitalism), order, sameness, and identity are death itself.[14] We long to escape from the forces that form and conform us. Accordingly, movie after movie plays out the story of the lone individual's triumph over corruption and hostile forces or the hero's discovery and expression of his/her true self despite overwhelming odds. Their success is our fantasy and a cinematic paean to our indi-vidual uniqueness, for which we all pay the same ticket price unless we have coupons or passes.[15]

The movie *Pleasantville* nicely expresses this modern myth.[16] After an advertise-ment for the "Pleasantville" marathon, touting "pure family values," the movie begins with two adolescents, David and Jennifer, in the 1990s in less than ideal circum-stances. Their world is a dangerous, threatening place, as teacher after teacher depressingly observes. Further, David and Jennifer are the children of a broken home. Their harried mother gets no relief from their absent father. David escapes into the nostalgic world of 1950s sitcoms—his favorite is "Pleasantville"[17]—and Jennifer escapes into a world of adolescent sexuality.

The movie's initial complication arises when David and Jennifer both wish to commandeer the TV on the same evening, David to watch a "Pleasantville" marathon and Jennifer to watch a music concert with her current boyfriend. Their struggle breaks the TV remote and renders their TV useless. Out of nowhere, a mysterious TV repairman arrives with thunder and lightning, of course, in the background. After quizzing David's knowledge of "Pleasantville," the repairman offers David a special remote with "a little more oomph in it. . . . You want something that'll put you right in the show." As David takes the remote, there is more lightning and the camera abandons horizontal momentarily to look down upon David and the repairman. The repairman leaves amid yet more lightning. As David and Jennifer struggle over the remote, they are "put right in the show," the black and white—or "pasty"—world of "Pleasantville" as Bud and Mary Sue. The TV repairman, now on a TV screen in Pleasantville, declares their translation a miracle. When David and Jennifer want out, the TV repairman whines about their lack of gratitude and walks off the TV screen in a huff.

David/Bud adjusts quickly to this translation. It realizes his nostalgic fantasy for a simpler, more manageable world. No longer the nerd, because he knows all the scripts in advance, he quickly becomes sage and hero. Jennifer/Mary Sue is less satisfied. For her, this world is drab and boring, but she "comes around" when she sees her handsome boyfriend, Skip. Soon, Mary Sue and Bud begin to change the 1950s world they have entered. Fearing her advanced sexual mores, Bud tries to keep Mary Sue away from Skip, but his efforts cause the boy to miss a basketball shot for the first time. As a result, Bud decides that she has to date Skip. He fears that if they mess around with the script, they may never get home. Nonetheless, Bud himself soon teaches Mr. Johnson, the soda shop owner, to deviate from his script in running the soda shop. Mary Sue acts even more willfully by introducing Skip to the joys of sex. When Skip tells his friends about his experience, no one on the basketball team can make a basket.

Bud is frightened, but Mary Sue revels in the changes—the gradual colorization and the arrival of double beds, rock-and-roll music, and books—of Pleasantville. The town fathers, led by Mayor Big Bob and George Parker, worry, too. The women are understandably more intrigued by difference. Soon, Betty Parker asks Mary Sue about sex. After her daughter introduces her to masturbation, Betty reaches climax for the first time, and a tree bursts into colorful flame outside her bathroom window (a 1990s burning bush?). Soon, difference colorizes certain inhabitants, including Betty. For a time, however, Betty hides behind gray pancake makeup.

Bud gradually decides for change, too, when he accepts the cookies from Margaret scripted for Whitey and begins to tell Pleasantville young people about the outside word and about literature (blank pages in the books fill in as Bud tells the stories). He also brings an art book, from the newly popular library, to Mr. Johnson, whose one great pleasure has been to decorate the soda shop windows for Christmas. Intriguingly, one of the first paintings that Mr. Johnson sees is an expulsion from Eden. Mr. Johnson's fascination with colors and the fortune of people who can see them inspire Bud, and he, abandoning the script, asks Margaret out.

Bud's willfulness earns him an angry visit via TV from the TV repairman. The repairman wants to remove Bud and Mary Sue from Pleasantville. Bud, claiming bad reception, simply turns off the TV.

Bud's date with Margaret wonderfully inverts the Genesis Eden story. In a beautiful park, after they talk about the outside world, Margaret offers Bud a brilliant red apple. Meanwhile, Betty visits the soda shop, lured by Mr. Johnson's artistically painted window, and they become romantically involved. Mary Sue rejects a date in favor of reading, and George Parker sits in his dark house alone. Thunder, lightning, and a gentle rain punctuate the changes. It has never rained in Pleasantville before. Bud, of course, calms the frightened youth by frolicking in the rain. Despite his growing trickster-quality, Bud remains, at this point, in black and white.

The rain is hardly a divine judgment, even though a brilliant rainbow marks its end. The town patriarchs, however, decide to defend their order against frightening changes, like absent wives, absent dinners, and bad ironing. If this is not a sufficient parody of the divine judgment in Gen 3, another TV visit of the repairman underlines the god's loss of control. The repairman tries to bring Bud under control by replaying his eating of the apple, his violation of paradise. Bud does not deserve paradise, and the TV repairman demands the remote so that he can remove Bud and restore order. Bud, however, refuses to obey.

Violence in the streets against the coloreds, a gesture at the race problems of America in the 1950s and 1990s,[18] enables the city fathers to pass censorship laws against difference, color, and change. Bud finally comes to color himself when he defends Betty against a roving gang of black-and-white thugs. Bud becomes the leader of the resistance, and in an act of defiance, he and Mr. Johnson paint a colorful Chagall-like mural on the wall of the police station.

They are arrested and brought to "trial."[19] Bud objects to Big Bob's right to regulate Pleasantville, claiming that silly, sexy, and dangerous are better than imposed order. Further, Bud asserts that these "insidious" differences are already within all of us. Bud proves his point by colorizing both his father, by bringing him to acknowledge his love for Betty, and Big Bob, by making him sufficiently angry. As they are within, the colors cannot be stopped. In fact, the entire town is now in brilliant color. A color TV even appears in a shop window.

David/Bud and Jennifer/Mary Sue, or the 1990s, have forever changed this utopian 1950s fantasy. As George Aichele observes, something more like the world in which we live has invaded and transformed Pleasantville,

> a world that for all its faults is far more desirable than the monochrome and monotone world of "Pleasantville." Paradise is the place where one must follow the script without deviation, and it is eventually replaced in this movie by a messier but more human (and humane) world where "nothing is supposed to be." Even the transgressions of Betty and Mr. Johnson, quite outrageous in terms of 1950s middle-class morality, are vindicated in the movie's conclusion. Nevertheless, although the happy ending of the movie justifies the broken covenant, it is not an unambiguous vindication. The present illusion of freedom has been replaced by harsher circumstances. From now on, the people of Pleasantville must write their own scripts and suffer the fear and uncertainty that accompany such responsibility.[20]

In charge of their own destiny, Mary Sue decides to stay in Pleasantville while Bud departs to help his mother in the "real world." He promises, however, to return to Pleasantville. As Bud leaves, the TV repairman also drives away smilingly.[21]

If we read this movie vis-à-vis Gen 3, as I have rather allusively, the most notable variation is that there is no expulsion from Eden, wherever that Eden may be. In fact, if Pleasantville is Eden, change or salvation comes to Eden (and to its god?). The agents of change, David/Bud and Jennifer/Mary Sue are able to move from one "reality" to another without the constraints of any supernatural being. While the TV repairman initially introduces them to Pleasantville, he cannot "repair" their changes and, thereafter, can neither trap nor exclude them. If there are gods in Pleasantville, they are David and Jennifer, appearing in the guise of Bud and Mary Sue. More important, their story clearly valorizes movement and change (but not escape, as the final fates of the primary characters demonstrate), not stasis. In short, the values of this movie invert the values of the Eden of Genesis and the new creation of Saint Paul.[22]

Further, the movie challenges any nostalgic longing that we might have lurking within us for Saint Paul's redemption from the body, from the world, and from difference or for pure, asexual family values. Laid over against Saint Paul, the gradual colorizations within this movie reveal Saint Paul's frighteningly monochrome world.

> I therefore, the prisoner in the Lord, beg you to lead a life worthy of the calling to which you have been called, with all humility and gentleness, with patience, bearing with one another in love, making every effort to maintain the unity of the Spirit in the bond of peace. There is one body and one Spirit, just as you were called to the one hope of your calling, one Lord, one faith, one baptism, one God and Father of all, who is above all and through all and in all. (Eph 4:1–6)

If there is, in fact, only one body—a metaphorical reference to the community of believers, not a reference to actual human bodies—why does Saint Paul need to exhort his followers to unity so strenuously? Does Saint Paul's rhetoric simply lather a gray makeup over diversity and problems and, like nostalgic sitcoms, call the "pasty" result paradise? Regardless, the commitment to an inhuman "oneness" turns Saint Paul and his followers, as he himself notes, into "the *prisoner* in the Lord" (emphasis added). Paul and his followers are trapped in sameness, like the monochrome citizens of Pleasantville. Admittedly, verses in Ephesians discuss various gifts, but they all are "for building up the [metaphorical] body of Christ, until all of us come to the unity of the faith" (Eph 4:12–13). Actual bodies, real differences, are obviously lost.

Modernity, of course, lives for difference. It celebrates the myth of individual freedom. On our reading thus far, *Pleasantville* supports our myth of individualism and tolerance and challenges Eden, Saint Paul, and other traditional orders.[23] As Ebert nicely puts it, "The movie is like the defeat of the body snatchers."[24] Of course, the body snatchers are not sci-fi aliens but Paul, Paul's Christ, Paul's spirit, and Paul's one body. *Pleasantville*'s redemption of family values nostalgia exposes the rage for order in Saint Paul. Saint Paul becomes the comically ineffective TV repairman or the blustering, tyrannical Big Bob and his chauvinist pals.

Watching Paul Watching You

Moderns usually look askance at such blustering. Accordingly, as we saw in chapter 1, various interpreters have tried to distinguish the historical Paul from the Saint Paul who now seems a highly questionable defender of traditional orders. The redeemed Paul who is the fruit of these efforts typically supports modern ideological agendas. If Saint Paul is a hidebound conservative, the historical Paul of recent years is nicely "politically correct." In particular, historical critics have highlighted certain texts to argue that Paul, despite his episcopal reputation, is, in fact, an egalitarian. The classic proof texts are Rom 12:4–8; 1 Cor 12:4–31; and Gal 3:28.[25]

Boyarin, I think, has efficiently impugned the egalitarian nature of the last text.[26] He does so simply by focusing on the latter part of the text, "for all of you are one in Christ Jesus," rather than on the earlier, purportedly egalitarian, portion of the text. This focus, by the way, immediately resolves all manner of paradoxes in the Pauline literature. In particular, it answers scholars' inability to explain why the purportedly egalitarian Paul could on other occasions sound so chauvinistic, without recourse to textually unsupported claims of interpolations. The most famous text, supposedly so interpolated, is 1 Cor 14:33b–36, a passage that the NRSV reduces to a parenthetical comment with the feeblest of notational comment. The paradox vanishes, of course, because the egalitarian possibilities of Jew or Greek, slave or free, male or free have already vanished into the "one in Christ Jesus" in Gal 3:28. No wonder, then, that the difference between Jew or Greek vanishes into the one body of Eph 2–4, that slavery becomes a non-issue in 1 Cor 7, and that the distinction between male and female vanishes altogether in 1 Cor 12:13 and Col 3:11. No one here, least of all Paul, is fundamentally committed to equality. Paul, long before becoming the bishops' saint, rages after imperial order.

The other two politically correct passages can be dispatched similarly. While both passages mention diverse gifts or diverse parts of the *one* body, they both focus on the *one* body. The passage in Rom 12 follows Paul's demand that the individual believers sacrifice their living bodies (Rom 12:1, 3). That self-abnegation leads to one's asexual place in the one body. The subsequent verses demand asexual love (Rom 12:9–10), a love that demands, not surprisingly, subjection to the empire (Rom

13:1–7),[27] commitment to neighbor (Rom 13:8–10), and a sacrifice of one's opinion for the sake of the weak in the community (Rom 14:1–15:13). Certainly, those who obey these demands have "put on the Lord Jesus Christ" and made "no provision for the flesh." They have made no provision for any noticeable personal differences that they might have (Rom 13:14). They are lost, imprisoned in the one Lord.

The passage in I Cor 12 is similar. That text also occurs in a long paean to Pauline order. Once again, Paul calls for the sacrifice of individual opinion (I Cor 8; 10) and the submerging of individual spiritual gifts for the good of the metaphorical body of Christ (I Cor 12–14). Notably, asexual love (I Cor 13), as defined by Paul's own sacrifices (I Cor 9) and expressed in terms of sacrifice for the metaphorical body, dominates the whole section. In particular, the so-called paean to equality stands under the following heading:

> For just as the body is one and has many members, and all the members of the body, though many, are one body, so it is with Christ. For in the one Spirit we were all baptized into one body—Jews or Greeks, slaves or free—and we were all made to drink of one Spirit. (I Cor 12:12–13)

The distinction between male and female in Gal 3:28 has now completely vanished. Moreover, the whole passage (I Cor 12:14–31) appears under the superintending, imperial determination of the one God: "God arranged the members in the body, each one of them, as he chose" (I Cor 12:18; see also 12:24, 28). The passage also leads into the most famous paean to love in the New Testament (I Cor 13). Once again, it is an asexual love defined as actions edificatory to the metaphorical body of Christ (I Cor 14:1–5). Given the overall direction of the passage, how can anyone be surprised that women are told to be quiet for the sake of godly order (I Cor 14:33b–36)?

Castelli has explored the Pauline rage for order in the Pauline demand that his followers imitate him (I Thess 1:6–7; 2:14; Phil 3:17; I Cor 4:16; 11:1). This Paul is no egalitarian. His rhetoric of mimesis valorizes sameness over difference; gives the apostle a privileged, authoritative position; strives, unsuccessfully, to write the identity of the model over the copy; and damns those who differ:[28] "To stand for anything other than what the apostle stands for is to articulate for oneself a place of difference, which has already implicitly been associated with discord and disorder."[29]

Further, throughout the mimesis rhetoric, there is a perceptible slip-slide between Paul, Christ, and God. This slide furthers Paul's own divine status. Thus, in I Thessalonians, Paul moves at will between "our gospel" (1:5), the "gospel of God" (2:2, 8, 9), and the "gospel of Christ." What, then, is the difference between the authority of Paul, Christ, and God?[30] The fact that only Paul speaks, that he is the Voice, quickly obscures any difference. Castelli traces the same authoritative slide in I Cor 4:16 and 11:1.[31] First Corinthians 11:1 is most blatant and most similar to the rhetoric of Acts and of the Pastoral Epistles: "Be imitators of me, as I am of Christ." The apostolic/episcopal hierarchy is quite clear.

The same Christ-Paul-followers hierarchy is evident in the call to mimesis in Phil 3:17, but the surrounding passage there makes the stakes even clearer:[32]

> Let those of us then who are mature be of the same mind; and if you think differently about anything, this too God will reveal to you. Only let us hold fast to what we have attained.
>
> Brothers and sisters, join in imitating me, and observe those who live according to the example you have in us. For many live as enemies of the cross of Christ; I have often told you of them, and now I tell you even with tears. Their end is destruction; their god is the belly; and their glory is in their shame; their minds are set on earthly things. But our citizenship is in heaven, and it is from there that we are expecting a Savior, the Lord Jesus Christ. He will transform the body of our humiliation that it may be conformed to the body of his glory, by the power that also enables him to make all things subject to himself. (Phil 3:15–21)

Paul's way is mature. Paul ways are God's ways. Those who do not agree with Paul and God obviously need a special revelation. Of course, Paul has already had such an apocalypse and, because of that, works for his followers' salvation (see 1 Cor 10:33, which the NRSV blocks in the same paragraph with 1 Cor 11:1). Those who do not fall into the hierarchy of God/Christ/Paul will not receive the divine/Pauline salvation. They are headed for destruction.

The text preceding this call to mimesis, particularly the parallel resumes offered about Paul's self-humiliation unto glory (Phil 3:4–14) and Christ's kenosis (Phil 2:5–11), the latter of which seems an expanded, hymnic form of Paul's death-resurrection gospel, suggest that Paul's followers' imitation of him calls for suffering and humiliation (see Phil 1:27–2:5). Of course, it certainly aids episcopal oversight if one's followers commit themselves to passivity, humility, and suffering in the prospect of future recompense. It helps, too, if this acquiescence leads them to "think the same" (Phil 2:2; 3:15; 4:2). The result would be a quiet order indeed.

Castelli explores Paul's rhetoric and strategy of power through the lens of Foucault. She accepts Foucault's notions that power is a quality that inheres in relationships, not a "thing," and that no system is ever absolute but is always engaged in a struggle to advance its ideology. She also follows Foucault's focus on the special institutions and practices whose disciplinary knowledge shapes the human subject and creates and manages deviance.[33] This analysis brings her, of course, to Foucault's understanding of the power relationships and struggles in Christianity, which he calls "pastoral power":

(1) It is a form of power whose ultimate aim is to assure individual salvation in the next world.

(2) Pastoral power is not merely a form of power which commands; it must also be prepared to sacrifice itself for the life and salvation of the flock. Therefore, it is different from royal power, which demands a sacrifice from its subjects to save the throne.

(3) It is a form of power which does not look after just the whole community, but each individual in particular, during its entire life.

(4) This form of power cannot be exercised without knowing the inside of people's minds, without exploring their souls, without making them reveal their innermost secrets. It implies a knowledge of the conscience and an ability to direct it.

(5) This form of power is salvation oriented (as opposed to political power). It is oblative (as opposed to the principle of sovereignty); it is individualizing (as opposed to legal power); it is coextensive and continuous with life; it is linked with a production of truth—the truth of the individual himself.[34]

We have already had occasion to observe the "necessary" connections in Paul's rhetoric between his communities' recognition of his apostolic privilege and their salvation (items 1, 5 above). Further, we have repeatedly explored Paul's boasts about suffering on behalf of his communities (item 2 above).

Items 3–5 deserve further comment. Pastoral power is all-encompassing. It completely surrounds the individual. Accordingly, Paul's followers are prisoners of Paul and the Lord. They cannot escape the divine/apostolic gaze. Further, that gaze penetrates to the secret things of the heart, to the conscience and its direction, to the very "truth" of the individual.[35] On first blush, that sounds more like Orwell's *1984* and a host of subsequent sci-fi movies than it does ancient apostles like Paul.

We must not overlook, however, the mechanics of Pauline mimesis. Castelli finds two features in that mimesis that lead to self-policing. First, Paul's call to mimesis is generally quite vague.[36] It does not specify details. It calls one to the general pattern of Paul/Christ and to the general values of sameness, identity, and order. As a result, Paul's followers must always consider what Paul would do before they can actually imitate him. In the fashion of some contemporary evangelicals sporting T-shirts and jewelry emblazoned with WWJD (What would Jesus do?), Paul's followers metaphorically bear upon their vanishing bodies WWPD. Despite Stendahl's contention that the modern introspective conscience is anachronistic as applied to Paul, Paul's mimetic demand is the precursor of modern reflective selves. With WWPD, Paul struggles to make himself, his Christ, and his Spirit a part of what we would call his followers' superegos.

Second, the call to mimesis is a call to failure. No one can ever successfully become the other. The copy can never quite merge with the model. Constant failure only intensifies the striving of the fervent.[37] Accordingly, Paul becomes the precursor not only of modern introspection but also of the divided self. The believer constantly tries to become or to imitate Paul/Christ and constantly fails. Mimesis makes Paul's followers into Donnie Darkos (see chapter 2). Surely, Paul's constant references to an indwelling Christ/spirit play a role here, too, for Paul urges his believers to heed and to conform to this colonizing presence, a presence transforming their difference into sameness. Paul is not only keeping watch on his communities, then, through letters, emissaries, and visits (actual or threatened), but he is also setting up sentinels—Paul, Christ, the spirit—within the lives of each of his followers. Paul watches them, they watch Paul, and they watch Paul watching them. Surely this is a Foucaultian power, a pastoral power that encompasses the entire individual, explores his/her soul, and produces his/her "truth."[38]

Who, then, is watching whom? *The Truman Show* raises precisely this question. Truman Burbank is the star of a live, twenty-four-hour-a-day "reality show." Five thousand cameras chronicle almost every detail of Truman's life. The movie opens with credits for the TV show and an interview with Christof, the show's producer/director.[39] We know, then, from the beginning that we are watching a TV show with actors. The novelty is that Truman does not know we are watching or that he is a celebrity.[40] The movie, which offers us repeated reminders that we are watching a TV show by offering interviews with actors and scenes of fans watching avidly, depicts Truman's enlightenment.

Truman's education unravels his life in an idyllic paradise called Seahaven. Part of the revelation comes simply from the difficult logistics involved in putting a "life" on TV. A camera falls from the sky at Truman's feet. An exiled actor returns. A wall is not where it is supposed to be, and Truman sees behind the set. Gradually, Truman begins to notice the "scripted" quality of the characters around him. Most important, Truman wants to travel to Fiji. Christof, however, has engineered a boat crisis in Truman's youth, which supposedly claimed his father's life and instilled a fear of water into Truman that keeps him captive on his island paradise. At the heart of Truman's desire to travel is his nostalgia for his lost love, Lauren, whom he thinks has moved to Fiji. Christof banned her from the show because she attempted to tell Truman the truth about his scripted, controlled existence. As the "real-life" Sylvia, she continues to watch the show and to pray and campaign for Truman's escape.

As true love beckons, the contrived machinations that keep Truman in paradise make him even more suspicious of his reality. All the posters in the travel agency depict the perils of travel; the bus driver strips the gears of the bus headed out of town. When Truman finally makes it out of town despite several orchestrated traffic jams, he encounters a forest fire and a nuclear plant disaster. Finally, his wife campaigns for a baby, a desperate, last-ditch stab to entrap him. After a violent confrontation with his wife, Truman goes to an unfinished bridge with his friend Marlon and succinctly states his deep suspicions: "Maybe I'm losing my mind, but it feels like the whole world revolves around me somehow. . . . Everybody seems to be in on it."[41] Marlon's lies, fed to him by Christof, and a tear-jerking reunion with his supposedly dead father on the bridge temporarily distract him. The next night, however, Truman digs out of his basement to freedom, hiding the hole behind a travel poster in a fashion reminiscent of the escape in *The Great Escape*.

When Christof discovers Truman's escape, he sends the entire crew into the night with flashlights, marching in lockstep, to find Truman. When that fails, Christof "cues" the artificial sun and turns night into day. Gradually, Christof realizes that Truman has taken to the sea. When he finds Truman's boat, he "cues" a storm to incite Truman's carefully implanted fears. Truman, however, defiantly shakes his fist at the heavens. Enraged, Christof increases the storm, capsizes the boat, and almost drowns Truman. When Christof finally relents, Truman sails, with his picture of Lauren/Sylvia constructed from magazine ads, to the end of his world, running his boat into the solid dome that covers his world. Like Michelangelo's Adam or Spielberg's E.T., he reaches out a hand tentatively to this dome. Then, departing the boat, he walks on the water and up a staircase to a door leading to the outside world.

To save Truman, Christof tries a last, desperate theophany. He introduces himself to Truman for the first time, answering Truman's question about his identity: "I am the creator . . . of a television show that gives hope and joy and inspiration to millions. . . . You're the star." When Truman asks if anything was real, Christof responds:

You were real. That's what made you so good to watch. Listen to me, Truman. There is no more truth out there than there is in the world I created for you. The same lies, the same deceit. But in my world, you have nothing to fear. I know you better than you know yourself. [Truman: You never had a camera in my head.] You're afraid. That's why you can't leave. It's OK, Truman. I understand. I've been watching you your whole life. . . . You can't leave Truman. You belong here, with me. Talk to me. . . . You're on TV. You're live to the whole world.

With his trademark salutation, a grin, and a wave, Truman walks out the door into the dark. We cannot see where Truman goes. We never see Truman again. In the denouement, we see Sylvia grab her coat and run out to meet Truman, we suppose. Other fans exult at Truman's triumphant escape and then look for something else to watch.

Like *Pleasantville*, *The Truman Show* inverts the values of Eden and Saint Paul's new creation. Instead of a secure life in some divine/apostolic script, the movie celebrates heroism and love, both of which the movie offers as means to overcome our fear and our willingness to accept a superintended security. While both movies play with the overlap between TV and "our reality," *The Truman Show* adds an element of voyeurism that *Pleasantville* does not foreground. This voyeurism brings the film into interaction with Paul's mimesis and his other surveillance devices.

The hero of "The Truman Show" discovers and escapes Christof's surveillance. He literally walks into the impenetrable dark at the movie's end. As such, Truman enacts our own fantasy of escaping from the forces that have normalized us. Foucault, for one, is hardly so sanguine about our escape; however, near the end of his career, he did suggest that we might practice an aesthetics of the self or explore an "arts of existence":

> What I mean by the phrase are those intentional and voluntary actions by which men not only set themselves rules of conduct, but also seek to trans- form themselves, to change themselves in their singular being, and to make their life into an *oeuvre* that carries certain aesthetic values and meets certain stylistic criteria.[42]

Vis-à-vis Paul's order and sameness, Castelli similarly suggests that we reinscribe difference. To do so, she asks us to consider carefully our perspective and, in par- ticular, to reflect upon what we consider "normal" or "natural."[43]

Even *The Truman Show* is not as sanguine about escape as I have suggested. After all, we may not be Truman. Numerous scenes in the movie, particularly the "mock- umentary" interviews with various actors and Christof, make us voyeurs, like Christof and the fans, of the TV show as well as of the movie. We also watch fans watching the program. Most tellingly, we watch viewers look for something else to watch as "The Truman Show" goes off the air. That scene nicely parallels Truman's own vanishing act. That disappearance, the end of the TV show, and the end of the movie leave us in an interesting position. Are we—that is, do we identify with— Truman or with Christof and the channel-surfing TV viewers?

Two scenes in the movie suggest that watching traps one as much as being watched does. Like Truman's tentative reach toward the wall of his prison, they are both reminiscent of Michelangelo's *Creation of Man* and both of them feature Christof, the creator of the TV world that we are all watching. First, just before Truman's escape, Christof alone in his aerie perch reaches out lovingly to caress the wall-size TV screen that shows Truman sleeping. Later, as Truman reaches for the handle on the door to freedom, Christof caresses the TV monitor by which he watches Truman. In both cases, the media comes between the touch and the touched.[44] Even the creator cannot bridge the media gap between simulation and "reality." Christof is as trapped as Truman.

Despite the fantasy of Truman's escape into an unwatched world, the movie also reminds us that there are watchers there as well, if that world is, in fact, what we ordinarily take for our reality. In that reality, too, as Christof says, we readily "accept the reality of the world with which we are presented." We do so particularly when the media presents the reality that we wish to see. If we substitute the word "normal" or "natural" for "reality," the connection between the circle of voyeurism in *The Truman Show*, in our "reality," and in Paul becomes painfully obvious. Only a single-minded focus on Truman's escape or Paul's salvation obscures the traps for both watcher and watched. *The Truman Show* lets us see quite clearly that Christof and Truman's other viewers need liberation as much as Truman does. In conversation with Paul, Christof makes Paul's need for salvation painfully clear as well.

In this respect, *The Truman Show* becomes a question about the extent to which the media, particularly TV, defines and normalizes us and our reality.[45] When we watch, who watches us? Perhaps more important, what spectacles do we use? If we recognize that our vision is a perspective, we will at least escape the trap of the Vision, that is, the arrogant illusion that our vision is reality.[46] Multiple visions will undercut the Vision and liberate us from apostolic surveillance, just as a cacophony of voices denies the dominance of the Voice. Against the media and Paul, we must reject passivity. At the very least, we should have questions "about the reality of the world with which we are presented."

No Complete System

Foucault contends that no coercive system is complete. All power relationships are continuously contested, inscribed anew, and/or revised. Truman's escape suggests the possibility of at least temporary difference in the face of normalizing forces. This escape incarnates the deepest fantasies of the modern individual, the desire to be different, unique, or free. *The Truman Show* is hardly alone in playing to and enforcing this myth. Generally, modern movies—following the lead of the novel—privilege the individual vis-à-vis the institution, society, community, or system. Unlike the Capra-quality of *The Truman Show*, sci-fi movies often explore darker dystopias, the fears of modern individuals that their bodies and freedoms will be snatched by systems (government) or machines. Despite their dystopian quality, these movies, too, often ease our anxieties about our potential, or present, loss of freedom. Like Foucault, they contend that no system, however seemingly complete, will conquer us.[47]

Spielberg's *Minority Report* is an excellent example of this type of movie. Technological advances have made Foucault's Panopticon a reality. Not only does "Big Brother" watch over everything, but the Department of Precrime sees and stops murder before it ever occurs. Our worries about violent crime are over, and the streets are safe again. Our freedom, however, may also be a thing of the past. As Danny Witwer, an investigator from the attorney general's office, remarks, "I'm sure you all understand the legalistic drawback to Precrime methodology. . . . We are arresting individuals who have broken no law. . . . But it's not the future if you stop it. Isn't that a fundamental paradox?"[48]

As the movie opens, we see Precrime at work. Precognitives have visions of a murder. John Anderton manipulates the images for clues as to the time, place, and people in the vision. Locating the predicted crime, he and his SWAT team swoop down upon the potential offender and arrest him before he can murder his wife and her lover.

The complication is that Lamar Burgess, director of Precrime, wishes to make Precrime a national institution. As a result, the attorney general has sent Danny Witwer to investigate the system, "to look for flaws." As we have already seen, Danny is suspicious of the system. John, the true believer, dismisses Danny's worries. Eventually, John takes Danny into the "Temple" itself, the vat housing the three precogs. Danny, an ex-seminarian, compares the precogs to the deity, because they can forecast the future, and thinks of them as a miracle, a possible indication of the existence of the divine. When John demurs, Danny admits that the priests— John and his operatives—have always been the real source of power, "even if they had to invent the oracle." Danny's mission is to thwart abuses of or within that pastoral power. Tellingly, Danny knows that any flaw will be "human." Eventually, of course, he decides that John is the flaw because John takes illegal drugs and truly believes in the system. John does both in order to deal with the pain of the loss of his son, Shawn.

While John remains alone in the Temple, Agatha, the dominant precog, lurches from the vat and grabs John, saying, "Can you see?" As she does, we see the murder of Ann Lively. John, of course, begins to investigate the crime despite a warning from Gideon, the keeper of the criminals and their records: "You dig up the past, all you get is dirty." John soon discovers that dozens of previsions are missing, along with Agatha's vision of the murder of Ann Lively by John Doe.

Immediately after John tells Lamar Burgess about this problem, the precogs have a vision of John's murder of Leo Crow. John flees, with the requisite chase and fight scenes. As he flees, his movements are tracked by eye scanners that reveal his location to the police. In one amusing scene, he enters a mall and is personally greeted by advertisements—keyed by eye scans—one of which intones that a road diverged in the desert and he is on the less traveled one!

John makes his way to the house of a mad scientist, Iris Heneman, joint-creator along with Burgess of the Precrime system. She tells him about the existence of minority reports, visions of alternative futures, roads less traveled. The system covers up these reports because the system cannot afford to be less than perfect. John is aghast that he may have imprisoned innocent people and is even more certain that he is not a murderer. He must then find his minority report, which Heneman tells him will be in Agatha, the dominant precog.

To penetrate the Temple, he has to lose his eyes; therefore, he goes to the Sprawl to a sleazy plastic surgeon, whom he once arrested, in order to have his eyes replaced. John then enters the Temple in disguise and steals Agatha by pulling the plug on the vat. John and Agatha "go down the drain" ahead of the police. Danny, however, simply tracks their future location by reviewing the previsions of John's murder of Leo Crowe. Meanwhile, John has a sleazy computer programmer hack Agatha's mind to find his minority report. He finds none, but he sees the murder of Leo Crowe again, with Agatha asking again, "Can you see?"

Following clues to the site of the anticipated murder, John finds Leo Crowe's apartment and pictures of missing children, including his son. He knows then that the previsions are right. He will kill Leo Crowe. Agatha, however, insists that he has a choice. Unlike other potential murders, he has seen his future and can change it. When Leo arrives, John dramatically overcomes his murderous designs and reads Leo his rights. The system is not perfect. Even without a minority report, John is not a murderer. Leo, who needs to be murdered in order to gain money for his family from a mysterious conspirator, grabs John's gun and commits suicide. It looks like murder, so John and Agatha flee.

When Danny arrives, the "orgy of evidence" tells him that the murder was a setup. He also investigates Ann Lively's murder and discovers that someone who knows how Precrime works used a failed murder attempt to kill Ann, the mother of Agatha. When Danny tells Lamar, Lamar shoots him and goes undetected because the precogs do not work in Agatha's absence.

Eventually, the police track down and arrest John and Agatha at John's wife's house. They do not do so, however, before John discovers that the whole affair concerns Ann's murder. An inadvertent slip by Lamar tells Lara that he is involved, and Lara uses John's eye and gun to free him. John goes to the celebration for the nationalization of Precrime and plays Agatha's vision of Lamar's murder of Ann for the crowd as he talks to Lamar on the phone: "You created a world without murder. And all you had to do was kill someone to do it. . . . I'm talking about Agatha's mother, Ann Lively." She wanted her daughter back, but Lamar needed her for Precrime.

In a final rooftop confrontation, Lamar faces a final dilemma after a prevision of John's murder. John describes the problem:

Lamar, it's over. The question you have to ask is, what are you going to do now? No doubt the precogs have already seen this. . . . You see the dilemma, don't you? If you don't kill me, the precogs are wrong and Precrime is over.

If you do kill me, you go away, but it proves the system works. The precogs
were right. So what are you going to do now? What's it worth? Just one more
murder. . . . All you have to do is kill me. . . . Except you know your own
future. Which means you can change it if you want to. You still have a choice,
Lamar, like I did.

Somewhat surprisingly, Lamar's choice is suicide. His dying words to John are
"Forgive me, my boy."

In the denouement, we learn that Precrime has been closed. All the imprisoned
have been released. John is reunited with a pregnant Lara. The precogs are free at
an undisclosed location.

Minority Report is a typically modern rejection of the perfect, complete system that
disallows human freedom. The system purports to be divine. Various characters
describe it as a "miracle," "infallible," "absolute metaphysics," "more than human,"
and a "perfect system." The system, that is, plays God.[49] The police become clergy
and the heart of the station becomes the Temple. The problem with the system, as
concisely stated by Danny, is inevitably human. No system tolerates the human well.
Human weakness and imperfection are annoyances. Further, the godlike system is
unable to admit its own murderous imperfections.[50] Meanwhile, true believers, like
John and Lamar, oil the cogs of this system, cover up its flaws, and facilitate the
demise of their own humanity.

By contrast, Danny's cynicism recovers lost humanity. At least Danny is the cat-
alyst that sparks John's heroic resistance. John is in the Temple and meets Agatha's
imperious question—"Do you see?"—only because of Danny. John's refusal to
murder—and Lamar's similar refusal—proves that the system is flawed. Despite
previsions, people can choose alternate futures. Lamar does so without actually seeing the precog's prevision of his murder, although he assumes it. The visions—like
the connection of John, a gun, and a dead man—need interpretation. Although
Precrime's clerics provide the official interpretations—as the canon does for Saint
Paul—Danny, John, and Lamar show that other interpretations remain possible.

In addition to Danny's refusal to deify the system (despite a speech that sounds
like such an endorsement), the heart of the liberation is John's loss of faith and his
refusal to play his scripted role. He refuses his predicted future; nonetheless, the
system encloses his resistance. Even after Lara frees him, the system threatens to
close around him again. Only Lamar's family feeling for John finally stops the system. Unfortunately, Lamar was a different father for Danny.[51] Danny's dark fate
reminds us that John's escape, like Truman's, may simply be a heroic fantasy for an
audience of modern individuals trapped themselves in various normalizing disciplines. Certainly, Danny's fate testifies to the difficulties that systems present to
struggles for difference.

A Repentant Paul?

Vis-à-vis *The Truman Show* and Saint Paul, a dominant motif in *Minority Report* is sight and blindness. Like *Oedipus Rex* and *King Lear*, the movie repeatedly suggests that true sight comes through or in blindness. More so than Truman's departure from the stage, this motif has the potential to challenge voyeurism and the Panopticon. In a movie based on the sci-fi premise that precogs can see some of the future, salvation ultimately comes from a hero who deliberately blinds himself in order to see differently. He has to reject the sight, in particular, that situates him in the system in order to elude the system.

Not incidentally, this resembles Castelli's suggestion vis-à-vis the normalizing influence of Saint Paul. To allow difference we have to refuse the sight—both that of the apocalyptic vision and that of the mimetic model—offered by Paul. To allow difference, we have to see differently. We have to see, that is, unnaturally or non-normatively. We have to view Saint Paul and his world askew.

Paul does not play with the motif of blind sight.[52] Why should he? Paul's apocalypse provides a prevision of Paul's salvation of the Gentiles. The canon enforces the authority of this prevision for a gentile church. The blind—those not granted Paul's apocalyptic visions—do not need to see. There is no different vision possible for them. They simply need to hear or read what Paul has already seen and what has been enshrined as canon. Appropriately, then, Paul imagines that his followers already see, although darkly, dimly, or enigmatically (I Cor 13:12). What is more important in Paul's Panopticon is that we are already known (I Cor 13:12). We do not need to see; Paul and his system see us.

In *Minority Report*, such an all-seeing system is fatally flawed. It does not see well. What it sees still requires interpretation. Most of all, it plays God, as all systems do, and forgets its human (inhuman?) creation. In *Minority Report*, humanity returns only when the characters shatter this divine mirror.

The shattering of the Precrime/prevision system has its costs. The city loses its "safety," but as in *Pleasantville* and *The Truman Show*, this Eden is no paradise. The Edenic system sacrifices our freedom to our fears. To be human is to live with fear and to live with the possibility of death. Thus, only when John loses his true belief and his drug addition, both of which cover his inability to deal with loss, can he live again. Only when he faces his loss does he find his pregnant wife, again.

The precogs are an even more blatant example of restored humanity. As the cleric-police admit, the system depends on denying the humanity of these visionaries. They are mere cogs in the system. They lose this reified status only when John exposes the murder that reified them and the system comes crashing down in Lamar's suicide.

There, even Lamar finds some semblance of humanity. Although a double murderer, he finds a line that he will not cross. He can murder Ann and Danny. He can frame and imprison John to ensure his system, but he cannot murder "his boy." While this repentance is hardly Ivan Karamazov's refusal to live in a world founded upon the suffering of even one innocent, Lamar's refusal does stand in stark contrast to Paul's gospel about God's murder of his Son. Unlike Lamar, Paul is quite willing to be complicit in the creation of a system that stands upon "just one murder" or, at least, one innocent death (see chapter 3).

Nonetheless, Lamar is hardly Eugene in *Playing God* or Stu in *Phone Booth*. Eugene's humility and Stu's confession mark them as more genuinely human. Lamar's repentance does not extend so far. Like Christof, he does relent and refuse the destruction of his "son," but neither Lamar nor Christof manage the TV repairman's enigmatic smile at the end of *Pleasantville*. Why does that figure smile? After all, the "Pleasantville" script has come undone. Is he, too, converted to difference?

The repairman's smile makes him an intriguing foil for Saint Paul. As we have seen, Saint Paul's voyeuristic surveillance system is doomed to failure at the individual level. At best, then, Saint Paul is as comically ineffectual as the TV repairman. His claims to divinity are misplaced. What would happen, then, if Saint Paul recognized his rage for order as a grab at divinity and repented of it? What if Saint Paul also enigmatically smiled as the world spun beyond his control?

That is a fantasy, of course, that goes beyond *The Truman Show*. Saint Paul is beyond repentance. We can hardly save Paul from his sainthood or from the canon, but we can, as scholars have, place Pauls alongside the Saint. The very existence of those Pauls renders Saint Paul suspect. Those Pauls call attention to the incompleteness of the Saint Paul system. Other interpretations exist. In that pluralism, Saint Paul becomes an ideological construct, like all other Pauls, but with, of course, far more institutional backing.

Saint Paul, like his God and Christ, is an image that we employ or resist. If we imagine a Saint Paul, we imagine an authoritative apostle playing at being God. Saint Paul is a normalizing force, an icon of pastoral power. Of course, the real power, as Danny Witwer observes, is always in the priests/clerics/interpreters/ideologues. In short, if we imagine a Saint Paul, we render our own ideology unassailable and inhuman. We become true believers oiling the cogs, covering the flaws in the system, and hastening our own demise. If we imagine, by contrast, a smiling Paul, we may be able to reject Saint Paul's rage for order. We may begin to reinscribe difference, as Castelli suggests. At the very least, we call attention to images, voices, and ideologies. Thereby, we resist the Voice and the Panopticon. Instead of blindly accepting Saint Paul's salvation from our bodies and from our difference, we insist that Saint Paul needs to repent, that he needs his own liberation.

The fantasy of Saint Paul's repentance implies something like the reciprocal redemption that George Aichele finds in *Pleasantville*:

In this movie redemption is not a one-way gift. Instead, it is an exchange. The redemptive exchange takes place not only between Margaret and David, but also between levels of reality. For both David and Jennifer, the fantasy world transforms the realistic world, and vice versa. Underneath the allure of the fantastic lies a desire for reality, and it is only by passing through fantasy that they encounter reality—different realities, as it happens. The ideological relation between the realistic and the fantastic is exposed and inverted, and the fantastic becomes real.[53]

In this analysis, the redeemers, too, are redeemed.[54] Aichele imagines this process as an interpenetration of reality and fantasy. I am working with similar conceptions vis-à-vis Paul here. Reality is a construct of our ideology. Given the presence of the Saint Paul image in our culture, either we reject the image of Saint Paul on the basis of our ideology, or we use that image to endorse our ideology. Neither is fantastic and neither entails reciprocal redemption. For our liberation and Paul's, we need something that eludes our ideological control. Imagining multiple Pauls and bringing those images into dialogue with contemporary movies is a start. It places multiple voices in dialogue and values that dialogue over the Voice's monologue. Imagining Saint Paul repentant is, of course, not really imagining any activity on the part of a real Paul. It simply visualizes our refusal to reject or conscript Paul. It denies the totality and divinity of the system, and our own grab for divinity. Imagining Saint Paul repentant erases *Saint* and the capitalization in *Voice*. It returns us all to simple humanity. I can hardly imagine any of the Pauls I have considered here agreeing with this project, but then, I have never imagined any of them smiling before either.

Notes

1. Other than the descent/ascent of the camera that marks the beginning and end of the film, the most overtly religious element in the movie is the opening music, "Operator," which includes the line, "Get Jesus on the line."

2. If we ignore the opening voiceover, we could read the story as another cinematic interpretation of Job. Claire (Satan) brings Eugene (not quite the righteous Job) to the attention of Raymond (playing God). Raymond uses Eugene and everyone else for his own purposes (as does God in Job). Certainly, the plot concerns the trial of a not-very-just man. Unlike Job, Eugene succumbs to temptation.

3. See Walsh, *Reading the Bible*, 474–85.

4. Mystery is a common apocalyptic trope. Should it bother us that the content of the "mystery" differs from one Pauline document to another? Generally, the mystery relates to Paul's gentile mission (Rom 11:25; 16:25–26; 1 Cor 2:7; 4:1; Eph 1:9–10; 3:3–4, 9). Sometimes, the mystery refers to details of the final apocalypse (Rom 11:25; 1 Cor 15:51; 2 Thess 2:7). Sometimes, the mystery refers to the spiritual union of Christ and the believer (Eph 5:32?; Col 1:26–27; 2:2; 4:3) or to spiritual gifts (1 Cor 13:2; 14:2). Finally, mystery can simply mean the faith/creed (1 Tim 3:9, 16). As the referent changes, it becomes clear that what is truly important is the mystery's custodian and spokesperson: Paul.

5. Scholars credit Stendahl, "The Apostle Paul and the Introspective Conscience of the West," for moving scholarship from Paul's conversion to his call. Segal, *Paul the Convert*, has returned the notion of Paul's conversion to scholarly discussion by refining the concept. For Segal, Paul converts to a "heretical" form of Judaism (ibid., xii). This refinement removes the anachronism and anti-Semitism implicit in the idea that Paul converted from Judaism (as if there were such a thing) to Christianity (as if there were such a thing).

6. See Walsh, "Three Versions of ~~Judas~~ Jesus," 156–61.

7. Peter's own "conversion" to the gentile mission is itself narrated twice, but in rapid succession (Acts 10–11). As a result, it does not dominate the book of Acts in the way that Paul's conversion does.

8. The delightful story of Paul's shipwreck en route to Rome and the salvation of the crew "with Paul" is an anecdotal version of this point (Acts 27:24). Fulfilled prophecies and a Eucharist (Acts 27:33–37) make it tempting to read the Pauline ship allegorically as a/the gentile church.

9. The slide between Paul and God/Christ in the "late" New Testament documents is akin to the slide between Christ and God in John. Is the Johannine Christ a vehicle to God ("I am the way") or God ("I am the life")? Of course, the Pauline texts make the slide more covertly.

10. See A. J. Mattill, "The Jesus-Paul Parallels and the Purpose of Luke-Acts: H. H. Evans Reconsidered," *Novum Testamentum* 17 (1975): 15–46; and Talbert, *Literary Patterns*.

11. Castelli, *Imitating Paul*, 134, summarizes her analysis of Paul's rhetoric tersely: "I am arguing that Christian discourse is radically over-extended in the arena of identity."

12. Jewett, *Saint Paul at the Movies*, 148–61, uses 2 Tim 1:3–7 and *Dead Poets Society* to discuss the need for interplay between tradition and individual charisma. He finds the Pastorals overinvested in tradition and the movie too romantic (Keating skips the Realist poets altogether). Alone, both are deadly, as Puck's fate sadly discloses in the last case. I do not find Jewett's attack on tradition as unstinting as his attack on romanticism. I agree wholeheartedly with him, however, that Saint Paul, the unquestionable authority, is an unreal figure (ibid., 150–51). As we have already seen, in chapter 1, Jewett abandons the traditional Saint Paul more thoroughly in later works, like *Paul the Apostle to America*.

13. Vis-à-vis Christian sameness, Castelli calls for reinscribing difference (*Imitating Paul*, 135–36). She, of course, relates her project to Derrida (ibid., 124–28). In the interactive study of film and biblical studies, Erin Runions, *How Hysterical: Identification and Resistance in the Bible and Film* (New York: Palgrave Macmillan, 2003), has engaged difference far more strenuously than anyone else with whom I am familiar.

14. In the last chapter, we discussed the human need for order. It is now time to consider the other side, the human need for freedom.

15. See Walsh, *Reading the Gospels in the Dark*, 38–39, 173–85, for a discussion of movies and the myth of individualism. The scene in *Monty Python's Life of Brian* when the crowd, which wishes to make Brian a messiah, ritually intones after him, "We're all individuals," concisely expresses the paradox of the myth of individualism. As we declare our individualism, we adapt ourselves to the myth of our consumer society. We become like everyone else in our society as we scramble to identify ourselves by our consumer choices. See Jewett, *Saint Paul at the Movies*, 158, for a discussion of the scene in *Dead Poets Society* where Keating has the boys march and clap to demonstrate to them how hard it is to maintain individual freedom. Nonetheless, like most Peter Weir movies, *Dead Poets Society* is a paean to the "out-of-place" individual who struggles to express himself vis-à-vis a contrary world. It is fully complicit in individualism itself.

16. For quite diverse readings of *Pleasantville*, see George Aichele, "Sitcom Mythology," in Aichele and Walsh, *Screening Scripture*, 100–119; and Adele Reinhartz, *Scritpure on the Silver Screen*, 144–65.

17. Aichele, "Sitcom Mythology," explores at length the various realities in the film: *Pleasantville* the movie, "Pleasantville" the sitcom, and Pleasantville the town to which David and Jennifer are transported. As a further challenge to reality, they have new identities there as Bud and Mary Sue. Aichele's point of interest is the "redemptive exchange" taking place "between levels of reality. For both David and Jennifer, the fantasy world transforms the realistic world, and vice versa" (ibid., 119). See below.

18. Ibid., 110–11.

19. The set recalls *To Kill a Mockingbird*. As in that earlier film, the accused and the "pasty" citizens and judges are on the ground floor, while the "coloreds" are in the balcony.

20. Aichele, "Sitcom Mythology," 114–15.

21. I return to this enigmatic smile below.

22. Reinhartz, *Scripture on the Silver Screen*, 20–22, 145, 192 n. 25, calls attentions to readings of myth and Genesis that privilege human responsibility and development rather than static hierarchy. She does admit, however, that various films subvert the values of Gen 2–3 (ibid., 20, 186).

23. Ibid., 148, and Aichele, "Sitcom Mythology," 116.

24. Roger Ebert, *"Pleasantville,"* http://www.suntimes.com/ebert/ebert_reviews/1998/10/102302. html (accessed October 9, 2003).

25. Castelli, *Imitating Paul*, 130.

26. Galatians 3:1–7 is the base text for Boyarin, *A Radical Jew*, 5.

27. Romans 13:1–7 is particularly problematic for modern egalitarians. See Elliott, *Liberating Paul*, 75–79, 181–83, who claims that that one passage more than any other has made Paul into the servant of oppressive powers. Elliott interprets the passage in a more liberating fashion, in a manner consistent with his view of Romans as an assertion of God's justice vis-à-vis the oppressive injustice of the Roman Empire (ibid., 217–26). Incidentally, others even dare to strike the passage altogether as an interpolation (not Elliott's view, but see ibid., 25–27). While I am sympathetic with Elliott's politics, I do not see that Paul's imperial ethos in Rom 13:1–7 differs from the imperial ethos that he advocates in the ethic of submission in Rom 12 and in the larger argument in Romans about the apostle's place in God's imperial plan. N. T. Wright, "Paul's Gospel and Caesar's Empire," in Horsley, *Paul and Politics*, 164, seems more on target when he asserts that Paul is not against empire; he is against Caesar's empire. Compare Cynthia Briggs Kittredge, "Corinthian Women Prophets and Paul's Argumentation in 1 Corinthians," in Horsley, *Paul and Politics*, 103–9.

28. Castelli, *Imitating Paul*, 15–22, 49–57, 87, 130–31.

29. Ibid., 87.

30. Ibid., 90–93.

31. Ibid., 97–115.

32. Ibid., 95–97.

33. See ibid., 35–58.

34. Michel Foucault, "The Subject and Power," 214ff., cited in ibid., 47. The fifth paragraph is not numbered in Castelli.

35. Foucault's works are often about the various "modern" disciples that produce the individual and the norm. He discusses surveillance and self-policing in his *Discipline and Punish: The Birth of the Prison*, trans. Alan Sheridan (New York: Vintage, 1979). See particularly his discussion of the Panopticon (ibid., 195–228). The idea of confession, both religious and psychological, is important in his *History of Sexuality: An Introduction*, vol. 1 of *History of Sexuality*, trans. Robert Hurley (New York: Vintage, 1990).

36. Castelli, *Imitating Paul*, 32, 109.

37. Ibid., 13.

38. Scholars often remark that Paul uses two kinds of rhetoric: (1) hierarchical and (2) familial. Some stress the second in order to minimize Paul's rage for order and authority. Aside from the patriarchal, hierarchical conception of "father" in Paul's culture, this interpretation mistakes a rhetorical strategy frequently used by tyrants who move between hierarchical and familial rhetoric as it suits their needs. Most of us probably work at places that use "it's a business" rhetoric when we have needs they do not intend to service and "it's a family" rhetoric when they want that little extra from us.

39. I read *The Truman Show* here as if Christof is the analogue to the God of Gen 3 or to the watchful Saint Paul. Sylvia is another intriguing divine, extraterrestrial figure. If Christof is God/Paul, then Sylvia is the adversary. On another reading, however, she might easily become sophia/logos, or the story might become a contest between rival gods, as Aichele, "Sitcom Mythology," imagines happening in *Pleasantville*.

40. While the most obvious and dominant biblical precursor for the film is Gen 3 (see Reinhartz, *Scripture on the Silver Screen*, 5–23), this opening and Truman's ignorance are reminiscent of Job's prose introduction as well. The confrontation at sea bears some resemblance to Job's whirlwind as well. In fact, we might compare the film to various biblical texts. In addition to Job's whirlwind, the storm at sea recalls both the ark and the story of Jonah. The final theophany is reminiscent of Exod 3–4.

41. The unfinished bridge is a concise visual metaphor for Truman's quandary.

42. Michel Foucault, *The Use of Pleasure*, vol. 2 of *History of Sexuality*, trans. Robert Hurley (New York: Vintage, 1990), 10–11. This aesthetic focus follows the lead of Nietzsche and Camus. Foucault deliberately rejects the "know thyself" program of philosophy and the liberal arts for aesthetic self-creation because, in his analysis, the knowable self is the creation of the normalizing disciplines that Foucault contests.

43. Castelli, *Imitating Paul*, 133–36. Runions, *How Hysterical*, calls for more revolutionary political action in the battle for difference against the forces of normalization.

44. Admittedly, in Michelangelo's famous fresco, the hands of Adam and God do not touch either, but at least they inhabit the same medium.

45. See Reinhartz, *Scripture on the Silver Screen*, 15, 19.

46. Exposing the cultural construct as such, rather than as the natural order it purports to be, is the illuminating aim of Barthes, *Mythologies*.

47. This paean to freedom does not always occur. In *eXistenZ*, for example, the "game" so completely swallows reality that no one "wins" or is ever safe from entrapment in some other reality. While *The Matrix* is a fairly typical assertion of heroic freedom, a dark underside is also present in the Oracle's "lie" to Neo. The Oracle cannot tell Neo, the self-reliant, self-made hero, that he is the hero, or Neo will resist his destiny. Does the Oracle's knowledge and lie, then, determine the hero without his knowledge? That determination becomes central in *The Matrix Reloaded*. That installment leaves any human freedom (and any human existence?) completely in question. John Connor in *Terminator 3* also struggles unsuccessfully against his destiny.

48. The film is based on, but differs from, Philip Dick's "The Minority Report," in *The Philip K. Dick Reader*, 323–54. In Dick's story, a pre-audition (the police interpret the babbling of their idiot precogs, not their visions) names Anderton, the head of Precrime (there is no Burgess character), a murderer. He ultimately does murder the man named in the pre-audition to save the police Precrime unit from a military takeover (Lamar, of course, refuses to murder John in order to save Precrime). More important, Dick deals far more seriously with the paradoxes caused by knowledge of the future, while the movie seems intent simply on asserting the hero's free will. The precogs do not know *the* future. One sees a future, the next sees another future that includes knowledge of the first's prediction, and the third sees another future including knowledge of the two prior predictions. No majority report exists. In this case, only minority reports exist, and Anderton "chooses" his future. Further, Dick's story is even less concerned with the humanity of the precogs—called "idiots" and "monkeys"—and with the other possible innocents condemned by Precrime than Spielberg's movie is.

49. In *Equilibrium*, the police who track down social dissidents are called the Tetragrammaton Clerics. That name makes the system's divine role even more obvious, as does the figure of the Father. In the movie, set after World War III, people willingly take Prozium to prevent emotions, because they fear that such unruly elements might cause another war. Those who dissent are "sense offenders." The hero, a member of the clerics, becomes a sense offender and brings the system, led by the Father, crashing down. We might also compare this movie to Paul's attempt to crack down on sense offenders, to his reduction of the Father/God to an image in his writings, and to his use of familial imagery and rhetoric to ensure the submission of his followers.

50. According to Michael Serres, *The Parasite*, trans. Lawrence R. Schehr (Baltimore: Johns Hopkins University Press, 1982), if a system succeeds in eliminating noise, parasites, and other flaws, it arrives at the stasis of death.

51. Obviously, like Paul's use of familial language, Lamar's family feeling leaves certain hierarchies and exclusions in place. See nn. 38, 49.

52. He does play with the notion of blindness and the veil in 2 Cor 3–5, but those characterize Paul's precursors and opponents, not the Pauline "in Christ" community. Paul himself does not have to be blinded in order to see. Of course, matters are different in Acts 9:1–22.

53. Aichele, "Sitcom Mythology," 119.

54. Ibid., 115.

Epilogue: Watching Paul(s)

Therefore, my beloved, just as you have always obeyed me, not only in my presence, but much more now in my absence, work out your own salvation with fear and trembling. (Phil 2:12)

A Plethora of Pauls: A Brief Review

We began, in chapter 1, with a project that I called "saving Paul." By that phrase, I mean the appropriation of Paul by some ideological agenda. The domesticated Paul appearing most commonly of late is some version of the liberal Paul, a Paul who anticipates our politically correct culture or who speaks for humanity against empire. Purged of unacceptable elements, the "liberal" Paul is a noble figure, our ideological friend and ally. Given the dominant form of modern religion, this Paul represents individual transformation and acceptance. This Paul has dominated historical-critical studies.

Over against a similarly liberal Jesus, the result of the nineteenth-century quest, Albert Schweitzer "discovered" an apocalyptic Jesus. Schweitzer then concluded that the quest was a success and a failure. Its success was the discovery of the apocalyptic Jesus. Its failure was that same discovery, for that alien Jesus is hardly the precursor of any form of modern Christianity.[1] Of course, Schweitzer's apocalyptic Jesus was the fruit of his culture and became the precursor of several Jesuses "discovered" in the apocalyptic twentieth century.[2] Nonetheless, his criticism still stands. Apart from existentialist modifications, or some other individualizing transformation of ancient apocalyptic, the apocalyptic Jesus fails "to found" any modern/liberal Christianity.

Following Schweitzer's lead, I suggest that the apocalyptic Paul, a common construct in twentieth-century scholarship, is equally alien in modernity. Given this image of Paul, Paul's grace is not individual transformation or acceptance. It is an anarchic interruption of the world, a disruptive miracle, a hierophany, or an apocalypse. Such grace—obscured and domesticated by priest, evangelist, and historian—appeals, as Nietzsche clearly recognized, to the socially dislocated, the marginal, and the criminal in society.[3] The apocalyptic Paul's anarchic grace also clearly alienates him from modernity and from our ideological designs, whether religious or academic. After all, both traditional religion and historical criticism have as their chief design eliminating any distance between us and ancient texts.

Despite the focus on the apocalyptic Paul in several chapters above, I am not arguing that the historical or real Paul was apocalyptic. I do find apocalyptic motifs—like Paul's visions and the focus upon the resurrection—in the Pauline texts. Nonetheless, I deliberately, consciously chose the image of the apocalyptic Paul for the express purpose of questioning the use of Paul as a warrant for modernity and for modern religious projects. That apocalyptic Paul is admittedly merely a construct, not the real, true, or "historical" Paul.

Accordingly, I challenge the apocalyptic Paul in chapter 2. The canon validates Paul's visionary claims and domesticates his unsettling claims about the resurrection; however, apart from canonical approval, the sanity of the visionary Paul is highly questionable. Paul's apocalypse reveals two secrets. First, Paul is the most important individual in history. He is God's representative at the end of this evil age. Second, this age is so evil that salvation comes only through death, either of the enemy or of the self. Seen so, apocalyptic is a violent superhero fantasy endangering the continuance of the world. Vis-à-vis this Paul, I suggest laughter, the kind of laughter that arises when one joins the apocalyptic Paul with Jake Blues or Elwood P. Dowd, rather than with Douglas Quaid, Adam Meiks, or Donnie Darko. Such laughter, of course, forgoes apocalyptic certainty, providence, and election. By decentering Paul, it may also enable us to go on living and working out our salvation.

Of course, that decentering reverses the trajectory of chapter 1, where I deconstruct the liberal Paul with appeals to an apocalyptic Paul in order to alienate Paul, to make his domestication by a modern ideology impossible. In chapter 2, I deconstruct the apocalyptic Paul with appeals to reason and tolerance, significant planks in the liberal agenda. There, I try to liberalize Paul. Further, while chapter 1, following Stendahl, questions Paul's status as the precursor of the introspective conscience, chapter 2 situates Paul as the precursor of modern psychosis and of the divided mind of religions like Christianity. Incidentally, this connection still fails to validate popular estimations of Paul or to legitimate any modern religion.

The apocalyptic Paul is obsessed with a death-gospel. Chapter 3 focuses on that obsession and traces its continuance as the heart of cruciform Western Christianity. The huge success of Gibson's *The Passion of the Christ* underlines that obsession's continuing appeal. That focus, however, debases humans as sinners and as deserving death and conceives God as executioner. It enshrines suicide as the foundation of Christianity and offers Paul's followers the fantasy of dying to become gods. The obsession is sadomasochistic. Vis-à-vis the lure of death, I affirm this life and claim that people do not deserve to die. They simply die. Rejecting the notion that people deserve to die, of course, also turns one away from the Western obsession with divine forgiveness. In its place, I placed a concern for human forgiveness. Those affirmations reject the apocalyptic Paul—and also the pre-Vatican II and evangelical Paul—in favor of "liberal" affirmations. Put differently, those affirmations are at home in William James's "healthy-minded" religion, not in the apocalyptic and evangelical Paul's "sick-souled" religion.[4]

The focus on this life makes Paul's apocalyptic grace quite suspect. Accordingly, chapter 4 considers Paul's own problems with grace. Romans, Paul's great attempt to justify grace, fails miserably. It succeeds in obscuring the question of God's justice only by debasing humans (we all become sinners) and by accepting the loss of the innocent Christ and the betrayed Israel. If justice is our concern, grace is dangerous. I affirm this life and human responsibility rather than fantasies about deus ex machinas. Amid life's admitted pain, we would be better off laughing and dancing than expecting transcendent help. Further, instead of expecting divine deliverance from our "sins," we might take responsibility for our own lives. Intriguingly, as Paul tried to build communities of character, he himself set up new social norms (for example, Paul, Christ, and the spirit). That is, Paul never thought grace alone sufficient. The dominance of anti-Semitic interpretations of Paul in the West, both in the churches and in the academy, has obscured Paul's continuance in some form of Judaism. Accordingly, chapter 4 privileges a Jewish Paul rather than the image of Paul as founder of Christianity. That focus calls attention to the necessary interplay of both order (norms) and freedom (for example, grace) in human life. In Pauline studies, that focus is salutary because Paul tends to stand—with the help of the canon—for a rhetoric/system of sameness, oneness, and identity from which we now need liberation. In brief, Paul's emphasis on the one gospel of grace has left us in need of a new grace, of a deliverance from him and his Christian system or its heirs.[5]

Chapter 5 continues to raise questions about Paul's imperial system and the irrefragable authority of Saint Paul, mythic apostle to the Gentiles. Questioning the value of imperial orders, like Eden and Saint Paul, I assert that Saint Paul plays God. He is the Voice creating the very identity of his followers. Vis-à-vis that pastoral power, I advocate difference, individual self-expression, and "arts of existence." Fortuitously, the plethora of Pauls in existence already deconstructs the Voice of the Saint Paul system. That, of course, is the justification for this book and the reason that I have moved at will from a liberal Paul to an apocalyptic Paul to a psychotic Paul to a Christian Paul to a Jewish Paul and to Saint Paul.[6] In sum, the Saint Paul system is not complete, for Pauls exist. All we have to do, then, is to listen to the voices rather than passively accepting the dominance of the one Voice. That attention will bring us into a dialogue with voices, or Pauls, and into the kind of negotiation that Jonathan Z. Smith has described as the heart of the religious enterprise. It will involve us, that is, in the negotiation of a human space to live amid Pauls and others.[7] Notably, playing God—that is, the Saint Paul system— sacrifices such humanity.

If we are to regain humanity (difference) and humility, we are not able to save Paul for our ideological agenda. I cannot imagine any of the Pauls considered here accepting my agenda. Accordingly, I choose to imagine Paul repentant. Admittedly, that is a fantasy. There is no real Paul to repent, and I cannot imagine the liberal Paul, the apocalyptic Paul, the psychotic Paul, or the Christian Paul repenting. With the image of the repentant Paul, I am trying to conjure up a Paul who does not belong to my or any other agenda. I am trying to imagine a Paul who can move redemptively from one system to another and thereby challenge all systems. Of course, that Paul simply expresses my own wish for "lines of flight" that challenge the dominant.[8] Most importantly, with the image of a repentant Paul, I am trying myself to repent, to eschew the human desire to play God.

To the images of Paul that I have considered here, then, all of which can arguably be based on some reading of the Pauline texts, I wish to add this last, more fantastic image, a smiling, repentant Paul. That Paul stands against our arrogant claim that our ideology is divine, natural, or right. That Paul stands for continuing debate and revision. That Paul's repentance just might redeem us, too, and allow us to work out our own salvation. I would like to close, then, with a vision of Paul repentant.

Watching Paul

Religious leaders have fared badly in recent film. Hollywood tends to portray them as charlatans or as weaklings in need of a crutch.[9] Surely, the most famous of all such questionable evangelists is Elmer Gantry. The movie of that name opens with Elmer drunk in a Prohibition-era speakeasy on Christmas Eve.[10] When a demure woman comes in and unsuccessfully collects money for orphans, Elmer takes her collection box and rakes in the money with a sermon on Jesus and love as "the morning and the evening star . . . divine love, not the carnal kind." His sales pitch and his life, however, are incongruous. He wakes hung over on Christmas morning, with a woman from the bar. After hopping a train to leave town and losing his shoes to hoboes, Elmer arrives barefoot at a black church service where he joins in the singing of various spirituals, including "I'm on My Way Up to Canaan Land." Importantly, the black minister who befriends him tells Elmer that he sounds like a minister.[11]

Unsuccessful as a traveling salesman and as a gambler, he decides to enter evangelism after he sees an attractive revival singer and the milk buckets full of money that Sister Sharon Falconer's revival brings in. He is unsuccessful, however, in joining Sister Sharon's revival because she and her manager, Bill Morgan, rightly see him as a con man. He joins the revival train anyway by seducing Sister Rachel.

Gradually, Sister Sharon warms to Elmer's talents, and together they concoct a story about his conversion with a Gideon Bible (Ps 18) in a hotel room. In Elmer's repertoire, his conversion made him a successful salesman, a moment of truth in a rhetoric stoked with hypocrisy. While Elmer often returns to his refrain about divine, not carnal, love, his main function is to berate the audience with a message of hellfire and damnation as a warm-up for Sister Sharon's message of love. Although he has an awed, religious look on his face as the crowd first responds to his invitation and when he preaches thereafter, his real attraction is Sister Sharon. His attentions are, however, unrequited. Sister Sharon knows he does not really believe. Bill Morgan reports Elmer's shady past, and Jim Lefferts, the atheist reporter, considers Elmer the head clown at the circus.

When Elmer convinces Sister Sharon to take her revival to the city of Zenith, local ministers oppose the revival by claiming that it degrades religion by improperly mixing it with business and entertainment. George Babbitt, one of the most prominent businessmen in the city, however, lends his support to the revival, which, he feels, nicely combines American religion and business. Nevertheless, the revival starts slowly in the face of urban cynicism and Lefferts's editorial that dismisses it as a circus sideshow and an unregulated business.[12] When Babbitt's support wanes in light of the editorial, Elmer saves the revival by blackmailing Babbitt with his knowledge of Babbitt's shady business connections with speakeasies and brothels. More important, Elmer's attack on Lefferts's blasphemy, atheism, and bigotry convinces the newspaper editor to allow Elmer a rebuttal on his radio station (a half-hour show a day for two weeks, paid for by Babbitt).

Sister Sharon's admiration for Elmer's victory on her behalf finally paves the way for her seduction by Elmer. Soon, Elmer takes over the revival and begins to lead police raids on speakeasies and brothels. On one of those raids, Lulu Baines, a deacon's daughter seduced by Elmer as a young girl (she describes him as having "rammed the fear of God into me so fast that I never heard my old man's footsteps") and reduced to prostitution thereafter, meets Elmer. She arranges to have Elmer photographed in a compromising position with her, and every newspaper in town, except Lefferts's, prints the photo.[13] Not surprisingly, the revival falls on bad times, hecklers egg Elmer, and the revival's demise leaves Sharon sobbing, "My God, why hast thou forsaken me?"[14]

Surprisingly, Elmer comes to the aid of Lulu, rescues her from her abusive partner in blackmail, and apologizes to her. Even more surprisingly, Elmer decides to leave the revival. As he and Lefferts drink and laugh in the ruined tabernacle, Lefferts explains why the mob was so enraged: "The mob don't like their gods to be human." Elmer's response expresses his more relaxed religious philosophy.

Well, the way I got it figured, you're up, you're down. You sin. You're saved. You do the best you can and you leave the rest to the Lord. [Lefferts: You really do believe in the Lord, don't you?] You're damn right I do. It does a man good to get down on his knees once in a while. That's why people come to a place like this. Because they're scared or sick or because they got no money or too much money or before a war or after a war. Praying is the cheapest first-rate medicine I know. That's why Shara was so good for them. . . .

Even though Lulu has recanted, Elmer's "reputation" is saved, and the crowds have returned to the revival, Elmer vanishes for three days. On his return (resurrection?), he asks Sister Sharon to leave with him for a "normal life" "like most folks."

Sharon, of course, will not leave her people. In the finale, after the unexpected healing of a deaf man, Sister Sharon's tabernacle catches on fire because of a carelessly tossed cigarette. Despite Elmer's attempts to save Sister Sharon, she, flushed with her miracle, rushes deeper into the flaming tabernacle, telling the crowd that those who trust will be saved. She perishes in the flames. Standing amid the rubble with a cross prominently in the background on the next day, Elmer tells the people that Sister Sharon forgives them and loves them and that love is "the morning and evening star." After he sings "I'm on My Way Up to Canaan Land" with Sister Rachel, he leaves, telling Bill Morgan, "When I was a child, I spake as a child. I understood as a child. When I became a man, I put away childish things. Saint Paul. I Corinthians 13:11. So long, Bill."[15]

Clearly, this movie negatively portrays evangelical religion, which we might see as a modern successor of Paul's apocalyptic evangelism. Its premier ministers, Elmer and Sister Sharon, are respectively a clownish con man and a visionary so hopelessly out of touch with reality that she perishes needlessly in a fire. Evangelical Christianity is anti-intellectual, impractical, and hopelessly outdated. At best, it provides entertainment. Further, the atheist reporter, Jim Lefferts, is clearly the most appealing figure in the movie and provides a lens for a 1960s audience to look back at a religion already out of date in the 1920s.[16]

Nonetheless, the movie does not dismiss religion altogether. There are those urban ministers who worry about the revival's degradation of religion. Further, when the revival falls on hard times, one of those ministers even visits the revival to see if he can be of any help. More important, despite his hypocrisy, Elmer himself sees some value in religion. It helps some people, including Elmer, cope. As there is something appealing about the big-hearted, life-embracing Elmer, this opinion is hardly insignificant. Further, ironically, the hypocritical Elmer is overwhelmingly sincere throughout the movie. In this, the contrast between Elmer and Scorsese's Paul, for example, is dramatic. While Scorsese's Paul dismisses questions of truth in favor of salvific illusions, Elmer does not raise the question of truth (except in his staged debates with Lefferts). His approach is as pragmatic as Scorsese's Paul, but hardly as jaundiced.[17]

More important, the movie traces Elmer's "salvation." Elmer begins and ends the movie with paeans to love, but Elmer's view of love changes. His opening love-speech is a seduction, claiming money and a woman. His final speech is a paean to his lost love, Sister Sharon, and garners him nothing materially. In fact, his desire to leave the revival with Sharon for a "normal life," despite its renewed success, suggests a quite different Elmer, as does his forgiving treatment of Lulu. What precisely causes his transformation is not quite clear. After all, after his successes in the city, he uses Sister Sharon's admiration for him to seduce her. Surely, this is Elmer at his most despicable.[18] Thereafter, however, Elmer is different. He is far more committed to Sharon than he has been to other women. He resists Lulu's advances in the name of Sharon and near the end of the movie still wishes for a normal life with Sharon.

Perhaps we should simply assume, given Hollywood discourse, that romantic love has saved Elmer.[19] But Elmer's love goes unrequited when Sister Sharon chooses the revival over him. As a result, that which figures more importantly than this romantic interlude is Elmer's platonic, regretful, forgiving relationship with Lulu. Elmer is sorry for what he has done to her and bears her no ill will, despite her malicious actions. As he forgives rather than judges, he creates the prospect of community. In fact, it is rather difficult to imagine Elmer alone.

This "salvation," however, takes him beyond evangelistic religion and the revival. Once again, then, the movie is suspicious of religion. If the revival is a modern analogue for Paul's evangelism, Elmer is the analogue for a modern rejection of that evangelicalism. Elmer even quotes Paul's words about leaving behind childish things to explain his final departure from the revival (1 Cor 13:11). Elmer, then, stands for a practical acceptance of this life, of love and spirituals, and, most importantly, of common humanity. If he bears any resemblance to Paul, he is a repentant Paul who has given up his evangelistic certainty or, better, his hypocritical claim to speak for God. When and why Elmer repents are, however, admittedly not clear.

Jonas Nightengale is a far less appealing and far less repentant evangelist in *Leap of Faith*. When his traveling revival breaks down in rural Kansas, Jonas decides to throw a few extra shows to make a little extra cash. That is his only goal. As the movie tagline states, Jonas and his team offer "real miracles, sensibly priced." They understand "miracles," of course, simply as a good show, reasonably priced entertainment, featuring singing, preaching, dancing, and drama.

The poor farming community to which Jonas's team has come is in the midst of a long-term drought. Furthermore, the sheriff of the town, Will, sees Jonas and his team rightly as con men whom the desperate town will easily fall for but can hardly afford. Jonas, however, has an answer for the cynical sheriff and dispatches his comely assistant, Jane, to change the sheriff's mind. The chemistry between the two gives Jonas permission for his show, but it also begins to make Jane question the direction of her life.

Soon, Jonas has the tent set up and the show going. Jonas brings "miracles" to the town with the help of spies and impressive computer equipment run by Jane. A spy detects a problem and informs Jane, who informs Jonas, who impresses the crowd with his specific knowledge of their particular problems. "Miracles" ensue, and the money roles in. Will, of course, remains skeptical.

Complications arise when Jonas develops feelings for a lovely young waitress, Marva. Problematically, she has a crippled brother, Boyd, who has already been disappointed by faith healers. Accordingly, Marva distrusts Jonas and is unresponsive to his attentions. To woo her, Jonas dances along a fine line. He needs to do "miracles" in order to bring in money, but he must not and does not want to hurt Boyd, whom he genuinely cares about. Accordingly, Jonas warns Boyd away from the revival and dismisses his desperate hopes repeatedly. Finally, however, pressures and greed overcome Jonas, and he decides to go for the big miracle. Sneaking into the revival tent, he paints tears on the statue of Jesus.

The miracle brings national attention to the revival, as well as hordes of people willing to pay for the sight and the possibility of miracles. Jonas is delighted with the money but anguished about the pain that he fears will come to Boyd. Surprisingly, in the film's finale, Boyd rises from his wheelchair and walks. No one is more surprised than Jonas, who abandons his revival team and catches a ride on a truck going out of town as rain begins to fall on the thirsty community.[20]

The critics liked the first half of this movie. They admired the movie's criticism of faith-healing evangelists. They did not like the second half, or "message" part, of the movie.[21] I, however, enjoy the idea of a visionary, miracle-producing evangelist hoisted on his own petard. I like the idea of a conniving evangelist reduced to human helplessness in the face of events larger than himself. We do not need to call those larger forces God. Such mysteries[22] nicely insist on human limitations and, in particular, on the imperfect humanity of evangelists and apostles. However hungry and desperate we may become for deus ex machina deliverances, evangelists and apostles are hardly in charge of such. They would be as surprised by a miracle as we.

The ending is unsatisfactory if we are deeply concerned for the character of Jonas Nightengale. We know less, and can imagine less, of what becomes of him than we can of Elmer Gantry. Further, in no sense does he repent. His one human moment is when he tries not to take advantage of Boyd. He eventually turns away from that humanity, sticks to his evangelical guns, and is surprised by a miracle. While that miracle has the potential to return him to his humanity, we do not see that happen. In the end, he simply runs away. As a result, Jonas is far more like the unrepentant Saint Paul than Elmer is.

Although Elmer is a better gesture at the repentant Paul for whom we are looking, he still rejects Paul too decisively. If we wish a "redemptive exchange"[23] between ourselves and Paul, we will need to be less superior than a stance with Elmer or against Jonas offers us. Fortunately, Robert Duvall has made a wonderfully sympathetic portrayal of a modern-day evangelist in *The Apostle*. That film and Duvall's portrayal of the main character, Sonny Dewey, render an all-too-human evangelist without seductively offering us a divine, moral high ground from which to view the foibles of this figure. That juxtaposition offers the possibility of "redemptive exchange."

The film opens with a shot of Sonny's youth in a black holiness church in depression-era south Texas. Moving rapidly to the present, Sonny stops his Cadillac on the side of the road beside an accident. Rushing to the wrecked car, he lays his Bible on the car's roof and begins to proselytize the injured young man inside. As the boy accepts Sonny's Jesus, a skeptical policeman runs Sonny off, saying, "I guess you think you accomplished something in there, huh?"[24] Sonny replies, "I know I did. All I know is I did not put my head through that window in vain. . . . I'd rather die today and go to heaven than live to be a hundred and go to hell." Sonny's illogical reply and the policeman's query nicely juxtapose the two attitudes that Duvall's movie holds redemptively in tension throughout: (1) a cynicism about evangelists eminently justified by recent events and virtually required in Hollywood film; and (2) Duvall's realistic, human portrayal of Sonny's (and evangelical Christians') otherworldly faith.[25] Underlining the otherworldly character of this faith, Duvall allows us a shot of an ambulance—that is, practical help—arriving as Sonny and his mother drive away singing.

After several scenes establishing Sonny's human character and his commitment to a traveling revival ministry, the movie's complication occurs. Sonny discovers that his wife, Jessie, is having an affair with Sonny's youth minister, Horace. Adding insult to injury, Horace and Jessie also steal Sonny's large, prosperous church from him. Sonny goes home to his mother's and spends the night "shouting" angrily at God.[26] Sonny finds no peace, for he soon appears drunk at his kids' ball game. There, he strikes Horace with a baseball bat in a rage, leaving Horace in a coma.

Like Elmer and Jonas, Sonny leaves town. Unlike those other movies, *The Apostle* has only begun at this point. While he prays for God's direction (complete with an interesting shot of his car at a crossroads from above), he fakes his death. After spending time in prayer and fasting at a black man's fishing camp, he baptizes himself anew as the Apostle E. F. On one level, of course, this name change is simply another part of his attempt to hide from the consequences of his "sins." On another level, Sonny has re-created/resurrected himself for a new life. Once again, that is, Duvall has nicely juxtaposed secular cynicism and sectarian faith.

Making his way to Bayou Boutté, Louisiana, the Apostle E. F. goes to work as a mechanic for Elmo and convinces a retired black minister, Charles Blackwell, to help him reopen Blackwell's closed church, One-Way Road to Heaven. When Blackwell agrees, E. F. opines, "It's resurrection time." E. F. takes another job, in a fast-food restaurant, to bring in more money for materials to speed up the refurbishment of the church. E. F. also convinces Elmo to give him time on a radio station that he also owns (although E. F. has to pay before he prays!).[27] His performance is so powerful that the station receptionist, Toosie, begins to fall for him. After a date with Toosie, E. F. sits before his church and prays:

> Lord, let this church live. Just pray you'll let that man Horace live. In the name of Jesus, let him live. I don't know how long it's gonna last, Lord, cause they could be coming for me. . . . But in the meantime, we've done something, haven't we? We've done something. I want to thank you for that.

While the church starts slowly, Blackwell and E. F. eventually start to draw more people. Another problem arises, however, when a redneck troublemaker comes to the church to start trouble. He despises E. F. and his integrated church. When the redneck refuses to leave, E. F. beats him soundly while the congregants sing "There Is Power in the Blood." Afterward, E. F. apologizes to the church. He knows he should have turned the other cheek, but he will not let anyone take his church.

After E. F. hears of his mother's death, the church holds a picnic celebrating its one-month anniversary.[28] The redneck arrives on a bulldozer, threatening to "take out" E. F.'s church. E. F. stops the redneck by laying his Bible, open to Ps 91, before the bulldozer and telling the redneck that God will strike him down if he moves the book. E. F. leads his congregation in a repeated chant: "Nobody moves that book." When the redneck kneels to move the Bible, E. F. kneels with him and witnesses to him, telling him, after the fashion of Paul, that he was a worse sinner than he is. The conversion of the redneck, broadcast live on radio by Elmo, is E. F.'s most dramatic success, as the congregation sings "Victory Is Mine" in the background.

Shortly thereafter, E. F. confesses his past to Reverend Blackwell and asks his advice. Blackwell responds, "Whatever you want to do. We love you. You've helped many, many people in the town."[29] E. F. rejoins, "If and when they come, take my gold, my watch, my jewelry; hock 'em. Get every penny you can to help this ministry stay alive. I love this little old church. You never know how long the Lord's gonna let you hang around." Soon, Jessie hears E. F. on the radio selling prayer scarves and reports him to the authorities. They arrive en masse as E. F. preaches. As the police wait, E. F. leads the church in a testimonial service of thanks. His last sermon (Jesus has his eye on you; you cannot escape) converts his friend Sam.[30] As they kneel together, E. F. says, "Saint Paul says any man who accepts Christ as his savior is a saint. You're a saint here tonight, Sammy. You're going to heaven and I'm going to jail . . ." (as the congregation sings "Softly and Tenderly, Jesus Is Calling"). E. F. takes his leave of the church, chanting, "I'm on my way to heaven," as they all sing "I'll Fly Away."[31]

As the music continues in the background, the police arrest Eulis F. Dewey for murder. To the end, then, Duvall continues the juxtaposition of secular reality and otherworldly religion. E. F. leaves Sam his Bible and leaves his jewelry for the church. As the credits roll, we see Sonny working in a road gang, leading the prisoners in Jesus chants, and then we hear a black choir singing "I'm a Soldier in the Army of the Lord."

I remarked in the introduction to this book that Paul has had little movie exposure. *The Apostle* is a dramatic exception to that general observation. Sonny/the Apostle E. F. is Paul, albeit in "disguise." By "disguise," I mean that E. F. is a Paul figure in a fashion similar to the characters in film that we sometimes describe as Christ figures, because they bear some allusive resemblance to Jesus. E. F.'s resemblance to Paul is, however, hardly so allusive. The matter is much closer to the interplay between Christ figure (Daniel) and Jesus (the role played by Daniel in the passion play he produces) in *Jesus of Montreal*. Sonny/E. F. deliberately lives his life after the fashion of what he understands of the New Testament. As he does so, his character and story come to resemble the portrayal of Paul in Acts,[32] as he tries to live "in Christ."

Like Saul/Paul, Sonny grows up in the bosom of a religious tradition. *The Apostle*, of course, substitutes Pentecostalism for first-century Judaism. Further, Sonny is zealous for this tradition and travels in support of his faith. A significant crisis changes all of that. For Saul, the crisis was a blinding hierophany. For Sonny, it is the loss of his family and his murder of his wife's lover.[33] While the violent act sets Sonny in flight, it does not take him away from his religion. Instead, he enters into an intensive period of religious searching from which he emerges as a new man, the Apostle E. F., like Saul becoming Paul in Acts. In harmony with modern understandings of the individual nature of religion and self-transformation, Sonny becomes the Apostle E. F. by his own baptismal hand. By contrast, Saul's transformation, in keeping with the "all apostles" theme of the book of Acts, is far more communal.[34]

After this religious rebirth, the Apostle E. F. travels, like Paul, "in the service of the Lord." Like Paul, he frequently seeks spiritual guidance in the exact direction that he should go. Like Paul, he supports himself in this service by manual labor. Eventually, with the help of an older minister (Barnabas?), he founds one integrated church (Antioch?) among the poor and socially disadvantaged (Gentiles?). One church is a significant reduction compared to Paul's ministry, but E. F. also has a large ministry on the radio, a technological advance over Paul's letters. The miracles of his ministry, of course, are not Paul's supernatural acts. They are modern miracles of acceptance and transformation like those in *Tender Mercies*. Finally, while E. F. does not write letters for the church, he does leave his Bible and his appointed ministers to his church. Imprisoned by the state, the last scene shows E. F. preaching his gospel "without hindrance" (Acts 28:31).

Despite the fact that E. F. teaches a "one way to heaven" gospel, the disguised portrayal of the apostle deconstructs any tendency toward the Saint Paul system. The element of disguise also frees Duvall's movie from slavish devotion to the literal text of Acts. While this apostle resembles Paul, he is not Saint Paul. The result

Toward a repentant Paul?

is a movie far more like Pasolini's *San Paolo* script than the nostalgia of Young's *San Paolo*. Pasolini and Duvall both assay—and foreground—a redemptive exchange between tradition and the present.[35]

Accordingly, Duvall's movie sets Paul loose in modernity, free from canon, nostalgia, and myth. If E. F. is a "saint," he is one going to jail for murder. As a result, despite his religious devotion, Sonny is a Paul in need of repentance and redemption.

He is a fully human apostle. With *The Apostle*, the irrefragable *Saint* and *Apostle* are forever gone.

Unlike Scorsese's treatment of Paul and the criticism of religion so pervasive in *Elmer Gantry*, however, Duvall still imagines a practical, salutary place for religion. Even more than Elmer, Sonny is sincerely, devoutly religious.[36] Further, Sonny's religion "saves" him. Even though he flees from justice, we may see Sonny's flight as an imposition of his own religious discipline upon himself.[37] Further, he repeatedly states that "they" will come for him, so he does not expect to escape justice. Instead, he seeks a respite in order to do something "good." Accordingly, he pays for his crimes in his own way and then according to the laws of the state of Texas. His brief flight is a resurrection, both for himself and for Reverend Blackwell's church. Despite the otherworldly air of Sonny's religion, these resurrections are quite material and this-worldly. They do not so much escape the world or condemn the world apocalyptically as they make a way within the ongoing world. Accordingly, the movie begins and ends with church services that spew the apostle out into the world first as roadside evangelist and then as chain-gang preacher. This human Paul, then, is working out his own salvation "with fear and trembling" (Phil 2:12).[38]

Duvall's apostle cannot be dismissed easily to the mythic realms of either sainthood or evil. He lives in the human space between them.[39] He is a human apostle working it out as he goes. Given his human flaws and his crisis, he is simply striving to re-create his life as best he can, using the tools at his disposal. In Sonny's case, the tools are the Christian Bible and various religious hymns filtered through Pentecostal religious experience.

Camus once remarked that we should forgo myths of the gods for terrestrial myths, for myths with human faces.[40] Saint Paul is the former. Sonny is the latter. Consequently, E. F. is an apostle worth hearing. Consequently, we need not accept his authority passively nor condemn his impractical otherworldliness and "sinfulness" from some superior position. We need not look up to him as saint or down upon him as charlatan, nut, or weakling in need of a crutch. Duvall crafts a movie between those two options, between an otherworldly, sectarian religion and modern cynicism. In this place lies the fantastic, redemptive possibility of a repentant, human apostle. If Sonny is not Paul, maybe Sonny provides a lens through which we can imagine a human, repentant Paul. If we can, maybe we will have an image, or images, of Paul worth our reflection and dialogue.

Notes

1. See Schweitzer, *The Quest for the Historical Jesus: A Critical Study of Its Progress from Reimarus to Wrede*, trans. W. Montgomery (New York: Macmillan, 1968), 398–99; Miles, *Christ*, 266; and Walsh, *Reading the Gospels in the Dark*, 45–68.

2. See Jeffrey L. Staley, *Reading with a Passion: Rhetoric, Autobiography, and the American West in the Gospel of John* (New York: Continuum, 1995), 14–15; and Walsh, *Reading the Gospels in the Dark*, 173–85.

3. See Nietzsche, *The Gay Science*, 353; idem, *The Antichrist*, 42–43.

4. For a description of these two different types of religious experience, see James, *The Varieties of Religious Experience*.

5. Recent philosophers have turned to Paul for precisely this reason.

6. Each of the Pauls considered here has positive and negative features. An apocalyptic Paul, for example, nicely challenges complacent hierarchies. An insane or a comic Paul nicely challenges the certainty and violence of an apocalyptic Paul. A Jewish Paul nicely challenges the obsession with death in a Christian Paul. The main gain of multiple Pauls is the possibility for conversation about the relative values of these Pauls.

7. See Smith, *Map Is Not Territory*, 289–309.

8. See Gilles Deleuze and Félix Guattari, *A Thousand Plateaus*, trans. Brian Massumi (Minneapolis: University of Minnesota Press, 1987), 501–14; and Richard Walsh and George Aichele, "Preface: Interpretive Thieves," in Aichele and Walsh, *Those Outside*, vii–xvi.

9. See Miles, *Seeing and Believing*, 5–25, 48–67.

10. In fact, the famous first lines in the Sinclair Lewis novel on which the film is based are "Elmer Gantry was drunk. He was elegantly drunk, lovingly and pugnaciously drunk." The opening visuals—including several crosses and a manger scene—strongly contrast Christianity and Elmer. By contrast, the closing visuals connect Elmer and Christianity. A cross and Elmer stand in the midst of—and dominate—the rubble.

11. Incidentally, Elmer refers to Paul's dramatic conversion in his conversation with the black minister.

12. After Sister Sharon's opening sermon in the city, Elmer dismisses the adoring crowd and leaves Sister Sharon clothed in white, sleeping peacefully on the bed. That visual contrasts nicely with the woman in red whom Elmer leaves on the hotel bed in the movie's opening.

13. Lefferts refuses to print the photos because (1) they only prove Elmer is human, and (2) they are blackmailing lies.

14. The mob, which has destroyed her office, has painted "Repent" on her wall.

15. Incidentally, the cross remains prominent in the background as Elmer walks away smiling and then as the end credits begin.

16. In this, Lefferts resembles the role and function of Lucius in *King of Kings*. Both figures stand between modernity and religious tradition. Of course, *King of Kings* handles the tradition more positively than does *Elmer Gantry*. Lefferts is also a far more human character than Lucius. Our connection with him ebbs (when he attacks Sharon in the newspaper office) and flows (when he refuses to print the blackmail photos).

17. We have discussed Scorsese's Paul on several occasions. See, for example, the introduction.

18. Danél Griffin sees Elmer Gantry as an evil man, Jonas Nightengale as an opportunist, and the Apostle E. F. as a holy man. See his review, *"Leap of Faith,"* http://uashome.alaska.edu/%7Ejndfg20/website/leapoffaith.htm (accessed July 26, 2004). Elmer is an "evil" character if we hold him responsible for Sister Sharon's demise. The temptation scene, in which Elmer wishes to tear off Sharon's holy wings and make her into "a real woman," does suggest this reading. In the final scenes, however, it seems that Sharon's otherworldly faith, not her temptation by Elmer, destroys her. With Elmer, she might have

found a "normal life." We can also read the movie "nonredemptively" if we read it as a progressive unveiling of a character—Elmer's tagline sermon does remain the same throughout—from beginning to end. Compared to Sinclair Lewis's novel, however, the movie is clearly more sympathetic to Elmer. The novel's craven, cowardly Elmer pushes other people into the flames to escape and only pretends to try to save others after he is safe.

19. In the charred rubble of the tabernacle, a sign that once proclaimed "God's Love" now only says "Love."

20. Perhaps we should read this film in tandem with the story of the reluctant, disobedient Jonah. Of course, Jonah receives the miracles—God's pursuit of him and the deliverance of Nineveh—that he knew would come but did not want. Jonas is far more surprised by his miracle. Further, Jonas's story ends far earlier than Jonah's. We never know what happens after Jonas runs away.

21. See Roger Ebert, "*Leap of Faith*," http://www.suntimes.com/cgi-bin/print.cgi (accessed July 25, 2004); and Hal Hinson, "*Leap of Faith*," http://www.washingtonpost.com/wp-srv/style/longterm/movies/videos/leapoffaith13hinso (accessed August 8, 2004).

22. *Leap of Faith* is perfectly at home in the culture of films in the late 1980s and in the 1990s. Although reluctant to offer traditional Western depictions of God or religion, film became quite enamored of "mystery." See *Grand Canyon, Powder, The Green Mile*.

23. I borrow this phrase from Aichele, "Sitcom Mythology," 119.

24. Sonny's Bible atop the car is the centerpiece for most of this scene. The physical Bible appears prominently again in the confrontation with the redneck on a bulldozer and in the scene where E. F. takes his leave of the church and Sam, his young protégé. In short, the Bible dominates this film visually and textually. In fact, E. F. punctuates almost every event with a scripture text, reference fully supplied. Reinhartz, *Scripture on the Silver Screen*, 114–28, has an interesting discussion of the Bible as talisman in this film. She instructively compares the film's use of the Bible to the notion of the salvific, abiding, textual word in the Gospel of John.

25. I am tempted to add a third element to the mix: the constant quotation of the Bible, its physical presence, and the religious music that is sung by characters or offered as background music. These elements are hardly an attitude though. I see them, then, as part of Duvall's realistic portrayal of Pentecostal religious experience.

26. If one wished to read Sonny as mentally disturbed, one could easily begin with this scene.

27. In contrast to Elmer and Jonas, the Apostle E. F. does not seem motivated by greed. In this scene, it is Elmo who discusses money matters at length. Further, E. F. works two jobs to support the building of the church and leaves the church all his worldly goods when he is arrested. We do, however, toward the end of the movie, see him selling prayer scarves on the radio.

28. In *Tender Mercies*, another movie starring Duvall, a new family "saves" Mac Sledge. By contrast, in this movie, E. F.'s new church replaces his lost family. In fact, Duvall often cuts from family failures or crises (like the death of E. F.'s mother) to church successes (like the one-month anniversary celebration). Further, at the end of the movie, E. F. leaves his worldly possessions to his church, not his family.

29. Sam listens to this conversation from outside an open window. His subsequent conversion, then, is a kind of "redemptive exchange" within the movie itself.

30. Of course, a picture of Jesus hangs on the wall behind E. F. during the sermon.

31. Religious music dominates the film. The most important songs are "I'll Fly Away" and "I'm a Soldier in the Army of the Lord," both of which are repeated. They help create the impression that E. F. is on a journey to a better place. The opening and closing visuals contribute to the same impression. In both, a church service leads to an evangelistic scene "in" the world.

32. See Reinhartz, *Scripture on the Silver Screen*, 119–22.

33. I see no real connection here to the stoning of Stephen; however, in both Acts and *The Apostle*, the hero's significant religious experience follows a violent death.

34. Paul's account in Gal 1–2 is not an emphasis on individual self-appointment. Its denial of other human input is an attempt to arrogate divine authority for Paul's mission. Of course, in modernity, the individual is god, so the difference may be insignificant.

35. Pasolini assays a redemptive exchange between Catholicism and Marxism. See also Walsh, *Reading the Gospels in the Dark*, 107–12.

36. The fact that flight ends the story of Elmer and Jonas and begins the story of the Apostle E. F. means that this movie can explore the issues of redemption and responsibility much more thoroughly than those movies.

37. See Danél Griffin, "*The Apostle*," http://uashome.alaska.edu/~jndfg20/website/apostle.htm (accessed August 8, 2004).

38. Of course, I have to omit the earlier part of the verse and the subsequent verse in order to delete Paul's typical rage for order and sameness.

39. The similarity to J. Z. Smith's understanding of religion is, I hope, evident. See his *Map Is Not Territory*, 289–309.

40. *The Myth of Sisyphus*, 117–18.

Movies Cited

The Apostle. Directed by Robert Duvall. VHS. October Films, 1997.

Babette's Feast. Directed by Gabriel Axel. VHS. Orion Pictures, 1988.

Bad Day at Blackrock. Directed by John Sturges. VHS. Metro-Goldwyn-Mayer, 1955.

Barabbas. Directed by Richard Fleischer. DVD. Columbia Pictures, 1962.

Barton Fink. Directed by Joel Coen. VHS. Twentieth Century Fox Film, 1991.

A Beautiful Mind. Directed by Ron Howard. VHS. Universal Pictures, 2001.

Being John Malkovich. Directed by Spike Jonze. VHS. USA Films, 1999.

Being There. Directed by Hal Ashby. VHS. United Artists, 1979.

The Big Lebowski. Directed by Joel Coen. DVD. Gramercy Pictures, 1998.

Blood Simple. Directed by Joel Coen. VHS. Circle Films, 1984.

The Blues Brothers. Directed by John Landis. DVD. Universal Pictures, 1980.

Braveheart. Directed by Mel Gibson. VHS. Paramount Pictures, 1995.

Bruce Almighty. Directed by Tom Shadyac. DVD. Universal Pictures, 2003.

Commandments. Directed by Daniel Taplitz. VHS. Gramercy Pictures, 1997.

The Confession. Directed by David Hugh Jones. VHS. Conprod, 1999.

Cool Hand Luke. Directed by Stuart Rosenberg. VHS Warner Brothers, 1967.

Crimes and Misdemeanors. Directed by Woody Allen. VHS. Orion Pictures, 1989.

Dances with Wolves. Directed by Kevin Costner. VHS. Orion Pictures, 1990.

Dead Man Walking. Directed by Tim Robbins. VHS. Gramercy Pictures, 1995.

Dead Poets Society. Directed by Peter Weir. VHS. Buena Vista Pictures, 1989.

Donnie Darko. Directed by Richard Kelly. DVD. Pandora Cinema, 2001.

Elmer Gantry. Directed by Richard Brooks. VHS. United Artists, 1960.

End of Days. Directed by Peter Hyams. VHS. Universal Pictures, 1999.

Equilibrium. Directed by Kurt Wimmer. VHS. Dimension Films, 2002.

The Evil Dead. Directed by Sam Raimi. VHS. New Line Cinema, 1981.

E.T. the Extra-Terrestrial. Directed by Steven Spielberg. VHS. MCA/Universal Pictures, 1982.

eXistenZ. Directed by David Cronenberg. VHS. Dimension Films, 1999.

Fargo. Directed by Joel Coen. VHS. Gramercy Pictures, 1996.

The Fifth Element. Directed by Luc Besson. VHS. Columbia Pictures, 1997.

The Firm. Directed by Sydney Pollack. VHS. Paramount Pictures, 1993.

Flatliners. Directed by Joel Schumacher. VHS. Columbia Pictures, 1990.

Forrest Gump. Directed by Robert Zemeckis. VHS. Paramount Pictures, 1994.

Frailty. Directed by Bill Paxton. DVD. Lions Gates Films, 2001.

The Gods Must Be Crazy. Directed by Jamie Uys. VHS. Twentieth Century Fox Film, 1984 (1980).

Grand Canyon. Directed by Lawrence Kasdan. DVD. Twentieth Century Fox, 1991.

The Great Escape. Directed by John Sturges. VHS. United Artists, 1963.

The Green Mile. Directed by Frank Darabont. VHS. Warner Brothers, 1999.

Harvey. Directed by Henry Koster. VHS. Universal International Pictures, 1950.

High Noon. Directed by Fred Zinnemann. VHS. United Artists, 1952.

High Plains Drifter. Directed by Clint Eastwood. VHS. Universal Pictures, 1972.

The Hudsucker Proxy. Directed by Joel Coen. VHS. Warner Brothers, 1994.

Il Vangelo secondo Matteo (*The Gospel according to St. Matthew*). Directed by Pier Paolo Pasolini. VHS. Continental, 1964 (1966).

Intolerable Cruelty. Directed by Joel Coen. DVD. Universal Pictures, 2003.

Jakob the Liar. Directed by Peter Kassovitz. VHS. Columbia Pictures, 1999.

Jesus. Directed by Roger Young. VHS. CBS TV, 1999.

Jesus of Montreal. Directed by Denys Arcand. VHS. Orion Classics, 1990 (1989).

King of Kings. Directed by Nicholas Ray. DVD. Metro-Goldwyn-Mayer, 1961.

The Last Temptation of Christ. Directed by Martin Scorsese. VHS. Universal Pictures, 1988.

Leap of Faith. Directed by Richard Pearce. VHS. Paramount Pictures, 1992.

Lethal Weapon. Directed by Richard Donner. VHS. Warner Brothers, 1987.

Levity. Directed by Ed Solomon. VHS. Sony Pictures Classics, 2003.

Life Is Beautiful. Directed by Roberto Benigni. DVD. Miramax Films, 1998.

Mad Max. Directed by George Miller. VHS. Orion Pictures, 1979.

The Man Who Wasn't There. Directed by Joel Coen. VHS. USA Films, 2001.

The Matrix. Directed by Andy Wachowski and Larry Wachowski. VHS. Warner Brothers, 1999.

The Matrix Reloaded. Directed by Andy Wachowski and Larry Wachowski. VHS. Warner Brothers, 2003.

Miller's Crossing. Directed by Joel Coen. VHS. Twentieth Century Fox Film, 1990.

Minority Report. Directed by Steven Spielberg. VHS. Twentieth Century Fox Film, 2002.

Monty Python's Life of Brian. Directed by Terry Jones. DVD. Orion Pictures, 1970.

O Brother, Where Art Thou? Directed by Joel Coen. VHS. Buena Vista Pictures, 2000.

Pale Rider. Directed by Clint Eastwood. VHS. Warner Brothers, 1985.

The Passion of the Christ. Directed by Mel Gibson. DVD. Twentieth Century Fox
    Pictures, 2004.

Patch Adams. Directed by Tom Shadyac. VHS. Universal Pictures, 1998.

Phone Booth. Directed by Joel Schumacher. VHS. Twentieth Century Fox
    Film, 2002.

The Pianist. Directed by Roman Polanski. VHS. Focus Features, 2002.

Places in the Heart. Directed by Robert Benton. VHS. TriStar Pictures, 1984.

Playing God. Directed by Andy Wilson. VHS. Buena Vista Pictures, 1997.

Pleasantville. Directed by Gary Ross. VHS. New Line Cinema, 1998.

Powder. Directed by Victor Salva. VHS. Buena Vista Pictures, 1995.

Raising Arizona. Directed by Joel Coen. VHS. Twentieth Century Fox Film, 1987.

San Paolo. Directed by Roger Young. DVD. Radiotelevisione Italiana, 2000.

Seven. Directed by David Fincher. VHS. New Line Cinema, 1995.

Shane. Directed by George Stevens. VHS. Paramount Pictures, 1953.

The Sixth Day. Directed by Roger Spottiswoode. VHS. Columbia Pictures, 2000.

The Sixth Sense. Directed by M. Night Shyamalan. VHS. Buena Vista
    Pictures, 1999.

Star Trek II: The Wrath of Khan. Directed by Nicholas Meyer. VHS. Paramount
    Pictures, 1982.

Stigmata. Directed by Rupert Wainwright. VHS. Metro-Goldwyn-Mayer, 1999.

Strange Days. Directed by Kathryn Bigelow. DVD. Twentieth Century Fox
    Film, 1995.

Sullivan's Travels. Directed by Preston Sturges. VHS. Paramount Pictures, 1942.

The Tao of Steve. Directed by Jenniphr Goodman. VHS. Sony Pictures
    Classics, 2000.

Tender Mercies. Directed by Bruce Beresford. VHS. Universal Pictures, 1983.

Terminator 3: Rise of the Machines. Directed by Jonathan Mostow. VHS. Warner
    Brothers, 2003.

To Kill a Mockingbird. Directed by Robert Mulligan. VHS. Universal International
    Pictures, 1962.

Total Recall. Directed by Paul Verhoeven. DVD. Twentieth Century Fox Film, 1989.

Train of Life. Directed by Radu Mihaileanu. VHS. Paramount Pictures, 1998.

Trainspotting. Directed by Danny Boyle. VHS. Miramax Films, 1996.

The Truman Show. Directed by Peter Weir. VHS. Paramount Pictures, 1998.

Unbreakable. Directed by M. Night Shyamalan. VHS. Buena Vista Pictures, 2000.

Unforgiven. Directed by Clint Eastwood. VHS. Warner Brothers, 1992.

Witness. Directed by Peter Weir. VHS. Paramount Pictures, 1985.

The Wizard of Oz. Directed by Victor Fleming. VHS. Metro-Goldwyn-
    Mayer, 1939.

Works Cited

Aichele, George. *The Control of Biblical Meaning: Canon as Semiotic Mechanism*. Harrisburg, Pa.: Trinity Press International, 2001.

——. "Sitcom Mythology." In *Screening Scripture: Intertextual Connections between Scripture and Film*, edited by George Aichele and Richard Walsh, 100–19. Harrisburg, Pa.: Trinity Press International, 2002.

Anderson, Bernhard. *Out of the Depths*. New York: Board of Missions, United Methodist Church, 1970.

Anonymous. "Review of *San Paolo*." http://www.imdb.com/title/tt0270621/plot summary (accessed August 7, 2004).

Babcock, William S., ed. *Paul and the Legacies of Paul*. Dallas: Southern Methodist University Press, 1990.

Badiou, Alain. *Saint Paul: The Foundation of Universalism*. Translated by Ray Brassier. Stanford: Stanford University Press, 2003.

Bainton, Roland H. *Behold the Christ: A Portrayal in Words and Pictures*. New York: Harper & Row, 1976.

Barr, David L. *New Testament Story: An Introduction*. 3rd ed. Belmont, Calif.: Wadsworth, 2002.

Barthes, Roland. *Mythologies*. Translated by Annette Lavers. New York: Hill and Wang, 1972.

Beker, J. Christiaan. *Paul the Apostle: The Triumph of God in Life and Thought*. 2nd ed. Philadelphia: Fortress, 1984.

Berardinelli, James. "*The Big Lebowski*." http://movie-reviews.colossus.net/movies/b/big_lebowski.html (accessed June 21, 2004).

——. "*Jakob the Liar*." http://movie-reviews.colossus.net/movies/j/jakob.html (accessed July 8, 2004).

——. "*The Passion of the Christ*." http://movie-reviews.colossus.net/movies/p/passion_christ.html (accessed May 17, 2004).

————. "*Stigmata.*" http://movie-reviews.colossus.net/movies/s/stigmata.html (accessed June 21, 2004).

————. "*Train of Life.*" http://movie-reviews.colossus.net/movies/t/train_life. html (accessed August 23, 2004).

Berger, Peter L. *A Rumor of Angels: Modern Society and the Rediscovery of the Supernatural.* New York: Anchor, 1990.

————. *The Sacred Canopy: Elements of a Sociological Theory of Religion.* Garden City, N.Y.: Anchor, 1969.

Boer, Roland. "Editorial." *The Bible and Critical Theory* 1, November 2004. http:// publications.epress.monash.edu/doi/full/10.2104/bc040001 (accessed January 18, 2005).

————. "Non-Sense: *Total Recall*, Paul, and the Possibility of Psychosis." In *Screening Scripture: Intertextual Connections between Scripture and Film*, edited by George Aichele and Richard Walsh, 120–54. Harrisburg, Pa.: Trinity Press International, 2002.

Bonhoeffer, Dietrich. *The Cost of Discipleship.* Rev. ed. Translated by R. H. Fuller. New York: Macmillan, 1963.

Boyarin, Daniel. *A Radical Jew: Paul and the Politics of Identity.* Berkeley: University of California Press, 1994.

Brooks, Xan. "*Frailty.*" http://film.guardian.co.uk/News_Story/Critic_Review/ Guardian_review/0,4267,786804,00 (accessed May 28, 2004).

Bultmann, Rudolf. *Theology of the New Testament.* 2 vols. Translated by Kendrick Grobel. New York: Charles Scribner's Sons, 1955.

Burnett, Fred. "The Characterization of Martin Riggs in *Lethal Weapon 1*: An Archetypal Hero." In *Screening Scripture: Intertextual Connections between Scripture and Film*, edited by George Aichele and Richard Walsh, 251–78. Harrisburg, Pa.: Trinity Press International, 2002.

Campbell, Joseph. *The Hero with a Thousand Faces.* Princeton: Princeton University Press, 1972.

————. *The Masks of God.* 4 vols. New York: Penguin 1969.

Camus, Albert. *The Myth of Sisyphus and Other Essays.* Translated by Justin O'Brien. New York: Vintage International, 1991.

————. "Nobel Prize Acceptance Speech." http://www.nobel.se/laureates/ literature-1957-acceptance.html (accessed November 1, 1999).

————. *The Rebel: An Essay on Man in Revolt.* Translated by Anthony Bower. New York: Vintage, 1956.

Castelli, Elizabeth A. *Imitating Paul: A Discourse of Power.* Louisville: Westminster John Knox, 1991.

Cohen, Stanley, and Laurie Taylor. *Escape Attempts: The Theory and Practice of Resistance to Everyday Life.* 2nd ed. London: Routledge, 1992.

Cossé, Laurence. *A Corner of the Veil.* New York: Scribner's, 1999.

Crossan, John Dominic. *Raid on the Articulate: Comic Eschatology in Jesus and Borges*. San Francisco: Harper & Row, 1976.

Crossan, John Dominic, and Jonathan L. Reed. *In Search of Paul: How Jesus' Apostle Opposed Rome's Empire with God's Kingdom*. New York: HarperSanFrancisco, 2004.

Deleuze, Gilles, and Félix Guattari. *A Thousand Plateaus*. Translated by Brian Massumi. Minneapolis: University of Minnesota Press, 1987.

Dick, Philip K. "The Minority Report." In *The Philip K. Dick Reader*, 323–54. New York: Citadel, 1997.

———. "We Can Remember It for You Wholesale." In *The Philip K. Dick Reader*, 305–22. New York: Citadel, 1997.

Dirks, Tim. "*Bad Day at Blackrock*." http://www.filmsite.org/badd.html (accessed July 16, 2004).

Dodd, C. H. *The Epistle of Paul to the Romans*. Moffatt New Testament Commentary. New York: Harper & Brothers, 1932.

Donaldson, Terence L. *Paul and the Gentiles: Remapping the Apostle's Convictional World*. Minneapolis: Fortress, 1997.

Droege, Arthur J., and James D. Tabor. *A Noble Death: Suicide and Martyrdom among Christians and Jews in Antiquity*. New York: HarperSanFrancisco, 1992.

Dunn, James D. G. Introduction to *The Cambridge Companion to St. Paul*, edited by James D. G. Dunn, 1–15. Cambridge: Cambridge University Press, 2003.

Ebert, Roger. "*Frailty*." http://www.suntimes.com/cgi-bin/print.cgi (accessed May 28, 2004).

———. "*Jakob the Liar*." http://www.suntimes.com/cgi-bin/print.cgi (accessed July 8, 2004).

———. "*Leap of Faith*." http://www.suntimes.com/cgi-bin/print.cgi (accessed July 25, 2004).

———. "*The Passion of the Christ*." http://www.suntimes.com/ebert/ebert_reviews/2004/02/022401.html (accessed May 17, 2004).

———. "*Pleasantville*." http://www.suntimes.com/ebert/ebert_reviews/1998/10/102302.html (accessed October 9, 2003).

———. "*Stigmata*." http://www.suntimes.com/cgi-bin/print.cig (accessed June 21, 2004).

Eliade, Mircea. *Myth and Reality*. Translated by Willard R. Trask. New York: Harper & Row, 1963.

———. *The Sacred and the Profane: The Nature of Religion*. Translated by Willard R. Trask. New York: Harcourt, Brace & World, 1959.

Elliott, Neil. *Liberating Paul: The Justice of God and the Politics of the Apostle*. Maryknoll, N.Y.: Orbis Books, 1994.

Erasmus, Desiderius. *The Praise of Folly and Other Writings: A New Translation and Commentary*. Translated by Robert Adams Martin. New York: W. W. Norton, 1989.

Foucault, Michel. *Discipline and Punish: The Birth of the Prison*. Translated by Alan Sheridan. New York: Vintage, 1979.

———. *History of Sexuality: An Introduction*. Vol. 1 of *History of Sexuality*. Translated by Robert Hurley. New York: Vintage, 1990.

———. *The Use of Pleasure*. Vol. 2 of *History of Sexuality*. Translated by Robert Hurley. New York: Vintage, 1990.

French, Philip. "Into the Heart of Darko." http://film.guardian.co.uk/News_Story/Critic_Review/Observer_Film_of_the_week/0,4267 (accessed June 1, 2004).

Friedman, Richard Elliott. *The Hidden Face of God*. New York: HarperSanFrancisco, 1997.

Furnish, Victor Paul. "Pauline Studies." In *The New Testament and Its Modern Interpreters*, edited by Eldon Jay Epp and George W. MacRae, 321–50. Philadelphia: Fortress, 1989.

Gager, John. *Reinventing Paul*. Oxford: Oxford University Press, 2000.

Grady, Pam. "*Harvey*." http://www.reel.com/movie.asp?MID=536&buy=closed&PID=10090203&Tab=reviews&CID=18 (accessed June 3, 2004).

Greene, Graham. "The Destructors." http://www.gmtech.com/rocktheband/the_destructors.html (accessed June 2, 2004).

Greene, Naomi. *Pier Paolo Pasolini: Cinema as Heresy*. Princeton: Princeton University Press, 1990.

Griffin, Danél. "*The Apostle*." http://uashome.alaska.edu/~jndfg20/website/apostle.htm (accessed August 8, 2004).

———. "*Leap of Faith*." http://uashome.alaska.edu/%7Ejndfg20/website/leapoffaith.htm (accessed July 26, 2004).

Harnack, Adolf von. *History of Dogma*. 7 vols. Translated by Neil Buchanan. London: Williams & Norgate, 1894.

Hays, Richard B. *Echoes of Scripture in the Letters of Paul*. New Haven: Yale University Press, 1989.

Hengel, Martin. *The Atonement: The Origins of the Doctrine in the New Testament*. Translated by John Bowden. Philadelphia: Fortress, 1981.

———. *Crucifixion: In the Ancient World and the Folly of the Cross*. Translated by John Bowden. Philadelphia: Fortress, 1977.

Hick, John H. *Philosophy of Religion*. 2nd ed. Englewood Cliffs, N.J.: Prentice-Hall, 1973.

Hinson, Hal. "*Leap of Faith*." http://www.washingtonpost.com/wp-srv/style/longterm/movies/videos/leapoffaith13hinso (accessed August 8, 2004).

Hornblow, Deborah. "The Cash-In of the Christ." *The Fayetteville Observer*, April 2, 2004, E1.

Horrell, David G. *An Introduction to the Study of Paul*. London: T & T Clark, 2000.

Horsley, Richard A., ed. *Paul and Politics: Ekklesia, Israel, Imperium, Interpretation: Essays in Honor of Krister Stendahl.* Harrisburg, Pa.: Trinity Press International, 2000.

————. "Rhetoric and Empire—and 1 Corinthians." In *Paul and Politics: Ekklesia, Israel, Imperium, Interpretation: Essays in Honor of Krister Stendahl,* edited by Richard A. Horsley, 72–102. Harrisburg, Pa.: Trinity Press International, 2000.

Hume, David. *An Inquiry concerning Human Understanding.* Indianapolis: Bobbs-Merrill, 1955.

James, William. *Varieties of Religious Experience: A Study in Human Nature.* Glasgow: William Collins Sons, 1960.

————. *The Will to Believe and Other Essays in Popular Philosophy.* New York: Dover, 1956.

Jewett, Robert. *The Captain America Complex.* 2nd ed. Santa Fe, N.Mex.: Bear & Co., 1984.

————. *Paul the Apostle to America: Cultural Trends and Pauline Scholarship.* Louisville: Westminster John Knox, 1994.

————. *Saint Paul at the Movies: The Apostle's Dialogue with American Culture.* Louisville: Westminster John Knox, 1993.

————. *Saint Paul Returns to the Movies: Triumph over Shame.* Grand Rapids: William B. Eerdmans, 1999.

Jewett, Robert, and John Shelton Lawrence. *The American Monomyth.* Garden City, N.Y.: Anchor, 1977.

Johanson, MaryAnn. "Choose Your Own Psychotic Breakdown: *Donnie Darko.*" http://www.flickfilosopher.com/flickfilos/archive/014q/donniedarko.shtml (accessed June 1, 2004).

Käsemann, Ernst. *New Testament Questions of Today.* Translated by W. J. Montague. Philadelphia: Fortress, 1969.

Kermode, Frank. *The Genesis of Secrecy: On the Interpretation of Narrative.* Cambridge, Mass.: Harvard University Press, 1979.

Kierkegaard, Søren. *Fear and Trembling.* Translated by Alastair Hannay. New York: Penguin, 1985.

Kittredge, Cynthia Briggs. "Corinthian Women Prophets and Paul's Argumentation in 1 Corinthians." In *Paul and Politics: Ekklesia, Israel, Imperium, Interpretation: Essays in Honor of Krister Stendahl,* edited by Richard A. Horsley, 103–9. Harrisburg, Pa.: Trinity Press International, 2000.

Klassen, William. *Judas: Betrayer or Friend of Jesus?* Minneapolis: Fortress, 1996.

Kreitzer, Larry. *The New Testament in Fiction and Film: On Reversing the Hermeneutical Flow.* Sheffield: Sheffield Academic, 1993.

————. *Pauline Images in Fiction and Film: On Reversing the Hermeneutical Flow.* Sheffield: Sheffield Academic, 1999.

————. "The Scandal of the Cross: Crucifixion Imagery and Bram Stoker's *Dracula.*" In *The Monstrous and the Unspeakable: The Bible as Fantastic Literature,* edited by George Aichele and Tina Pippin, 181–219. Sheffield: Sheffield Academic, 1997.

Lévi-Strauss, Claude. *The Naked Man: Introduction to a Science of Mythology.* 4 vols. Translated by John and Doreen Weightman. New York: Harper & Row, 1981.

Maccoby, Hyam. *The Mythmaker: Paul and the Invention of Christianity.* New York: Harper & Row, 1986.

Mack, Burton L. *Who Wrote the New Testament? The Making of the Christian Myth.* New York: HarperSanFrancisco, 1995.

Malina, Bruce J. *Christian Origins and Cultural Anthropology: Practical Models for Biblical Interpretation.* Atlanta: John Knox, 1986.

Malina, Bruce J., and Jerome H. Neyrey. *Portraits of Paul: An Archaeology of Ancient Personality.* Louisville: Westminster John Knox, 1996.

Martin, Thomas M. *Images and the Imageless: A Study in Religious Consciousness and Film.* 2nd ed. London: Associated University Presses, 1991.

Matthews, Peter. *"Jakob the Liar."* http://www.bfi.org.uk/sightandsound/reviews/details.php?id=269 (accessed July 8, 2004).

Mattill, A. J. "The Jesus-Paul Parallels and the Purpose of Luke-Acts: H. H. Evans Reconsidered." *Novum Testamentum* 17 (1975): 15–46.

Meeks, Wayne A. *The Writings of St. Paul.* New York: W. W. Norton & Co., 1972.

Miles, Jack. *Christ: A Crisis in the Life of God.* New York: Alfred A. Knopf, 2001.

———. *God: A Biography.* New York: Vintage, 1996.

Miles, Margaret. *Seeing and Believing: Religion and Values in the Movies.* Boston: Beacon, 1996.

Moore, Stephen D. *God's Gym: Divine Male Bodies of the Bible.* New York: Routledge, 1996.

———. "Ugly Thoughts on the Face and Physique of the Historical Jesus." In *Biblical Studies and Cultural Studies: The Third Sheffield Colloquium,* edited by J. Cheryl Exum and Stephen Moore, 376–99. Sheffield: Sheffield Academic, 1998.

Morrow, James. *Blameless in Abaddon.* San Diego: Harcourt Brace & Co., 1996.

———. *The Eternal Footman.* San Diego: Harcourt Brace & Co., 1999.

———. *Towing Jehovah.* San Diego: Harcourt Brace & Co., 1994.

Munck, Johannes. *Paul and the Salvation of Mankind.* Translated by Frank Clarke. Atlanta: John Knox, 1977.

Nietzsche, Friedrich. *The Antichrist.* In *The Portable Nietzsche,* edited and translated by Walter A. Kaufmann. New York: Viking, 1954.

———. *Beyond Good and Evil: Prelude to a Philosophy of the Future.* Translated by Walter A. Kaufmann. New York: Vintage, 1966.

———. *Daybreak: Thoughts on the Prejudices of Morality.* Translated by R. J. Hollingdale. Cambridge: Cambridge University Press, 1982.

———. *The Gay Science.* Translated by Walter A. Kaufmann. New York: Vintage, 1974.

Olafson, Frederick A. "Camus, Albert." In *The Encyclopedia of Philosophy,* edited by Paul Edwards, 2:15–18. 8 vols. New York: Macmillan, 1967.

Pagels, Elaine H. *The Gnostic Paul: Gnostic Exegesis of the Pauline Letters*. Philadelphia: Fortress, 1975.

Petersen, Norman R. *Rediscovering Paul*. Philadelphia: Fortress, 1985.

Petrakis, John. "*The Passion of the Christ*." *The Christian Century* 121.6 (March 23, 2004): 40.

Pippin, Tina. "Of Gods and Demons: Blood Sacrifice and Eternal Life in *Dracula* and the Apocalypse of John." In *Screening Scripture: Intertextual Connections between Scripture and Film*, edited by George Aichele and Richard Walsh, 24–41. Harrisburg, Pa.: Trinity Press International, 2002.

Preston, Peter. "God and the Father." http://film.guardian.co.uk/News_Story/Critic_Review/Observer_Film_of_the_week/0,426 (accessed May 28, 2004).

Räisänen, Heikki. *The Torah and Christ: Essays in German and English on the Problem of Law in Early Christianity*. Helsinki: Finish Exegetical Society, 1986.

Reinhartz, Adele. *Scripture on the Silver Screen*. Louisville: Westminster John Knox, 2003.

Roetzel, Calvin. *Paul: The Man and the Myth*. Minneapolis: Fortress, 1999.

Runions, Erin. *How Hysterical: Identification and Resistance in the Bible and Film*. New York: Palgrave Macmillan, 2003.

Sanders, E. P. *Paul, the Law, and the Jewish People*. Philadelphia: Fortress, 1983.

————. *Paul and Palestinian Judaism: A Comparison of Patterns of Religion*. Philadelphia: Fortress, 1977.

Sanders, James. "Hermeneutics." In *The Interpreter's Dictionary of the Bible*, Supplementary Volume, edited by Keith Crim, 404–7. Nashville: Abingdon, 1976.

Schrader, Paul. *Transcendental Style in Film*. Berkeley: University of California Press, 1972.

Schreib, Richard. "*Flatliners*." http://www.moria.co.nz/sf/flatliners.htm (accessed June 7, 2004).

Schüssler Fiorenza, Elisabeth. *In Memory of Her: A Feminist Theological Reconstruction of Christian Origins*. New York: Crossroad, 1987.

————. "Paul and the Politics of Interpretation." In *Paul and Politics: Ekklesia, Israel, Imperium, Interpretation: Essays in Honor of Krister Stendahl*, edited by Richard A. Horsley, 40–57. Harrisburg, Pa.: Trinity Press International, 2000.

Schweitzer, Albert. *The Quest for the Historical Jesus: A Critical Study of Its Progress from Reimarus to Wrede*. Translated by W. Montgomery. New York: Macmillan, 1968.

Seeley, David. *The Noble Death: Graeco-Roman Martyrology and Paul's Concept of Salvation*. Sheffield: Sheffield Academic, 1990.

Segal, Alan. *Paul the Convert: The Apostolate and Apostasy of Saul the Pharisee*. New Haven: Yale University Press, 1990.

Serres, Michael. *The Parasite*. Translated by Lawrence R. Schehr. Baltimore: Johns Hopkins University Press, 1982.

Smith, Jonathan Z. *Map Is Not Territory: Studies in the History of Religion.* Leiden: E. J. Brill, 1978.

Stack, Oswald. *Pasolini on Pasolini: Interviews with Oswald Stack.* Bloomington: Indiana University Press, 1969.

Staley, Jeffrey L. "Meeting Patch Again for the First Time: Purity and Compassion in Marcus Borg, the Gospel of Mark, and *Patch Adams.*" In *Screening Scripture: Intertextual Connections between Scripture and Film,* edited by George Aichele and Richard Walsh, 213–28. Harrisburg, Pa.: Trinity Press International, 2002.

———. *Reading with a Passion: Rhetoric, Autobiography, and the American West in the Gospel of John.* New York: Continuum, 1995.

Stark, Rodney. *The Rise of Christianity: A Sociologist Reconsiders History.* Princeton: Princeton University Press, 1996.

Stendahl, Krister. "The Apostle Paul and the Introspective Conscience of the West." In Krister Stendahl, *Paul among the Jews and Gentiles, and Other Essays,* 78–96. Philadelphia: Fortress, 1976.

Talbert, Charles H. *Literary Patterns, Theological Themes, and the Genre of Luke-Acts.* Missoula, Mont.: Scholars, 1974.

Taubes, Jacob. *The Political Theology of Paul.* Edited by Aleida Assmann and Jan Assmann in conjunction with Horst Folkers, Wolf-Daniel Hartwich, and Christopher Schulte. Translated by Dana Hollander. Stanford: Stanford University Press, 2004.

Terrien, Samuel L. *The Elusive Presence: Toward a New Biblical Theology.* San Francisco: Harper & Row, 1978.

Tilley, Terrence W. *The Evils of Theodicy.* Washington, D.C.: Georgetown University Press, 1991.

Travers, Peter. "*The Passion of the Christ,*" *Rolling Stone,* February 23, 2004. http://www.rollingstone.com/reviews/movie?id=5949551&pageid=rs.ReviewsMovie Archive&pageregion=mainRegion (accessed May 17, 2004).

von Rad, Gerhard. *Old Testament Theology.* 2 vols. Translated by D. M. G. Stalker. New York: Harper & Row, 1962.

Walsh, Richard. *Mapping Myths of Biblical Interpretation.* Sheffield: Sheffield Academic, 2001.

———. "On Finding a Non-American Revelation: *End of Days* and the Book of Revelation." In *Screening Scripture: Intertextual Connections between Scripture and Film,* edited by George Aichele and Richard Walsh, 1–23. Harrisburg, Pa.: Trinity Press International, 2002.

———. *Reading the Bible: An Introduction.* Notre Dame: Cross Cultural Publications, 1997.

———. *Reading the Gospels in the Dark: Portrayals of Jesus in Film.* Harrisburg, Pa.: Trinity Press International, 2003.

———. "Three Versions of ~~Judas~~ Jesus." In *Those Outside: Noncanonical Readings of Canonical Gospels*, edited by George Aichele and Richard Walsh, 155–81. New York: T & T Clark, 2005.

Walsh, Richard, and George Aichele. "Introduction: Scripture as Precursor." In *Screening Scripture: Intertextual Connections between Scripture and Film*, edited by George Aichele and Richard Walsh, vii–xvi. Harrisburg, Pa.: Trinity Press International, 2002.

———. "Preface: Interpretative Thieves." In *Those Outside: Noncanonical Readings of Canonical Gospels*, edited by George Aichele and Richard Walsh, vii–xvi. New York: T & T Clark, 2005.

Weber, Max. *The Sociology of Religion*. 4th ed. Translated by Ephraim Fischoff. Boston: Beacon, 1963.

Wiesel, Elie. *The Trial of God*. New York: Random House, 1979.

Wiles, Maurice. "The Domesticated Apostle." In Wayne A. Meeks, *The Writings of St. Paul*, 207–13. New York: W. W. Norton & Co., 1972.

Williams, Peter. *Symbolic Change and the Modernization Process in Historical Perspective*. Englewood Cliffs, N.J.: Prentice-Hall, 1980.

Williams, Sam K. *Jesus' Death as Saving Event: The Background and Origin of a Concept*. Missoula: Scholars, 1975.

Wright, N. T. *The Climax of the Covenant: Christ and the Law in Pauline Theology*. Minneapolis: Fortress, 1993.

———. "Paul's Gospel and Caesar's Empire." In *Paul and Politics: Ekklesia, Israel, Imperium, Interpretation: Essays in Honor of Krister Stendahl*, edited by Richard A. Horsley, 160–83. Harrisburg, Pa.: Trinity Press International, 2000.

Žižek, Slavoj. *On Belief*. London: Routledge, 2001.

———. *The Puppet and the Dwarf: The Perverse Core of Christianity*. Cambridge, Mass.: The MIT Press, 2003.

Author Index

208

Movie Index

Scripture Index